The Popes against the Protestants

The Popes against the Protestants

THE VATICAN AND EVANGELICAL CHRISTIANITY IN FASCIST ITALY

Kevin Madigan

Yale UNIVERSITY PRESS

New Haven & London

Published with assistance from the foundation established
in memory of Calvin Chapin of the Class of 1788, Yale College.

Yale University Press books may be purchased in quantity for educational, business, or promotional use. For information, please e-mail sales.press@yale.edu (U.S. office) or sales@yaleup.co.uk (U.K. office).

Set in Adobe Garamond type by Newgen North America.
Printed in the United States of America.

Library of Congress Control Number: 2020949521
ISBN 978-0-300-21586-1 (hardcover : alk. paper)

A catalogue record for this book is available from the British Library.

This paper meets the requirements of ANSI/NISO Z39.48-1992 (Permanence of Paper).

10 9 8 7 6 5 4 3 2 1

Amandae Optimae Figliarum

Contents

Preface

In this book I tell the story of Catholic resistance to Protestant and especially Anglo-American attempts to send missionaries, establish churches, and transplant evangelical Christianity to Italy. Even more precisely, it is a story of how Protestants did this in fascist Italy, that is, in an authoritarian and right-wing, national, ethnological regime that was, by and large, intolerant of much that America and Britain symbolized and, religiously, all that the reformed congregations represented. In short, this book treats the Vatican response to what it termed "the Protestant invasion" or "the Protestant danger" in the fascist period in Italy. I concentrate therefore on a period during which the Roman Curia was attempting to establish a new Catholic world at the same time that, to the profound dismay of the pope and the Vatican hierarchy, Anglo-American evangelical churches were trying to Protestantize that world. Church and state, joined politically in 1929, were generally united in what they opposed. As the historian John Davis has observed in *The Jews of San Nicandro,* "While in many respects the objectives of the political movement that Mussolini had founded in 1919 were unclear, there was no uncertainty when it came to identifying its enemies." Quite true. While this story has not been ignored by scholars, mine is the first volume, I believe, to have benefited from the vast and rich resources of Vatican and Jesuit archives for this period, which were made available only in 2006. Because these archives hold documents corresponding to the pontificate of Pope Pius XI, my story will begin in 1922 and end in 1939. Fortunately, those are the years to which the anti-Protestant campaign largely corresponds, as the pressures of war and the priorities of a new pope moved to the fore in 1939.

The approach I have adopted is basically chronological. Since neither the evangelical nor the Vatican campaign was static but changed quickly in tactics over time, I have been able to link new themes with the chronology and to mix narrative, description, and analysis in an effort to chart a rapidly developing interaction over time. Dominating all chapters is the Vatican confrontation with the evolving "Protestant danger"; the ambitions of the pope to establish a confessional state; the tactics and legal thinking of his point man on Protestant affairs, Francesco Borgongini-Duca; the vast resources the Vatican brought to bear in suppressing the Protestants; the frustrations of the Vatican with governmental officials as well as with their bishops and priests; and the remarkable resilience of the persecuted evangelical groups, which, though harassed, persecuted, and in some cases criminalized, outlasted all efforts to contain or suppress them.

There are scores of interesting themes upon which I have not touched and archival sources not used here. Limitations of time and space as well as the overwhelming richness of the newly available archives themselves suggested I not try to do more than was possible in a single book. My focus, again, is on the unfolding Protestant invasion and the campaign against it organized from the Vatican. While many of the narratives I analyze involve ordinary parishioners, I view them, if critically, through the lens of documents produced by those sympathetic with the pope's desire to neutralize the effectiveness of Protestant proselytizing. Much, much more can be done, though perhaps with sources different from those I have relied upon, on the regional and local effectiveness of the anti-Protestant campaign.

In some cases, the paucity of archival materials on key aspects of the anti-Protestant campaign startled me. Though I had intended to say much about the role of Catholic Action, one of the principal organs of Catholic resistance to evangelical missionizing, the Vatican Archives contained relatively little about it; and though I spent time at the Institute for the History of Catholic Action (ISACEM) in Rome, the materials it has preserved for *this* topic were, by and large, ones I had already examined at the Vatican Archives. This key dimension of the anti-Protestant campaign remains for other researchers to pursue, and I do hope some choose to do so. Because so much of the activity of Catholic Action was organized locally, even if encouraged by the national offices, diocesan archives may bear more fruit than the Vatican's for a detailed study of its role and effectiveness. Here I do attempt to give a general picture of the efforts on the part of Catholic Action against the Protestant campaign, one based on reports submitted by Catholic parishioners and prelates to several congregations at the Vatican and to the powerful Jesuit Pietro Tacchi Venturi, in whose archives and those of the Jesuits in Rome they are now preserved. This picture, I stress, will leave to other scholars the important work of describing the work of Catholic Action on a local and diocesan basis in the 1930s.

In the course of my research at the Vatican Archive I discovered material compiled by the Missionary Union of the Clergy. The material had to do with a vast plan conceived in the late 1930s, when all previous efforts to inhibit proselytizing and conversion and even to eradicate evangelical Christianity had failed. The plan describes something like an ecclesiastical Overlord, involving forty-four thousand priests going out, apostolic style, to preach the true gospel and thus to push the evangelical occupier back and defeat evangelical Christianity. The plan involved rigorous educational preparation on Protestantism in such institutions as the Gregorianum, which had agreed to provide tuition. Because the Vatican archival materials on my subject ended in 1939, with the pontificate of Pius XI, I could not, even by examining other Roman and Italian archives, determine if the plan was ever implemented. I doubt it was, in part because of the pressures of looming war as well as, perhaps, the priorities of a new pope. That said, I have written a chapter-length treatment of this "vast and arduous plan." If other scholars could determine what, if anything, happened to this plan, they will have contributed an important chapter to this story. Because I could not tell how this chapter of history ended I have consigned it to an appendix, though in truth the story it tells cannot, I think, be ignored. It expresses something about the seriousness of Vatican intentions when all else had failed.

Two more words about my hopes and intentions for this book. First, I stress that my focus, as a historian of Christianity, is on the Roman curia's views of Protestant proselytizing and on the motivations and means of suppressing it. I write here as a historian of Christianity. I encourage specialists in Italian fascism, social scientists who have studied migration and conversion, and other scholars to address more fully the questions that lie outside my scope—and those of the archival materials—and competence. To have attempted to address all questions would have meant that I had addressed none. Second, in part because these archival sources have not been studied, I chose to include much detail and narrative. I hope nonetheless that the forest will still be visible in the profusion of trees.

In the preparation of the volume I have benefited especially from the remarkable resources of the Vatican Archives and the Jesuit Archives in Rome. I thank their directors and staffs as well as those of the many other archives from whose riches I have profited. The support of many friends and colleagues has been essential. I want specially to thank my friend David Kertzer, not only for his work on the Catholic Church and antisemitism but also for his personal advice, support, and ongoing encouragement. It was he who suggested that I pursue this fascinating topic. My debt to him will be recognized in the echo of the title of this book to Professor Kertzer's *The Popes against the Jews.* I thank David and John Davis for their careful reading of an early draft. Their scrutiny of the manuscript saved me from many errors, and they both made many useful suggestions. If I could not follow up on all of their generous suggestions, it is only because of the limits to which I have just alluded. I am profoundly and gratefully indebted to my dear friend Dr. Roberto Benedetti, who, though busy with his own historical and editorial work, introduced me to archives and archivists, helped me locate key documents, and otherwise aided in locating the massive volume of primary research on which this book is based. I don't have the words to express my gratitude for his invaluable help and friendship. The support and feedback of friends Paolo Zanini, Raffaella Perin, Kevin Spicer, Robert Ventresca, Charles Gallagher, Jon Levenson, David Hempton (whose decanal support included granting me a year's leave from teaching), David Holland, and Catherine Brekus have put me in their debt. I'd like to thank the members of the North American Religious Colloquium at Harvard, then run by Professors Brekus and Holland, for helpful questions. In the last stages of writing I found the generosity and keen reading of chapter drafts of David Hall invaluable. My students Courtney Sender and Erin Aslami gave indispensable help with admirably careful editing and proofreading. Thanks to Susan Laity and Larry Kenney of Yale University Press for exceptionally sharp editing. Finally, my wife, Stephanie Paulsell, and daughter, Amanda Madigan, spent a magical year in Rome with me in 2015–16, during which I completed much of the archival research for this book. Our time together in the Eternal City was unforgettable. It is to my daughter and great Italianist Amanda, best of daughters, to whom I dedicate this book.

The Popes against the Protestants

Introduction

In 1934 the Vatican secretary of state received a letter that he forwarded to the Vatican's point man on Protestant affairs, Francesco Borgongini-Duca, the Vatican's new nuncio to the State of Italy. A retired railwayman, the author of the letter was named Riccio Michele di Lorenzo. Di Lorenzo had lived all his life in Ariano Irpino, one of the communes in the province of Avellino, now in the Campania. A member of the parish of St. Andrew, he had, over the past few decades, seen much that disturbed him about the religious life of his and similar regional parishes. A Franciscan tertiary, or third-order Franciscan, di Lorenzo was quite devout, not to mention principled and stubborn. He had twice before written to the Vatican regarding the shameful religious conditions the parishioners of Ariano had had to endure. Nothing so jeopardized the quality of parochial life, though, as the issue about which he wrote to the Vatican now: an invasion of Anglo-Saxon Protestant missionaries intent on converting Italian Catholics to evangelical Christianity.[1]

Ariano Irpino is spread out beautifully over three hills; for some time it therefore bore the name Città del Tricolle (City of Three Hills). Roughly equidistant from the Adriatic and the Tyrrhenian, the commune lies in a critical strategic position, near a natural mountain pass between Campania and Puglia. The hills began to be occupied, then fortified, when the Lombards, to stave off the Byzantine Greeks and the Goths, built citadels and fortresses, the ruined walls of which are still visible. The site on which the town was founded, and its vulnerability to natural disaster, shaped its future. The Byzantines were the first to exploit the mountain pass. They damaged but did not conquer the city. Some five centuries later the Normans vanquished it (1140). This marked the beginning of a dizzying series of defeats, then centuries of subjection to foreign powers familiar to all parts of Italy since the Middle Ages. In the following century (1255) Ariano was conquered by the son of Frederick II. In 1265 the town's cathedral, Santa Maria Assunta, was destroyed by marauding Saracens. Eventually controlled by the Capetians, the town was in turn conquered by the Spanish at the time of the Sicilian Vespers (1282). It finally became a city-state dependent upon the Kingdom of Sicily.

Roughly one decade before Benito Mussolini came to power, the city was so poor and housing so vulnerable to earthquake that a sizeable part of the community, their domiciles ruined, dwelt in caves. The painful experience of defeat, conquest, occupation, subjection: these were part of the cultural and national memory of Italy's now united citizenry. That memory—made raw by the recent ignominy of Caporetto, still a symbol in Italy of preventable calamity—helped motivate some Italian Catholics to resist the Anglo-American Protestant invasion that arrived shortly after the Great War.[2] The city's history in some ways mirrored that of much of the rest of Italy, repeatedly traumatized and splintered by invasion and occupation or disintegrated by natural disaster. Still, the intensity and duration of suffering over the centuries were uncommon, freakish almost. Ariano had known remarkable sorrow. Its tenth-century Romanesque cathedrals, repeatedly weakened by earthquakes, bear mute witness to Ariano's millennial agony. Since the Byzantines had tried to conquer it, almost the only thing holding the town together structurally and socially was the binding power of Catholicism.

Socialists had arrived when the railwayman was a youth; they, along with communists and secret societies, Freemasonry among them, were despised and condemned by the nineteenth-century popes. As socialism relinquished its grip over the population, di Lorenzo reports, another claimant for the hearts and minds of the citizens of Ariano appeared: evangelical Protestantism. This was an import from Britain and America. Fatefully, it had arrived at the same time as—indeed as a result of—the Risorgimento. This momentous development was accompanied by the triumph of anticlerical armed forces. With their victory came religious tolerance. The champions of the new liberal political order extended an open welcome to non-Catholic religious confessions, even as they celebrated the loss of papal power over central Italy and especially Rome. These changes opened the way for a flood of Protestants, especially evangelical missionaries from England and America.

Evangelical Christianity had arrived in Italy much earlier and in far different though quite propitious political circumstances. Prior to the Risorgimento, the Protestant community in Italy was tiny. Aside from settlements of foreign merchants, the Protestant presence in Italy was made up overwhelmingly of members of the Waldensian church. Claiming ties to a medieval reform movement begun in France in the twelfth century, the community was confined, geographically, to three valleys of the western Piedmont. By the nineteenth century three centuries of Waldensian history had been marked by the memory of persecution at the hands of Catholic religious and political authorities. Profoundly shaped by their martyrological past, the Waldensian community regularly memorialized their slain saints. As it was largely Occitan and French speaking, the Protestant community was not Italian culturally, linguistically, or religiously. Insofar as it looked outward at all for historical links and religious association, it was to England and to continental Europe. It really was an Alpine ghetto.

By the late nineteenth century, intellectual and political earthquakes had struck. On 20 September 1870, Italian armed forces captured Rome, the last unconquered territory of the Papal States, thus unifying the country. The movement for unification was won by politicians, soldiers, and thinkers who were, by and large, anticlerical. Most supporters of unification were happy to see overlordship of Rome and central Italy transferred from the papacy to the king, no Christian group more so than the Waldensian church. The Risorgimento dramatically transformed conditions for that church and soon for all Protestant communities in Italy, not to mention—though in the opposite direction—for the ancient Catholic church. Once the liberal legislation of the Sapaudian Piedmont was generally conceded, the way was open for Waldensian, Italian Protestant, and Anglo-American evangelical churches to spread and attempt to propagate their versions of Protestant Christianity.[3] Geographical spread and numerical growth were accelerated by the anticlerical history and political sentiments of the leaders of the movement for unification. The association of evangelical missionaries with the liberal regime of the mid and late nineteenth century would make it possible for Protestant groups to preach and spread. Later, that association would enable Catholic polemicists, in the far different political circumstances of the *ventennio* (the period c. 1922–43, the roughly twenty years of fascist rule in Italy), to label Protestants as anti-Italian enemies of the government as well as of the church.

The Law of Guarantees (1871), a parliamentary attempt to govern relations between the Holy See and the state, made the pope a subject of the Kingdom of Italy. Unsurprisingly, the papacy refused to accept the new political order or the loss of prestige and independence it associated with temporal rule of the Papal States. Pope Pius IX (1792–1878) condemned the king, Victor Emmanuel II (1820–78). He and his three immediate successors refused to accept the government's proposal to keep a tiny corner of the last papal state, the Leonine City. For the next fifty-nine years no pope would leave the Vatican; to do so would be to recognize the authority of the Roman government over the whole of the city of Rome—not to mention the epochal shift in the traditional political order. Excommunicating the king, complaining bitterly about the "sacrilegious usurpation" of papal authority, and refusing to leave the papal palace, Pius IX and his successors famously became "Prisoners of the Vatican."[4] Unification, the arrival of evangelical missionaries, and the loss of papal power and stature—the popes, once independent princes, were reduced in stature to subjects of the political Kingdom—seemed to have happened simultaneously. They would be linked in the minds of twentieth-century prelates opposed to the spread of Protestant Christianity in the capital city of Catholic Christianity. The once-liberal Pius IX, chastened by rapid changes of which he by no means approved, refused to accept the authority of the new Italian government; he excommunicated the king. The bad feeling linked with these dramatic changes would long be bound up in clerical minds with the arrival of Anglo-Saxon missionaries.

Pius IX's reaction to the collapse of the old political order put into motion a series of proclamations that attempted to buttress the traditional orders of politics, religion, and thought. Those declarations roundly condemned a wide spectrum of modern philosophical, religious, and political ideologies. A comprehensive riposte to both "liberalism" and many facets of modernity, this reactionary response was a rejoinder to the insistence that the papacy ought to accept either. This retort culminated on 8 December 1864, when Pius IX issued the encyclical *Quanta Cura.*[5] Along with this letter to the bishops Pius IX published the *Syllabus of Errors,* a document of eighty theses previously condemned by the Catholic church. A thoroughgoing repudiation of political, religious, and philosophical modernity, the *Syllabus* would govern papal attitudes for nearly a century. Among the modern errors the *Syllabus* condemns are ones mentioned by the railwayman. Many aspects of the evangelical faith Protestants encouraged Italian Catholics to adopt had been condemned in the *Syllabus of Errors,* including Bible Societies. This latest of invasions—this one Anglo-Saxon—had begun decades earlier, when di Lorenzo was very young. Yet nothing, when he wrote in 1934, had weakened Protestantism's crusading zeal or impeded its success, least of all the Catholic clergy, about whose indolent performance he complains quite bitterly. Indeed, the railwayman repeatedly states his conviction that, among other grievous ecclesiastical disorders, the sorry state of the Catholic clergy had greased the wheels of what now appeared to be an unstoppable evangelical express.

The spread of Protestant Christianity into both urban and rural areas of northern Italy slowed until the dawn of the twentieth century. Then, in the first decade of the 1900s, the number of Italian Protestants nearly doubled. Why? Part of the answer has to do with the newly accentuated social emphasis of Protestant preaching. This was reflected in a novel kind of conversionary preaching that targeted the lower classes and the peasantry, a message readily received in areas where socialism had spread and left-wing political views and administrations had taken hold. The association of socialism or communism with evangelical Christianity would soon be held against evangelical proselytes, as would the sense that, having once been contained to a few valleys in the Piedmont, they soon appeared to have spread ubiquitously. Until the early twentieth century southern Italy and Sicily had been on the periphery of Protestant expansion. Now, a variety of Protestant and evangelical sects established a throng of centers, many of them still small, over a vast swathe of continental Italy and Sicily.

It was from these regions of the country that many millions had emigrated across the Atlantic, especially to America, in the nineteenth and early twentieth centuries. A small but significant number of them converted to some form of evangelical Christianity while in the United States. When these so-called *americani* returned they brought evangelical Christianity, which underscored the obligation of each to convert others to the true faith, with them. Alongside centers established by indigenous reformed groups, the americani formed hundreds of small Protestant communities, many of them in remote or mountainous regions, in the provinces of the South and Sicily. In short, evangelical Christianity luxuriated in soil emigrants had regarded as hopelessly arid and from which emigration had been most intense.

In the aftermath of the First World War, Italian Catholic anxieties about the power and intentions of global Protestantism mushroomed. With the victory of the Entente powers, the influence of the United States and Britain grew—and alarmingly so in the eyes of clerics at the Roman curia. The period following the British Mandate was characterized by an increasingly strong

Protestant presence in Palestine, as missionaries poured into a space still quite precious to its small Catholic population and to the Roman curia. The Catholic Austro-Hungarian empire had collapsed. American and Protestant influence seemed to be swelling in South America and the Caribbean; the Vatican seemed impotent in the face of these incursions into traditional spheres of religious ownership and power. However alarming Anglo-Saxon infiltration could be, from the perspective of the Vatican, some areas of missionary activity were on the periphery of the Catholic world. Because Europe retained a place of privilege in the Catholic imagination, Protestant proselytizing in the recently established Kingdom of Poland caused more anguish. There, Methodist missionaries had established several impressive settlements in an East European country culturally Catholic and faithful to Rome. Even closer to home, Methodist missionaries had made inroads in the Kingdom of Belgium, as had American missionaries in the Netherlands. Protestantism increasingly seemed to pose a global threat to the Catholic church, as it jeopardized its religious hegemony in Europe. But the attempted conversion of Italy in the interwar period especially caused Vatican anxieties to spike.

In 1919 a writer for the widely read and influential journal *Civiltà Cattolica* claimed, with some exaggeration, that the number of converts in Italy had doubled since the war began just five years earlier. He expressed fear that this number would only increase as travel became easier and more common, as converts returned from America to Italy, and as well-financed organizations from the Anglo-Saxon countries made Protestantism seem, in many respects, more appealing than the insipid Catholic fare ladled out indifferently by demoralized priests at home.[6] His fear was not utterly irrational. As the historian John Pollard has observed, "In the 1920s and 1930s, Italians returning from America would bring with them the seeds of the first serious Protestant dissent in Italy in modern times, nuclei of Baptists, Jehovah's Witness [*sic*], Pentecostal and Seventh-Day Adventist organisations, especially in the south."[7] Little so irritated Roman clerics as the Methodist attempt to build an educational and religious citadel on Monte Mario, overlooking the Vatican Hill, not to mention the Wesleyan attempt to acquire land on Castel Gandolfo, the traditional summer residence of the Holy See. The audacity and scope of the Protestant invasion initially caught the Vatican off guard, but it would not be long before it regained its balance—and its determination to resist.

In response, Catholic writers launched a strident, widespread polemical offensive that, in its vigor and violence (rhetorical, legal, physical), contrasted sharply with the sluggish performance or disregard of weekly ceremonial practice in thousands of sleepy parishes throughout the peninsula. A campaign of proselytizing was, from the standpoint of the railwayman, not to mention many Catholic polemicists, by 1920 dangerously metastasizing across the peninsula. Aggressive proselytizing by Methodists, especially, agitated many Catholic prelates, and it was against them and the YMCA, with which the Methodists were associated, that a pamphlet war began. By the late 1920s it was common for Catholic writers in Italy to compose alarmed pamphlets on "the Protestant danger" (*il pericolo protestante*) or, more ominously, "the Protestant Conquest of Italy."[8] Each of these was the title of at least one published polemical pamphlet (including one written by Pope Pius XI) or private, often highly sensitive ecclesiastical reports. The titles were widely understood shorthand for an ordeal by which many Italian Catholics, well before the pontificate of Pope Pius XI (1922–39), were exasperated, even panicked.[9]

Contemplating this offensive, Pollard has justly observed that "Roman ecclesiastical anti-Protestantism was as virulent as anti-Judaism" would come to be.[10] While the former was never lethal, it nonetheless superseded the anti-Jewish campaign in cultural space and gravity, verbal and sometimes physical ferocity, and duration. To begin with, the anti-Protestant campaign lasted from c. 1920 to 1939. In the archives of the Vatican Nunciature to Italy is a letter from Secretary of State Eugenio Pacelli to the nuncio, Borgongini-Duca, warning him of Protestant propaganda in meridional Italy. The date? The twenty-fifth of March, 1938, about eight months before the promulgation of the notorious Racial Laws and roughly four months before the publication of the "Racial Manifesto."[11] It was no accident that campaigns against foreigners, Protestants and Jews especially, overlapped—chronologically, thematically, rhetorically—especially after 1935, when Italy's fortunes in war plunged and relations with the international community of nations, Britain above all, became strained.

The anti-Protestant campaign initially had little effect—not in 1922 or in 1927, when the first widely read pamphlet, Pietro Tacchi Venturi's *The Protestant Danger* (*Il Pericolo Protestante*), had been published, or even in 1929, when in the Lateran Accords the Italian government declared Roman Catholicism to be "the Religion of the State." It has been said that the rise of fascism marked the end of a kind of golden age of Italian Protestantism. In some respects true, the observation nonetheless cries out for qualification. Demographically it was still the case, at the beginning of the fascist period, that only one in ten thousand Italians was Protestant, a fact Mussolini repeatedly harped on when implored by the pope to do more to impede the Protestant invasion. Irrational anxiety, paranoia, religious hatred, not to mention the monocultural imperatives of Italian fascism, would soon imaginatively transform the tiny community into a grave threat to religious and national integrity. Second, though some communities, especially the Methodist or those linked with the political left, were persecuted in the 1920s, not much changed for most of the Protestant churches until 1931. Again, it is sometimes said that the Lateran Agreements (1929) marked a turning point in relations between the Catholic and Protestant churches; or that the slow collapse of the liberal state in 1922–26 marked the beginning of a dark period for Italian evangelicals. But this, too, needs to be carefully qualified. The dramatic political changes overturning the liberal political order did not, at least not initially, result in disaster, reversal, or even serious adversity for most Italian Protestant communities. In fact, Mussolini soon put in place legal protections to which the pope would strenuously object. Almost immediately after the Lateran Pacts made Roman Catholicism the Religion of the State, the government passed a law on "permitted religious organizations" (*culti ammessi*). These were laws published essentially in conjunction with the Lateran Accords and intended to demonstrate that non-Catholic religious groups, including evangelicals, had certain rights—like that to free speech on matters religious—despite the recognition of Roman Catholicism as the state religion. The laws were also passed to show the world that the fascist government had not simply capitulated to Catholic demands, that Mussolini, at least, had no plans to cooperate with the Vatican in making Italy a confessional state—the grand dream of Pope Pius XI. Legally, the law changed the status of Protestant sects in Italy from merely tolerated to permissible, satisfying both Italian Protestants and their patrons in England and America.

Initially, the fascist religious program, if one can use so grandiose a term, encouraged Protestant leaders in Italy and abroad. Mussolini had no coherent religious program and even less a predisposition of hostility or repression toward the Protestant confessions. In fact, some powerful anticlerical fascists, like Roberto Farinacci, the Ras of Cremona, would take up the Protestant side in some interconfessional disputes in the 1930s to frustrate the designs of the Catholic church and to advance the anticlerical agenda. Circumstances, not legal or ideological principle, often dictated policy, as when church and state quarreled over an issue regarding Catholic Action in 1931. Until that issue was resolved, the national government coolly refused to respond to Vatican pleas to intervene in this or that dispute with evangelical communities.

Being the religion of the State meant nothing concrete for Catholic prelates when it came to the suppression of Protestants. This was a period during which Catholic bishops and priests were virtually powerless and thus evangelical communities essentially unmolested. In addition, local governments, to the everlasting frustration of Vatican prelates, often established alliances with Protestant pastors or churches, refused to curb evangelical preaching or construction or to respond to alarms from the Vatican. One member of the Roman curia was able, eventually, to recruit Guido Buffarini-Guidi, the powerful, sometimes pitiless undersecretary of the interior, as well as some of the few highly placed fascists who were also devout Catholics, to its cause. More characteristically, the Roman curia, beginning with the pope, would find itself frustrated with the failure of the government to perceive the magnitude of the problem or flummoxed when local fascist officials, for reasons unknown in Rome, refused to follow the law (as interpreted by the new nuncio Borgongini, especially) or honor Vatican requests for suppression of evangelical communities or projects. Some governmental officials appear not even to have known what the law was or how to interpret it. Others, for local social or familial reasons, simply ignored the law.

Occasionally, frustration with the stubborn problem of Protestant propaganda and the slowness of the slumbering local governments to recognize it as a problem boiled over. Protestants had long been represented as heretics, but as the ventennio wore on they were made ciphers by anti-Protestant hawks at the Vatican for much that, in its view, was iniquitous, injurious, and immoral in modernity. This they could symbolize only in the rhetoric of the end-times. In 1937, for example, one cleric, frustrated with the impotence of local ordinaries and governmental officials and, above all, with the astonishing resilience of evangelical, especially Pentecostal, Christians, angrily asked why some Italian clerics could not summon the energy to overpower "the Antichrists of our day."[12] Many Italian bishops, beginning with Pope Pius XI, incensed by Protestant presence, proselytizing, and propaganda, hoped that agreement between church and state would herald the establishment of a Catholic confessional state. In any confessional state, including the one the pope was trying to build in Italy, dissidents were regarded not only as minority communities, nuisances, and an irritation but also as heretics. In the eyes of Catholics, heretics traditionally had no civil rights, and so Catholic hardliners, whose imaginative cosmos had hardly changed in five centuries, would be infuriated to see Protestant denominations granted toleration and religious liberties.

Exasperation among Catholics with the presence and aggressive, supposedly deceitful proselytizing of the Protestants was especially pronounced after the passage of the culti ammessi laws. Many bishops and parish priests reported an uptick in evangelical activity, and almost all imputed the new aggressiveness of the Protestants to rights and privileges recently enshrined in the new laws. As the crisis of Catholic Action (1931) receded into the past and as evangelical propaganda seemed to spread in the years 1929–31, the church began to organize its campaign against the Protestants. Led by the pope, congregations, and bishops associated with the Holy See as well as by thousands of parish priests, this was a campaign in which the Vatican also applied systematically for recourse to the powers of the state, though, as indicated, not always successfully.

Issues related to the sociology of knowledge have to some extent, and inevitably, shaped the presentation of this campaign. As Pietro Scoppola once observed in an important historiographical article written in 1973, scholarship on the evangelical churches in the fascist period had then, as now, been written largely by scholars of evangelical schooling, affiliation, and sympathy. The image they had collectively produced is of a church—or group of evangelical churches—having suffered grievous blows from the dictatorship and "largely negative repercussions, for religious minorities." While this judgment was, by and large, well founded, it was, Scoppola persuasively argued, "a bit impoverished and too simpli[stic]." To begin with, Italian Protestant scholars had relied wholly on evangelical sources and testimonies. He recommended that scholars take advantage of state archives, especially those of the police. These, he argued, gave one a better sense of a "variable equilibrium"—this in contrast to the static picture he thought had emerged from Protestant historians—among the evangelical groups, the intentions of the regime's legal authorities, and the objectives of the Catholic church. "Only thus," Scoppola wrote, "could the topic emerge from the isolation in which it has remained." He then went on to exemplify the approach he had recommended by offering several ways in which the documents preserved at the Central State Archives for the fascist period might enrich the picture of the evangelical churches in the fascist regime.[13] That Scoppola's appeal was sensible was proven when evangelical scholars, notably Giorgio Rochat and Giorgio Spini, undertook studies whose distinction was founded on the sort of approach the Catholic Scoppola had recommended.[14] That said, the narrative still had a gaping hole at its center: the story of the campaign from the perspective of those Catholic prelates and priests who launched and sustained it.

In this book I tell the story of the anti-Protestant campaign from the point of view of the Vatican, a perspective closed off not only to Italian evangelical scholars, by both perspective and resources, but even to the Jesuit Scoppola, by chronology and fortune.[15] Documents recently made available at the Vatican and Jesuit archives in Rome since 2006 shed new light on a narrative that, to date, has been produced largely by the aforementioned Italian Protestant historians, to whom the fathomlessly rich sources of the Vatican had not been available. Those sources enable one to understand much more about the anti-Protestant campaign in fascist Italy. They especially enable one to see more clearly how Catholic prelates viewed Protestant Christianity, to chart the unfolding invasion of evangelical missionaries in relation to contemporary Italian history, and to glimpse as well evangelical motives, means, and, finally, the effectiveness of Catholic resistance.

If the prevailing view of the period is that of a powerful division of priests acting in concert with a cooperative and equally determined state to suppress a tiny and helpless band of evangelical invaders, this book reveals a very different view of that history. Throughout the anti-Protestant campaign key figures at the Roman curia would be overcome with frustration: with the nonchalance of Mussolini, with the obliviousness to national law of regional governmental officials and police, with the strength of local communal bonds, and, above all, with the boldness and impudence of the evangelical missionaries, and then, after repression, the evangelicals' chameleon-like capacity to blend into the landscape and reconstitute themselves, often under different names. Evangelicals at the end of the decade felt unjustly persecuted and harassed—injustices and emotions that evangelical scholars have emphasized. But the new archives demonstrate truths never contemplated by historians of Italian Protestantism: at the end of the decade Catholic prelates were also bitter, but at the *failure* of their campaign, which they could blame, not entirely unjustly, on the indifference of Mussolini and the government he commanded and the insufferable continued presence in Italy of anti-Catholic Protestant churches and Christians.

The Vatican had a perspective on the entire country, and, as I rely so heavily here on its records, so my own scope here is quite broad. I aim in this book to understand and represent that general perspective, though I have tried throughout to bring the Vatican's point of view into conversation with evangelical and governmental sources. One has to begin by attempting to grasp the aspirations, methods, achievements, and self-reported failures of the evangelical missionaries. These can be appreciated only by understanding how evangelical missionaries understood themselves; how they viewed Roman Catholicism and its history; the religious, educational, and sometimes political aims they set for themselves; and the conditions they faced when first arriving in Italy during the nineteenth century and then during the fascist period. Many disparate groups, with different geographical and theological origins, participated in the attempt to evangelize Italy; they could not always be distinguished by Italian priests and virtually never by laymen. This was in part attributable to ignorance, but it was, more importantly, because most of these communities were part of a broader religious movement that had as its principal aim the restoration of the simplicity and purity of New Testament Christianity. To evangelical proselytes, this was a sacred obligation, enjoined upon them by God, an obligation grounded in the presumed clarity of the New Testament. It was incumbent upon them to liberate Rome from priestly, especially papal, tyranny, which had clouded the purity of the earliest teaching of the church. The ambition and awesome scale of the task were only heightened for many by the sense that they were participating in the events of the last days and hence accelerating the return of their Lord. Thus the Risorgimento, which had prepared the way for evangelicals to enter the stronghold of Roman Catholicism, was part of the divinely prepared plan for humanity, now in its final stage. Many shared the politically liberal and anticlerical sentiments of the leaders of the Risorgimento. In the long run those sentiments would make them threats in the eyes of both the fascist regime and the church, as would their Anglo-Saxon origins and culture, not to mention their tantalizing wealth. Perhaps nothing would make them so despised by many prelates in the Vatican as the fact that they had been joined, in significant numbers, by ex- or apostate priests, now their severest and most credible critics.

The first serious critic of the Protestant danger was the powerful Jesuit Pietro Tacchi Venturi, intermediary between the pope and Mussolini. His polemical treatment of evangelical missionaries—and especially his insistence on yoking Anglo-Saxon Protestantism with political, social, and economic movements and figures that had been denounced by church and state—deeply influenced the ways in which evangelicals would be viewed by Catholics throughout the fascist period. Especially noteworthy is his making of the apostles of Protestant Christianity not only heretics, that is, enemies of the church, but fifth columnists, that is, enemies of the fascist state. Tacchi Venturi would succeed in making evangelicals not only anti-Catholic but anti-Italian and antifascist and thus open them up not only to Catholic critique but also to the far more sinister surveillance of the fascist state. He made them seem especially threatening by exaggerating or fabricating their connections with political movements (communism and socialism), societies (Freemasonry), religious traditions (Judaism), political and legal heresies (latitudinarianism, tolerance, indifferentism), economic systems (capitalism, plutocracy), social and moral practices (birth control, abortion, women's rights), and cultural conventions and usages (Anglo-Saxon)—all of which had been condemned by popes in the nineteenth and twentieth centuries. Tacchi Venturi gave special attention to Methodism as a "most dangerous sect," one that succeeded only, he argued, by proselytizing through gifts of cash, and to the YMCA, which he regarded, not entirely wrongly, as a Methodist proselytizing institution. This tactic of very grave guilt-by-association would prove effective. It made the most innocent Bible vendor an archenemy, a dark adversary whose capacity for evil justified the application of repressive measures by the Catholic laity, the institutional church, even, if not consistently, the fascist regime. These would come to include mob violence, incarceration, and confinement.

No Italian priest agonized more over Protestant proselytizing than Pope Pius XI, especially as reports of the first attempts at evangelical conversion began to trickle into the Vatican. As the pope's private ambassador to Mussolini, Tacchi Venturi had hoped to alert Il Duce to the grave political dangers to the fascist regime posed by the Protestant invaders. To the immense frustration of the pope, which only intensified over the 1930s, Mussolini could not then be convinced of the danger posed by (as Il Duce insisted) a tiny minority of the population. Focused on the demographics of the Protestant sects, he would never be persuaded that they posed a threat to the continuity of his government; and, responsive to world opinion, he was especially sensitive to the reactions of their Anglo-Saxon patrons. Partly for that reason he pushed through laws that extended legal recognition and protection to them. To the pope this seemed to contradict a number of the principal clauses of the Concordat, which in his view made Protestant propaganda illegal. His disenchantment with Mussolini, who seemed alarmingly nonchalant in the face of the threat, and with the growing presence of evangelical missionaries on Italian soil would only grow over the remainder of his pontificate, which concluded with utter despondency when he died in 1939. By then he had brought all the clerical resources at his disposal to bear on strengthening Italian Catholicism and impeding the Protestant advance. Though formidable, these had, at best, transient and fluctuating effectiveness over time and space. Early in the 1930s he confessed that the success of the Protestant project,

Mussolini's indifference, his laws protecting Protestant speech and activity—all became his "greatest cross to bear." Nine years later, after a bitterly fought war of words, he would say something almost identical as, in resignation, he grimly recognized that all of his efforts were, in effect, made in vain and that his trust in Mussolini had proven to have been, in multiple respects, costly, fruitless, and embarrassing.

Still, he began the decade by launching a vigorous campaign. This began with a serious attempt to determine everything he could about the evangelical invaders so as to neutralize them more effectively. He commissioned three trusted clerical colleagues to produce reports on patterns and methods of evangelical proselytizing. Again, what he learned deeply troubled him. All three clerical colleagues reported that, as a result of the passage of the culti ammessi laws, Protestant activities had intensified in the North, central, and, above all, southern parts of the peninsula. Missionaries had success in part because they could provide money, educational and medical services, and other amenities unknown in poor Italian communities. They used these especially to target youth and military. The energy of the Protestant missionaries contrasted sharply with the indolence of the parochial clergy and the lack of initiative from almost all bishops. Ordinary people, often unlearned and destitute, were evangelized by foreigners, repatriated Italians from the United States (americani), and, most loathsome of all, ex-priests. In some cities relations between Protestant and Catholic clergy were warm—positively galling to the Roman curia—the latter sometimes participating in the religious and educational ceremonies of the former. For the first few years leaders of the evangelical campaign were flush with victory. They took territory as did the Wehrmacht in the early phase of Barbarossa. In the early 1930s it seemed as if Anglo-Saxon missionaries were ubiquitous; they had occupied Italian territory everywhere. Some evangelical groups were literally living at the gates of the Vatican. Their momentum seemed unstoppable.

The Vatican would attempt to push back, sometimes with extraordinarily vigorous polemical, rhetorical, and legal force. Repressive energy was concentrated on no other locus as heavily as the tiny Villa San Sebastiano. Still, despite the efforts of local Catholic grandees, of Tacchi Venturi, of many Jesuits and several high-ranking prelates from the Vatican, the British Methodist congregation, though tested by severe repressive measures and persecution by the state, would not disappear. This is one of the Protestant communities studied by Italian historians of evangelical Christianity in Italy. Documents available in the Vatican Archive give a dramatically new perspective on the motivations of some of the principal governmental officials and Catholics of the Villa. In light of these documents, it seems as if powerful Catholic families were instrumental in bringing Wesleyan Christianity to the Villa. Their mysterious reasons for doing so have less to do with the appeal of evangelical Christianity than with social tensions—familial slights and vendettas in a shame-and-honor culture. The Vatican concentrated enormous rhetorical, polemical, and legal energy at the Villa. It was a hill they were, so to speak, willing to die on. Despite all their efforts, nonetheless, they failed to eradicate Protestant Christianity from the Villa. They were crippled by long-secret animosity felt for the local bishop, incomplete information, the mystifying cooperation of Catholic fascist officials with the Wesleyan community, and even the attempt by the profoundly anticlerical Ras of Cremona, Roberto Farinacci, to stymie the Catholic effort at suppression.

If Tacchi Venturi was the face of the anti-Protestant campaign before the Concordat, the new nuncio to Italy, Francesco Borgongini-Duca (1884–1954), would manage it, with inflexible dedication and ruthlessness from c. 1931 to 1939. He is the protagonist of this account, if an unsavory and unsympathetic one. He was recognized by fellow priests at the Roman curia as an intellectual mediocrity, but his stubbornness, personal ambition, and slavering to be appreciated nonetheless made him the leading enforcer and interpreter of the culti ammessi laws, which he naturally read to the disadvantage of evangelical groups. Basing his reading of the law on the new fascist penal code of Minister of Justice Alfredo Rocco (1875–1935), Borgongini argued that proselytizing should not be interpreted as a form of protected speech. Private religious meetings held for the purposes of conversion, he argued, took on a public purpose and, in view of their illegal and public character, could be shut down by law enforcement—a view that rendered evangelical leaders dumbstruck. He also interpreted a number of Mussolini's remarks on religion so as to make proselytizing not merely an offense against the sensibility of simple Catholics but something far graver: a crime against the state. Although intended to command the attention of Mussolini, Borgongini's inflationary rhetoric never did so. However, it did persuade Mussolini's powerful undersecretary, Buffarini; he would criminalize Pentecostalism at least partly based on Borgongini's arguments, which he heard in person many times and at points of inflection in the decade, not least on the infamous occasion on which, in the summer of 1935, he criminalized Pentecostalism and the Jehovah's Witnesses.

Nonetheless, Borgongini would be frustrated, as would the pope from whom he accepted his mission and to whom he reported—for the entire period under discussion—at local governmental authorities' ignorance of the law or refusal to enforce it. Even though he boasted, in the wake of the Buffarini Decree of 1935, that *he* had abolished the Pentecostal cult in Italy, Borgongini would be startled, then infuriated to learn that his boast had been quite premature. Borgongini would be able to rout neither the Pentecostals nor any other evangelical group. Even when it seemed, as it did in 1935 to certain Vatican congregations, that the anti-Protestant campaign had succeeded in diminishing or defeating the evangelicals, the same congregations would soon report, in letters crushing to the spirit of Pius XI, that evangelical groups had reconstituted or reorganized themselves. Victories in the Catholic crusade against the Protestant infidel proved dishearteningly ephemeral. No matter how severely persecuted, evangelical groups, for the most part, refused to submit to defeat. What seems today like communal resilience and conviction of right appeared to the Vatican, its prelates, and the bishops, à la Moyen Âge, as diabolically inspired dissidence—heresy.

The railwayman had written to the Vatican just at a time when the Protestant invasion had gained momentum. This was when it seemed as if, with swift action from Rome, it might be arrested. At the end of the fascist period, evangelical communities were still, as Mussolini had described them at its beginning, a tiny drop in a sea of a country that remained, culturally and demographically at least, Roman Catholic. Measured against the Catholic attempt to purge Italy of Protestants, Italian evangelicals outlasted the campaign intended to discomfit and rout them. The enormous energy invested in rhetoric and suppression hardly matched the hoped-for results. Even in 1939 there is little evidence that the number of Italians drawn to Protestant or evangelical Christianity had declined. Groups confidently pronounced extinct, like the Pentecostals, violently suppressed by the regime, simply went underground or appeared under a new guise. That said, at the end of Pius XI's pontificate in 1939, the evangelicals, it was clear, would fall well short of realizing their grand, apocalyptic dream of Protestantizing Italy. The anti-Protestant campaign had produced an enormous volume of sound and fury, but in the end it had almost nothing to show for it, except, perhaps, a legacy of vicious and immoral suppression.[16]

CHAPTER I

The Evangelical Confessions in Italy (c. 1861–1922)

From 1861 both indigenous and Anglo-American missionaries tried to convert Catholic Italy to evangelical Christianity—and to deconvert it from popery, priesthood, and paganism. In the long run Protestant organizations and leaders from Britain and especially America would guide and fund the efforts of their missionaries.

Evangelical missionaries brought with them a package of religious convictions, which they would induce potential converts to accept. These largely grew out of the religious revival known as the Great Awakenings and included articles of faith: the belief that Christian churches should be based only, in matters of faith and practice, on structures and criteria laid out, by all accounts with limpid clarity, in the New Testament; that new churches and the old had to be restored to New Testament Christianity, from the purity of which many had fallen away; that this restoration would occur through the agency of missionaries in a worldwide operation it was a true Christian's obligation to undertake; that no church had so corrupted the apostolic ideal as the Roman Catholic and that it, therefore, should be the first to be improved and converted, beginning in the worldwide center of apostasy; and that the colossal project of worldwide conversion had to be consummated before the near coming of the millennium. Fortunately—providentially—recent political developments in Italy had prepared the way of the evangelical project. An anticlerical army had defeated the forces of the Papal States. Papal rule and prestige had suffered profound diminishment. A new liberal political order had been installed. Legal protection was extended to non-Catholic religious groups, including indigenous Italian Protestants and Jews. Little impeded the arrival of evangelical missionaries from England and America to begin their work of conversion. The resurrection of Italy, the establishment of a kingdom, and a new political order would now proceed, as missionaries, moved by grand dreams and visions, set to work restoring the religion of Christ and the apostles in the land where bishops and popes had so outrageously polluted it.

From a demographic point of view the outcome of the efforts to re-Christianize Italy, into which so much energy, hope, and money had been poured, was unimpressive, as more than one evangelical writer mournfully noted at the time. An unbiblical abomination, infant baptism in Italy remained all but universal in the late nineteenth and early twentieth centuries. In the period from unification to the First World War—despite the anticlericalism expressed by Italian liberals, nationalists, and monarchists in the nineteenth century—Italy remained, demographically as in other respects, overwhelmingly Roman Catholic. Nor did secularization significantly shrink the percentage of the population identifying itself with Rome.[1] In 1914 only 1 out of every 1,000 Italian citizens was Protestant.[2] The census of 1881 demonstrated that there were more diocesan priests (76,560) than Protestants (62,000) in Italy, which had a total population of roughly 29 million; that is not even to count the thousands of monks, brothers, nuns, and others in religious life.[3]

In subalpine Italy, the message of the reformers found rocky soil. Partly for this reason historians prefer to speak of a Reformation in Italy rather than an Italian Reformation. Still, a number of historical developments paved the way for some Italians, including prominent Augustinian friars, to incline their ears to the reformed bulletins pouring out of Geneva in the sixteenth century. Ironically, it was in Italy, home to the papacy and the institutional center of the Roman church, that the oldest group of European dissidents and the oldest "Christian minority" of the Western church found its home.

It is customary for historians of Protestantism in Italy, and critical to the self-understanding of the first Italian Protestants, to trace the history of the Waldensian church back to the Poor of Lyons. Nonetheless, it would be difficult to argue that the Italian Waldensians had much in common, theologically or organizationally, with the reform movement inaugurated by the twelfth-century Waldensians, who would not have recognized or appreciated, much less adopted, many of the doctrinal or organizational beliefs characteristic of reformed Christianity. Scholars of all denominational stripes, including the Waldensian, have conceded that Waldensians were not Protestants. None anticipated central reformed doctrines like justification by faith, to take the simplest and most obvious example. That said, some important continuities do exist—like the priority of scripture in faith and practice—and so I will follow historiographical convention here.

INDIGENOUS MISSIONS

Originating in the late twelfth century, the followers of the erstwhile merchant Waldo (or Waldes) of Lyons (c. 1140–c. 1205) spread from France to several western and central European countries. Eponymously christened the Waldensians, a name that took hold only well after their "founder's" death, the Poor of Lyons had been driven from their home diocese for having preached in the face of an archiepiscopal ban on doing so. For defying this ban they were anathematized by Pope Louis III in 1184 and excommunicated by the Fourth Lateran Council (1215).[4] Ironically, pursuit of heresy often diffused it more widely. In this case it sent the followers of Waldes to the Alpine fastnesses of France and the western Piedmont—still called the Waldensian valleys and, by devotees, the "Israel of the Alps."[5] There they first successfully evangelized families that gave them refuge. Already in the fourteenth century Milan had become a center of Waldensian expansion. Waldensian nuclei were soon established in Apulia and Calabria. Eventually, the European diaspora came to include Bohemia, Transylvania, and Poland, and it stretched to the plains of the Black Sea.[6]

Having broken decisively with Rome, the Waldensians in the sixteenth century were brought into the household of the reformed churches. Some Waldensians, after encountering influential reformers, including William Farel (1489–1565) and Martin Bucer (1491–1551), were soon integrated into the Genevan wing of the Swiss reform. Their geographical position in the Piedmont valleys functioned as a channel from which Reformation ideas could flow down from the north. From 1532 they would frame their theological ideas, practices, and governmental structures within the framework established by the Swiss reformed churches. This meant that as a small gathered community the Waldensian church would preserve its commitment to the primacy of scripture, intense opposition to idolatry, and, in polity, reformed models of self-governance. They also adopted a non-Lutheran, non-Zwinglian, and non-Catholic view of Eucharistic presence.[7] Italian Protestants, many having taken refuge in Switzerland from the aggressive measures of Catholic counter-reformers, used Geneva as a base from which to take the Protestant message to Italy.[8]

Their connection with the reformers made Italian Waldensians vulnerable to Catholic authorities, both religious and religiopolitical. Waldensians in Calabria as well as in Provence faced terrible persecution, including imprisonment, as early as the 1530s. The establishment of the Holy Office (or Roman Inquisition) in 1542 by Paul III, and the appointment as general the following year of the Dominican inquisitor Antonio (Michele) Ghislieri, heralded a new era of suffering, a time of agony prolonged when Ghislieri became Pope Pius V (1566–72). John Henry Newman memorably said of Pius V that this soldier of Christ had established "martial law . . . in a spiritual sense."[9] Naturally, the Waldensians did not hallow him as a saint nor did his campaigns of suppression feel anything but unholy. The tribunals made martyrs of scores of Waldensians throughout the country. Those not martyred or incarcerated fled. As the Catholic missionary counteroffensive gained strength in the last quarter of the sixteenth century, reformers and their families flew from the northern centers of Lucca and Modena; they would settle in Geneva. Communities in other regions were less fortunate. Inquisitorial fire nearly extinguished the large communities in Calabria, Apulia, and the western Piedmont. Tacchi Venturi was hardly the first Catholic historian to defend the tribunals. The dark instruments of torture and fire, he explained, were necessary: they had prevented the triumph of the Reformation heresy in Italy.[10]

Discriminatory edicts issued by the House of Savoy followed in the seventeenth century, as did aggressive Jesuit and Capuchin missionizing. Pitiless military campaigns ensued. Carnage enacted by troops of the Duke of Savoy in 1655 infamously jeopardized the physical survival of the Waldensians. The poet John Milton, in the opening couplet of his sonnet "On the Late Massacre in Piedmont," would, after the forces of Savoy had completed their butchery, memorably implore the Deity:

> Avenge, O Lord, thy slaughter'd saints, whose bones
> Lie scatter'd on the Alpine mountains cold.[11]

Justice did not arrive; worse would follow. In the long run, suffering supplied a martyrological element to Waldensian historiography, crucial to the refinement of the church's identity. The geographical term "Alpine ghetto," first heard in 1798, reflected and reinforced the separatist, sectarian ethos of the church.[12]

A momentous turn would put a term to the church's suffering and transform its relationship to the state. After the Waldensians had endured centuries of persecution, the Sardinian king Charles Albert finally issued a set of letters securing civil rights for Christians and Jews on 17 February 1848. As there was no other significant Protestant minority in Italy at the time, the decree was meant to protect the Waldensian churches as well as Italy's Jewish community. The first Protestant Italians to become citizens, Waldensians and soon all Italian Protestants would be linked historically and politically with tolerant, integrative, and liberalizing movements—changes of which the Catholic church would, in both near and long term, cordially disapprove.

For their part the Waldensians wished to leave no doubt about the extent of their gratitude or the sincerity of their loyalties. Inhabitants of the valleys were especially scrupulous about participating in "national" holidays and carrying out what were now perceived to be patriotic duties, especially the Festival of the Statuto, which became an important celebration in the Kingdom of Sardinia in 1851. As if suddenly divorced from its pacifist traditions and history, some Waldensian newspapers urged members not to avoid military service. Others insisted on their loyalty to Victor Emmanuel II; they thanked the sovereign for the freedom his predecessors had granted. Waldensians participated with unfamiliar ecstasy in the festival of the Taking of Rome, which celebrated the end of the Papal States and prelatical power. This they celebrated (again fatefully) with delegates from continental Protestant churches, Jewish communities, and delegates from the Masonic community, many of them English. Waldensian links had, until 1848, been much stronger with England and Protestant Europe than with Italy. Legend has it that when Porta Pia was breached, two members of the British and Foreign Bible Society—Waldensian, of course—brought with them into Rome the first Italian translations of the Bible, then banned in Rome. It seemed as if the Waldensians had been integrated into a subalpine, political, civil, and Italian national society.[13]

In practice, the Waldensians were barely tolerated. The establishment of a new ministry in towns was often greeted with physical assault. Missionaries were sometimes stoned, beaten, or intimidated—by clergy as well as by parishioners. Spini has provocatively suggested that Waldensians were tolerated in the way that social deviance or nuisance are reluctantly accepted.[14]

Nonetheless, after the establishment of an Evangelization Board, Waldensians, despite impediment, were able to evangelize the Italian peninsula. They would soon be joined by Italians returned from exile, largely in London, as well as by Baptists, Methodists, and other English and especially American missionaries.[15] Simple, self-taught itinerant evangelists began to establish pocket communities throughout the peninsula. Itinerant salesmen distributed the first Italian translation of the Bible from north to south. In Turin the Waldensians built a church, or temple, intended to symbolize their right to preach. Later transferred to Rome, the Waldensian Faculty of Theology at Torre Pellice, a commune some thirty miles southwest of Turin (and still the global center of the Waldensian community), was founded in 1855.[16] Many charitable and cultural institutions followed, as did Claudiana, a distinguished publishing house that is still bringing out many important works in the historiography of Italian evangelicalism. More sophisticated pastors, either graduates of theology school or, infuriatingly to the Roman community, ex-priests, attempted to evangelize new communities. Schoolteachers also served as evangelists.[17]

Together, these proselytes founded many new if numerically tiny communities: in the North, Milan, Bergamo, Como, Pavia, Brescia; Tuscany; and Sicily and Naples, when taken by Garibaldi, and Rome in 1870, with the fall of the Papal States. Until the establishment of the Kingdom, therefore, the history of Italian Protestantism is essentially that of a French-speaking community of roughly twenty thousand souls, marooned, so to speak, in the far northern "Protestant island" hugging the French border. Socially speaking, the Waldensians were made up largely of peasants and some lower-middle-class merchants involved in the sale of textiles. A second, small but considerable minority consisted of a fairly well-educated group of teachers and pastors; it was among their tyrannized ancestors, some of whom had contact with Swiss reformers and many of whom had read the works of Rousseau, that Reformation ideas first took hold.[18]

Along with the Waldensian church two other Italian evangelical churches were founded in the wake of the granting of religious freedom and civic emancipation. One came to be known as the Free Christian Church of Italy.[19] It lasted from 1852 to 1904. Many evangelicals were, again, former ("apostate") clerics, a large number of them once diocesan priests or friars. Among these, Alessandro Gavazzi (1809–89), generally understood to be the founder of the Chiesa Cristiana Libera d'Italia, had become a Barnabite monk at the age of sixteen. Four years later he left the church. Having quit both the church and

Italy, he became internationally renowned for shocking anti-Roman diatribes. Having launched his public Protestant career polemicizing against Jesuits and sacerdotalism in England, Scotland, and North America, the onetime monk's lectures in Montreal and Quebec were so virulently anti-Catholic that they caused riots in both cities. In Montreal five died and many were wounded. The following year Gavazzi's body would be burned in effigy in Quebec City, which only enhanced his reputation in liberal Italy. In 1870 Gavazzi became the leader of the Free Church of Italy; in 1875 he founded a theological college in Rome. There he would teach until his death in 1889. In addition to having started an influential journal, he wrote several anti-Catholic books, one with the characteristically expressive title *No Union with Rome* (1871).[20]

After organizing Italian Protestant exiles on the Continent, Gavazzi returned in 1860 to Italy and became chaplain to the army of Garibaldi. His support of Mazzini, champion of the cause of unification, made him persona non grata in Rome. So, too, did the enthusiasm of many of his followers and clergy with Freemasonry. Catholic polemicists would truthfully, if perniciously, scar Protestant pastors with participation in the anticlerical Craft, which did nothing to heighten evangelical popularity among those loyal to Rome. Along with his Garibaldian and Mazzinian ties, Gavazzi's links with the lodges made him a successful evangelist among the anticlerical and antipapal, those aggrieved with parochial Catholicism, and Italians enthusiastic for the prospect of political and cultural liberalism.[21]

Gavazzi was hardly alone in his passion for the heroes of the Reformation or in his general anticlericalism and opposition to papal rule.[22] The churches he founded in the Po Valley, like those founded by Giorgio Appia in Sicily and Naples, embraced the democratic and republican ideas he had championed. These Gavazzian communities were often identified or overlapped with communities of Masons or with the rapidly escalating number of those involved in labor movements. As in the case of the Waldensians, Gavazzian support for the project and leaders of the Risorgimento would heighten Roman Catholic antagonism. Political and religious differences brought out the hostility of the Catholic population, especially in the far southern regions of the country. A riot that broke out in Barletta (Puglia) on 19 March 1869 resulted in the death of six evangelical preachers.[23] Occasionally, Catholic communities in the fascist period would react to itinerant preachers or to colporteurs with similar displays of violence.

A second non-Waldensian evangelical denomination founded in this period came to be known as the Evangelical Christian Church of the Brethren

(Chiesa Cristiana Evangelica dei Fratelli). The name was intended to underscore both the Italian and the nondenominational character of the organization. By contrast to the Gavazzian churches, those founded by Piero Guicciardini (1808–86) and Pietrocola Rossetti (1825–1917), a cousin of Gabriele, were largely apolitical. The movement was focused, geographically, in Tuscany and especially Florence. Originally influenced by the Schwarzenau Brethren, the denomination came to incorporate important theological and disciplinary features from the Plymouth Brethren; it came also to be influenced by the work of American Baptist missionaries. Like other groups stemming from the Anabaptist tradition, the Church of the Brethren's clergy underscored conversion and the possibility of a life of individual sanctification.[24] Though in many senses harmless, Guicciardini was nonetheless exiled for professing the evangelical faith. Eventually he arrived in England, where he encountered leaders of the Plymouth Brethren. Sometimes referred to in archival sources as Darbisti, the Brethren were established in England in 1830 by a former Anglican priest named J. N. Darby, then resident in Plymouth. In fact, they had been founded some years earlier in Ireland; there they were known as Brethren and only later, after settling, as Plymouth Brethren.

Influenced by elements of Calvinism and Pietism, they were austere and disciplinarian, renouncing all secular occupations except those deemed compatible with the New Testament. Darby preferred an absolute separation of believers from the world. He aimed not merely to avoid the temptations of the profane realm but to avoid contamination by any form of Christianity that had ever, in his view, collectively apostatized. Like some American congregational churches, local churches were completely autonomous; the Brethren have no organized ministry. Like the Churches of Christ, they laid stress on the unity of all Christians and, similarly, were themselves ironically fragmented by theological rows. Like them, too, the strong expectation of the coming millennium propelled expectant Brethren missionaries to continental Europe, including Italy.[25]

Although he had met Darby personally, Salvatore Ferretti (1817–74), one of many exiles from Italy to land in England, rejected the world-denying ethos of the founder of the Brethren. Ferretti, a distant relative of Pius IX, had been destined for the priesthood as a young man. He then met a young girl, with whom he fled Florence. His path to London went through Geneva, where he embraced the evangelical faith and began a writing career. Deeply moved by the plight of poor children in London, he wrote scenes of urban misery suggestive of Dickens, then set up a hostel for Italian children in his own home. He preached the gospel of Mazzini, by whose writings he had been deeply influenced. In 1847 he began publishing the periodical with the telling name the *Echo of Savonarola.* The motto of the journal was *Italia renovabitur,* "Italy shall be renewed," the *ipsissima verba* of the fiery late-medieval Dominican reformer. Both the title and motto expressed the hope that Italy would regenerate itself religiously and politically. Savonarola, who went to his death for his convictions—including his unflinching critique of the papacy—was to many Italian evangelicals a hero and in their eyes a "forerunner of the Reformation."[26] Like many exiled evangelicals, Ferretti would return to Italy just after the establishment of the Kingdom.[27] The independence and pride of Florence in some ways made it the capital of evangelical Italy, despite the importance to Italian Protestants of the project of retaking Rome, a precondition for stripping temporal power from the papacy and reuniting Italy.[28]

Like other evangelical missionaries, the Darbyites arrived in Italy during the Risorgimento. All exhilarated in the prospect that political liberalism might herald a new religious age in Italy. Despite that shared conviction, efforts to cooperate with Baptist and Methodist missionaries failed. Darbyites were even said to have believed that they, not the Waldensians, were the only genuine evangelists of Italy. This claim was based in part on social class and regional pride. The Brethren, centered on Florence, spoke the pure Italian of Tuscany, the Waldensians a dialect of Italian influenced by French. One of their historians concludes that the Darbyites had apocalyptic hostility toward the Roman church but that they also disapproved of other evangelicals—and, with Catholic exclusivity, preferred no fraudulently evangelical denominations in Italy.[29]

ENGLISH AND AMERICAN MISSIONS, 1861–1922

Indigenous Italian missions would soon be joined by evangelical missionaries from England and America. These would come to command the evangelical operations in Italy, in converts, personnel, influence—and in the wrath they generated. Four Anglo-American missionary denominations were active in Italy from 1861: the Methodist (or Wesleyan), the Baptist, the Adventist, and the Salvation Army. Missionary operations were supplied almost exclusively by British and American members of these creeds. That was not the case with the Pentecostals, who became active in Italy in 1908. By and large

Pentecostalism was brought to Italy not by foreign missionaries but by Italians, most of whom had converted in the United States and, on their return home, proselytized their Italian countrymen.[30]

Possibly a term of opprobrium, "Methodism" grew out of an evangelical organization at Oxford called the Holy Club. Eventually, it became a term generally applied to the system of religious beliefs and practices promoted by the brothers John (1703–91) and Charles Wesley (1707–88), along with the astonishingly prolific preacher George Whitefield (1714–70).[31] A movement that would ultimately become known for pervasive and deep anti-Catholicism, Methodism was also perhaps equally opposed to focal aspects of Calvinist theology, especially its deterministic predestinarianism. The movement spread rapidly. By the time of John Wesley's death some fifteen thousand Methodists were enrolled. Many more had come under the influence of Methodist ideas. Methodism would go from strength to strength in England and Wales as a voluntaristic and progressively noncredal movement. Its representatives in Ireland would deplore the effects of Roman Catholicism on the native population, among whom Methodism would never become popular.

The decision of Whitefield to move to America would profoundly shape the future of Protestant Christianity in the United States as well as globally. Whitefield preached tens of thousands of sermons to millions in the great revivals in North America known collectively as the Great Awakening. In the view of many historians of American Christianity, the Great Awakening would inspire the creation of evangelical Christianity, a cross-denominational movement established on a package of theological beliefs, not least the sacred calling to evangelize the heathen nations, among which they certainly included the Catholic. By 1792 an evangelical Missionary Society, the Baptist, was created. Other such societies would soon follow.[32] Their sincerity would be received in Italy as insufferable presumption.

In accord with the emergence of a new global order in the eighteenth and nineteenth centuries, Methodism expanded worldwide; its near immediate global expansion was breathtaking. In Italy it would be spread by both English and American agents. Like so many Anglo-Saxon missionaries, Henry Piggott (1831–1917), the son of a former missionary to Sierra Leone, was drawn to Italy by glimpsing new opportunities for mission introduced with the Risorgimento.[33] Remaining in Italy for forty years, he hoped to marry Italian religious to ongoing political revolutions by creating a national evangelical church. Having given up that idea as impractical, Piggott would soon join forces with Bartolomeo Gualtieri (1817–45), another ex-priest. After founding churches in the North and in the Veneto, Gualtieri established his base in Rome. An admirer of Gavazzi, he eventually founded a network of communities in the north, central, and southern regions of the peninsula.

The American Methodist Episcopal church would soon join their British Wesleyan counterparts, one year after Rome was added to the new Italian State (1871), when Leroy Monroe Vernon (1838–96) was sent by the Missouri-Arkansas Conference to establish an outpost. Both communities, British and American, established themselves primarily in urban centers; they aimed first to convert members of the upper classes, including intellectuals. In 1874 Vernon incorporated the first Episcopal Methodist church of Italy; the following year he opened a temple in Rome. There, the Methodist church would erect buildings, some said by evangelical admirers to be as impressive and elegant as the ambient classical and ecclesiastical architecture. Construction of such buildings was designed to enhance visibility and prestige and thus to serve as an instrument in conversion.[34] Marked by the memory of domination, anti-evangelical Catholics regarded construction, especially in Rome, as foreign occupation, at best undesirable, at worst unacceptable. Deeply antagonistic to the papacy and an admirer of Gavazzi, Piggott would write with zeal against Roman Catholicism.[35] The anti-Roman theme, expressed by most missionary activists, would receive special emphasis from Wesleyan writers. As the Methodist expert David Hempton has put it, "Nothing is more ubiquitous in the pages of Methodist missionary reports than anti-Catholicism." Catholicism was "portrayed as despotic, priest-ridden, superstitious, illiberal, and ignorant. . . . [It] was the creed of the old world enslaving superstitious victims in the New."[36] Piggott and other evangelists in Italy were perpetuating a tradition already heard in the writings of the Wesley brothers, who were reproached by Catholic intellectuals almost immediately, if vainly, for gross anti-Roman sectarianism and bias.[37] It was a theme given unusual stress in Rome, to which language from a nineteenth-century missionary bears eloquent witness: "The might of ancient Rome vanished before the presence of our northern barbaric ancestors. Why may not this new and mightier Rome be conquered by weapons of Gospel truth?"[38] Here the missionary positions himself at a portentous moment in salvation history: at the beginning of a final apocalyptic struggle between the papal Antichrist and the Protestant Sons of Light. The bishop in charge of Methodist Foreign Missions from 1904 to 1912, E. B. T. Spencer, once said of Catholicism, "It is pagan in all but name." He also unambiguously articulated, in the martial rhetoric common to all, the ambitions of the Methodists in Rome: "The Protestant legions must gather all their energies and assail Popery, in its citadel, in Rome. . . . Before evangelizing the world, we must evangelize Rome."[39] The successes of the Methodists in Rome were as considerable as the hostility they inspired. The church established a theological school, a college for boys, and a publishing house. Day schools were established in many cities, from Venice, Genoa, and Turin to Naples. Little wonder that Catholic polemicists in the ventennio would write as if surrounded everywhere by the Enemy.

That said, the failure of missionary endeavors in Italy reflects realities registered elsewhere in the Latin and wider religious worlds. As Hempton has observed: "[The] sober reality of the missionary reports is that Methodism did not do well in Catholic and non-English-speaking regions" of the world.[40] In Italy Methodist proselytizing efforts were frustrated because of the perceived arrogance of missionaries, their connections to imperial America and England, and, above all, their undisguised, uncompromising, unrelenting anti-Catholicism. We ought not to overlook one other factor: American and Italian Methodists were especially linked with Freemasonry, a connection rarely left unsaid by Catholic controversialists.[41] Methodist proselytes were touched, by the end of the century, by two social movements which affected the targets of their preaching and framed the way in which they would be perceived and presented by Italian Catholics—and eventually by the fascist government. The first movement of significance was the emergence, especially within the American Methodist church, of a movement captured in one word: *massonevangelismo.* Waldensian, Baptist, Free Christian, and other churches had many leaders who had experience with, even leadership positions among, the Masons. But when Bishop William Burt arrived in Italy in 1889 he made American Methodism, as Spini has noted, the "stronghold [*roccaforte*] of *massonevangelismo.*" Methodists were quick to make common cause with Italian Freemasonry, whose heartfelt anti-Catholicism at the time rivaled that of the Methodists. Indeed, Saverio Fera (1850–1915) caused a schism in Italian Freemasonry by forming a group of anti-Catholic, evangelical Freemasons.

Giorgio Spini spoke often and with sensitivity, in print and in public, on the need for evangelical Christians to link with the Masonic movement in Italy. "The great risk evangelical Christianity faced after the end of the Risorgimento," he explains, "was to find itself enclosed . . . in a pietist sacristy . . . detached from Italian reality. With the holiest intentions in the world, that detachment from the 'world,' which pious evangelicals expressed, according to the spirit of the [Great] Awakening, risked being translated into something worse than an escape from reality. . . . *Massonevangelismo,* with all its obvious limitations, still represented for evangelicals an escape from the pietist sacristy and their first awareness of their responsibilities as Christians toward their Italian brothers."[42] Spini asked readers to remember the tradition of resistance to political and pontifical tyranny, which had made martyrs of many Masons. Quite true. Nonetheless, Methodists gave a hostage to fortune, not only to Catholic but to many Protestant critics who, in the long run, regarded the association as damaging and Freemasonry as a movement from which they sought to dissociate themselves. During the fascist period Catholic opponents strove to delegitimize evangelicals by associating them with Freemasonry and hostility to the fascist government. This was a successful effort that would cause the lodges to cease their activity in Italy. Spini, not wrongly, regarded these links as honorable. He therefore underlined the degree to which Masons resisted fascism not only in Italy but also in Spain.[43]

The second social movement influential in Italian Methodism might weakly be called religious socialism. Many Methodist preachers either took a socialist perspective on worldly misery or emphasized the social implications of evangelical Christianity—an enormously influential development in Christianity, to which official Catholicism was initially and for a long time opposed.[44] As a result Methodist missionaries over time directed their message to the lower classes in the cities. With funding from the American Methodist church especially they also established many social service organizations for which their traditional clientele of intellectuals and the affluent would have little use: orphanages, schools, kindergartens, and educational and welfare institutions.[45] In 1946 the two branches of Methodism, English and American, would merge to create a single church. The united church would then, in 1975, merge with the Waldensian.

The genesis of Baptist theology and Baptist churches is somewhat complicated, but, for my purposes, I can say that the Dutch separatists and Anabaptist wing of the Reformation in Zurich were primarily concerned with establishing (reestablishing, in their view) the baptism of believers rather than all in a Christian society in infancy. This, they maintained, was ordained in the New Testament. The first English Baptist churches were established in 1612, and in 1630 in America, in Providence, Rhode Island. Though Calvin himself was vehemently opposed to Anabaptism, the Baptist churches were Calvinist in theology and in many other respects. Again, Baptists were among the many congregations that came under the influence of the Great Awakening in New

England, which led to a transatlantic exodus of Baptist missionaries and rapid growth on the Continent as well as to internal missionizing that led to the same in the southern states of North America.[46]

The first Baptist center in Italy was established by British and American missionaries. In 1863 they settled in Bologna, which would become a base, known as the Gospel Mission of the Italians. The missionary Edward Clarke (1820–1912) would soon install an important, much more durable center of missionizing in the strategic gulf port of La Spezia, thus targeting both the young and the military.[47] This center of Baptist propaganda (throughout the fascist period "propaganda" simply signified proselytizing personally or through publication) was a target of special prelatical and governmental concern during the fascist period. The Baptists introduced their first missionaries to Rome in the very year that Porta Pia was breached, the same moment the American Southern Baptists established a presence in the city. A northern Baptist, William C. van Meter, dedicated himself to opening evangelical schools. William K. Landels influentially preached in Rome and Naples in 1875 and 1877, respectively. In 1884 the two churches united to form the Opera Cristiana evangelica battista d'Italia. It then had 51 communities and, tellingly, 2,240 members.[48] Virtually all their communities were numerically Lilliputian.

Italian Baptists introduced the theology and practice of "believers' baptism" in Italy. Like the Wesleyans, they emphasized the social meaning of Christianity. Their pastors consciously ministered to the proletarian classes, to which they preached their message of social redemption and among whom, like many other evangelical groups, they achieved their greatest successes. In Gioia del Colle (Puglia) an important community was established by the socialist pastor Liutprando Saccomani.[49] In June 1920 his followers occupied the lands of local landlords in protest. Six peasants died. The whole episode made the Baptists seem a political danger.

Later Baptist leaders' writings and publications would be perceived as a threat to the fascist regime. Dexter Gooch Whittingill (1866–1956), an American missionary, would carve out a prominent place in the cultural and religious milieu of European Protestantism. He created in 1901 the influential journal *Bilychnis,* where he published articles to which Catholic polemicists would often respond. He founded a second review, *Conscientia,* published from 1922 to 1927. Over the course of time the magazine became increasingly antifascist; it was suppressed in 1927 by the regime. Another review, significantly entitled *Gioventù Cristiana,* would be founded; it, too, was crushed by the fascist regime. During the fascist period the Baptist churches, like others, were persecuted. Some were forced to close. Saccomani and other Baptists would be tried, convicted, and sentenced *in confino.*[50] Suspicions about political loyalty, born years before, would haunt their churches and persist throughout the 1930s and beyond.

The Adventists—a name adopted in 1861—are the largest of a cluster of sects, originating in the first half of the nineteenth century in the United States, that focus both on the Second Coming of Christ and on the importance and biblical foundation of observing the sabbath from Friday dusk to Saturday sunset. Like many evangelical churches, the Adventists grew out of the Second Great Awakening. In this case the Adventists drew many from Methodist, Presbyterian, and Congregational churches; their members came to believe the Adventist prophecy, made on the basis of a reading of Daniel 8:14 that Christ would soon return. The group emerged in 1831 when William Miller (1782–1849), then a Baptist, prophesied that the return of Christ in glory would occur in 1843, later recalculated for 1844. When he began to share his prophecies with others, a movement coalesced around him.[51]

When Christ did not return in 1843 or in 1844, a nonevent dubbed the Great Disappointment, some of Miller's followers defected. The visionary Ellen White (1827–1915), around whom the largest group of Adventists would gather, founded with her husband the Seventh-day Adventist church. White famously argued that Christ had in fact come to prepare for the final judgment, which she thought would take place quietly. Under the influence of White, the Adventists came to hold some beliefs, as in the authority of scripture, in common with other evangelicals. In addition, they maintained that Christ would come again imminently and that the command to obey the sabbath was intended for both Jews and Christians. Some Adventists held distinctive beliefs about the state of the soul after death. Living austere lives of temperance, they abstained from alcohol and tobacco and were discouraged from consuming tea, coffee, or meat. Originally vegetarian, they long emphasized what one today might call wholeness in body and mind, a theme important in the writings of White, who wrote on agriculture and health and promoted vegetarianism. The Adventists quickly became known and regarded for the quality of the medical and educational provision emphasized in their missionary work, spurred by a vision of White in which God told her to send missionaries abroad and expand internationally.[52]

As was true of other American sects, the Italian Adventist church emerged first in the Waldensian valleys.[53] In fact, the first two Italian Adventists were converts from the Waldensians. It was in the Waldensian valleys that the onetime Franciscan friar, former Baptist, and, finally, self-sent missionary Michał B. Czechowski began to spread the Adventist message.. For Italian Adventists the question of sabbath observance, not eschatology, was central. If missionary activity began in the North, it was in Naples that the Adventists, in the nineteenth century, would have their greatest impact and which they would make the principal target of their missionary activity. That said, there were twenty-two Adventists in Naples in the late nineteenth century.[54] When Mussolini, in 1932, protested to the pope that evangelical communities were a speck in the sea of Catholics, it was presumably with demographic numbers like these in mind.

Adventist belief, along with the pacifist convictions of some members, made them suspect. So did the anti-Catholicism of some of its leaders and writers. Adventists came to be associated with Pentecostals and cast thus as subversives, antisocial, and antimilitaristic. During the years of fascism, they, too, were charged with being a danger to social health.[55]

The Churches of Christ were one of three main denominations to have emerged from a movement begun on the American frontier by the Presbyterian leaders Thomas (1763–1854) and his son Alexander Campbell (1788–1866). In 1832 the reform movement led by the Campbells would merge with a similar movement of restoration led in Kentucky by Barton W. Stone (1772–1844). Emphasizing the unity of all Christians, the joined congregations simply identified themselves as Christians or Disciples of Christ. Persuaded that the historic creeds had split Christians, the Campbells led a reform movement that stressed reliance on scripture and that was emphatically nondogmatic. They aimed to establish a form of belief and practice that depended solely on the Bible in the hopes that, on the foundation of a single, common source of authority, they could bring together the "separated brethren" of the Christian world under the aegis of an austerely biblical and nontheological faith. Eventually disagreements over the biblical foundations of liturgical music shattered all attempts at unity.[56]

By 1906 disagreements caused one group, called Churches of Christ, to break off and form a separate denomination.[57] It was this denomination, based in the Upper South and more conservative than the liberal Disciples of Christ, that sent missionaries to Italy. They were strongly influenced by the apocalyptic outlook of their common founder, Campbell, who would begin a journal tellingly entitled the *Millennial Harbinger.* Two of their leading historians have observed: "Anyone seeking to understand [the] Churches of Christ must also understand the apocalyptic heritage of that tradition."[58] In that journal and elsewhere Campbell had prophesied that evangelical Christianity, purged of Romanism, its simple message restored, would unite all Christians and usher in the millennial age. In one number of his journal Campbell observed: "Popery was the great Antichrist so minutely delineated in the prophecies of Daniel . . . and in the book of Revelation. . . . [T]his antichristian power, after suffering a temporary depression (as Romanism has done since the 16th century), is in the 'last days,' to gather up its waning strength and allying itself perhaps with civil despotism, to make a final onset upon Christianity. . . . With these prophecies before you, we would ask you whether there is nothing ominous of evil in the recent movements of the Church of Rome?"[59]

It took little for twentieth-century missionaries to apply this prophecy to their own day and to identify fascism with civil despotism and the union of the Roman church and Italian state as an omen of adversity. The first of these missionaries is legendarily said to be an American soldier who, during the Great War, had been touched "by the pitiable conditions of the people of Italy." This young man "returned to America with a burning desire to return there as a soldier of Christ."[60] Whether or not the author of this account recognized that the soldier of Christ topos is an ancient staple of hagiographical literature (the onetime cavalryman Martin of Tours [316–97] is the first Western saint to have been called a soldier of Christ) is neither here nor there. This is an origin story. As such, it goes on to claim that others, similarly inspired, soon returned to Italy. Originally intending to center their operations on Milan, the missionaries decided on Rome instead. Aside from the presence of the American embassy and of many other evangelical groups there was another appeal: Rome was the "center of Apostacy [*sic*]." Her doom was "written and sealed." Campbell went so far as to divide Christendom into Popedom and Protestantdom. As in Jerusalem, the glory of the city had passed. The history of Rome was "more claimant, more soul attractive, more alluring" than that of second city Milan. And it was that city, Rome, that he aimed, religiously, to conquer.

The Salvation Army was founded in 1865 by William Booth (1829–1912), a former Methodist who, following an experience of conversion in 1844, became a revivalist preacher. A native of Nottingham, this partly Jewish Englishman later moved to London. Booth's aggressive preaching caused him to come into conflict with the Methodists, with whom he broke in 1861. He then established a revival movement of his own in Whitechapel, initially called the Christian Mission. In addition to evangelism, it understood social and rescue work to be central to its mission. In the last two decades of the nineteenth century, the mission spread to America, Australia, the European Continent, and elsewhere. In 1878 it received its present title—it is organized along military lines—and Booth became the first general of the Salvation Army. Though the religious teaching of the Salvation Army corresponds largely to traditional evangelical belief, it rejects all sacraments, including those commonly honored by other Protestant groups. Rather, the moral and social elements of Christianity receive special attention, including care of criminals, workers, and the sick.[61]

The history of the Salvation Army in Italy begins in Rome in 1887. Because of the militaristic name of the organization it was misunderstood. Public witnessing, which was a hallmark of the Army, was publicly derided, and police authorities could refuse, as the Roman curia hoped they would, to grant them permission to hold open meetings. The center established in Rome was closed after only two years, but the Army reconstituted itself in 1890 in the Waldensian valleys. The return of americani resulted in the spread, in the north and south of the country, of the organization. Unlike other foreign cults, the Salvation Army was never granted public recognition. The fascist regime was deeply hostile. It frustrated many of the activities of the Army, and by 1940 all activities ceased. Along with the Pentecostals and Jehovah's Witnesses, the Salvation Army was the denomination most heavily persecuted during the fascist era.[62]

Pentecostal Christianity is distinguished by the expectation of receiving the same experience and spiritual gifts as did the first Christians "on the day of Pentecost" (Acts 2:1–4). Believers therefore underscore the importance of gifts like glossolalia, prophecy, and healing, spoken of in the Acts of the Apostles and in the First Letter of Paul to the Corinthians. These gifts are usually received spontaneously in public, common acts of worship. The power to exercise these gifts is given at first in an experience commonly called baptism in the Holy Spirit, so as to distinguish this experience both from sacramental baptism and from conversion. Since the early twentieth century "Spirit baptism" has normally been marked by the experience of glossolalia, or spontaneously speaking in unknown tongues. Those baptized in the Holy Spirit may receive other supernatural gifts, including the ability to heal, prophesy, or interpret glossolalia. Like the Baptist and Methodist Holiness churches from which they first emerged, early Pentecostalists emphasized the importance of conversion, moral rigor, and the inspired interpretation of the Bible, gifts they thought common in the earliest church. Unlike other American churches, they never formed a single congregation. Instead, single congregations came together; they formed a variety of denominations. It is that group of denominations which make up the Pentecostal movement.[63]

The movement emerged in contemporary Protestant history at the Bethel Bible College in Topeka, Kansas. The director of the college, Charles Fox Parham (1873–1929), had been influenced by the American Holiness movement. Persuaded that a cold and formalistic church needed rejuvenation, he urged his ministers to wait for the outpouring of the Holy Spirit. In 1901 several of his students began to speak in unknown tongues, which Parham claimed as evidence that they had been genuinely baptized in the Holy Spirit. He further understood recurrences of the Pentecost experience prophetically: they were signs of the end-times. Motivated by a sense of the nearness of the end and the consequent urgency of converting the unbaptized, Pentecostalists set out on a mission to evangelize the world.[64]

As their earliest missionaries were ridiculed or ignored, the Pentecostal movement almost collapsed. Parham saved the church in 1903 by resurrecting the practice of faith healing, which in turn became a hallmark of Pentecostalism. The movement spread widely in Texas, Alabama, and Florida as well as in Kansas and Missouri. National and international expansion ensued, largely as a result of the Azusa Street Revival at the Apostolic Faith Gospel Mission in Los Angeles. Under the direction of its one-eyed pastor, William Seymour, who had been influenced by Parham's teachings in Houston, Azusa Street became a great center of Pentecostal experience. Seymour's congregations cut across many social and racial lines, attracting the wealthy and destitute, blacks and whites, Hispanics and so-called Anglo-Saxons.[65]

Some pastors who embraced Pentecostal practices left their mainstream churches and joined the Church of God, headquartered in Cleveland, Ohio. But many other pastors lost their pulpits, and parishioners speaking in tongues were expelled from their churches. Resistance from Protestants operating within the established framework of reformed communities caused many Pentecostal practitioners to withdraw from their churches and to form new ones. Some of these, by the start of the Great War, were housed in storefront missions in both urban and rural settings. The potential for unity was shattered by divisive doctrinal debates over the significance of the baptism in the Holy Spirit. Other religious and ethnological beliefs, including pacifism and views on racial difference, also had fissiparous potential. In the Deep South the movement became segregated along the very racial lines initially rejected in Los Angeles but familiar to older denominations in the South.[66]

The apocalyptic expectation of early Pentecostalists and their conviction that the gospel had to be preached throughout the world before the end brought Pentecostalism to Italy.[67] In 1908 Giacomo Lombardi received baptism in the Holy Spirit at about the time the Azusa Street Revival founded a new center in Chicago. An immigrant, he returned home to Italy in 1908. Establishing assemblies in Calabria, Abruzzi, and Rome, Lombardi, along with many other americani, diffused the Pentecostalist message throughout the country. Within twenty years almost 150 centers had been established in Italy, before growth was brought to a halt with the signing of the Lateran Pacts.

The regime was more hostile to the Pentecostals than to any other sect. Persecution began in earnest in 1934; in the following year the famous Buffarini Decree criminalized the entire denomination. Many pastors were sent in confino, to camps, or to prisons. To the dismay of Vatican officials and the fascist government, initially persuaded that they had abolished the cult, the movement went underground, reconstituted itself under other names, and met in private homes as well as in caves or cellars. While Pentecostalism was restored under the Allied occupation, it came to suffer persecution under the Christian Democratic regime.[68] Like other Protestant denominations, the church is well represented in the South. Early patterns of settlement reflect realities today: more than half of its congregations are in the provinces of Apulia, Basilicata, Calabria, the Campania, and Sicily.[69]

The founder of the International Bible Students Association, Charles Taze Russell (1852–1916), was also instrumental in the development of the Jehovah's Witnesses. Russell had left both Presbyterianism and Congregationalism. A chance encounter with members of the Adventist movement persuaded him that the Bible could be interpreted so as to prophesy the shape of God's plan of salvation, including the end of the world. Russell's apocalyptic viewpoint would have tremendous influence on the theological outlook and millennial expectation of the Jehovah's Witnesses: for them, the end was truly nigh. As one of its historians has said: "Almost from the moment of its foundation, devotees have lived in anticipation of a new Messianic Kingdom, in which all earthly wickedness would be destroyed and paradise be inaugurated."[70]

In 1881 Russell founded a monthly religious journal entitled *Zion's Watch Tower,* the name he gave to a religious society he incorporated in 1884. An extraordinarily prolific writer, Russell composed countless articles, tracts, and sermons for the journal. Strongly influenced by the writings of Millerite Adventists, he was convinced that Christ had returned invisibly in October 1874 and that only a few years remained before the final return of Christ. It was the duty of later Witnesses to spread this apocalyptic word, though only a tiny community of elect, 144,000 in all, would participate in the coming millennial kingdom. Russell published a six-volume Bible commentary originally entitled *Millennial Dawn.* The titles of these books are telling: *The Time Is at Hand* (1889) and *The Battle of Armageddon* (1897). After his death, a schism split the society. Those who had maintained their ties with the Watch Tower Society were given the name Jehovah's Witnesses.[71]

These followers were now convinced that the New Kingdom would come only when the true word of God—of Jehovah—had been brought to the ends of the earth: thus the missionary fervor of many decades of Witnesses. They have often been regarded as political dissidents, religious deviants, or both. Some of the practices of the Witnesses have caused misunderstanding, hostility, and even repression: their door-to-door style of ministry, the public sale of their writings, a taboo against blood infusions, their reluctance to mix with non-Witnesses. Most seriously for my topic, they have always refused to honor the symbols of nationhood and the obligations, especially military conscription, of citizenship.

In 1891 a group of Italian immigrants first encountered a band of students formed by Russell. That same year Russell had visited Italy. There he met with Daniele Rivoir, a Waldensian and professor of languages at Torre Pellice. Though Rivoir never became a Witness, he was deeply interested in the biblical interpretations of Russell and, indeed, wished to translate his interpretive work into Italian and circulate it. In 1903 Rivoir translated Russell's *The Divine Plan of the Ages* and began to translate *The Watchtower.* In the same year a group of Russell's students in Pinerolo held its first meetings in the home of Fanny Lugli, a Waldensian. Two years later the Bible Students held their first assembly in Pinerolo. It was there that *The Watchtower* was published. Already sensitive to the fascist authorities, the seventy students who attended the first meeting of the Bible Society disguised it as a wedding celebration. By that time Remigio Cumminetti, a Bible Student, had become the first conscientious objector in contemporary Italian history. For this, he received a prison sentence of more than three years from a military tribunal in Alessandria (1916). He spent the interwar years translating materials imported from America into Italian.[72]

The fascist regime monitored the sect closely. There is an odd disproportion between the number of Jehovah's Witnesses in Italy and the attention they garnered. In 1939 there were no more than 150 Witnesses in the whole of the country. Spies nonetheless generated an immense amount of espionage literature, available today in the Central State Archives in Rome. This was not only because of their proselytizing but also because of their extensive correspondence abroad. Many letters from the United States, the Witnesses' then-headquarters in Brooklyn, were monitored. Religious publications enclosed in packages were always seized, the name of the addressee carefully recorded in official police logs. The letters monitored would often spark police investigations. Indeed, the Naples Prefecture had directed an espionage report to the Ministry of the Interior. More would soon follow. Eventually, an import ban was imposed, ignored by many Witnesses; evangelizing through a very wide distribution of tracts, other books, and the Bible was central to their self-understanding. Confiscation of publications steadily increased. In September 1929 the Ministry of the Interior sent out to prefects the names of roughly 60 subscribers to *The Watchtower.* Fascist police would go as far as Bern and even to Brooklyn to gather information on the Bible Students. Many students were harassed over the years, even more so at the outbreak of the Ethiopian War (October 1935), when refusal to join the army resulted in sentences of up to five years in confino. Others would be so sentenced for continuing to preach despite orders to desist. In 1939–40 no fewer than five circulars were issued by the Ministry of the Interior regarding the threat of the Witnesses and how to deal with them.[73]

Having stressed the unique origins, developments, and characteristics of the Anglo-American evangelizing communities, I want to recognize what these groups had in common. After all, for most lay Catholics in Italy, "Christian" and "Catholic" were synonymous. They had never before heard terms like "Methodist" or "Baptist," and they would not have heard of them as words to modify "Christian." The same was true of the overwhelming number of diocesan priests in Italy, whose ignorance Vatican officials recognized and took measures to overcome. Insofar as the great mass of Italian Catholics thought of Protestant missionaries at all, it was as an undifferentiated group that shared a number of undesirable characteristics.

First, each of these communities was part of a broader movement of restoration, or the attempted reconstruction of an ancient, original, and sacred order, which all, despite many differences, affirmed to be based on the simplicity and discipline of New Testament Christianity. Ernesto Comba, a missionary to Italy, put it like this: the grand attempt of the evangelical churches was "to restore the simplicity and purity of primitive Christianity; to separate religion from the political elements which cause it to degenerate into clericalism; to demonstrate that every legitimate progress of civil life is not only compatible but indissolubly connected with true and genuine Christianity; to offer hospitality to souls who [are] emancipated from sacerdotal tyranny . . . [and to cause] the leaven of the eternal Gospel to penetrate into the Italian soul."[74]

This statement, while nowhere expressly anti-Catholic, is everywhere implicitly so. All the evangelical cults, though perhaps to different degrees, saw the Roman church as a corruption of the apostolic ideal: neopagan, priest-ridden, and hopelessly tied up with the flawed world and corrupt political order. Though many of these denominations would come to break apart—essentially over rival readings of the New Testament text—none doubted that their own doctrines and practices mirrored those practiced and taught by leaders in the early church, as set out with limpid clarity in the New Testament. As this conviction implies and as every evangelical Christian stated, Christians had no need of an authoritative magisterium. Indeed, the papal church had only clouded the pure stream of ancient Christianity. The awesome, millennial Protestant project was to decontaminate the pool the popes had sullied.

Second, all of the missionizing denominations were proudly associated with the Risorgimento and had linked their fortunes to the liberal political order. Many of the confessions sent missionaries to Italy around 1870 because they were persuaded that a new political order would pave the way for a religious transformation of Italy. Some even viewed the events of 1861–70 in apocalyptic terms: unification was the divinely designed, auspicious moment at which pure Christianity could be reintroduced—in the land that had done more than any other to defile it. Evangelical enthusiasm for political liberalism and the anticlerical sentiment of many leaders of the Risorgimento would pave the way for the evangelical denominations to enter Italy.

In the long run, however, those associations would not be forgotten, as the liberal order gave way to fascistic politics in the wake of the humiliations suffered in the First World War. In the fascist period Catholic writers reminded readers that Protestantism was not only heretical: it was the source of all modern errors, most of which the Catholic church had condemned in the nineteenth and twentieth centuries. The church had turned its back on modernity, of which evangelicals were despised as foreign, alien carriers. Popes, for example, had repudiated liberalism and all its work. Even elements of evangelical Christianity that Roman Catholicism came, eventually if cautiously, to adopt—the social implications of the gospel, ecumenism—popes first shunned as dangerous, nonapostolic perversions of the gospel.

The British and American origins of the missionaries also made them suspect. The backing of prosperous Anglo-Saxon nations caused many Italians to distrust all foreign missionaries, especially those bringing gifts, like the American dollar. (Those who went over to Protestantism were derided as "dollar converts.") Objectionably foreign, they brought a culture, a worldview, and an economic outlook—not to mention a religious style and message—almost entirely strange and unfamiliar. As I have noted, some had strong links with deeply anticlerical Freemasonry, itself condemned by the Roman church. All of this suggested that, once the liberal period had passed, Protestants would face intolerance and worse, and they did.

The following point requires emphasis, though in 1922 no Roman cleric would have thought so. Far from thinking that the Roman Catholic church had fallen away from the original, ancient order, all Catholics believed and affirmed weekly in the liturgical creed that theirs was the true—the "one, holy, apostolic"—church. This was a theme that anti-Protestant polemicists underscored in the fascist period: no other church could trace its origins to the apostles or claim an unbroken chain of continuity with them. The Roman church alone had handed down the gospel from Christ through the Apostles and, from them, to the uninterrupted line of episcopal succession. The true gospel was in the custody of the Roman pope alone. Like ancient heretical gnostics, Protestants were fragmented. They were as arrogant as ancient gnostics, too. Missionaries gazed at Italy as Keats's "Cortez" did the Pacific. Few things so irritated Catholic polemicists as the idea, which they considered as self-important as it was ludicrous, that Italy was missionary territory.[75] Perhaps only one thing aggravated them more: that the Protestant message was being spread, in part, by ex-priests. This was *trahison des clercs* with a vengeance. Former brothers had broken their vows. Apostates, they had embraced false religion—heresy. They, too, were hungry for American dollars. And, as the sharpest critics of the Roman church they once served, they were feared. For all these reasons Vatican officials would track them carefully after they left the priesthood.

Little had changed over three centuries in Catholic Italy. In his *Apologia,* John Henry Newman, explaining why he had embraced Catholicism, called both Lutheranism and Calvinism heresies, as bad as fifth-century Monophysitism (an ancient Christological error). In fact, these communities were not "churches" at all.[76] This view of Protestant confessions has endured at the highest levels of the Roman church. In 2000 Joseph Ratzinger (later Pope Benedict XVI [2005–13]), reflecting ecclesiological views that prevailed during the fascist period, has maintained that the word "church" could not be given to non-Roman "ecclesial communities." Lacking "elements considered essential" to Roman doctrine, these communities did not (among other things) "accept the Catholic sense of church," he declared, as then-prefect of the Congregation for the Doctrine of the Faith, in the declaration *Dominus Iesus* (2000).[77] If such thoughts could be expressed by the worldwide leader of the Catholic church at the dawn of the twenty-first century, it takes little imagination to grasp the resolve with which popes and prelates resisted evangelicals, their claim to represent true Christianity or the "gospel of Christ," and their efforts at conversion in the mid-twentieth century and in the global capital of Roman Catholicism.

In 1925 an Italian émigré from Basilicata, by then an active and successful proselyte in America, composed a pamphlet in which he addressed potential converts back in Italy: "BROTHERS! The word of God commands us to leave behind Babylon.

"Listen: 'Then I heard another voice from heaven saying, "Come out of her, my people, lest you take part in her sins, lest you share in her plagues"' (Apocalypse 18:4). All true Christians prefer to be faithful to the religion of Christ as taught in the New Testament and reject human inventions, paying heed to the warning of St. Paul, who says: 'But even if we or an angel from heaven should preach a gospel other than the one we preached to you, let him be anathema.'" Within years this pamphlet would land in the hands of Roman Catholic priests and, finally, in the Archives of the Vatican.[78] The apocalyptic tone and anti-Roman summons to leave the Babylonian church, addressed to Italians, would soon panic Roman Catholics, including the most powerful among them in Italy. They would react first with alarm and, then, a fierce determination to suppress.

CHAPTER 2

Before the Concordat

TACCHI VENTURI AND *THE PROTESTANT DANGER* (1922–29)

The most influential response to the Protestant danger came from Father Pietro Tacchi Venturi, who composed a widely read polemical pamphlet. Tacchi Venturi was extraordinarily effective in sounding the alarm in part because he wrote with obvious distress and in a panicked tone that matched the evangelicals in apocalyptic fervor. In addition, he linked evangelical Christians with virtually all liberal groups, movements, and philosophies that had, by the time he wrote in 1927, already been condemned by the church. He also raised fears that evangelicals were bringing to Italy a "civilizing" form of Christianity in the service of a diabolically inspired scheme that had enlisted a hated team of reprobates: cosmopolitan Jews, anticlerical Freemasons, and antifascists. This coterie of enemies intended not only to topple the fascist government but to displace Latin culture and replace it with Anglo-Saxon plutocracy. Evangelical Christians were not innocent as doves; they had planned a religious, political, and cultural revolution.

The Jesuit priest Pietro Tacchi Venturi was among the most formidable clerics in fascist Italy. When the Lateran Accords (1929) brought church and state in Italy into union, after sixty years of mutual alienation and hostility, Tacchi Venturi would enjoy a particular rise in power. Christened by Italian contemporaries Mussolini's "Confessor" (and by a German newspaper Mussolini's "Rasputin"), Tacchi Venturi served as Il Duce's handpicked emissary to the Roman curia and to Pope Pius XI. By the time Mussolini was deposed in 1943 Tacchi Venturi had had hundreds of meetings with him. Yet he saw himself as no mere intermediary; nor, in fact, was he. Indeed, he has recently been described by one American historian as a "power broker extraordinaire."[1]

Tacchi Venturi became a Jesuit at the age of seventeen. A well-educated historian, he would become the author of a massive history of the order and editor of Matteo Ricci's letters. Eventually he was appointed official historian of the Italian Jesuits and secretary of the Society of Jesuits from 1914 to 1921. Since Włodzimierz Ledóchowski (r. 1915–42), then superior general of the Jesuits, was considered Austro-Hungarian and thus a citizen of an enemy nation, he had to remain in Switzerland during much of the Great War. During that time Tacchi Venturi was the de facto general of the order. Tacchi Venturi would help to bring the Vatican and the government into negotiations and played some yet-to-be-written role in the substance of the accords finally signed in 1929.

Though he presented himself as one who merely shunted messages back and forth between the Vatican and Mussolini, Tacchi Venturi attempted to persuade the pope and Mussolini that they were insufficiently alert to the dangers to Italy of its Jewish population, which, at something like one-tenth of 1 percent of the population, was tiny. To Mussolini, who initially disbelieved him, Tacchi Venturi insisted that "Talmudic Jews" and "Judaized Bolsheviks" sought to destroy and dominate Italy. His role in Mussolini's decision to pass the Italian Racial Laws (1938), if any, has yet to be established.[2] Tacchi Venturi worked, though not alone, to persuade Mussolini (the pope needed no convincing) that Protestants on the peninsula were far from harmless evangelical missionaries. By that time, however, he was no longer the Vatican's point man on the Protestant affair; Borgongini would take that role. However, he was the leading anti-Protestant polemicist in the period around 1922–29. In league with the Jews and others of Italy's perennial enemies, evangelical missionaries, he feared (or affected to fear), represented a threat as dangerous to Italian fascism as to Roman Catholicism.

In 1926 Tacchi Venturi sent a highly classified four-page letter, with three attachments from informants (one of them a spy on antifascist exile in Paris, Gaetano Salvemini [1873–1957]), to Secretary of State Cardinal Pietro Gasparri (r. 1914–30).[3] The letter was entitled "Some Observations on the Current Antireligious [i.e., anti-Catholic] Campaign in Italy and Means of Confronting It." Tacchi Venturi began it by observing that for all Catholics it was an occasion of great joy that the current fascist government was then binding itself ever more tightly to the interests of Catholicism.[4] He rejoiced over the "indissoluble links" then beginning to yoke church and state in Italy. Regrettably, this "consoling phenomenon" of the recent Catholic religious revival, animating dioceses everywhere, was then being frustrated. Why? Because aggressive Protestant missionaries had been allowed to fan out across the peninsula. Even worse, the evangelical proselytes had allied themselves with other "sectarian" enemies of Italy: Jews, Freemasons, and Bolsheviks.

Though the Protestant danger was surely distressing, the sectarian alliance of which it was a component was far more treacherous—and already alarmingly well organized. Indeed, the nemeses of Italy had, Tacchi Venturi warns, come to an agreement on a neat division of labor to achieve their malicious objectives: "The Jewish lords of high finance, the Protestants who are solidly established in Italy to conquer it, the Masons who dominate the bureaucracy, the Bolsheviks who make up the rest: all work tirelessly and with formidable means, against Catholicism [religione] and the church at the special service of an Anglo-Saxon hegemony. . . . [They have] a vast plan of conquest, of our dear Italy, that is today religious, tomorrow political!"[5]

Tacchi Venturi underscored the national and cultural character of the evangelical threat. Protestant churches and missionaries, most from the United States, were taking orders from Jews, Masons, and Bolsheviks; they in turn were linked to the powerful imperialistic interests of plutocratic British and Americans. Anglo-American actors aimed in manipulating Protestant missionaries first to undermine the Catholic church and then to bring the Italian national government to collapse: "We need to be vigilant of the vast action of propaganda that occurs under Anglo-Saxon Protestantism," Tacchi Venturi warned. "It works feverishly," he continued, "for the de-catholicizing of Italy, and for its subservience, first religious and then political, under the Plutocratic and Anglo-Saxon hegemony."[6] In the Italy of the 1920s élite, highly educated, accomplished, and intelligent Catholic clerics and other leaders could and did believe, or so it seems, that a Jewish-Masonic cabal could manipulate and was manipulating the powers of western Europe as well as England and America—and it was doing so through the efforts of American and British missionaries. Critically, the powerful and respected Tacchi Venturi gave this view credibility, dramatically raising the stakes of what might have appeared to others, like Mussolini, to be an innocuous incursion of unarmed American and British proselytes, some of them pacifist. Tacchi Venturi did nothing to quiet the anxieties of Pope Pius XI by expressing these views; nor did he (or the pope) ever persuade Mussolini that he should *worry more.* Though the pope seems not to have accepted the extreme claims of his Jesuit deputy, especially regarding the putative sectarian alliance, his own alarm was both reflected in and intensified by Tacchi Venturi's maximal picture of the threat.

In fact, in later, published writings Tacchi Venturi expressed fear that the religious project of Anglo-Saxon Protestants was relatively innocuous when understood against the background of a broader, more portentous Protestant plan of domination. In his view the Protestant deconversion campaign was merely a stalking horse for the political conquest of Italy. This is why "plutocratic-imperialistic Anglo-Saxon and North American elements, notoriously influenced by international Jewish and Masonic sectarianism," had sunk capital in Italy so lavishly.[7] Protestant missionaries were hardly motivated by altruistic concerns in pouring so much money into Italy. Rather, they were driven by antifascist hatred, and they aimed to sabotage and finally abolish the government and eradicate fascist ideology. The Protestant danger was thus not just a religious but a national danger. It aimed not just to de-Catholicize the Italian people; it wanted to denationalize it and de-fascitize it.[8] To Tacchi Venturi the danger of "plutocratic Protestantism," which was "allied with Masons, Socialists, and subversives of every stripe," was particularly acute, as it could penetrate the Italian masses so easily, oblivious as they were to the insidious methods of the Protestants.[9] Rhetorically, Tacchi Venturi's strategy was effective, if tethered loosely to realities on the ground.

One reason that Tacchi Venturi believed in an alliance between antifascist Bolsheviks, Jews, and Freemasons is that he had several spies working for him in some of the capitals of Europe. These spies persuaded him that such networks existed, were cultivating Protestant missionaries, and were actively working against the fascist regime and the church, with the cooperation of many political and intellectual luminaries. These claims were not entirely untrue. In January 1927 one such spy wrote Tacchi Venturi a letter summarizing his recent investigations in Paris:

> In Paris, in his lodging at the Pension de Famille, 44 Rue Madame, Professor G.S., opening his soul to an old acquaintance, having rabidly vented, as he is accustomed to doing, his antifascist phobia, entered into particulars regarding the antifascist movement, in Italy and abroad. He spoke at length about a new program of action, which

> would have Protestant religious propaganda, of the Anglo–North American type, as its solid foundation, in opposition to the Roman Catholic faith (*religione*).
>
> He specified that certain Americans, having direct and secret contacts with international antifascist organizations, would establish themselves by obtaining permission to acquire lands and buildings, in Rome and in the Mezzogiorno, where they would more easily penetrate the Anglo-American churches and confessions, in open opposition to the Vatican, and, in covert fashion, to the fascist project.
>
> The propaganda of the Protestant faith would, according to Prof. G.S., give cover to prepare resolute souls to combat fascism and the works of the Church. The methods of the Organization would be in the hands of International Freemasonry, and one part of this activity would originate from Brussels.
>
> Prof. G.S. is in close relation with Émile VANDERVELDE and with Signora VANDERVELDE, about whom it is known that they participate actively in every international anti-Catholic and Masonic movement.
>
> Other than this, Prof. G.S. said that, next year the famous Annie BESANT would consider making a propaganda tour in Italy, along with the young Krishnamurthi, where, [among] theosophical Italians, a program of action is even now being prepared. . . .
>
> Prof G.S. . . . demonstrated a certain willingness to act with international Masonry . . . to achieve the goal of ruining fascism and destroying all the means and factors that establish a link between the fascist state and the Vatican.
>
> He spoke of other international politically responsible spheres that tacitly encouraged this program of penetration with apparently innocuous aims, but secretly pernicious for the fascist regime and for the politics of valorizing religion.
>
> The investigation can, at an opportune moment, be deepened.[10]

The G.S. to whom the spy refers was Gaetano Salvemini (1873–1957).[11] In 1925 Salvemini was arrested for opposing the new fascist regime. He left Italy that year and would not return until 1949. He would eventually make his way to the United States. For almost two decades he taught history at Harvard and wrote several books on the fascism in Italy. Before leaving for the United States, Salvemini did indeed attempt to organize resistance from France and

England.[12] To some extent, then, the anonymous spy was right in some particulars. Salvemini was a leader of antifascist movements centered outside of Italy. Émile Vandervelde (1866–1938), a Belgian statesman and law professor, was in fact an antifascist activist and among the most well-known writers on socialism in the West.[13]

Much of the rest of the spy's report is uncertain or doubtful. The claim about Vandervelde's anti-Catholicism seems overdone, though, in fighting for universal suffrage, he urged liberals and socialists to join together against Catholics who opposed it.[14] Also of interest is the spy's claim that Protestant propaganda would give cover to missionaries, and that it would do so to combat not only the church but also the fascist regime and the link between them.

The difficulty with this alliance of Protestants, Jews, Freemasons, and Anglo-Saxons is that it so perfectly mirrors the views of Tacchi Venturi. It is very hard to know whether this spy report helped to shape or merely reflected Tacchi Venturi's already-formed views. It is perfectly possible that his spy was another of Tacchi Venturi's acolytes, who supplied a report that confirmed Tacchi Venturi's known views. On the other hand, it is also possible—and perhaps slightly more likely—that influence ran in the opposite direction, that is, that this report deeply shaped the Jesuit's views and, with the particulars it supplied, gave him reason for alarm. The writings Tacchi Venturi published after receiving this spy report certainly demonstrate that the Jesuit appears firmly to have believed in just the sort of international antifascist cabal whose plans the spy puts into the mouth of Salvemini. The private writings of Tacchi Venturi *also* reflected belief in such a cabal.

Because of the influence of Tacchi Venturi, the Bolshevik-Jewish link and the support it would lend to the Protestant project of cultural and political conquest were repeatedly, almost compulsively, underlined by Catholic polemicists in the years c. 1920–35. So, too, was the imagined threat of Anglo-Saxon hegemony that aimed, ultimately, to colonize Italy by means of religious conversion. Tacchi Venturi would again and again emphasize these motifs in his writings. As is well known, promoters of the conspiracy of Jews–Masons–Bolsheviks would soon train their rhetorical guns, and worse, on Italy's Jewish community—with mortal consequences.[15] Tacchi Venturi was the first and certainly the most powerful ecclesiastical figure to argue that Protestant proselytizing, however objectionable in itself, was a mere prelude to the larger aim of Americanizing Italian and even Latin culture. If these themes became common in the vast anti-Protestant literature produced after the Concordat, it was in no small part due to the influence of Tacchi Venturi.

In this case, the report Tacchi Venturi submitted to Gasparri on 22 October 1926, however genuinely felt, was simply an edited, more elegant version of a four-page letter written to Mussolini's Jesuit only nine days earlier by the obscure, even unknown Filippo Maria Tinti (b. 1870). The author of a pamphlet entitled *Zionism and Catholicism* (and, eventually, eight more short opuscula), Tinti held an unsatisfying bureaucratic position in the police headquarters in the town of Bari, a hotbed of Protestant proselytizing in the southern province of Apulia.[16] Seeing himself as a defender of Catholicism and fascism, he corresponded often with the sympathetic Tacchi Venturi. How or when they met is not known. Put next to Tacchi Venturi's "Observations," Tinti's letter reveals several things of interest. First of all, examining the letter in the Jesuit Archives, we see that Tacchi Venturi annotated Tinti's letter in his instantly recognizable, tiny hand script and edited it heavily, excising whole sentences, even paragraphs, and rewriting others. Both verbally and conceptually he also borrows heavily—very heavily—from Tinti. Virtually everything that Tacchi Venturi says above about the welcome renaissance of Catholicism in Italy, the support of the national government for this renewal, the Jewish-Protestant-Masonic conspiracy against the church and the national government, the pervasive secular mentality of the period: all of this is lifted virtually verbatim from Tinti.[17]

Tinti, Letter to Ciriaci	**Tacchi-Venturi, "Observations" to Gasparri**
Se è per ogni cattolico motivo di grande gioia constatare ogni giorno il fermo proposito dell'attuale Governo di stringere sempre più nell'interesse della Religione, legami indissolubili tra la Chiesa e lo St'ato, e di imporre nel miglior modo, la Religione stessa, è anche motivo disconforto constatare che alla periferia non si degne seriamente, quasi da nessuno, le direttive del Governo, mentre è oramai noto, che il consolante fenomeno del	Se è per ogni cattolico motivo di grande gioia il constatare ogni giorno il fermo proposito dell'attuale Governo di stringere sempre più nell'interesse della Religione, legami indissolubili tra la Chiesa e lo Stato, e di imporre nel miglior modo, la Religione stessa, è anche motivo di sconforto *l'osservare* che alla periferia non si degne seriamente, quasi da nessuno, le direttive del Governo, mentre è oramai noto, che il consolante fenomeno del risve-

risveglio religioso, che dovunque si sviluppa, sta per essere frustrato dal multiforme settarismo degli ebrei, dei protestanti, dei massoni, e dei bolscevici, tutti sempre ben e potentemente alleati contro la religione, contro la contro la Chiesa, e contro lo stesso Governo Nazionale.	glio religioso, che dappertutto si sviluppa, sta per essere frustrato dal multiforme settarismo degli ebrei, dei protestanti, dei massoni, e dei bolscevici, tutti sempre e potentemente alleati contro la religione, Se ne Chiesa, e contro lo stesso Governo Nazionale e prova di ciò la mentalità laica che pervade ancora quasi tutta l'attività sociale italiana la prova della mentalità laica che pervade ancora quasi tutta l'attività sociale italiana.

Though no one knew it then, the powerful Jesuit intermediary and correspondent with the Vatican secretary of state relied for his ideas and even his language on an obscure police official rusticated, Tinti keenly felt, to the *petit bureau de travail.* There, in Bari, he had been condemned to pushing papers for inferiors who had benefited as he had not from the patronage system.

It was a secret that would never be discovered. We know next to nothing about Tinti. Nor can we begin to guess why one of the most powerful men in Mussolini's Italy chose to befriend and rely heavily on him. We do know they saw eye to eye on politics, religion, and the threat posed to Italy by Protestants, Jews, Masons, and Bolsheviks. Tinti's fear and loathing of Masons, who seem to have impeded his career progress, are especially pronounced. It is again not entirely clear, nonetheless, in which direction the influence flowed. It could be that Tinti sat at the feet of Tacchi Venturi and replicated in writing things the latter had said in conversation. If not, then Tacchi Venturi would have given his imprimatur to ideas that in their origin were those of the obscure Tinti.

TINTI'S "STUDIO" AND TACCHI VENTURI'S IL PERICOLO PROTESTANTE

A second instance of literary dependence between the two figures, this one bolder, involves a lengthy "Studio" on the dangers of Protestantism by Tinti, which Tacchi Venturi edited lightly and then brought to publication.

A stray remark made by Tinti in a letter written in January 1927 to Tacchi Venturi makes explicit that some sort of prearrangement for ghostwriting and publication had been made between the two men.[18] Summarizing his recent literary activities to the Jesuit, Tinti divulges that he is finishing editing his "Studio," to which he had given the title "I Protestanti alla conquista dell'Italia?" In the next sentence he adds, "We will publish it in the form of an article by you."[19] One page later Tinti refers to "my opusculum" *Zionism and Catholicism.*[20] Thus the author of *Zionism and Catholicism,* whom we know to be Tinti, was the same man who wrote a "Studio" on the Protestant conquest of Italy.[21]

The understanding to which the two had come was as follows. The "Studio" would, with Tacchi Venturi's emendations, be published. Observing, with no little understatement, that it contains "some repetition" (but, he declared risibly, "no errors"), Tinti promised to correct the manuscript according to Tacchi Venturi's specifications: "In any way you emend it, I will correct it," he promised the Jesuit.[22] Tinti's "Studio," as edited by Tacchi Venturi, was indeed published.[23] It bore the title *The Protestant Danger* (*Il Pericolo Protestante*). However, it did not bear the Jesuit's name. Instead, it was published, in Tinti's hometown of Bari, in 1927, under the pseudonym "Veritas"—"Truth."[24] It was brought out by the Lega del Beni in Bari. This was the same small publishing house that had brought out Tinti's *Sionismo e cattolicismo.*[25] The Lega also had the same address as the letterhead of Filippo Maria Tinti.[26] Publishing was his cottage industry.

It was not the last time Tinti would serve as a ghostwriter, sometimes without his knowledge or approval, for Tacchi Venturi. Both men were intensely, irrationally suspicious and distrustful—though not, it appears of each other—preoccupied with buried motives, certain that their beloved church and dear *Patria* were being persecuted; and that an alliance of enemies as unholy and omnipotent as it was implausible was out to subvert the national government of Italy. It was their duty to resist, using the pen as sword in the imminent, apocalyptic confrontation with the enemies of Catholicism, Italy, and fascism; and resist in this way, together, they would. The first danger they would face was that posed by evangelical missionaries to the religious and national integrity of Italy.

Tinti was persuaded that the Protestants were dangerous, in part, because their founding ideas were, in the potted history of the Reformation with which he begins his "Studio," plainly heretical and foolish. What good ideas could sprout from so contaminated a source? A presumptuous man, Calvin foolishly dared to try to reform the Catholic church. He had an "extremely cruel spirit," which is why he "burnt everyone who did not think as he did!" (Needless to say, Tinti does not advert to the history of the medieval, Spanish, or Roman Inquisitions.) Tinti claims that the English Reformation had its origins in the king's predilection for polygamy. Risking a disingenuous compliment to Methodist piety, Tinti comments that the immoral conduct and corruption of Henry VIII so disgusted John Wesley that he felt compelled to "reform the reform." Wesley loses all credit for reform, however, as he was the author, ultimately, of American Methodism, which both Tinti and Tacchi Venturi agree is the most sinister Protestant sect, a claim that was to have wide influence. Luther was an apostate and schismatic crazed by a mania, the imbecilic idea that each Christian could, without the authoritative guidance of the *magisterium,* interpret the scriptures according to his own lights and for his own convenience. Moving to the modern day, heretical and apostate Protestantism had facilitated the development of "untold numbers of liberal, liberalistic, atheistic and agnostic philosophical theories"—like, for example, "humanitarianism—which had subverted the intellectual, moral, political, and social order."[27]

Not surprisingly, much of the Catholic critique of the Protestant missionary effort centers on the Protestant view of revelation, the allegedly subjective and individualistic mode of reading the Bible by Protestant sects and the consequences of permitting, indeed encouraging, the free interpretation of the sacred text. These were issues at the core of the Protestant Reformation in the sixteenth century. Occasions of war in the early modern period, they remained points of theological and political conflict into the twentieth century. The result? Religious anarchy, as each Protestant sect now had "its own savior" and even its own form of Christianity, creating "a true intellectual, moral, religious, and social anarchy."[28]

Worst of all, though, were the dangerous, indeed heretical ideas, both theological and moral, to which biblical interpretation unencumbered by magisterial authority or interpretive limitation could lead—and had led. Lugubriously, Tacchi Venturi observes, "The throng of interpreters of the Bible unfailingly grows," with the result that Protestants had rejected many fundamental creedal propositions. Most troubling—almost monstrous—some Protestants no longer acknowledged the divinity of Christ, a heresy traceable back at least to Arius and the Arians in the early fourth century.[29] In Catholic eyes this was simply to cut the heart out of traditional creedal, Chalcedonian Christianity, which had been established in antiquity (451 CE), had endured through the centuries, was a tenet of belief for which many fought and some died, and without which, in the eyes of most, Catholicism would cease to be Christianity.[30] This was worse even than the Anglican episcopate suppression of the mention of Hell in the creed.[31]

The chaos in Protestant biblical interpretation mirrored and was caused, Tacchi Venturi maintained, by the multitude of Protestant confessions, itself the result of liberal interpretation of the holy text of Christianity. Because of the free interpretation of the Bible, without the limiting restraints of the Catholic magisterium, there were "still so many species of Protestantism: Anglicans, Methodists, Lutherans, Calvinists, Adventists, Presbyterians, Waldensians, Evangelicals," and so forth.[32] Though divided from one another theologically by profound and fundamental disagreements, only one malevolent motive united these disparate confessions: their "desire to battle Catholicism, Catholics, and all the governments of the Catholic nations."[33]

Later in *The Protestant Danger* Tacchi Venturi gives his reasons for believing, additionally, the theory that Protestantism success would lead inevitably to atheism. As always when construing such remarks, one must remember that for Tacchi Venturi as well as for Tinti, Protestantism was so insidious a danger because it was linked to and supported by socialism and communism, to which it inexorably led in the end: "Socialism," Tacchi Venturi declares, "is essentially atheistic and a fulfillment of materialism and of Judaism, which tends toward Communism."[34] Supporting this view, Tinti observes that, insofar as it is essentially materialistic, Judaism is, in his words, a forerunner to communism. In the words of Tacchi Venturi, as communism is "essentially atheistic" it "is a realization of the materialism of Judaism."[35] Every Protestant sect is propagated willingly by "Jewish-Masonic sectarianism, the most ruthless enemy of Catholicism." For that reason Protestant confessions "quickly degenerate into atheism, or moral and religious agnosticism."[36]

This is one of a considerable number of instances in the writings of Tinti and Tacchi Venturi in which the anti-Protestantism of each writer is fed and informed by his deeply felt antisemitism.[37] One strain of Jesuit antisemitism that pervaded the influential Jesuit journal *Civiltà Cattolica* in the nineteenth and early twentieth centuries and then clerico-fascist writings in the mid-1930s was that Judaism was not a religion, like Protestantism or Catholicism, but a race.[38] Emphatically *not* absent is the conviction that "Talmudic" Judaism was, at its core, materialistic and, in this sense, little different than atheistic Bolshevism (which Tacchi Venturi states, almost ritually, to be dominated by Jews).[39] Indeed, according to this thinking, the essentially materialistic orientation of Jews explains why they were putatively allied with the plutocratic Anglo-Saxons.

Other anti-Protestant polemicists during the fascist period in Italy could argue, more bizarrely, that Judaism was in effect the originator and instigator of Protestantism. Like Luther, Jews emphasized the plain rather than Christological sense of the Hebrew Bible. The reformers' plea, particularly that of Calvin, to retrieve the texts of early Christianity in practice resulted in the implementation of Old Testament Law and "the spirit of Judaism." Like the Jews, Puritans "considered themselves the elect people." Lutheran Münster had anachronistically attempted, between 1524 and 1536, to establish a "Bolshevik"—that is to say, a Jewish—form of government. (The recent attempt [1919] in the wake of the Great War, by a German group dominated by Jews, to establish a Soviet-style republic in Munich, though quickly repressed, was surely fresh on clerical minds.)[40] These two tiny religious communities, Jews and Protestants, together made up less than 1 percent of the Italian population. Yet they would both be targeted by the fascist government and many clerico-fascists for suppression. It is little wonder their opponents found them not only conspiratorially but historically linked. They were also linked with yet another overrepresented group in the international conspiracy: Italy's twenty thousand Freemasons.

Though Tinti, like Tacchi Venturi, habitually links Judaism and Freemasonry, it would be difficult to exaggerate Tinti's hatred for, more like pathological suspicion or terror of, the latter. To be sure, Catholic suspicion and hostility toward Freemasonry practically coincided with its establishment. Many popes, beginning in the early eighteenth century, excommunicated those affiliated with Masonic lodges. Rather like Jews and Judaism, the Masons would, in the dominant Western Catholic worldview of the nineteenth and twentieth centuries, shoulder much of the blame for the disasters of the French Revolution, European secularization, and, in Italy, for the Risorgimento and the dissolution of the Papal States. They were resented for presenting an alternative to traditional Catholicism and for bringing Protestants, Jews, and atheists into association with Catholics. Invoking a hoary anti-Semitic slur, Pope Leo XIII (r. 1878–1903) even effectively branded Freemasons as Jews; Masons were, he alleged in his 1884 encyclical *Humanum genus,* "a synagogue of Satan" (see Apocalypse 3:9).[41] He was not the last to view Masons in anti-Semitic terms. When the papal chamberlain monsignor Rudolph

Gerlach was accused of leading an Italian espionage ring, Pope Benedict XV could conclude that Gerlach, against whom the evidence had been weak, had been convicted by a "Masonic Sanhedrin."[42]

By the late nineteenth century influential international Catholic periodicals, such as *Civiltà Cattolica,* would make the relationship between Jews and Masons unambiguous and real. The two were part of an evil international conspiracy, guilty of sedition and treachery wherever they were found. Socialists, then Bolsheviks, would soon swell the number of groups hostile to healthy Christian societies and conspire with Jews and Masons to subvert them. The conspiracy, being worldwide, by definition operated ubiquitously.

If Masons had little appreciation for Catholicism, many clerical Italian Catholics despised Italian Masons. They appear in the rogues' gallery of international conspirators, at least in part, because many deeply resented clerical power and papal influence. No less a figure than Giuseppe Garibaldi (1807–82), the popular "father of the [Italian] Fatherland," who held anticlerical and antipapal views, was an Italian Mason. Like Garibaldi, the military champion of Italian unification, most Italian Masons were pleased to see the abolition of the Papal States, the separation of church and state, and the expropriation of ecclesiastical property for secular purposes. Staunch supporters of a unified nation and the national government, Italian Masons applauded the loss of the papacy's secular and political power. Hoping to secularize public education, they, with the assistance of highly placed political colleagues, helped to drum clerics out of the schools, a change reversed only by the Lateran Pacts in 1929. It is hardly any wonder that Catholic profascist writers regarded Masons as enemies opposed to Catholicism and to fascism. Many were.[43]

Embellishing the point, Tacchi Venturi and Tinti declare that Protestant sects were "always and everywhere composed of elements associated with International Masonry," a "systematic enemy of Catholicism, of Italy, and of Fascism."[44] They were among the few groups, along with Italian Jews, said to be opposed to the Conciliation and the Lateran Pacts.[45] Neither Tinti nor Tacchi Venturi could overemphasize this theme. In the document composed by Tinti and passed on to Gasparri by Tacchi Venturi, Tinti (a policeman, as noted earlier) objects to fascist surveillance of the Catholic clergy. To Tinti, this seemed odd, insulting, and wasteful, given the putative love the Catholic clergy and indeed all the Catholic church had for Il Duce and the regime. Elements positioned recklessly at the very heart of the regime had purposely confused the police. Highly placed actors in the ministries—especially Masons, Tinti specifies—had an interest in making the police believe the clergy and Catholicism were inimical to fascism.[46] The international cabal was busy deceiving the fascist regime into harboring suspicions about its champions.

The letter reflects Tinti's deep loathing for bureaucrats and the "big shots" at the ministries, especially the Ministry of the Interior. These, Tinti asserts with no trace of self-doubt or efforts at nuance, are "either Jews or Masons." While the police were wasting their time investigating the clergy, they were oblivious to the threat posed by the "deceitful and subversive Jews, Masons, and Protestants." Under the naked lie of being admirers of fascism, they are its enemies—a fact no one had apparently communicated to "our beloved Duce."[47] In Tinti's view, the Jews and Masons were not simply external, nonresident antifascists, though he acknowledges that many were resident abroad. What made the Jewish-Masonic threat so alarming is that Italian Masons had penetrated to the heart of the fascist government. For Tinti, the most dangerous and powerful enemy to both the church and to the regime was not "the usual anarchists, republicans, vulgar delinquents, or even antifascists." Rather, it was "the Jews, Masons and Protestants."[48] Later, during the Abyssinian war, Tacchi Venturi would reveal to Mussolini in a private conversation that Freemasonry (which, he thought, also dominated the League of Nations) was leading the campaign to bring down Il Duce, destroy fascism, foment a revolution, and establish a Bolshevik kingdom in Italy.[49] Yet Catholic Italy would, with the aid of those same Bolsheviks, have to be Protestantized and Americanized first.

Many Catholic polemicists naturally emphasized the disastrous effects for religion and the churches of the recent Bolshevik revolution. But some saw lurking behind even the Mexican Revolution (1910–20), perceived by Tinti and Tacchi Venturi to be "directed exclusively against Catholics and Catholicism," the long tentacles of the Anglo-American Axis and the international conspiracy led by Jews.[50] In *Il Pericolo Protestante* Tacchi Venturi states that, one monsignor, a bishop in Oklahoma, revealed that the Bolshevik revolution in Mexico was nourished, if quietly, by Jewish-Masonic sectarianism in the United States.[51] These sectarians were, both Tinti and Tacchi added, supported by "dominant elements" in North America, including the "famous anti-Catholic sect" the Ku Klux Klan (which both Italians call the Ku-Klu-Kan).[52] The powerful North American elements that had supported the socialist revolutions were silent during the years of the Mexican Revolution, in compensation for which they were, according to the eccentric theory of Tinti and Tacchi Venturi, given possession of almost all the petroleum fields of Mexico.[53]

Needless to say, much of this is sheer nonsense. That said, Deborah Baldwin has recently argued that Mexicans who had been converted by American Protestant missionaries did enthusiastically support the revolution. In addition, they lobbied the United States to intervene militarily. Once "converts had already broken with traditional religion," Baldwin concluded, they found it easier to "break with the established political order."[54] These same North American elements influenced the unjust triumph of Zionist Judaism, the "diehard enemy of Jesus," in the Balfour Declaration of 1917. Not coincidentally, this was the same year as the Russian Revolution—which allowed the "deicide people" to reconstruct a Jewish nation in the "holy country of Jesus." Tacchi Venturi disparages this nation (Israel) as "the ruthless denier and irreducible enemy of Jesus."[55] Here again is an instance in which the authors harness anti-Semitic language and myths for the campaign against Protestants, another religious and even national rival. The conspiracy theories Tacchi Venturi employs to pillory Jews and Zionism are nearly identical to those he uses to inveigh against the Protestants. Both Jews and Protestants are attempting to invade and occupy a land not theirs to take, under the influence of "the international conspiracy."

"THIS DEADLY ASSOCIATION": THE YMCA

One central way, institutionally speaking, by which not only young Italian Catholics but also émigrés were thought by Tacchi Venturi to be Protestantized and Americanized was through the seventy or so YMCAs spread across the peninsula.[56] The link between the YMCA, Methodism, and evangelization was not entirely imagined by Catholic polemicists. Founded in 1844 by George Williams (1821–1905), the YMCA was designed originally to supply a haven to working-class men in the squalid conditions of industrial England. Williams also intended the Y to furnish a decidedly Christian environment amid the temptations of the city (London). Time was set aside each day for the men to pray and to study the Bible. Within ten years of its founding in London, Ys could be found in North America. In 1854 the Y held an international conference at which traditional congregational boundaries were not recognized. This was an augury of things to come. In the nineteenth century Protestants with ties to YMCAs in the cities were evangelizing the urban populations of the United States and Canada. No less a figure than Dwight L. Moody (1837–99), a conscientious objector, joined the Y during the Civil War and thus bent the arc of its future. He concentrated on evangelizing troops, especially men who were nearing death as a result of wounds suffered in battle.

A much more profound influence on the YMCA was exercised by John Mott (1865–1955). An American Methodist and a zealous missionary, he held several important positions in the Y. Indeed, he brought together—theologically, in his own person, and in the self-understanding of the international YMCA—the three elements that Catholics perceived to be such a danger when linked and supported by the international conspiracy: Methodism, mission, and the YMCA. The language with which Mott has always been associated was the purpose he gave to the Y: "The evangelization of the world in our generation." This ambitious aim became the title of one of his books as well as the watchword for many student organizations and evangelical associations.[57] The Y was understood to be a Protestant rather than a broadly Christian institution, and many Catholic clerics warned their parishioners away. Indeed, one priest in Connecticut felt compelled to warn his congregation in the nineteenth century that the YMCA was explicitly an "anti-Catholic institution." He added that Canon Law did not allow Catholics to join a YMCA. Indeed, they could not even participate in its activities. Some after-school organizations were founded for Catholic youth solely to prevent friendships from developing with Protestants.

Just after the First World War the YMCA would involve itself in the growing ecumenical movement, to which the papacy was viscerally opposed. It also sent ministers to help soldiers in the battlefields of Europe in the First World War. Anti-Protestant polemicists perceived this as an insidious effort on the part of the Y to integrate itself into Italian culture and especially to ingratiate itself to young people for purposes of propaganda. After the Second World War Mott helped found the World Council of Churches and was made its honorary president in 1948. Although Rome was disturbed at the success of the council, it was not tempted to participate in ecumenical discussion and was distressed that the Eastern Orthodox church was in the least enthusiastic. The Catholic church dismissed with hauteur the idea that it had a coequal sister. This, it stated, was a symptom of modern *indifferentismo*—not religious apathy or indifference but a failure to distinguish the historic, the divinely ordained, and true from the modern, the human, and false. The only unity it would entertain was a return by the heretical sects to communion with Rome. With its emphasis on Christian unity and evangelism and its association with heresy, the YMCA represented much that popes from Benedict XV (d. 1922) through Pius XII (d. 1958) would emphatically reject. So surprising was it as late as 1961—months before the Second Vatican Council would begin—that non-Protestant Christians were exercising and socializing at YMCAs in large numbers in the United States that *Time* magazine reported, with some amazement, that perhaps one-fifth of the Y's participants were Catholic.

Tacchi Venturi warned that, if permitted in Rome or other Italian cities (as indeed it had been), the Y would discharge legions of Protestant missionaries to undertake "an intense and insidious anti-Italian Protestant campaign" associated in Italy with the "famous American association, the YMCA."[58] In every large city, Tacchi Venturi writes, the Protestants had purchased or constructed large buildings for schools, kindergarten, cooperative societies, recreation clubs, classes, and so forth. These were attractive to women, especially to young mothers. Tacchi Venturi was supported by reports submitted by his countless informants, many of which he sent as attachments to the secretary of state, and which contained lists of YMCAs, with addresses, in all Italian cities.[59] In at least one private audience with Mussolini, Tacchi Venturi brought up the issue of the YMCA, but because of the laconic nature of his records—they are merely handwritten agenda notes—it is unfortunately not known what was said or to what action, if any, Mussolini agreed.

Already by 1919 *Civiltà Cattolica* was claiming that the sole motivation of the YMCAs, in league with American Methodists, was to lure Catholics away from the Roman church.[60] So loathed and, in the Italian Catholic imagination, so tightly linked to the YMCA were the American Wesleyans that Tinti and Tacchi Venturi interpret the institutional acronym to mean the "Young Methodist Christian Association."[61] Among other things, it was the internationalism and cosmopolitanism of the Ys, characteristics it shared, supposedly, with international Jewry, Masonry, and Bolshevism, that so troubled its Catholic critics. With headquarters in Geneva, home of Calvinism, the YMCA, Tinti observes, with some exaggeration, had "an infinity of directorial centers in all the world": "from Toronto to Rio di Janeiro, from Washington to Buenos Aires, from New York to London, from Paris to Tokyo, from Berlin to Peking, from Rome to Athens, from Jerusalem to Melbourne and from [city inked out] to Moscow."[62] (Bolsheviks shut down the Moscow Y, only one of several in major Soviet cities, in 1919.) Also deeply troubling was the putative duplicity of the Y as an institution. Tacchi Venturi was obsessed by the conviction that YMCAs were ubiquitous. In this respect they were a well-organized and handsomely financed worldwide society, rather like "Anglo-Saxon plutocracy" or "international Jewry." As such, they were a danger not only to Catholics living in Italy. They were a threat to Italians, to the countless expatriates living in New York and Chicago, to countrymen and women planning to leave Italy for economic reasons, and to Catholics across the globe. Converts returning home would soon become a threat—one the Jesuit does not mention—to the souls of their neighbors as they quickly turned to the business of proselytizing.

Moving to the larger, cultural issues energizing his polemic, Tinti asserts that the Y at Torino was in fact organized to dupe emigrants and, above all, to erase their *italianità*.[63] One entered the Y at Torino, preparing for life in America, Catholic in religious affiliation, and Italian in ethnic identity and culture. Once educated, the emigrant left as a potential, if not actual, Protestant convert, shorn of attachment to Latin culture, now sympathetic to the values and norms of Anglo-Saxon plutocratic civilization, dazzled by the spectacle of an "idyllic Puritanism."[64]

Even before the passage of the laws on permitted cults a Roman policeman sent Tacchi Venturi a confidential report on the grandeur, sadly unmatched by any analogous Catholic institution, of the Y on Via Indipendenza, whose many educational and recreational facilities an enthusiastic convert was pleased to show the officer in their magnificent entirety.[65] Clerics sometimes despaired at the possibilities of keeping Catholic boys out of these buildings, so appealing to energetic, talented, or ambitious adolescents and utterly unrivaled by comparably glorious Catholic institutions. This Y was feared because especially attractive to a precious subcategory of youth: the military.

Several tactics used by the YMCAs were, evidently, effective. Particularly telling in this respect is a letter Tacchi Venturi received in October 1926 from a captain of the Carabinieri Reali, a branch of the Italian police, which Tacchi Venturi would send to Gasparri along with his letter on the Protestant campaign in Italy. Walking in the evening on Piazza Indipendenza in Rome, the captain came across a domicile with the inscription, "House of Young Christians." Curious, he knocked and was warmly received by a secretary. She introduced him to one of the young men living there, who showed him around the house. "The house," the captain reports, "is one of a kind in Italy." It had a wonderful gym, a theater, a library, schools of language, music, and stenography, rooms for fencing and boxing: "In sum, it was furnished with everything that a young person could desire"—and was, the captain added, an "extremely effective means of religious propaganda." Thinking at first the house to be Catholic, the captain asked to see the chapel. "Imagine my surprise," he reports to Tacchi Venturi, when he was told that the house and everything in it belonged to Protestants. Interrogating the young man, he was told that, although the boy was raised Catholic, his religious convictions had been much changed after having frequented the house. Indeed, he now "felt more Protestant than Catholic." The captain closes by warning that the "danger for youth is extremely grave." He recommends any means necessary to eliminate so grim a danger. Either the Protestant house should be destroyed or an even better Catholic one should be erected. In any case, "it is not right that in Rome the best house for youth is Protestant." What really made this house dangerous, in the captain's eyes, was the obvious affluence of those who had financed it. Their power might make it difficult to close.[66] A recurrent theme in the anti-Protestant polemics of the period, American riches and the material comfort that proselytes could provide was an allure that Italian Catholics would find impossible to match. More unique about this report is the obviously sincere concern expressed by an evidently sincere Catholic policeman.

By the time Tinti wrote his "Studio," he could complain that the Protestantism then spreading across Italy worked, "it is clear, not for the Christian religion" but for the imperial, colonizing American government. Emphasizing a theme that would be picked up by subsequent polemicists, it was an "American, civilizing" form of Christianity to which Italian Catholics were being converted.[67] Plutocratic, "international Jewish-Masonic sectarianism" had lavished vast quantities of capital on Italy so that antifascist and anti-Catholic elements, placed unwittingly by the fascist regime in high positions of the government, would cooperate in the "de-Catholicizing and Americanizing of the Italian people."[68] These dark imperialistic aims terrified Tinti; they also inspired a determination to resist. Or he would patriotically place his faith in the head of the national government. Such imperialistic intentions, Tinti declares at one point in the "Studio," would not escape "the vigilant eye of His Honor Mussolini."[69] Tinti was wrong about many things. Time would prove him never more deluded than in this expression of confidence in the Head of Government's alertness to the many dimensions of the Protestant danger.

"THE MOST DANGEROUS SECT": METHODISM AND AMERICAN IMPERIALISM

Methodism, in Italian Catholic eyes, was the Protestant sect most closely tied in with the American imperial project. Another Jesuit writer, Camillo Crivelli (1874–1954), who wrote prolifically on Protestantism in Catholic countries in Europe and Latin America, asserted that the postwar offensive was principally American as well as principally Methodist.[70] The American historian R. Laurence Moore captures the sources of the Italian Catholic wariness of Methodism and the cordial antipathy of Italian clerics, who were simply insulted by Wesleyan critique: "American Methodists . . . courted unpopularity in Italy in the late nineteenth and early twentieth century. One Methodist leader after another attacked Italian Catholicism as pagan, intellectually sterile, bacchanalian and downright evil. They made it their mission to show the Italian people that Roman Catholicism is not Christianity."[71]

That is certainly true. In the late nineteenth century the Methodist missionary Everett S. Stackpole (1850–1927) published a memoir of his nearly five years in Italy in which he recalls his approach to Rome with this remarkably revealing perception and question: "There, across the Tiber, is the massive pile of St. Peter's and the Vatican. Here at last is the citadel of the hostile forces. Here is the centre of that huge system of error and superstition that we have come so far to spend our life in opposing. The might of ancient Rome vanished before the presence of our barbaric ancestors. Why may not this new and mightier Rome be conquered by the weapons of the Gospel truth?"[72] The Methodists more than any other sect sought to launch an underhanded "war on Catholicism." They wrapped themselves in the wool mantle of sheep but only so they might seize the souls of Italian Catholics, whom they would then use, with the help of Masons, socialists, and communists, to bring down the Italian State and its official religion.[73] Harmless as doves, it seemed, they were sly as serpents.

Methodists were also the denomination almost all anti-Protestant polemicists recognized as most hostile to the Roman Catholic church and to the papacy. One historian has talked even of the "savagery of Methodist vilification of the Roman church and especially of the papacy."[74] As much as any Methodist leader, Bishop William Burt stressed the putatively moribund and pagan character of Romanism. Burt wholly embodied all the characteristics of radical anti-Catholicism. His aggressive missionizing clerical Catholics despised, and his unwelcome arrival in the seat of Catholicism, along with his audacious aims—which encompassed the acquisition of territory overlooking the Vatican, the wholesale deconversion of the state from the state religion, and the exposure of the heathen core of Catholicism—incensed the Vatican and its sympathizers. Catholicism was pagan, Burt asserted, insofar as it had been uninfluenced by Protestantism. In a speech given in Belfast in 1906, Burt avowed: "Somehow I have a firm faith that Methodism is destined of God for the overthrow of Rome."[75] (Burt added that he was sure that Ireland, too, would soon be liberated from the shackles of Romanism.) This sort of condescension to the church of Rome infuriated clerics at the Vatican. A Vatican report from 1931 states that "in Protestant temples, but above all in Methodist ones, the anti-Catholic and polemical note is accentuated and aggravated."[76] Methodist audacity, arrogance, and aggression antagonized, and their fathomless reservoir of American dollars exasperated and demoralized. A commentator in *L'Osservatore Romano* observed in 1934: "The Protestant invasion is not like the invasions of Gaiseric or Attila. They sowed death with iron and fire. This is an invasion of souls attracted by the dollar."[77]

Catholic polemicists made much of the American Methodists' unsuccessful attempt to establish a "Protestant Vatican" on Monte Mario, the highest hill in Rome, though not one of the seven legendary ones.[78] In 1914 the American Methodist Episcopal church purchased land on Monte Mario.[79] This, Tacchi Venturi states, was an attempt to obscure the "indestructible glory of the real Vatican."[80] (In an irony too delicious to be untrue, the land was known in the ancient Roman period as the *Mons Vaticanus:* Vatican Hill.)[81] By the early 1920s the American Methodists had hatched a plan to build on top of the high hill an international *collegio* for boys. Only a short distance from the Vatican, the site commanded a view of the Basilica San Pietro and of the Vatican gardens. Many Catholics in Rome, clerics above all, regarded the establishment of such a school as antagonistic to the traditions of Italian culture, religion, and education. It was also a poorly disguised attempt to express Protestant contempt for corrupt Roman Catholic piety, as if the physical height of the mountain—"one-hundred physical feet, and 1000 spiritual feet higher than the Vatican"—somehow demonstrated evangelical Christianity's superiority to Catholicism.[82] As Moore has observed, the attempt to establish Monte Mario "made explicit how close to the surface was American Protestant disapproval of European religious practice"—by which he means southern European or Catholic practice.[83] Methodist plans for Monte Mario were taken as proof that Anglo-Saxon cultural and political views were soon to be imposed upon an unenthusiastic nation and indeed on all of Latin culture.[84] In short, the establishment of Monte Mario was, in Italian eyes, an imperialistic venture. As Moore has pointed out, "The American side termed it [Monte Mario] an effort to emancipate Italian youth from a church hostile to free thought." "For the rest of the decade," Moore goes on, "this educational institution became, from the viewpoint of Italian journalists and public officials, a symptom of American 'empire' building. It was an assault on national integrity."[85] To which American Methodist church representatives responded: the only imperialism intended was "the imperialism of a pure Gospel."

That, minimally, is how Italians interpreted it. As organs of Anglo-Saxon hegemony, they were broadly regarded as a threat against Italy and the traditions of the Latin world. Because the school was well regarded but did not advertise itself as Methodist or Protestant, many Catholic families enrolled their children. Catholics regarded this as an example par excellence of Methodist deception, one of their defining corporate characteristics. It offended the sensibilities of Catholic writers like Tinti and Tacchi Venturi that the Methodists were not simply attempting to conquer Italy religiously but were spreading the Protestant word "from Rome," which was for them "the Sacred Capital of Italy and of Catholicism."[86] In a private audience with Mussolini, Tacchi Venturi floated an idea, whose nature he does not specify, with Mussolini on how to deal with the troubling issue. Mussolini, the Jesuit noted briefly, liked the idea and promised to speak with the minister of internal affairs about it.[87] As early as 1923 the government stalled building plans, leaving the field open to Conrad Hilton to transform the magnificent Methodist collegio into a posh hotel. At a time when Catholic antagonists felt on their heels against an army of Protestant invaders, it was a welcome, if rare, victory.

Years later, news of a Methodist attempt to acquire property next to the papal villas on Castel Gandolfo temporarily generated anxiety in the Vatican. In February 1931 Borgongini learned that Methodists were attempting to purchase the Villa Ferri on Castel Gandolfo, which sat alongside the two papal palaces of the Castello at Pagnanelli. Five inheritors of the villa were ready to sell it; it was a matter of indifference to them whether the buyers were Protestant or Catholic. Apparently the Methodists hoped to establish a *collegio metodista* and other "undesirable institutes" on the property.[88] Three letters from the local bishop over the next two months confirmed Borgongini's suspicions. A letter in April reported that the Protestants had engaged an agent to negotiate sale of the property. Yet another letter indicated that the buyer was a "foreign man" who had been pleased at how "the property fully corresponded to his plans." Finally, a third confirms that the sale had gone through and the contract had been executed in Rome. Monsignor Marazzi offers to alert the prefect, presumably to do what he could to halt the sale. After engaging a lawyer, on the advice of Serafini, Borgongini finally discovered from the local bishop and a parish priest that "the villino [was] still available." No sale had been made. The Ferri heirs still intended to sell the property, but no serious offer had been made.[89] (All these events, to date, Borgongini summarized in an audience with the pope on 6 March 1931.) We cannot know why the sale was not made. Perhaps the property was simply too expensive for the Methodists. Yet it was another bold attempt to encroach on not just Catholic but papal territory.

Tinti and Tacchi Venturi feared the political motives of the United States, the country from which many of the Protestant missionaries—especially Methodists, Baptists, and Adventists—were being disgorged.[90] In one of his letters Tinti tells Tacchi Venturi an anecdote by way of illustrating the real and present danger of American imperial ambitions. At Gioia del Colle, a small town in Puglia near Bari, there was a small Baptist church. Its pastor was, according to Tinti, a Bolshevik who used to propagandize his congregation. Local hoodlums, he goes on to explain, found this so objectionable that they "invaded his church and destroyed it." This is likely only part of the story, though the destruction of an evangelical church happened more than once in Italy, especially before the Concordat and its implementing legislation gave Protestant churches a modicum of legal protection. In any case, according to Tinti, American authorities inquired into the incident, from which he concludes that the United States, "which did not bother itself over the war in Mexico," now involves itself because of the "invasion of a small 'Baptist' church situated in the tiny commune of Gioia del Colle." According to Tinti, the American government learned that the pastor was Italian and his church frequented only by a few Italians. To Tinti, this intervention by the United States government "demonstrates the political interests of the North American government even in the smallest affairs of Italy." The United States interferes in what are essentially Italian affairs so that "tomorrow the United States will be able to occupy Italian territory on the pretext of protecting Italian Protestantism."[91]

FOREIGNERS AND OTHER ENEMIES

In a circular published and distributed by the Vatican secretary of state Pacelli (later Pope Pius XII), the author begins by speaking of the Protestant danger. The very first point he makes is as clear as it is laconic: "The first danger comes from national and foreign ministers."[92] It has long been recognized that fascist regimes often attempt to unify a country and consolidate their grip on power by the scapegoating of enemies, in many cases foreigners. Less well emphasized, indeed virtually unknown, is that this was also a ploy often used by profascist clerics in Italy.

Another letter, this time from an unknown correspondent to Tacchi Venturi, illustrates the vigor with which Catholic polemicists stigmatized the Protestant as a foreigner and therefore untrustworthy and deceitful and, again, connected with Freemasonry.[93] The letter writer begins by complaining about the "tenacious, deeply rooted, profound propaganda undertaken by the Protestants in this miserable corner of Italy." That corner of Italy—far from miserable—was La Spezia, "the Seat of Protestantism in Italy." There the Protestants had hatched a plan "full of boldness." The leaders of the plan were not Anglo-Saxon but Swiss, "the foreigner nestled in our own home. . . . [T]hat stranger, who was a spy during the War but also, now in peacetime." The government should, he warned, be aware of such guests. Furnished with enormous capital, their plans are put together in heretical churches, which, except for the Waldensians, are composed of foreigners, Wesleyans, Methodists. "I would be curious to know," the writer comments, "how many dozens of Swiss, German, English and American foreigners are staying at Spezia to make it necessary [to have] three churches" and several chapels. These, in any case, existed only "to de-Christianize our churches through a false and foreign faith." These churches had taken the most strategic places and had vast resources so that, undisturbed, a foreign religion might freely proselytize.[94] In few other contemporary archival documents does such xenophobia, and the conviction that foreigners are untrustworthy simply because foreign, receive such repeated emphasis.

Part of the foreignness of these churches was that it was "absolutely certain" that they were planning a "Masonic and antifascist action." These Masons and antifascists wished to extend their "tentacles under the aegis of a Government that wishes to be the protector of Catholicism." For in those churches, the writer improbably suggests, bold plans were being made to capture "Spezia, a port precious to us and of vital maritime interests." As propaganda was being spread by a foreign religion, one of Italy's strategic military harbors was in danger of being lost. Under the cover of foreign religious propaganda, a radical antifascist action was unfolding as Italy was sleeping. As someone who agreed with the pope that Mussolini was not attentive to the developing Protestant threat, it is not surprising that Tacchi Venturi carefully read, kept, and edited this letter.

Interestingly, the writer connects this plan to a new enemy: the Swiss (and even, and improbably, to Swiss confessions), who were not, to say the least, involved in the campaign to convert Italy to evangelical Christianity. He blames the Swiss for spying for Italy's enemies during the Great War.[95] Now they were engaged in another act of espionage. This could not be unexpected, as Swiss belonged, in large numbers, to Masonry (not to mention to a reformed church congregation): "The Swiss banking cartel is completely Masonic. If you are not a Mason, you can never . . . conduct business." In Spezia alone, the writer asserts, there were more than forty lodges. Not only were these "seedbeds of heresy." But "this Protestantism is [engaged in] espionage against our naval ships and is a dangerous enemy to the Regime of His Excellency Mussolini."[96] Spreading Protestantism and making converts, again, was just a cover for the darker political work of Swiss Masonry, which was determined to capture strategic Italian military sites in order to bring down the fascist government.[97]

It is for this reason that the United States—or rather the Masonic–Protestant–Anglo-Saxon hegemony—maintained so many Protestant churches, whose tiny number concealed their grand ambitions and likely global impact.[98] According to a report in *Il Giornale d'Italia,* many Baptists resident in Moscow had enthusiastically embraced Bolshevism and even requested to be inducted into the Red Army for the defense of the Soviet regime.[99] Tinti can only conclude, quite doubtfully, that the Americans were so desperate to dominate Italy that they were willing to make common cause with the Soviet regime.[100]

In fact, some Catholic polemicists were nervous that conceptual and concrete affinities could be found to link Christianity and communism, so that conversion to Protestantism might in fact lead to sympathy for communism. In the slippery-slope scenario imagined here, conversion to certain forms of Protestantism could lead to becoming a fellow traveler and thus atheistic and materialistic, thus augmenting—Tinti begins chasing his tail here—the cultural force of Judaism. Tinti and Tacchi Venturi additionally report that, according to the witness of "reliable fascist journals," the presence of so many Protestants (especially Methodists) in Italy raised the specter of a red tide washing over the peninsula.[101] This was a fear that would live on in Italy, not without foundation, far beyond the fall of Mussolini and even beyond the Second Vatican Council.

Tinti and Tacchi Venturi were persuaded that among the Sons of Darkness was a circle of professors, especially in the universities in Rome; they were surely part of the Protestant menace. Indeed, some are "writers for Protestant journals."[102] In another letter to Tacchi Venturi, written in December 1927, Tinti declares that the number of professors and teachers in Italy who spread Protestant propaganda is infinite. He tells Tacchi Venturi that in a recent raid in Bari, made at the home of a Protestant pastor, police found thousands of addresses. Among them there "abound addresses of professors and teachers."[103] Yet no one seems to care or even notice. That short reference to a raid raises the possibility that Tinti, himself a policeman in Bari, likely the most hostile law enforcement officer in the region, was involved in it, but we cannot know.

One reason Protestant proselytizing so outraged Tacchi Venturi and other Italian Catholic polemicists had to do with race. The Italian clergy understood that Africa was—in their eyes not wrongly—a land ripe for missionizing. In the early twentieth century very few Catholic clergy would have objected to the conquest, colonization, and Christianization of supposedly uncultured, irreligious, and idolatrous Africa. What exasperated and indeed insulted Catholics in Rome was that Protestant missionaries, with their imperial overseers, outrageously regarded *Italy* in virtually identical terms. The grandeur that was Rome was, in evangelical eyes, a land of mission. To Catholic prelates it was outrageous to link racially inferior, pagan Africans with the superior religious culture, history, and people of Italy and of the Latin peoples in general. Igino Giordani, then an anti-Protestant crusader, wrote that the most active agents of Protestantization in Italy were the very same Protestants who missionize in Africa; insultingly, "one and the other [are] considered mission lands." In his pamphlet Tacchi Venturi concludes, as Tinti does in his "Studio," by asserting:

> It is necessary to make known to the leaders of the Protestant incursion that Italy is not some Boetia,[104] some sort of Papua New Guinea,[105] some indigenous African region[106] in need of being civilized. The Italy of today is the country that defeated at Vittorio Veneto one of the most powerful empires in the world, that at Vittorio Veneto caused the European war to end, leaving [the war as] victor after untold sacrifices. . . . [T]he Italy that is the cradle of Christianity and of Christian civilization: the Italy, in closing, of Benito Mussolini, the Man who today dominates the consciousness of the entire world. The Italy of today does not consent to this deceitful penetration, this insulting anti-Catholic and dangerous antinational propaganda; and is remembered by all to have been the Master of civilization and of progress; and that therefore it feels no need to take any element from Saxon or Anglo-Saxon culture, which can project its plutocratic and imperialistic will over the Sahara or Siberia—but not Italy.[107]

One of the many ironies marking the writings of Tacchi Venturi is the unwitting coexistence of his fear of American imperialism with nonchalant views on

Italian Catholic conquest, colonization, and Christianization of Africa. One form of cultural and religious imperialism was acceptable; another was not.

In the early modern period Italian dreams of a Catholic society, even hopes of reestablishing medieval Christendom, had been shattered by the political, social, and economic upheavals that rocked Europe after the French Revolution. One reason among many that the pope linked hands and destinies with fascism and Mussolini was the hope, perhaps delusional, that Il Duce would reestablish a confessional state in Italy. In reality, little interested the profoundly anticlerical Mussolini less. To Catholic clerics, the two principal challengers to the reestablishment of *Christianitas* were Jews and Protestants. Both, too, were viewed as primary carriers of the many errors of modernity. They were allies in a conspiracy that aimed to subvert Italian society and trigger the collapse of Catholicism. The risk they posed to the glory of Rome was real, imminent, and potentially catastrophic. For this reason both groups had to be resisted with great vigor. The story of fascist persecution of Italian Jewry is well known. Even before Italian Jews came under threat, evangelical missionaries encountered a fearsome campaign of resistance, one which involved an alliance of important Vatican prelates with functionaries high in the fascist government. The holy and the evil alliances were about to collide.

CHAPTER 3

After the Concordat

LEGISLATION ON PERMITTED CULTS (1929–30)

Fearful of negative reaction from Britain and America and not wishing to seem to have surrendered to the wishes of the church, Mussolini pushed parliament, after the Concordat was signed, to pass laws to protect the "permitted denominations" (*culti ammessi*) of Protestant Christianity. The passage of these laws and their implementing legislation were greeted with joy by Protestants. Joy diminished when the meaning of these laws would become unclear, as Catholic opponents, disillusioned with Mussolini for promoting the statutes and protecting the confessions, struggled to read the laws in a way most unfavorable to the evangelicals, then to promote their own, sometimes eccentric jurisprudence as normative and binding. The debate over their meaning and implications would last throughout the fascist period. In the end, the laws pleased neither side.

THE LAW ON PERMITTED CULTS

On the day after the signing of the pacts, the writer of an article on the front page of *OR* famously declared, "Italy has been given back to God and God to Italy."[1] But, as was obvious not only to Jews but to Protestants as well, it was the deity whom Catholics venerated who had been reinstalled in Italy and to whom the country had returned devotion. If this was not instantly obvious, the first article of the pacts scrubbed away any lingering doubt: "The Holy Catholic and Apostolic Roman Religion is the only State Religion."[2] In so declaring, the article reaffirmed the first part of the analogous clause of the *Statuto Albertino* (4 March 1848) while, crucially, neglecting to replicate its second part, which stated that other religions were tolerated by the law.[3] In fact, nothing in the Lateran Pacts recognized the liberty, or even toleration, of religious minorities. One hardly need underscore that this was not unintentional. Catholic satisfaction with the pacts was very near total.

Instantly, or so it seemed, the jubilation died down. Speaking before the Chamber of Deputies on 21 April 1929, King Victor Emmanuel III asked for legislation to regulate the status and treatment of non-Catholic religious groups. This appealed to Mussolini. A law that recognized and tolerated religious minorities would suggest that Mussolini had not simply capitulated to the Vatican's wishes; and this, in turn, would please anticlerical fascists. As the fascist government and its head recognized, such a law would also reassure the Americans and British, who would be relieved to learn that neither Jews nor Protestants would be maltreated. In the end Mussolini and the fascist government would win on two counts. First, Mussolini was celebrated by the Catholic world for resolving the Roman Question and restoring Catholicism to a place of primacy in Italy. Second, with new legislation, Mussolini became a hero to Protestants and Jews, a defender, as Peter D'Agostino has put it, of "religious minorities from Catholic repression and bigotry."[4]

On 24 June 1929, just months after the Conciliazione had caused elation among Italian Catholics, legislation was passed by the fascists to protect religious minorities.[5] In September 1929 Mussolini commented on the new law and its relationship to the Conciliazione: "We have recognized the preeminent role that the Catholic church plays in the religious life of the people," he began. But, he stated emphatically, "it goes without saying that the other denominations that, to this point, have been tolerated, should not now be persecuted, suppressed, or even harassed."[6] Persecuted, suppressed, and harassed they would be, by both church and state. Yet the law afforded them some protection from outrage.

The law intended to protect foreign denominations is known by shorthand as Law 1159 (24 June 1929); it was implemented and fleshed out by Royal Decree 289 (28 February 1930).[7] Borgongini would remorselessly attempt to erect barriers around the law or to insist such impediments were implicit in the legislation. Be that as it may, partly because of Mussolini's known support, it was the only law among the implementing legislation to pass unanimously. In the first article of the law, non-Catholic creeds were "permitted" (the first article of the Albertine Statute had declared them "tolerated") so long as they did not "profess principles or follow rites contrary to public order or morality." Article 1 went on to state: "The exercise—even the public exercise—of such cults is free." Yet limits to the establishment and exercise of admitted creeds were ordained by the following article. It states that, like all such "moral entities," permitted cults are subject to the "control and supervision" of the state. Control and supervision fell to the director of cults, who was often in touch with and influenced by the Vatican nuncio, Borgongini. In the long run he succeeded in changing the meaning of the law by redefining both terms of "public exercise."

During the ventennio, the Directorate of Cults was housed in several governmental ministries. It eventually moved into the Interior Ministry, headed for a crucial period by the profoundly anti-Protestant Buffarini-Guidi. Borgongini would persuade the interior secretary to criminalize several foreign creeds (like Pentecostalism) on the charge that, by practicing rites contrary to public order and morality, they had violated the clause of the first article of Law 1159. Governmental control could be exercised less spectacularly by the undersecretary of the interior, who retained right of approval over any application to appointment to a position in religious ministry. Law 1159 also excepted non-Catholic students from the requirements of Catholic religious education.[8]

Neither side was completely pleased with the law. The application of government policy protecting the rights of non-Catholics was far from consistent throughout the 1930s. Preaching and propaganda plagued the pope; indeed, the mere presence of Protestants on Catholic soil distressed him. Nothing so tormented him, though, as governmental nonchalance in the face of what he felt to be a grave problem; this, for him, was a dereliction. This was a struggle (*lotto*) in which he would participate actively. But he needed the national government and local prefectures; he would never get their serious cooperation.

Though Protestants were initially delighted with the passage of laws protecting them, they shortly became disillusioned with the Catholic interpretation and fascist enforcement of them. Greeted by many evangelicals as a sort of Magna Carta of religious liberty in Italy, Law 1159 (1929) and the implementing decree (1930), along with the Concordat, nonetheless broke with the then-established practice of separation of church and state.[9] The law also established or recognized a preexisting hierarchy of religious faiths. The Concordat had acknowledged the primacy of the Catholic faith, which it named, echoing the Albertine *Statuto,* "the religion of the State." The Italian state had acknowledged the sacred aura with which the Holy See and Catholicism had permeated the Eternal City, and it had obliged itself, in the first article of the Concordat, to prevent in Rome "anything that might clash with that character." The state also obliged itself to enforce certain dimensions of Canon Law and clerical discipline. Thus it observed Catholic feast days; recognized the civil effects of the sacrament of marriage; extended Catholic education from primary to secondary school; acknowledged that religion teachers required ecclesiastical approval; recognized organizations forming part of Catholic Action; and agreed that apostate priests could not be appointed or continue as teachers of religion or other positions where they were in contact with the public. An insult to the Catholic church—or at least to the person of the pope—was a crime, an expression of contempt for the state religion. Yet Catholic polemicists could insult evangelical communities crudely without fear of social or legal reprisal. The evangelical communities may have been recognized, but it was a third-class sort of recognition.[10]

The protections, privileges, and power given legally to the Catholic church in the Concordat were nonetheless taken away in some respects by the implementing legislation, or, again, by the unclarity of its language and its openness to varying interpretations. This is true even when one appreciates that the legislation on admitted cults subjected all accepted cults, legally at least, to the stiff and potentially severe control of the state. In practice, that theoretical state control left many problematic issues unaddressed or at least unclear, to the advantage of the Protestant cults. No article of the implementing law would cause as much grief to Borgongini or Catholic polemicists as the fifth. Reinstituting the second article of the (then defunct) Law of Guarantees, Article 5 of the law on permitted cults (culti ammessi) stated that discussion on matters religious was completely free (*pienamente libera*). Here the architects of the law left a hostage to fortune. What Article 5 did *not* specify was what "freedom of discussion" in practice meant or what, precisely, "discussion" implied. Was it worship? Discussion of the Bible? Religious conversation? Invitations to religious services? Proselytizing? Protestants and Catholics would interpret the meaning of these words in contrary senses; the failure to spell out what the law meant left open a vast legal gridiron on which Catholics and evangelicals would clash at least through 1935. Borgongini would complicate what to evangelicals was well-defined legal language by redefining "discussion" so as to exclude proselytizing and, in so doing, opening the sluices to years of disputation and litigation. Antagonism would deepen when

Borgongini came to persuade authorities—based largely on his reading of the new fascist penal code[11]—to assume that private meetings, organized ostensibly for worship, had been established for proselytizing and so acquired a public quality. This meant they were a matter of state and police interest and therefore could legally be shut down. Enforcement of this interpretation of the law, in turn, would bring protests from evangelical leaders, which were sometimes effective, even more so when backed by the embassies of Britain or the United States.

Legislation left both sides feeling betrayed by the government, the Catholic perhaps more so, as they had expected so much more than had the minority religious communities. To begin with, Roman Catholic prelates were convinced that Protestant proselytizing on the peninsula had intensified in 1929–30; many complained that Law 1159 was to blame. It had legitimated evangelical propaganda. No one bore the consequences of Protestant proselytizing more heavily than the pope himself, who keenly felt that the presence of Protestants on his soil had become intolerable even before his single meeting with Mussolini (February 1932). His mood would not improve in the succeeding two years. In September 1934 *OR* reported that the pope was dejected by "the ruins Protestant proselytism made in Italy." In fact, Pius XI felt strongly that there were "few dioceses immune to this proselytism, and many are they that suffer greatly from it, from the Alps to Etna, from one sea to another."[12] Here the pope first deploys expansive, superlative language; he and other Vatican prelates, and fascist officials, would soon use such language to characterize a "Protestant pilgrimage" to Italy, planned in 1930. Pope Pius was the first but not the only cleric who thought the pilgrimage was covertly propagandizing in intent.[13] It would be the first event to make him worry that the implementing legislation could have grave consequences for the integrity of Italian Catholicism.

Protestant propaganda would so unsettle the pope because he was convinced—as Protestant jurists, if in the opposite interpretive direction, would be—that the law made things so very clear. Indeed, Pius XI, in view of the recently passed Concordat, was never in doubt about the meaning of the new law: the first article clearly called Catholicism "the religion of the State," with all the logical and juridical consequences of this Constitutional principle, *especially in regard to propaganda,*" that is to say, proselytism by Protestants.[14] Yet the verbatim reproduction of the Second Article of the Law of Guarantees[15]—"There is complete freedom of discussion as far as religious matters are concerned" (La discussione in materia religiosa è pienamente libera)—seemed to dash Catholic hopes that the pacts allowed Protestant proselytizing to be regulated by the *Statuto Albertino,* some of whose articles appeared to suggest that Catholic authorities could control Protestant activity.[16] "Tolerated"—as mentioned, the word used in the Law of Guarantees—might suggest that a cult was in a position of inferiority and could be restricted; but ammessi was harder, but not impossible (especially for Borgongini), to interpret in this sense. In an instant the new law seemed to change the status of the Protestant churches, in Protestant eyes, from "tolerated cults" (*culti tollerati*) to "permitted cults" (culti ammessi). Ironically, then, the Concordat and its implementing legislation, on which Catholics and especially the pope had pinned so much hope for the establishment of a confessional state, could seem to *strengthen* the legal position of non-Catholic Christians in Italy.[17] As tolerated Protestant denominations would soon learn, however, Catholic prelates and some powerful state actors vigorously attempted to set firm boundaries to what was free in Protestant speech and practice and to limit the frontiers of the wide field of discourse that "free discussion" seemed to have established. Catholic views of freedom in these cases became startlingly narrow over the course of the fascist period—not to mention potentially contrary to the laws enshrining toleration. Nonetheless, it bears repeating here that the laws exasperated both Catholic and evangelical communities. It would be wrong to suggest that only evangelical communities were troubled by them. Why Catholics were troubled has to do not just with the laws but with how the Roman church had viewed Protestantism for centuries.

"RELIGION FOR CHILDREN": PROTESTANTISM IN CATHOLIC PERSPECTIVE IN FASCIST ITALY

In an ecumenical, secular, and pluralistic culture like that of twenty-first-century America, it may be hard to appreciate the meaning and implications of the danger Protestantism posed and the imperatives, from the point of view of many twentieth-century Italian Catholic clerics, for vigorously resisting it. While many in Europe and America might today view the differences between Catholicism and Protestantism as an expression of the narcissism of petty differences, early-twentieth-century Protestants and, even more, Catholics and, perhaps above all, the pope, to say the least, did not. Truth—in particular, religious truth—was unitary, and there was one way, not multiple paths, to salvation.

A short pamphlet by an unknown Catholic cleric published in 1920, now found in the archives of the Holy Office, could not illustrate this sensibility more clearly.[18] Entitled *Due Domande,* the pamphlet addressed two questions: Could Catholics participate in the Protestant Italian Student Federation for Religious Culture or take its review, *Fede e Vita*? In both cases the response was categorically negative. This is because the teachers affiliated with the Federazione Studenti Italiani had, so the anonymous cleric argued, arrogated to themselves a teaching office that had been entrusted, by Christ, to the Roman church alone; because the federation had aspired to transcend creeds, confessions, and denominational boundaries; because it aimed to achieve an ever-higher religious ideal by encouraging "the free examination and private interpretation of the Gospel," an ideal that could also be achieved by meditation on the message of an infinite end given to all in the "intimate recesses of the soul."[19] Any Christian religion and all denominations, the federazione's teachers, particularly one Don Brizio Casciola (1871–1957), were said to believe, could benefit one in achieving this high aim, which was universal to the human spirit. Christianity had not come in any eternally fixed form. Rather, it was a perennial font of life; the religious seeker was permitted to choose any church—or none.[20]

To this notion, the anonymous Catholic cleric, indignant, responds, but not before calling the teacher of such an idea a modernist,[21] a movement associated in many clerical imaginations in Italy with Protestantism.[22] As early as 1914 *Civiltà Cattolica* had published an article entitled "The Cordial Harmony between Protestantism and the Modernists."[23] In any case, the anonymous cleric responds briskly to the notion that many forms of Christianity represent, despite differences, essentially the same interpretation of the gospel: "The one true religion [*l'unica vera religione*] is the one that Jesus has given to the Church. Therefore, it is necessary to accept the Holy Roman Church, with its pope, its seven sacraments, its new Code of Canon Law [1917];[24] and that its divine commandments were given to the Roman Church, and come exclusively from the Church, precisely according to the Gospel."[25] Truth was one; it was given by God to "the One True Church"; other churches or sects (*setti*), the pejorative noun preferred by Catholic polemicists, were, by definition, false and heretical; and the truth was to be interpreted authoritatively only by teachers in communion and agreement with the magisterial teaching of Rome. To be an evangelical Christian was one thing, but to be a true Christian—to be a Roman Catholic—was quite another. For Catholic writers,

Christianity—Roman Christianity—was an all-or-nothing proposition; one takes all or one takes nothing, that is, all of Roman Catholicism offered. Pondering recent British legislation that abolished certain restrictive legislation on Catholics, Tacchi Venturi declared that the growing number of English converts from Protestantism proved "they have finally understood how the strength and unity of the Church of Rome is the one road to salvation [*l'unica via di salvezza*] of all the nations."[26] The teachers of the Italian federation, agnostic as to the truth of the historical expressions of the Gospels, had led to a grave error of the time, repeatedly deplored in the published and archival documents of these decades: "religious indifferentism" (indifferentismo religioso). This is not meant to suggest apathy or indolence but something far more serious, and for the Catholic church, mortally dangerous in the history of modern ideas: a relativistic conviction that all churches, all forms of Christianity, are more or less equally instructive; and that more than one can be a True Church. Already in 1824 Pope Leo XII (r. 1824–29) had condemned indifferentism and, importantly, linked it with toleration and British Bible societies as among the most pernicious of modern errors.[27] An entire section of the *Syllabus of Errors* is dedicated to denouncing indifferentism (which it links with latitudinarianism); at least three papal encyclicals had denounced it by the time the syllabus was published in 1864.[28] Commenting on the Protestant invasion, one writer for *OR* (22 October 1934) declared, "It is an invasion . . . by Protestants who do not give faith to souls. They infuse them with indifferentism and skepticism."[29] This was a pervasive theme. "What is the Federation?" the author of *Due Domande* asks here, but "a free association of the church, respectful of every faith, every creed . . . free think[ers], heretics and schismatics, apostates, interested in the 'religious phenomenon,' not the dogmatic truth."[30] Almost needless to say, "respectful" here means, not civility, but a soft, reckless, and, finally, imbecilic pluralism. Something very like this form of inclusionism or pluralism Pius XI would condemn in *Mortalium Animos* (1928), which begins by lauding the aim of religious comity, but not at the cost, fatal to souls entrusted to Rome, of recognizing false forms of Christianity, which is to say, all forms save Roman Catholicism. Here Pius XI was targeting, among other things, the new ecumenical movement, which, in his view "professed a mutilated and corrupt version of Christ's teaching" and in whose discussions, therefore, Catholics were forbidden to participate.[31] Christ had founded only one church, the Roman; and it is only within the walls of that church that salvation was to be found.[32]

Casciola, therefore, is hypocritical when he says the evangelical churches do not proselytize in favor of any church. In fact, it is evident that he proselytizes for the Protestant churches. The goals of the federation are "distance from the Roman Catholic church, heresy in faith, schism, rebellion, Protestantism, modernism, indifferentism, rationalism, atheism . . . anticlericalism"—a very nearly comprehensive catalogue of modern errors condemned by the church. Casciola presides over a group composed of "free-thinkers, philosophers, seekers of the way." Its "ultimate aim," is to "propagate Protestantism . . . independent of ecclesiastical authority, the explicit exclusion of every dogmatic truth, absolute moral liberty of the individual and free study of the sacred scriptures."[33] In this connection, countless Catholic polemicists in these decades entitled their treatises and long letters not "the *Protestant* campaign" or even "the *anti-Catholic* campaign," but, tellingly, "the anti-*religious* campaign in Italy." Protestants in Italy aimed simply to destroy vera religione.

Given this point of view, it can hardly come as a surprise that, on 14 April 1920, the Holy Office went as far as to declare *Fide e Vita* "damned and proscribed."[34] Catholic anti-Protestant writers regarded their religious enemies as heretics and their religion as an expression of heresy—a fraught category, still—or an act of apostasy. Such writers also connected Protestantism with a host of modern political and social problems, above all, the rise and seeming triumph of secularism, often called *laicismo* in the archival and published documents from the period. In his 1925 encyclical *Quas Primas,* Pope Pius XI denounced *laicismo* as "the plague of our times."[35] Was there really doubt as to how to react to the Anglo-Saxon carriers of "the plague of our age"?

The responses of a Catholic cleric and the Holy Office were neither rare nor extraordinary. Rather, they were fundamentally characteristic attitudes of the Roman church's prelates and its approved theologians, especially when confronted with the Protestant menace in the early twentieth century. By then—much earlier, actually—the rhetoric of heresy has largely lost the punch it once packed in Latin Catholicism. That said, one can grasp the intensity, even ferocity, of the mutual polemicizing in the interwar period in Europe only if one perceives that, while attitudes toward the treatment of heretics may have softened, Protestants, in Catholic eyes, *were* and remained heretics. Clerical writers called them so over and again in the 1920s and 1930s. This is simply how Catholic clerics in early modern centuries and the fascist period viewed Protestants. In the eyes of some, like Tacchi Venturi (1861–1956), this was because, as carriers of the corrosive germs of modernity as well as false religion, they were even more dangerous than traditional religious deviants or apostates. Thus many insisted that they be subject to the full rigor of existing legislation, as they interpreted it, and the most powerful Catholics, who thought Mussolini deaf to pleas regarding the gravity of the problem, demanded that Il Duce live up to his name and *lead* on behalf of the one true church. He did not have to support an inquisition; but could he not enforce the law?

AN UNDESIRABLE AMERICAN PILGRIMAGE (1929–31)

Protestant activity on Italian soil confirmed many of Italy's leading clerics' worst fears, as the records of the freshly available Secret Archives reveal. Just months after the implementing laws were passed, word reached the Vatican of an American Protestant excursion designed to take evangelical pilgrims from Sicily to the northern provinces. Their journey, and reaction to it by priests, politicians, and journalists, reveals themes that would dominate relations between Italian Protestants and Catholics, the government, and the Vatican for almost a decade.

To begin with, an activity trumpeted as an educational and sightseeing journey was suspected, even presumed, of being inspired by an ambition to convert. Second, both seemingly powerful governmental and ecclesiastical authorities would try to frustrate the plans of the pilgrims but would—a harbinger of things to come—enjoy negligible success. Third, the journey was conceived by an *americano,* that is, by an Italian national who, while in the United States, had been converted to Protestantism. Many new evangelical communities would be founded, and missionary ventures spearheaded, by those who had returned home after having been converted to evangelical Christianity in America. Fourth, it would be led by a profoundly anti-Catholic leader of the American Methodists, seen, accurately, as the most aggressively proselytizing of all the sects, storming what the Wesleyans regarded with revulsion as a neopagan, idolatrous country in desperate need of cleansing by exposure to the true gospel. Finally, the pilgrimage heightened the already intense anxieties of Pope Pius XI over the revival of proselytism in Catholic Italy. It would also deepen his frustration over governmental powerlessness, or insouciance, in the face of what was, for him, so evidently a threat to his dreams of establishing a confessional state—yearnings for the very realization of which he had, after hesitation, tied his fortunes to those of Mussolini.

As would become a pattern over nine years, when news of troubling Protestant activity reached the Vatican, Pacelli, as secretary of state (1930–39), shunted the matter to the Apostolic Nuncio, Borgongini-Duca. The Jesuit Pietro Tacchi Venturi (1861–1956), chosen in 1923 by the pope and Mussolini as a go-between, would be called on by the pope to handle highly sensitive matters.[36] Yet it was the less subtle Apostolic Nuncio who, when it came to securing the perceived interests of Catholic Italy, would prove himself as coldly ruthless as Tacchi Venturi. As mentioned, he would quickly become the Vatican's eager and ruthless point man on Protestant issues. In the mid-1930s he joined forces with Mussolini's remorseless undersecretary of the interior, Guido Buffarini-Guidi (1895–1945). The man, who, infamously, would issue the decree to suppress all Pentecostal communities in Italy, Buffarini was, as the freshly available archives demonstrate, tirelessly counseled on points of the law for the lawyer Buffarini, and he guided him to the severe measures that have brought him infamy (achievements for which Borgongini characteristically claimed credit). At this moment, however, Borgongini, appointed new Nuncio (ambassador) to Italy in 1929, would collaborate with Dino Grandi (1895–1988), whom Mussolini designated the same year his minister of foreign affairs (1929–32).

Ultimately, Borgongini, Giuseppe Pizzardo (1877–1970), secretary to Pacelli, and Grandi (1884–1959) would all monitor the purposes of the pilgrimage, writing to American diplomats about it, and concurring on a policy of response. In the late summer of 1930 Borgongini first received news of the planned pilgrimage. He wrote to Grandi. An "American Protestant Pilgrimage to Italy" had been organized. A certain Reverend Moncada, an Italian American Methodist pastor, and his wife would lead it. For this reason and because the Methodist "bishop" William Burt (1852–1936) would accompany the group, the pilgrimage was evidently Methodist-inspired.[37] As the Methodists were the most profoundly feared—and cordially loathed—of all the evangelical groups, the Catholic response to the trip was not likely to be measured.

In part, the historic ambitions of Methodism made this likely, and the temperament of the Methodist leadership clinched the outcome. In the annual report written for the Methodist Missionary Society early in the twentieth century, one Bishop Vincent candidly stated the matter: "Where Romanism is, Methodism should be. We represent and stand for precisely what Romanism antagonizes."[38] Yet this hostility was expressed to different degrees in various parts of Europe. For example, while criticism of Catholic Austria was subdued, the language of hostility toward Italy was unrestrained.

Practically now a symbol of militant anti-Catholicism, Methodism embodied the features of aggressive, contemptuous missionizing clerical Catholics despised. Anti-Catholic sentiment was widespread and deep among both European and American Methodists, and it had found expression for decades before the planned pilgrimage. Condescension to the church of Rome infuriated clerics at the Vatican, from the pope on down, who firmly believed that the Roman church was ordained by God and the "only true church."

When news of the pilgrimage reached Rome, agents of neither the pope nor of Mussolini knew quite how to react; they knew it was wrong but could not quite say why. It was, as Grandi observed at the time, "the first attempt [at proselytizing] of its kind." Grandi was summoned by the pope for a personal audience on 15 July 1930. Deeply agitated by the renewal of Protestant activity in Italy, Pope Pius was among the first to perceive what kind of activity the pilgrimage was designed to promote—and conceal. Under the pretext of visiting Protestant churches and sites of historic interest, a "deplorable proselytism" was intended. In the memorable words attributed to the leaders of the pilgrimage, the Protestants aimed to "spread propaganda 'from Sicily to the Alps.'" Could the government do anything to frustrate the Methodists' travel plans?[39]

Here Pius established two important interpretive and polemical precedents. First, all Protestant activity ought to be presumed guilty of proselytizing before being proved innocent of it. Second, Protestant ventures could never be permitted to distress the tender sensitivities of the pious ecclesial parishioners of the Italian citizenry, the overwhelming majority of whom were faithful, at least nominally, to Rome; this was a theme expressed virtually ubiquitously in the 1930s, and it was written into law. Indeed, even Catholic journalists insisted on this. The author of an article entitled "An Undesirable American Pilgrimage," in the then-profascist daily *La Tribuna,* complained that it was not appropriate to have a Protestant pilgrimage "in the eighth year of the Fascist regime." Ignoring the fact that the regime, which the author identified, religiously, with Catholicism, had joined hands with the church only the previous year, the article dwelt on how grievously a Protestant pilgrimage would wound the country's Catholic population. At the same time, the article's author stressed that the pilgrims would be visiting places of Protestant martyrs, figures like Arnaldo da Brescia (c. 1090–June 1155) and the famous Florentine Dominican reformer Savonarola (1452–98). In addition, the Protestants would be visiting historic sites of sects that "more or less directly have their source in Martin Luther."[40] None of this suggests that the Protestants were in fact aiming primarily at the recruitment of Catholics. Still, this was wholly undesirable from the point of view of the Holy See, which framed the pilgrimage as exclusively proselytizing in intent.

With this view of the pilgrimage in mind, Grandi brought the wishes of the pope to his Apostolic Nuncio. Perhaps borrowing language from the pope, the foreign minister urged Borgongini to work with him to impede the "so-called" (*cosidetto*) pilgrimage and, above all, to prevent the Protestants from the manifestation, especially public, of any religious devotion that would be "an offense to the religious sensibilities of the Catholic population."[41] Grandi soon met with diplomatic authorities at the American consulate. He instructed the American diplomats to warn the leaders of the pilgrimage to do nothing that would upset the beliefs or religious sentiments of the Italian people. Given their mandate, the Americans assured Grandi that Reverend Moncada would receive these instructions and comply with them.[42]

Pope Pius was not in the least soothed. Grandi had already discovered that the renewal of Protestant activities in Italy had given new substance to the "apprehensions nourished by the Holy Father." Pius was quite sensitive to supposed governmental inertia. Indeed, he would soon complain quite bitterly: "The Government does not seem to preoccupy itself in an adequate way" with the "true and grave danger that menaces the religious and national unity of the Italians"—here, perhaps intentionally, echoing the words of Mussolini[43]—and that recurs "in the current surge of Protestant propaganda." The pope had cherished hopes for governmental as well as ecclesiastical zeal in "defense of the spiritual unity of the nation." Only if undertaken with energy and conviction could the campaign against "heretical and foreign propaganda" succeed.[44] With the use of the categories heretic and especially foreigner, the pope would give his imprimatur to the Catholic terms of the debate. If the force of the term "heretic" was weak among the peasant population, it was not so among schoolteachers, some governmental officials, and, especially, it was not so for Italian priests in most every diocese in the country. Catholic polemicists would for the entirety of the 1930s underscore that Protestants were foreigners (*stranieri*), as much a threat to national unity and political continuity as heretics would be to ecclesiastical integrity. Even if sincerely felt, the link between evangelicals and foreigners, insisted upon, was an attempt to alarm and thus involve the government in their suppression.

This was not always successful, especially with Mussolini. In a letter written to Gasparri, Tacchi Venturi noted that he had recently met with Mussolini to talk about the propaganda of the Protestants. How might the government help to stop it in the most effective way possible? "At first [Mussolini] found it hard to believe me," the Jesuit writes, "because His Excellency, like many others, harbored the opinion, which I always held erroneous, that Italy is not a land endangered by Protestantism." Given Tacchi Venturi's persistence, Mussolini promised an inquiry. But his skepticism regarding the magnitude and even the reality of a problem was something no Vatican cleric would ever succeed in changing.

THE CONSTRUCTION OF PROTESTANT MEMORY

The sites chosen by the pilgrims reveal something crucial about the construction of Protestant identity and memory. In the view of these American pilgrims—and virtually all contemporary Protestants—a small number of Protestant saints (most of them persecuted or martyred) had defied the corrupt papal church through the ages. These were Protestants before Protestantism, reformers before the Reformation. They had preserved the true gospel throughout the ages, and they made up a line of continuity and authority to the ancient pure church, one with which Protestants would associate themselves. The promotion of Protestant saints by evangelicals was a way to claim continuity with the ancient church. Whatever the pretenses of Rome to apostolic authority, it was the evangelical church that represented authentic (because ancient) Christianity. Pilgrimage to sites associated with them consolidated devotion to them and deepened Protestants' conviction that theirs was the truest, indeed the only true, form of the gospel.

An Augustinian canon who deplored the temporal power of the papacy and called on the church to renounce ownership of property, Arnaldo of Brescia imagined himself as a reformer. Yet he was hanged to death for heresy and burnt posthumously, after which his ashes were deposited in the Tiber.[45] The story of Savonarola is much better known. A member of the reformed Dominicans or Observants, Savonarola was a teacher at the famous priory of San Marco in Florence, where he initially functioned as a *lector,* or instructor in theology. Slowly he became a reformer and apocalyptic preacher of some renown. When Charles VIII of France (1470–98) invaded Italy, Savonarola's prophecy of a coming invasion from a new "Cyrus from the North" seemed to have been vindicated. (At the same time, Savonarola had incautiously predicted the deaths of the pope and Lorenzo de' Medici, a prophecy that would come back to haunt him.) With Florence under threat, the Dominican seer intervened with the French king, thus preserving the city. The Dominican's popularity soared, as the Fiorentini expelled the powerful Medici family and Savonarola established a theocracy; the king of Florence henceforth would be Christ. Savonarola's reputation was only improved when he declared that, purged of Medici presence, Florence would become the New Jerusalem, "richer, more powerful, more glorious than ever," and replace Rome as the capital city of Christianity. This, memorably, was accompanied by an austere program of laws against sexual transgression, immodesty, and the spectacle of the "bonfire of the vanities."

Savonarola's fortunes began to turn when, in 1495, he failed to join the pope's Holy League against the French. Summoned to Rome, he graciously declined the invitation, citing poor health. The pope, who had not forgotten his earlier prophecies, excommunicated him in 1497. He also threatened to place Florence under interdict. Popular opinion swung against the Dominican seer after a rival preacher suggested Savonarola undergo a trial by fire to test his prophetic credentials. Tortured, Savonarola was said to have confessed that he had fabricated his prophecies. His fate was thus sealed. Along with two other Dominicans, he was burnt in the Piazza della Signoria in May 1498.[46]

Yet the Protestants would not soon forget him. Indeed, they would deftly integrate him into their own history. In 1927 Monsignor Alberto Costa, bishop of Venosa, Melfi, and Rapolla, wrote to Tacchi Venturi, lodging a complaint about an evangelical minister named Alfredo Franco. He was guilty of every sin then imaginable for a Protestant pastor: he was deceitful, protected by Masonry, connected to the "too famous" YMCA, antifascist, and subversive. Finally, the local populace, indignant, was said to have confronted him and to have requested governmental intervention to shut his evangelical operation down. On 31 March 1925, by decree of the local prefect, the evangelical circle was closed down. Thus ended the brief history of the "Circolo G. Savonarola."[47]

Evangelicals would claim as their own other persecuted individuals and groups from the high and late Middle Ages as proto-Protestants, including the so-called Spiritual Franciscans.[48] Other groups embraced by the Protestants as reformers *avant le temps* included the British Wycliffites and the

Czech Hussites, whose leader, John Hus (1369–1415), was burnt at the stake at the Council of Constance in 1415—this after having been guaranteed a safe passage by the emperor Sigismund (1368–1437), who had convoked the council to solve the problem of the "great schism," when first two, then three candidates claimed to be rightful pope.[49] In all of these cases Protestants claimed that the papacy had burnt reformers who had challenged its authority. This was partly to express their own hostility toward the papacy, which all reformers denied was divinely ordained and whose exercise of power and tenure of lands it deplored.

Claiming medieval dissenters as their own suggests that Protestants were intent on constructing a history and memory of a particular kind. As has been often observed, antiquity counts in religion.[50] To put it directly, the more ancient a religion, the more likely it is, in the eyes of most, to be true. Luther memorably had to face the difficult charge that his "gospel" was a novelty. Catholic opponents, like the Swabian scholastic John Eck (1486–1543) and Cardinal Thomas Cajetan (1469–1534) taunted him: had Christ left the church to drift off its divinely ordained path for fifteen centuries before an obscure German friar could rescue it from doctrinal deviance and pastoral incompetence?[51] The Protestant response mirrored the early Christian response to Roman criticism that it was a novel religion. Early Christian apologists like Justin Martyr (c. 100–165) could retort by claiming that ancient Greek philosophers or Hebrew writers had captured fragments of the truth, the whole of which had now been revealed in the Christian gospel.[52] Fifteen centuries later the reformers could claim that Christian reformers persecuted by the diabolical power of the papacy had anticipated the fullness of the recovery of the gospel in the sixteenth century.

Turning back to the evangelical pilgrimage, it was precisely this strategy that was still being exploited by Reverend Moncada and colleagues in twentieth-century Italy. That is, against claims of novelty, evangelicals attempted to archaize their religious beliefs and practices (as indeed had occurred as early as the sixteenth century) by identifying supposed precursors or forerunners as exponents of true and pure Christianity who had criticized, then defied, and finally died at the hands of priests of a corrupt Catholicism.[53] Because these reforming forerunners had inevitably invoked the early church as their model for reform, evangelicals could claim that they, not the Catholic church, represented the truest, because earliest, form of Christianity.

Grandi was not impressed. Such a pilgrimage, and an Italian American one at that, was an affront to the fascist regime. It would offend the sensibilities of an Italian population that was almost entirely Catholic. As "the first attempt of its kind" to propagandize Italian Catholics, it was all the more mysterious and thus the more ominous.[54] Would this be the last of such pilgrimages? Or would there be more? If so, how should Catholics react? A brief note in the Vatican Archive suggests that the Holy Father wished that the Italian government not "simply indicate the measures taken to restrict the scandal of the evangelical pilgrimage, but rather to deplore the pilgrimage itself, as offensive to the Catholicity of the Nation."[55] It was in this context that Pizzardo complained to the Vatican Nuncio that the Italian government had proved insufficiently alert to the Protestant danger, a view all but universally shared among Roman clerics.

CANONIZING THE ANTI-PROTESTANT ANGELS

One way in which Pius attempted to ease his anxiety and to neutralize the Protestant threat was by canonization of saints. In our day Pope John Paul II (r. 1978–2005) was recognized as an unusually prolific saint-maker. Indeed, he canonized some 110 saints during a pontificate that lasted less than thirty years.[56] In his eight-year pontificate (2005–13) Benedict XVI canonized 45 virtuous holy men and women, increasing the rate at which his predecessor had made saints. On 8 March 2010 Benedict controversially moved Pius XII (1939–58) one step closer to canonization by declaring him venerable (*venerabilis*), which imputed to him a variety of "heroic deeds"; he thus asserted precisely what scores of scholarly *promotores fidei* ("devil's advocates") have found most in doubt about him during the Holocaust.[57] Already Pope Francis (2013–) has improved upon even the impressive tempo of his predecessors, averaging 7 canonizations for every year of his short pontificate.

Statistics tell some of the story here. But much more is revealed by those whom a particular pope chose to beatify or sanctify. These reveal much about a pope's preoccupations. Among others, Pius canonized Thomas More and John Fisher.[58] Why did Pius canonize *these* two men in 1935? What ecclesiological and political objectives were at stake? To respond to this question, one need ask only what characteristics and fate the men canonized by Pius XI shared. Born in the late fifteenth century, More (1477/78–1535) would become the leading English Catholic controversialist, a vituperative anti-Lutheran polemicist and a defender of Catholic orthodoxy against the new European reform movements. More cordially loathed Luther and all his works. In 1523 he wrote a response to his writings that was abusive and even defamatory.

As is well known, More was ultimately imprisoned in the Tower of London on 17 April 1534 for refusing to swear an oath (whose exact contents are unknown) on divorce and supremacy. After enduring several interrogations, he was tried and condemned for high treason in Westminster Hall. Executed on 6 July 1535, More was not England's first Catholic martyr. Yet his death caused a sensation throughout Europe, and his status as a martyr was immediately recognized. It would not soon be forgotten.[59]

Martyred before More was Bishop John Fisher (1469–1535), who became chancellor in the same year (1504) he was consecrated to the episcopate in Rochester. Like More, he wrote voluminously against Luther. He was also confessor to Catherine of Aragon (1485–1536). Fisher opposed the king's plans to divorce his wife, arguing that no man on earth could dissolve such a union. Eventually, he championed the supremacy of the pope over the king and church over kingdom. In 1531 he objected to the use by Henry VIII of the title Supreme Head of the Church of England. That was the act of defiance that sealed his fate. Fisher was almost immediately imprisoned. Like More, he was incarcerated in the Tower of London; during his incarceration Pope Paul III (r. 1534–49) made him a cardinal. Henry responded by remarking that the pope could send Fisher a red hat, but he would have no head to put it on. With this as background to his trial (17 June 1535), it came as no surprise that he was convicted and hanged. As he died, he proclaimed loudly that he was dying for the faith of the Catholic church.[60] More shares with Fisher a feast day, 22 June, the date of Fisher's execution.

It was no accident that Pius chose these two men to canonize, nor that they were canonized on the same day (19 May 1935). Most canonizations have broadly ecclesiological or political agendas. Saints are often made so their lives, or deaths, can be harnessed to the current aims and anxieties of the church; celebrations of the church's heroes are at the same time vilifications of its adversaries. No exception, these were men who were martyred for their defense of Catholicism against Lutheranism and Protestantism in general. Both canonizations were therefore meant to call to mind the deadly dangers of the Protestant peril that so preoccupied Pius XI in the 1920s and 1930s. They were meant to communicate to Catholic Italy the danger of tolerating Protestantism and to reiterate that Catholicism was, by history, demography, and law, the Religion of the State. They were tied to Pius's antipathy for Protestantism and his fear that his beloved Italy, or some of its Catholic parishioners, could follow, to the peril of their souls, the way of England and embrace what, in his eyes, was a form of false, even heterodox Christianity. The stakes were that high—salvation was truly at stake—which in part accounts for the ferocity, even the frequent ugliness, of the Catholic response. Anti-Protestant hostility, xenophobia, cultural pride, and fear of cultural imperialism account for much else.

The canonizations may, in addition, have been intended as a tacit message to another head of state, Mussolini, with whom the pontiff was often frustrated and, by 1935, profoundly disappointed.[61] At heart anticlerical and irreligious, Mussolini was no more in danger of converting to Protestantism than in becoming a fervently practicing Catholic. His chief failing in the eyes of the church with whom he had made an alliance and as head of a country whose only official state religion, as stated in the first article of the Lateran Pacts (1929), was Roman Catholicism, was apparent indifference to a Protestant menace whose dimensions and dangers tormented the pope—as well as many other clerics, not to mention a number of active and industrious lay Catholic groups and individuals.

BOCCHINI AND THE PREFECTURES

Perhaps the only way to get the Duce to focus on the menace was to present it as a threat to the Kingdom of Italy and especially to Mussolini's own fascist government. This was precisely the tactic taken by several anti-Protestant polemicists, many of whom deemed the threat not only credible and real but also profound and imminent. In less than twenty-four months Pope Pius XI twice sent his nuncio, Borgongini, to communicate his dismay with what he saw as the legal equalization of Catholicism and Protestantism interpreted (not, he would have contended, written) into the Lateran Pacts. If that did not get Mussolini's attention, then the message that the Protestant menace was the most serious threat to Italy and the government would; Mussolini would then, so the theory went, be motivated to act more forcefully.[62] In any case, most Catholic prelates and polemicists complained that Protestants had misinterpreted the term "permitted cults." As Camillo Crivelli, a Jesuit active in the anti-Protestant campaign, put it, evangelicals affect to believe that the term "culti ammessi" makes their "multiple sects" equal, in a legal sense, to the "Religion of the State."[63] On the basis of this same letter, Zanini observed in a recent article that "the Catholic perception was that the change of status of the Evangelical confessions from tolerated to allowed" was "the basic reason for the resumption of proselytism on their [the Protestants'] part."[64] In 1931 Cesare Maria De Vecchi, the Italian ambassador to the Holy See, wrote, "The Holy See has expressed grave apprehension about the revival of the Protestant movement, which has become stronger in Italy, thanks to the provisions of the law on 'permitted cults.'"[65] In the long run Mussolini himself did quite little to resist Protestant propaganda. As Rochat has observed, "The role of Mussolini in the determination of fascist policy toward the evangelical churches is 'singularly modest.'"[66] At least until 1935 Mussolini regarded the evangelical communities primarily as a pawn in delicate negotiations with England and America; but diplomats from the Anglo-Saxon nations, in general, were not acutely aware of the fortunes of the Anglo-Saxon congregations. Mussolini largely left oversight—and surveillance of the churches—to the police chief Arturo Bocchini (1880–1940).

In the wake of several attempts on his life, Mussolini dismissed the national police chief in 1926. At the suggestion of Federzoni, he replaced him with Arturo Bocchini, who had served as prefect of Brescia, Bologna, and Genoa for four years (1922–26). Bocchini would take control not only of the Polizia di Stato but of the Organizzazione per la Vigilanza e la Repressione dell'Antifascismo (OVRA) as well. Even before Bocchini took office, the regime, encouraged by the Vatican, had shut down several evangelical meetinghouses. Evangelical communities were an enemy that the government held in common with the Vatican. The regime had shut down Protestant meetings on a variety of factitious charges that nonetheless expressed the conviction that evangelical Christianity was not compatible with the principles of Italian fascism. And over the course of 1927–28 Bocchini would clarify the nature of the regime's opposition. At the end of April 1927 Bocchini issued a circular to his prefects. What motivated it is unclear, as it had no immediate repercussions, either in Rome or in the provinces. As Rochat himself has pointed out in explaining its origins, there was the simple fact that the evangelical communities "were objectively a source of problems for the police and that they could not be counted upon as supporters of the new government."[67] The circular was in addition likely part of Bocchini's efforts to establish a systematic mode of surveillance, information, and pacification of organizations that had not made common cause with the regime, an effort that, by the end of the year, had generated over one hundred thousand active files.[68] In any case, Bocchini ordered his prefects to supply him with reports on suspicious activity, mainly antifascist behavior.[69] After hearing from his prefects, Bocchini reported to Mussolini two months later that several provinces required careful observation, though none was a locus of disorder; he nonetheless concluded that all prefects should continue with "un'attiva vigilanza."[70] Evangelicals were clannish, partisan, doctrinaire, narrow-minded, fanatical, and for Bocchini that was enough.

Bocchini was particularly wary of, then distressed by, the presence of Pentecostals in Italy. At the end of 1927 he contacted the Italian embassy in Washington, DC. Was there, he asked, any connection between Pentecostalism and communism? In January an official of the embassy replied. Although no such connection could be established, he nonetheless warned Bocchini of several oddities, including what he took to be the neurotic and obsessional character of American Pentecostal religious commitment and propaganda.[71] In early April 1928, after apprising Mussolini of the presence and character of the Pentecostals, Bocchini sent a circular to seven prefects, including that of Rome: Pentecostals had been detected in all their provinces. Soon, Catholics from Rome denounced Pentecostals in their dioceses. On the basis of reports from Rome and from those he had sent to infiltrate their meetings, Bocchini would, on 9 October 1928, describe them fully.

The Pentecostal cult, he said, was sui generis. At a certain point in their worship service, their members, who were quite suggestible, claim to be invaded by the Holy Spirit. They cry, they exclaim, "they sing with a kind of public confession, with free readings. . . . [A]dolescents often participate in such meetings." Due to their incomplete constitutional development, the children's organisms, body and mind, are subjected to "continuous damage." For that reason the cult represents a "serious and continuing danger not only to religious morality but also to the health of the people who profess it." Bocchini concludes by asking the prefects to provide precise information on Pentecostals in their provinces, along with "concrete proposals."[72] Already in 1928 these were the terms with which Pentecostals were being represented—and stigmatized. If the other evangelical churches were mistrusted and surveilled, the Pentecostal community was regarded with deep suspicion and hostility. That said, the ability of all evangelical communities to worship was determined to a very great extent by local conditions, the quality of the provincial prefect, and his personal views toward the threat evangelical communities represented. But there is more. The newly available Vatican Archive demonstrates that, in some cases, prefects did not merely respond languidly or inconsistently to Bocchini's orders. In cases, they defied them, often for reasons of spite or anger or general dissatisfaction with diocesan bishops, other Catholic personnel, or the quality of religious life in a parish. In such cases—in Villa San Sebastiano, for example—the new evidence of the Vatican Archive requires a rewriting or at least revision of inherited stories. These were the stories Bocchini brought to Mussolini for special attention.

In the only meeting they had (1932), Pius surprised Mussolini by the item at the top of his agenda. Part of the pope's displeasure was with the language of the Concordat. He had preferred the traditional language. But the Concordat referred to admitted cults not merely as tolerated but as admitted. Taking advantage of this new language, evangelical communities had begun to speak of missions they had hoped to launch soon in Italy. Mussolini countered: Protestants constituted a tiny minority in Catholic Italy. This demographic argument the pope would never find convincing, and Borgongini would insist, over the coming years, that evangelical communities constituted a political as well as religious threat not captured by census data. The pope concluded by handing Mussolini a lengthy report he had commissioned, which suggested that Protestant missionary activity was intense or very intense in most regions of Italy.[73] The evangelical pilgrimage was merely a first sign of the invasion to come. Much to his dismay the pope could not persuade Il Duce of the magnitude of the threat. Disagreement between the two over youth and Catholic Action only deepened mutual misunderstanding and antagonism, which made it ever less likely that the pope would prevail on Mussolini to take on the Protestant danger with the gravity it demanded.

CHAPTER 4

The Pope's Anguish (1929–33)

In 1931 relations between Mussolini and Pius worsened. In many ways Mussolini still regarded the church as a foe or at least a challenger for the devotion and passions of the Italian people. This attitude mushroomed into a crisis over the issue of the loyalties of youth. Ill will was stoked by fascist charges that Catholic Action was supposedly organizing athletic activities and forming occupational groups. The issue came to a head because sporting events were expected to be the domain of the National Balilla Agency, formed in 1926 with the explicit aim of indoctrinating Italian youth. For his part, Mussolini deplored the practice of Catholic Action and other Catholic associations of displaying the papal flag in processions or other ceremonies. This suggested split loyalties to Il Duce, who scorned the papal banner as a "foreign flag." He decided to shut down Catholic Action.

This decision brought relations between the heads of the two states to a nadir. It was against the state's "resolve . . . to monopolize completely the young" in defiance of "the natural rights of the family and the supernatural rights of the church" that Pius angrily penned his 1931 encyclical *Non abbiamo bisogno*.[1] The irascible pontiff not only protested the many libels, falsehoods, and insults leveled at Catholic youth by the regime but vigorously reprehended Mussolini's decision to close down a group that Pius regarded as vital to the church's future.[2]

Ultimately, pragmatic confrontation with the reality that both sides had much to lose led to compromise, reached by the end of the summer of 1931. Mussolini even conceded, whether sincerely or not, that he was "well-disposed to the church playing a greater part in the organization of the regime." Clerics at the Vatican were relieved. Secretary of State Pacelli, whom De Vecchi had by then named as a sympathizer, was reported to be radiant when compromise was reached. By then the Vatican had agreed not to involve itself in sport and had settled on other restrictions the regime had imposed on political activity and oversight. The pope helped heal relations by remarking that fascism represented "order, authority and discipline; none of them contrary to Catholic ways of thinking."[3]

Mussolini helped to smooth feathers in February 1932 by making a formal visit to the Vatican. This did much to seal relations between the two parties. To the delight of the Vatican, Catholicism flourished in the 1930s. After the accord with the fascist regime, the number of priests and nuns grew. Yet so too did the number of Protestant ministers and the intensity of Protestant propaganda and proselytizing. These activities prompted some of the earliest complaints and actions taken by the pope. They also triggered some of the first recorded instances of police surveillance and harassment. At the same time, the pope's anguish was deepened by revelations that diocesan clergy were utterly unequal to the task of resistance with which he had charged them. If anything could have worsened his mood, it was the subsequent and surprising disclosure that the civil authorities had been derelict. All Catholic clergy were demoralized by the sense that propagandizing had intensified dramatically since the Concordat—and that the Protestants now felt confident, protected by the law.

THE POPE AND MUSSOLINI

After the signing of the Lateran Pacts, frustration with the legal status and activities of the Protestant sects shot all the way to the top of the Catholic hierarchy. In response, the Vatican created a Pontifical Congregation for the Preservation of the Faith and the Provision of New Churches (*Opera per la Preservazione della Fede e per la Provvista di Nuove Chiese*) in Rome.[4] This new office was established explicitly to battle heretics, that is, Protestants, in Rome and, as its name suggests, to build new churches. A letter written in 1937 from the Office of the Secretary of State indicates that requests for funds for the construction of new churches had been received from diocesan bishops. These requests were made explicitly to "counter Protestant propaganda."[5]

Occasionally, Pius XI would write editorials for *OR* on issues that particularly troubled him—or to alert Mussolini to his displeasure. Already in June 1929, the month during which legislation regarding religious minorities was being discussed, Pius had written a sharp-toned article that stated, among other things, that it was the duty of the Italian state to inhibit Protestant activity.[6] At the time of the culti ammessi debates, *OR* published a series of articles on the "pernicious threat" of Protestantism.[7] On 15 March 1931 Borgongini, having been summoned to the Vatican, had a private meeting with Pius XI. Borgongini reported that, in view of the recent census, the pope had recalled the nuncio's mind to the menace of Protestant propaganda.[8] In clerical eyes the threat was unnecessarily intensified by Mussolini's evident nonchalance in the face of it. Already by January 1927 Tacchi Venturi could write to Gasparri that, in one of his recent audiences with Mussolini, he had had an opportunity to speak of the Protestants' propaganda and of the necessity to resist it in the most effective way possible. Mussolini replied that Italy was not a land vulnerable to small attacks. To this observation, Tacchi Venturi commented in his diary: "Yet always this has been proven erroneous."[9] This was not the only time that Tacchi Venturi, or his correspondents, would doubt Il Duce's capacity to perceive the reality or the frightening dimensions and dangers of the presence of Protestant proselytes in Italy.

When Borgongini reported the pope's anguish to Mussolini, the Duce responded as he often did: by stressing how tiny the Protestant population of Italy in fact was.[10] Borgongini especially tried to jolt Mussolini from complacency by emphasizing the danger of foreign Protestants. Their intolerable foreignness was a theme that many—most—Catholic polemicists would take up from the pope. In much of the Catholic imagination, that foreignness included, was exemplified by, Methodists, Baptists, Adventists, Pentecostals, the Salvation Army, Jehovah's Witnesses, and those with links to Masonry; all were especially suspect, often surveilled, and vulnerable to interrogation, closure of churches, harassment and violence, and, finally, expulsion and governmental suppression. These denominations posed a threat not only to religious but to national unity.[11]

In the spring of 1931 the nuncio notified the Italian ambassador to the Holy See that the pope fervently wished that the government would put a halt to "this insane propaganda." De Vecchi responded by implying that a quid pro quo would satisfy the pope's wishes: the government would put an end to the Protestant menace if the Holy Father would stop hectoring Mussolini over youth groups, especially Catholic Action, an issue about which the two stubborn men had already begun feuding.[12] Finally, in 1933, Pope Pius confessed openly that evangelical success had become his "greatest cross to bear," a detail brought to Mussolini by Borgongini-Duca.[13]

Credit for perceiving that Protestant propaganda was growing was given by Pizzardo to the pope. In Pizzardo's account, it was Pope Pius who revealed just how menacing to both religious and national unity was the mounting evangelical threat. This was, to Catholic clerics, an unremarkable, honorific attribution, not a reflection of the truth. In a meeting of the two new ambassadors in early 1931, De Vecchi alerted Borgongini to the existence of a pastor in the Trentino–Alto Aldige region, a traditional stronghold of Waldensian churches, who was then publicly criticizing the fascist regime. Borgongini-Duca in turn alerted Pacelli, and the secretary of state passed the news on to the pope. Pizzardo reveals this in the very letter in which he quite improbably ascribes the discovery to Pius XI.[14] Whatever the string of transmission, this piece of news, which involved political criticism from a Protestant, must have seemed promising to the pope. Perhaps a Protestant propagandizing politically against the fascist regime could get the attention of the head of government. Presumably the same effect could be achieved another way: via a note written by hand in 1930 to the Apostolic Nuncio from Włodzimierz Ledóchowski, S.J. (1866–1942), then superior general of the Jesuits, indicating that Protestant propagandists were functioning as spies. If the note reached Mussolini, perhaps the head of government would choose to act.[15]

UNDER HIS VERY WINDOWS: PROTESTANTS OUTSIDE THE VATICAN WALLS

Mussolini was amazed at how seriously the pope took the Protestant threat—even that he had brought the issue up.[16] Yet the archival documents leave little doubt about how seriously the pope and his cardinals took the threat. In Borgongini's papers there are several folders dedicated to threats the pope perceived, which may seem to us minor, trivial, or nonexistent.[17] When it came to the attention of Borgongini that Protestants had settled in the neighborhood, he had Dom Marcello Urilli, superior of the Pontifical Oratory of Saint Peter (which listed an address of Piazza del S. Ufficio 7—that is, the address of the Holy Office in Vatican City), engage the commissioner, a certain Captain Redati, of the administrative district bordering Vatican City. Urilli asked the captain about the presence of Protestants thought already to be installed on Via Aurelia, a large road that runs along the face of the south wall of Vatican City. The captain then knew nothing; nor did Dom Urilli. Yet Redati promised that, as a "good Commissioner and a good Catholic," he would investigate more deeply. Lest one think that a *lack* of information about Protestants might not have been of interest to the worldwide head of the Catholic church, I note that Borgongini-Duca concludes his pro memoria by indicating the nuncio's record of his conversation with Redati and Urilli had been "read to the Holy Father on 12 April 1931."[18]

Less than a week later the commissioner had more information for Borgongini, which the nuncio recorded in a pro memoria written on the letterhead of the Pontifical Oratory of St. Peter, of which, again, Dom Urilli was superior. The commissioner had discovered that a Protestant couple had acquired an apartment on Via Aurelia, steps from the Vatican walls. With his report, he sent a Protestant pamphlet entitled "A Solemn Question: Is Your Soul Saved?"[19] The pamphlet had been stamped on the back with the following: Adunanza Evangelica, Via Aurelia 161. Evidently, evangelical meetings were being held at the newly acquired apartment at this address. Borgongini-Duca annotated this in pencil, identifying the names of the Protestant ministers and the leaflets they were distributing and even recording the names and the birth years of their daughter, Emmanuela (1915), and son, Cristiano (1918).[20]

Second, the captain reports on the existence of a group of dissidents in the Aurelian district. Mostly these consisted, he alleged, of fascists who had been expelled from the party for being politically republican or for "moral indignities." The dissidents were, he said, deeply anticlerical and, now, profoundly antifascist.[21] The captain indicates that the group would be watched by Public Security.

Here, however, while mention is made of the political character of the group, the focus of the archival documents centers on its religious activities. The Aurelian Circle had recently caused an incident, reported by Catholic neighbors, with the political-religious and provocative character of its proselytizing. The captain reports that a pastor had bribed children with money and distributed propaganda literature—"good books"—to local families. He spoke to them, the captain reports with some disgust, "about the redemption of Christ and the spilling of His Most Precious Blood, which has obtained from God entry for all to Paradise, without need for expiation and punishment for sin"—standard evangelical claims, in other words. Other anti-Catholic ideas were openly expressed there, beneath the very windows of the pope.[22]

In addition, the report documents that a Waldensian couple had acquired an apartment on Via Nicolo III, perhaps a five-minute walk from the southern wall of Vatican City. The American-born wife of the couple is described as a propagandist. The captain promised he would raid the couple's apartment. In the meanwhile, he had warned her not to "make propaganda among the youth" in the area, as, he added menacingly, he could not guarantee her safety. "All of this," Borgongini notes, "was reported to the Holy Father on 19 April 1931."[23] The pope, in other words, was receiving granular reports on the activities of small groups or even individuals from the front lines of the Protestant–Catholic skirmish. The pope made no objection to the captain's plans to disrupt the home of the young Protestant couple. Hawkish on the Protestant issue, the Apostolic Nuncio must have been encouraged in his belligerence by the Holy Father's silence or implicit approval. What mattered was the gravity of the threat they had brought to the very walls of the Vatican. The threat was just that serious.

THE 1931 CENSUS

Thanks to the evidence preserved in the lately available archives, we now know why it was that Pius was so preoccupied—to many, including Mussolini, irrationally—with the census. Several pieces of evidence suggest that the pope was alarmed by the results of the recent Italian census.[24] This is so even though Francesco Marchetti Selvaggiani (1871–1951) twice intriguingly indicates that, despite the intensity of propaganda, the number of formal conversions was not as high as was commonly alleged.[25] A Catholic prelate deeply involved in the anti-Protestant campaign, Selvaggiani is to be trusted. Nonetheless, Pope Pius communicated his alarm about the census results to Borgongini in a personal audience held on 15 March 1931. Some laymen, as well as clerics, in the spring of 1931 independently reported to the pope their sense that Protestant activity had quickened. On 13 May 1931, for example, the president of the Parish Council of the Church of Alanno, in the Diocese of Penne, reported that on that day the council had sent to Mussolini and to the prefect of the Province of Pescara a letter complaining about Protestant propaganda. It was the sense of the council that something needed to be done, as "it was not only Alanno that was visited by the Protestants" in recent months; rather, missionaries were active in many towns, selling books and holding public conferences.[26] Perhaps a sign of how seriously he took the problem and how grateful he was for help from any quarter, Pius took the extraordinary step of personally thanking the council president.[27] The issue meant that much to him.

At that time De Vecchi had alarmed the pope by claiming that the number of practicing evangelicals had grown alarmingly since the 1911 census. (That of 1921 did not record religious affiliation.) He predicted that the 1931 census would demonstrate that the number of Protestants in Italy, roughly 123,000 in 1911, had risen to over 200,000, and the number of active Protestant centers had grown by 20 to 25 percent. While this number was almost certainly exaggerated, De Vecchi asserted it with absolute certainty. As other fascist and Vatican officials would do in the next few years, he attributed the increase to the laws on permitted cults, which, De Vecchi states, had practically put Catholics and evangelicals on equal footing.[28] He added that evangelical religious propaganda had taken on a political character "certainly not in harmony with the spirit of the Regime." In his meeting with Il Duce, the pope claimed that, based on his bishops' reports presented to him by De Vecchi, Protestant proselytizing had increased "in almost all the dioceses in Italy."[29]

To date, it has been assumed that the pope was frustrated over the number of evangelicals represented in the 1931 census and the percentage change in growth over the 1911 census. That is certainly part of the story. In actuality, the pope's concern was not only statistical. Rather, it was the way in which those numbers could be inflated, in his mind fraudulently, that aggravated him and, he felt, ought to have incensed representatives of the government. In any case, the account of how numbers were rigged was, in addition, wrapped in a narrative whose ramifications touched on a whole host of sensitive issues at the Vatican.

This troubling narrative came to the pope from the small city of Riesi, some seventy miles southeast of Palermo. In April 1931 Ciriaci received a letter that he then passed on to Pope Pius XI. The letter was written to him by Archpriest D. Luigi Riggio Rutella, the parish priest of a church in Riesi in the diocese of Piazza Armerina in the Province of Enna, where he was local assistant to Catholic Action.[30] At the same time, Rutella copied the episcopal chancellery. Lest there be doubt about where his loyalties lay, he wrote both "G.M.G" (Gesu, Marie, and Giuseppe—the names of the Holy Family, which Catholic schoolchildren were taught to write at the top of any new page of writing) and "A. IX" (the ninth year of Mussolini's regime, aping ancient Roman imperial practice) at the top of his letter. Having established his philo-fascist and good Catholic credentials, the archpriest describes Riesi briefly. A city of some twenty thousand souls, Riesi had been home to "the Protestants" for about four decades. Recently, a certain Pastor Nisbet had flamboyantly arrived from "Alta Italia." A provocateur fond of ridicule, the pastor for months had barraged Riesi with a profusion of Waldensian pamphlets. As soon as the census was distributed by the officials, Nisbet "shamelessly" attracted the gullible from the poor quarters of the city. He then took the leaflets from the government officials. Before distributing them, however, Nisbet himself, in a column meant to indicate religious affiliation, "cunningly" marked "Evangelical" on all the forms before any of those gathered around him had a chance to do so. Appalled, the parish priest made a record of those who were thus inscribed fraudulently. That record he then put in the hands of public security. He had also alerted his bishop and the bishop of Caltanisetta; he hoped they would, with him, pressure Public Security for "just and exemplary sanctions." But he also wrote to Ciriaci, the president of the Roman Council, asking him to offer help "in a timely way." This was so because, as the archpriest declared, "I have the impression that this action is of a general nature in Italy and exemplifies the same fraudulent method." The archpriest urges Ciriaci and "our vast hierarchy": "Act, so that we may exorcise this evil spirit from the land."[31]

To be sure, the local clergy of Piazza Armerina were doing all they could to combat "sectarianism and its audacious propaganda." Unfortunately, the local clergy were simply overmatched. Or, to put it in the vivid words of the archpriest, "The clergy here are decimated." He and another chaplain were taking care of a second parish together. A third priest, then age eighty-four, was *inabile a tutto.* By contrast the Waldensians had a small church. In addition, they had an elementary school "with numerous children." These had been trained in the "intemperate and provocative" ways of Pastor Nisbet, who had taught an "audacious circle of youth" to be skeptical of and provocative toward the clergy and the claims of the Catholic church.[32] The provost of the cathedral in the diocese, Egidio Franchino, complains on behalf of his bishop in a letter to Pacelli: "Every day the [Protestants] become more audacious and are creating an attitude of hostility toward the Catholic Church." The evangelicals, he goes on, propagandize by a variety of methods "without fear and with arrogance." They "make anti-Catholic commentary that arouses at once both indignation and laughter"—and the local clergy seem powerless to stop it.[33] As with all accounts reporting on Protestant propaganda, claims of evangelical audacity must be understood in context. All Protestant proselytizing, no matter how quietly delivered, could seem to Catholic antagonists as hostile and impudent; any group of children in an evangelical elementary school might be characterized as numerous.

The provost then moves to what is the key, by-now-familiar issue in the bishop's mind: the Waldensians propagandize so boldly and provocatively because "they believe themselves to be *a group protected by the Government*."[34] That is, as an admitted cult whose members could discuss matters of religion freely, the permitted-cults decree gave the local Waldensians the protection of the law and discouraged local law enforcement from impeding their activity. This gave the cults license not simply to preach and propagandize but to provoke, or so the provost claims. On 24 March 1931 the bishop, Mario Sturzo (1903–41), himself followed up with a letter imputing the growth and temerity of the evangelicals to failure, "yet another time," on the part of the civil authorities.[35] Somehow these letters made their way up the chain to Pius XI. On 23 April 1931, "at the request of the Holy Father," Pizzardo forwarded the letter sent by the parish priest of Riesi to Ciriaci to Borgongini, indicating that it might prove quite useful if the results of the census "contain some surprises."[36]

An army of heretical and foreign propagandists had invaded Italy. Not only was the church in danger; so was the state. Yet the head of government seemed resigned to fiddling while Rome burned, while the local clergy seemed impotent. In order to act against the threat, the Vatican leader had to know much more about the concentration, targets, and methods of the alien invaders. In these circumstances, in the wake of the passage of the laws on permitted cults, the pope had to turn not to the languid, indifferent officials of the state but to trusted clerical colleagues within the Vatican. Alarmed by the arrival and aggressiveness of evangelical missionaries and frustrated by Mussolini's surprise and apparent indifference, Pius commissioned three trusted prelates to produce a report that would help him persuade Mussolini of the gravity of the problem.

MAPS OF WAR

In March 1931 the pope received from Federico Sargolini (1891–1969) a report on Protestant activity in every province of Italy. A priest in Camerino, a town outside Umbria, roughly forty miles southwest of Ancona, Monsignor Sargolini was, at the time he wrote, general assistant to the Youth of Catholic

Action.[37] This was an organization that would, at the request of Pius XI and with the encouragement of important cardinals at the Vatican, dedicate itself to the struggle against the Protestant danger.[38] Sargolini swiftly complied with the pope's request, sending out a questionnaire to every Italian diocese in the summer or fall of 1930. Having received many responses, he compiled his report, which he sent, in March 1931, to Pacelli.

Soon after he submitted his report, Sargolini asked Father Federico Mistrorigo, the parish priest since 1935 of the Church of San Agostino in Rome, to write a letter to Borgongini about information he had acquired regarding the conduct of several south Italian archbishops.[39] Mistrorigo then wrote up a short report of his own, which contains valuable, sometimes corroborating information, especially about Protestant activity and priestly indolence (a neuralgic problem of which Vatican authorities would soon become ever more lugubriously aware) in the southern provinces.[40]

Finally, a certain Father B., having been commissioned by the pope, wrote a lengthy report and was commended for having done it well by Francesco Cardinal Marchetti Selvaggiani.[41] Selvaggiani was a powerful man. Appointed in 1922 the secretary of the Congregation for the Propagation of the Faith, he was made cardinal in June 1930. One month later he was consecrated cardinal-priest of Santa Maria Nuova. Three months after commissioning his report, he was made vicar general of Rome by Pope Pius XI. (Given the extent of the pope's ordinary responsibilities to the worldwide church, the vicar general of Rome was then the de facto bishop of Rome.) In 1939, Selvaggiani was appointed secretary of the congregation of the Holy Office, and in 1948 he would become dean of the College of Cardinals. The Selvaggiani report is especially valuable for the rich information it provides on Protestant activity in Rome.[42] Whatever their shortcomings, the three documents furnish a reasonably clear glimpse into how interested prelates at the Vatican perceived the degree, agents, institutions, targets, instruments, and varying geographical intensity of—as well as several instances of resistance to—Protestant proselytizing in the years immediately following passage of the laws on admitted cults.

One hardly need underscore that, even if incomplete, such reports would represent—not reflect—what are sometimes casually categorized as realities on the ground. For one thing, it might be argued, though not persuasively, I think, that the reporters could find what they were looking for: evidence, for example, that Protestant propaganda had begun to intensify at the same time as and because of the admitted cults laws. That said, the reports are, historically speaking, quite dependable. They almost certainly represent, with a high degree of accuracy, the secrets the authors sought to unearth from the soil of the Italian dioceses. Why? First, such reports, conducted independently, tend to echo one another; the three analyzed here tend, by and large, to corroborate the findings of one another and of other reports commissioned at roughly the same time. But there are stronger reasons to believe them, by and large, credible and accurate. Second, the pope counted on as accurate, detailed, and true a picture as Sargolini, Mistrorigo, and Selvaggiani could produce. Why? Because the reports were not of mere academic interest. In fact, only with precise and rich reporting could the Vatican authorities use the reports for the reasons for which they were commissioned, namely, to ponder how most efficiently to resist the evangelical propaganda that was felt, if just inchoately, to be intensifying across the country. Faithful servants of the pope, these three trusted prelates regarded the Protestant missionaries, in medieval style, as heretical enemies of the One True Church, and they were highly motivated to produce a report Pius XI could trust. Finally, the documents contain several scathingly critical remarks about the conduct and performance of parish priests and the quality of local parochial life. Priestly indifference and indolence stood out by contrast to evangelical ardor and energy. There would have been no plausible motive to include this self-damning information, which, if discovered, could be exploited by Protestants, unless it were true—for which embarrassing discovery there was notable historical precedent.[43]

Each of the three reports conveys a general sense across many provinces that Protestant activity had intensified, in degree and kind, in the years since the passage of the culti ammessi laws. Protestant activity, especially efforts at conversion, was said to have been intense or very intense in many provinces, many of them in southern Italy. The propaganda in one town was not only "pernicious" but "insane." The intensity, confidence, and aggression of the army of false messiahs was a siren heralding the end-times.[44] Selvaggiani reports that all the evidence he had gathered suggested that the Protestants were planning a now-imminent campaign of propaganda tenacious and destructive in all the country, "but above all in meridional Italy."[45] Still, he adds, by no means were all propaganda efforts directed to the South:

> A real ring of iron is tightening around Spezia. Dioceses in the North, like Milan, Como, and Brescia [Lombardy], are experiencing the first attempts at penetration. Much alarming news arrives from Puglia,

> and, from Avezzano [Abruzzo], they write us that the danger grows closer every day. From Aquila, we are assured that the entire zone of Corcomello is infested with Protestants and pastors, who have come from Rome. Similar news comes from Chieti [Abruzzo], Rimini [Emilia-Romagna], and Civitavecchia [Lazio]. From Foggia [Apulia], they write us that the works of the Protestants become ever more zealous and, *especially now that the law protects them*. . . . We have other signals from Osimo [Marche], Gaeta [Lazio], Catanzaro [Calabria], Rossano [Cosenza], and Bari [Apulia].[46]

Many of these towns, just then experiencing the first attempts at Protestant propagandizing, would turn up over and again in the archival documents, a testament to the tenacity and conviction of Protestant proselytizing; to ambiguities in the law and ignorance of it in some cities; to the indifference of local law enforcement; and, in the view of Vatican authorities, to the apathy, ignorance, or penury of some diocesan priests. Viterbo, Grosseto, and Civitavecchia formed the vertices of a geographical triangle north of Rome within which quite a lot of Protestant activity was reported. Even in Rome the Protestants had been successful. Glumly, Sargolini concludes, evangelicals had penetrated the capital city's Catholic population even "more than one might believe."[47]

The text is representative in other ways, especially rhetorically. The language of successful entry into a religious market, and indeed the rhetoric of aggression and invasion, all chime throughout the archival literature. So too does the apocalyptic language of imminent or present injury. The Protestant invasion is a plague; it was spreading and would worsen. Utterly cataclysmic, it might, if unchecked, demolish the structure of Italian Catholicism and indeed of Latin culture—for good. (That Protestantism was a Germanic or Anglo-Saxon phenomenon that could not be grafted to Latin culture without damaging the host was a common theme of Catholic polemicists, including one later renowned for his ecumenism, then especially hostile to evangelical Christianity, Igino Giordani.)[48] Despite that somber warning, "negative" Catholic apocalyptic was paralleled by the "positive" Protestant: many Protestant denominations exhilarated in the prospective conversion of Italian Catholics from idolatry, superstition, and priestcraft. Conversions were propitious signs that, before the return of the Lord, the pure gospel was being restored—and in the land where it had been most corrupted by popery.[49] Finally, in this war, as in most twentieth-century conflict, the enemy, in this case proselytizing evangelical pastors, are cast as pestilential nuisances. In general, anti-Protestant literature like this was larded with the language of war. This is not of merely incidental or rhetorical interest. One historian, speaking perhaps more truly than he knew, has termed the anti-Protestant effort a campaign.[50] Its evangelical targets felt it to be offensive—not only insulting (intentionally, it was)—but a frightening blitzkrieg mounted by forces of church and the fascist police state, wholly disproportionate to the magnitude of the threat, if any, they represented. Like contemporary war efforts, this offensive finally involved disinformation and demonization as well as state surveillance, infiltration, and finally criminalization of religious and political rivals.[51]

It would be quite impossible, and perhaps undesirable, to reduce these reports to statistical degrees of certainty. Inevitably, we get a picture that is impressionistic rather than fully representational. That said, one can safely associate grades of intensity in proselytizing with three large regions of the country. First, in some provinces of central and north-central Italy, Protestant proselytizing was either unsuccessful or made no visible impact. It was quite inconsequential in the Marches and in Tuscany, with the exception of Grosseto, a target of intense recruitment. No mention of Protestant activity is even made in Umbria. In this case, the lack of allusion is likely not attributable to the incomplete nature of the report but rather to the scarcity of Protestants in the province, which remained rocky ground for evangelical seed throughout the fascist period. Second, Protestant propaganda was more intense in the north-central provinces of Abruzzo, the Veneto (above all in Gorizia), Lombardy, and Emilia-Romagna as well as in Lazio, especially in Rome. Finally, in the Piedmont and in meridional Italy proselytizing was generally intense and, from the evangelical point of view, effective. The provinces of Puglia, Campania, Basilicata, Calabria, the Salernitano, Sicily—all were territories in which the Protestant missionaries had concentrated their energies and, in Sargolini's characteristic phrase, "penetrated the population."[52] For reasons I will discuss in detail, they truly had. The evangelical heat grid glowed florid red in the broiling southern provinces.

Notable for industry among the continental missionaries were the cordially loathed Anglo-American Wesleyans, followed (in no particular order) by the Baptists, Seventh-day Adventists, Pentecostals, and those simply denominated evangelicals. The large national Lutheran and reformed churches were not involved; they catered almost exclusively to subjects residing temporarily in Italy and showed almost no interest in converting Italian Catholics. Only Italian Waldensians were, among continental churches, active as missionaries. Pentecostals were understood from the very early 1930s to be the cult most dangerous to the country at large (though to youth the YMCA was feared as the most dangerous sect). In meridional Italy and Sicily, Pentecostals were inciting a "worrisome growth," while in the Quartiere Urbano (Rome) they made "fanatical propaganda," especially among the vegetable and fruit sellers on Via Chiana—a clue to the importance of social class in this analysis. "Countless southerners" (*numerosissimi meridionali*) attended their meetings. Some communities in the South, like Palermo, were said to be swarmed by missionaries from all these sects. These were never dignified with the name churches (*chiese*), of which, from the Vatican's point of view, there was just one. Most Catholic polemicists branded evangelicals as heretics and their Protestantisms an expression of heresy.[53]

Apart from the Waldensians, these evangelical missionaries would be effectively stigmatized as foreigners (stranieri). Even when given legal capacity and recognition, evangelicals bore all the stigmata of outsiderhood and the frustrations outsiders face in becoming part of Italian society. Great importance attached to ancestry in being recognized, genealogically and culturally, as Italian; since being Roman Catholic was simply integral to *italianità,* the religion of Anglo-Saxon missionaries, aside from any other Anglo-American cultural baggage, physical distinctiveness, and habits, would have rendered them unfamiliar—other—in a society, in most relevant senses, quite homogenous.

The reaction they elicited may be imagined as somewhat akin to anti-gypsy feeling in the 1990s. Roma and Sinti were *nomadi;* even the principal Catholic welfare organization for them was called the Opera Nomadi. Gypsies were not ancient, nor Italian, nor Latin; nor were they Protestants. Protestants, however, were worse: they were non-Catholic Christians, non-Italian Protestants, non-Latin Anglo-Saxons, like historic invaders the French, Spanish, German, Swiss, and Austrians, only this time with an army of evangelical invaders. In a country no longer willing to function as a pawn in an international chess game, missionaries were presumptuous arbiters of the peninsula's religious and cultural destiny, apostates, spies, untrustworthy, deceitful—so that being straniero and being *subdolo* ("subtle," "deceitful") became almost indistinguishable.

As stranieri, they would attract the hostile attention of the fascist state, and so ecclesiastical polemicists would remorselessly draw attention to their alien origins. This had the grave effect of placing them outside the Italian national community, a maneuver calculated to attract the attention of fascist ideologues. They were enemies of the state and religious apostates. Who could trust them? Not, it seemed, the world of literature. The English writer Nancy Mitford was not the first to associate *foreigners* and *fiends.*[54] A recent book subtitled "Italian Protestants in the Catholic World," written by the Chicagoan Frank Cicero (his surname is also the name of an Italian immigrant municipality west of Chicago), is entitled, tellingly, *Relative Strangers.*[55]

Protestant leaders nonetheless confirmed their presence in the most inescapable fashion imaginable: by the erection of unignorable buildings. If many evangelical groups operated by stealth, others demonstrated their new self-assurance in several ways, many by ostentatious construction.[56] In Turin the establishment of a Protestant church directly across from the Catholic one was taken—and likely intended—as a provocation or at least as an unambiguous announcement that the Protestants were confident in their now-tolerated presence and uninhibited in their proselytizing.

By contrast, the privacy, secrecy, and undetectability of certain sects of evangelical proselytes were also emphasized. Already in 1930 Pentecostal communities were camouflaged, tucked away in covert loci, their eccentric ceremonials camouflaged by unremarkable buildings, sometimes underground, as was the one in Rome. In general, the Pentecostal communities had "secret churches."[57] Missionaries operated stealthily; converts prayed furtively. In many southern towns Protestants were not easily identified "because they are hidden among families" in private domiciles.[58] The "majority of Protestant activity," Selvaggiani indicates, occurred "in private homes."[59] Both impressive and alarming, evangelical missionaries would insinuate themselves into crowds of Catholics. Missionaries occasionally were said to be most active, if deviously, on market days, as in Novara (in the Piedmont). There they could hide in plain sight, mingling freely with merchants and shopkeepers, smiling agreeably, and distributing Bibles or recruitment literature.[60] Even the vendors of Bibles were fraudulent: they sold the Protestant version of Bibles to Catholics, who did not know what they were buying or, in many cases, were unaware even that there was more than one version.

The word widely, almost ubiquitously used to describe this sort of approach was *subdolo/subdola.* When used with admiration, which was exceedingly rare, it could signify what its English cognate expresses: subtle. Almost always, however, it was deployed in a pejorative sense. Protestant missionary methods, especially those of the Methodists, were cunning, devious, underhanded. Worming their way into the lives of the poor, who are necessarily venal, they operate by guile and deceit. They give subsidies, or bribes, to the unemployed and distribute medicines to the ill, food and clothing to needy families; and they do this cunningly, not "immediately requesting that [the recipients] apostatize," that is, convert to one or another denomination of Protestantism.[61] Clerics across the peninsula were adjured to be alert; these obscure proselytes were hard to spot in a throng.

Methodist missionaries were recognized as most hostile to the Roman Catholic church and to the papacy; theirs was the sect to which the adjective subdola was reflexively attached. Selvaggiani observes that "in Protestant temples, but above all in Methodist ones, the anti-Catholic and polemical note is accentuated and aggravated."[62] This is a claim corroborated, or at least repeated, by countless contemporary Catholic clerics. The Methodist Episcopal college on Monte Mario was institutionally deceitful. Its constitutions failed, intentionally, to make note of its Protestant character. Therefore, it had been able to attract several Catholic families, who unknowingly brought their children there to be educated.[63] In familiar Italian cultural terms, evangelists were regarded by Catholic opponents (*fessi,* naturally) as arch-*furbi,* that is, unprincipled, willing to resort to underhanded tactics to achieve their objectives, clever—but diabolically so. The intensity of the Methodists' anti-Catholicism would be matched by the fury of Catholic hostility toward them.

Deceit and secrecy linked many Protestant groups with hated Freemasons, as did the fact that many Protestant pastors, especially Methodists, had connections with the lodges or were themselves once Freemasons.[64] Long regarded with suspicion by the church for anticlerical views rooted in the liberal decades of the nineteenth century, Masons were also charged with being cosmopolitan in an atmosphere of hypernationalism, a charge that linked them implicitly, and quite often explicitly, to Jews and Judaism.[65] Evangelical cults had their own traditions of antisemitism, but for the Catholic church, Jews, in the words of Giovanni Miccoli, "became the symbol of hated modernization, . . . the inspirers and protagonists of the process of secularization."[66] The association of Jews with Protestants came very early in the polemical war. Some argued, quite bizarrely, that Jews had originated the theology of the anti-Catholic thought of Martin Luther.[67] Luther would have been dumbstruck.

Others contended that Judaism was a forerunner of communism. Irreligious and aggressively secularist, Bolshevism was simply a realization of materialistic Judaism. In any case, secrecy led to suspicion of Freemasonry, which led to charges of association with Judaism and, oddly, to evangelicalism. If association with the unhappy history of Giolittian liberalism were not enough, some Catholic polemicists anguished over supposed links between Protestant Christianity and communism. The Jesuit Tacchi Venturi, for example, was startled to report that the archbishop of Canterbury, according to a 1926 report in the Baptist journal *Bilychnis,* was said to have proclaimed that it "was impossible to ignore Communism." After all, the picture of the early apostolic community given in Acts 5, the primate asserted, was a communism of love; and he gave thanks to God that certain Brits who confessed that political creed were "very sincere Christians."[68]

Protestant self-confidence and energy could be expressed in other ways. Precious to many was the provision of childcare services—from temporary shelter to infant care to kindergartens to orphanages. A childcare center, to cite just one example, was opened, according to Mistrorigo, in Calabria.[69] Presumably this was welcomed by many Catholic mothers, who were happy, in exchange, to convert—or to appear to have converted. Some evidence suggests educational and recreational opportunities for the young could be gendered. While Prato is said to have established a school inviting youth of both sexes, Vallo Lucania, in the Campania, featured a workshop or studio of some kind, presumably artisanal, designed only for young women.[70] Novara, a populous city in the Piedmont, took pride in its "professional school for women."[71] Methodists in Rome ran an educational institute dedicated to the instruction and enrichment only of women. It offered instruction in a dizzying array of subjects, from infant care to foreign languages to domestic management, comparative literature, and the history of art. Day journeys to historic sites and exercises in gymnastics complete the picture. Troublingly, the school was "often frequented by Catholics." Worse, "while publicly committing themselves to the grandest principles of religious tolerance," proselytes subjected these women to "continuous and heretical propaganda." Similarly, at an Institute for Women on Via Balbo, under the veil of religious neutrality, one observes that real effort against the faith is undertaken—this in the shadow of the ancient Basilica Santa Maria Maggiore.[72]

To some extent, activities intended for women put evangelical communities in competition with the fascist regime, which, like the Catholic church, had laid stress on traditional moral and social norms, all the more where women, especially young women, were concerned. The only mission for which they were fit—and here the fascist regime emphatically approved and strengthened gender norms preferred by the church—was motherhood and childbearing. As is well known, propaganda put out by the fascists underscored the duty of women to raise large numbers of children. Here the state helped, in the most concrete ways possible—for example, with restrictive legislation banning women from teaching, which was the only occupation in which they had achieved widespread participation. Women were important insofar as they could produce what the fascists called numbers. Those not bearing children were opposed to the national demographic campaign and, ipso facto, antifascist. That many evangelical groups were suspected of being antifascist was brought into relief by the roles women assumed in the Protestant cults. It was thus that "gender disorder" was elevated to a threat to the state not only by Italian women who had invaded masculine space but also by female evangelists, who were, in addition, foreign. Evangelical women became, therefore, enemies of both church and regime.[73]

Women were not only the targets but the agents of evangelical activity—perhaps a source of their attraction to the Protestant confessions. Sargolini takes care to note that an unusual number of missionaries were women. In the central Italian town of Isernia, "almost all" the Protestant proselytizing was carried out by "a woman who had recently returned from America."[74] Perhaps intentionally exaggerated, the religious conviction of Pentecostal women was said to cause dreadful tensions in families.[75] So passionate was their commitment to Pentecostal piety and propaganda that they deviate "from their familiar habits and ignore their domestic obligations."[76] Here religious pressures caused tension not only between but within communities and families. (Much has been written about the causes of suppression of the Pentecostals; this should be more widely emphasized.) The sex of these missionaries would have been countercultural in a society, such as early-twentieth-century Italy, ordered along patriarchal lines—especially in the hypermasculine atmosphere of fascist Italy.[77] The language used to reprehend the entry of women into the masculine sphere of work was identical to that used to deplore the arrival of evangelical missionaries in traditionally Catholic Italy: both were an inappropriate, even scandalous invasion of spaces not theirs. Polemical tracts therefore underscored the many ways in which evangelicals violated the order of things: they were effeminate; they were foreigners; they were, in general, young—and their faith infantilizing, if far from guileless.

Because so much Protestant activity—preaching, lecturing, conversation, Bible study—happened in the home, the locus of heretical proselytizing was traditionally a domestic sphere dominated by women. Young women "secretly prepare the work of penetration in houses," where the work of missionaries is done.[78] Deaconesses, who had both medical and catechetical skills, visited the poor in their homes. They were said to be numerous and active and to have employed a *forma signorile* that attracted all, especially the poor. In the ancient parish of San Lorenzo female proselytes held small meetings for women and on Thursdays and Sundays for children. Selvaggiani notes with dismay, in this connection, the "fervid activity" on the part of "fanatical Pentecostal women."[79] That evangelical missionaries, be they male or female, operated in homes and were thus intimate with ordinary family needs made them, in the eyes of the hostile, feminine or effeminate. When undertaken by women, Protestant proselytizing tawdrily and unforgivably corroded the bonds of familial and social community, and women ministers refused compliance with the demand for religious and political purity.

Each report emphasizes that the means by which individuals or families converted were, above all, direct gifts of cash, often called subsidies. While this inducement to conversion has antecedents deep in the history of Christianity, it inevitably raises questions about the motives, authenticity, and depth—even the definition and meaning—of conversion to a Protestant sect. Protestant historians have sometimes objected to the allegation that evangelicals generated dollar converts by offering money or services. This question will never be reducible to statistics. That said, there is no question but that many, the indigent above all, were induced to convert by money and the many necessities it could buy for them, including childcare, medicine and health care, education, and more. The testimony of history and anthropology suggests that it has ever been so, or very nearly. In ways known even to those casually familiar with the history of Italy, political conversion operated there in essentially the same way. Various political parties essentially bought promised votes in exchange for free pasta. Some parties, rather like the evangelicals, served as service organizations. They made a difference, especially in the lives of the poor, as the evangelicals also did. Catholic opponents drew a bright line between religion and social services. Evangelical missionaries genuinely thought that the latter were implied in and obliged by the former. From one point of view this looks like buying converts. From another, it is simply ministering the gospel to the poor. Beneath the polemics lies a deeper but usually unexpressed disagreement over what Christianity meant in practice and especially in relation to social station. The conflict could not but come out into the open when Protestant ministers expressed sympathy with communism.

Missionaries persuaded some parents to allow their children to convert in exchange for cash. In Turin, for example, evangelical missionaries, it was said, were giving parents 500 lire—a handsome sum—for each child they "gave" to an unspecified evangelical community. Protestants in Gorizia were converted by "contributions of money."[80] The number of such examples could be boundlessly multiplied.[81] Expensive medicines unavailable or unaffordable to the poor and peasant were offered, along with care for the ill, inducing recipients to convert.[82] To the very sick, the destitute, and the medically deprived and ignorant, conversion must have seemed a negligible price to pay for the restoration of physical health. These stories testify to, among other things, the poverty, particularly desperate then in the South and in a time of worldwide economic collapse, of those targeted for conversion.

These inducements to conversion incensed Vatican prelates, who denounced them as unscrupulous, even illegal (though Catholic missionaries had used just such inducements for centuries). *OR* would publish many articles in the years after the passage of the permitted cults laws objecting to what, in its writers' view, amounted to bribery of the economically and educationally destitute. While the venal exist in all social and economic classes and while many can be bought for the right price, it was unsurprisingly—indeed, by definition—the unemployed, the uneducated, and the peasant who received *soccorsi ai poveri.* Countless Catholic polemicists would complain that, by contrast to a wealthy evangelical church, the diocesan church was at a competitive disadvantage as a *mendica pezzante,* a begging pauper.[83]

What conversion meant to those described as religiously ignorant and even more to those described as having "no belief at all" is an intriguing question.[84] It likely signified no more to the converted than a transition from desperate poverty to a modicum of security. Religious commitment, rebaptism, attendance at services and sermons—these were negligible costs for conversion from a state of destitution to marginal economic stability. Some evangelical organizations, like the one in Parma, were wealthy enough to have an associate pastor whose only charge was to recruit the poor.[85] In wealthier Rome, also the bureaucratic center of the state, one of the new ways to recruit was "the effort of Protestants to get members of their churches the highest and most influential posts in the bureaucracy," above all in banking.[86] Stable jobs proved an almost irresistible lure. Apparently, few converts feared that such a transaction might jeopardize the eternal destiny of their souls, or perhaps economic necessity simply eclipsed the soteriological in importance. The data and, even more, the complexity of human motivation defy our efforts to reduce these imperatives to numerical or statistical terms.

Because Protestants met so frequently in homes, their pastors were put in "direct contact" with "human needs and miseries," to which, as in Calabria and by contrast to the aloof Catholic clergy, they are reported to have responded immediately and sympathetically. Selvaggiani also suggests that Protestant responsiveness stands in egregious contrast to Catholic clerical indolence and indifference. This is a theme that would be expressed mournfully by Catholic prelates over the years of the fascist period. Again, as the home was a conventionally gendered space, the opportunity for women to exercise ministry—to have agency—was likely a potent motivation to conversion.

The intensity and energy of some Protestant proselytes astonished Sargolini. Two youths in Aquila had gone *in giro,* where car ownership was uncommon; they visited "almost all the families of the city and towns of the diocese." Their boundless energy galled, not least because it put into egregious contrast the general torpor of the diocesan clergy. So, too, did missionaries' modern methods and technology. Both the fascist government and the Catholic church regarded technology with misgiving, if to differing degrees and ways. For both, technology helped spawn modernization and urbanization, both of which undermined the healthy norms and traditions of agrarian society. It goes without saying that the fascist government's attitude toward modernization and technology was much too complex to be captured in these reports.

Insofar as evangelicals were almost exclusively Anglo-Saxon in origin, they were capitalist and plutocratic, ipso facto anti-Latin, anti-Italian, and, ominously, antifascist. The worldwide economic crash and resulting unemployment intensified suspicion of, even hostility toward, capitalism. During the 1930s the rural population in the South began to grow.[87] The growth in rural population made the problem of unemployment and underemployment worse. Ironically, Anglo-Saxon missionaries, associated in the minds of many Catholic critics with capitalism or plutocracy, made notable gains with the very populations said by critics to have been most severely victimized by the capitalist powers.

Overall, the impression communicated by authors of these reports was that the country was under religious assault, on its heels against a formidable Protestant crusade composed of indefatigable heretics and foreigners.[88] As many missionaries were Italian nationals, "foreigners" must be taken in an elastic sense. The agents of conversion are often identified as americani. By this term, Sargolini, along with all Italians, meant Italian nationals, usually from the South, who had converted to Protestantism after emigrating to the United States; they became active, often as leaders, in evangelical churches when they returned to Italy. In one southern province, for example, the adepts and missionaries were "almost all émigrés and the repatriated."[89] Mistrorigo was appalled to learn from the local police in Rapolla in the Basilicata that the *transatlantici,* led by an evangelical pastor, celebrated the Holy Supper in the local diocesan chapel after Catholic ceremonies had concluded. Their status as aliens made them objects of fear and hostility. Indeed, their foreign origins ipso facto rendered them suspicious among locals. They aroused exasperation, hostility, aggression, even paranoia, among the learned, who, as in the case of Tacchi Venturi, indignantly viewed them as British or American imperialists or, suspiciously, as spies. Anglo-Saxon missionaries regarded Italy as a *terra di missione,* its dominant religion pitiably pagan and priestly, the baptized sadly ignorant and superstitious, their culture obstinately Latin. Sometimes pastors who were designated foreign, particularly well-known or influential ones, were in fact non-Italian. Occasionally, influential foreign pastors would come, to great fanfare, to visit evangelical communities they had remotely launched. One, the English Adventist Reverend Pullen, is called one of the great engines (*propulsori*) of Protestant propaganda in Italy. This is a reference to *Arrigo* E. Pullen, described as "having conquered . . . entire regions, like La Spezia."[90] He tellingly appears in prelatically authored archival documents as *Amerigo* Pullen. Small wonder that his fellow Adventists were well organized, with clear plans and plots, lavish with subsidies, tenacious, even fanatical.

Not to mention disturbingly focused on youth in the strategic port of La Spezia, a concern communicated by the local bishop to the pope.[91] Throughout the anti-Protestant campaign many prelates expressed fear that military personnel and key strategic ports like that in Spezia were overrun by Protestant proselytes, out of all proportion to the number and size of congregations in military centers. It was not only the paranoid who gave voice to these anxieties. Given Spezia's strategic importance as a military port and the tiny size of the community, many prelates would wonder why so many evangelical pastors were in residence there.[92]

Equally concerned and perhaps impressed, Selvaggiani notes the way in which, whatever their nationality or ethnic origin, Protestant missionaries had sublimated their historic rivalries. Determined to maintain "every concentration of force against Rome," they demonstrated "a constant preoccupation with tactical unity."[93] Here again the language of warfare is striking. The special aim of the Protestants was to seize the home of the worldwide Catholic church and the fascist government of Italy, a country only recently established and, for centuries, one that had been conquered and controlled by many foreign Continental powers. The memory of occupation, even its place in Italian identity, made the Protestant invasion an exasperating bone in the throat.

Among so-called apostates particularly worthy of note—and brought to the attention of Tacchi Venturi, the Apostolic Nuncio, and others—were ex-priests exercising Protestant ministries.[94] These attracted the hostile scrutiny of the Sacred Congregation of the Council, which enlisted spies to report on their activities and on whom detailed reports were written.[95] According to Selvaggiani, the majority of teachers employed by evangelical Sunday schools were made up of "apostate brothers and priests."[96] Even if exaggerated, this claim would have put them in direct violation of the final paragraph of Article 5 of the Lateran Treaty: "Apostate or suspended priests may not be employed or continued in employment as teachers in any office or post that brings them into direct contact with the public."[97]

Ex-priests were overrepresented in the educational domain.[98] Priests despised these apostates for breaking their vows and for religious treachery. Even more, they dreaded them. Former priests were (or were believed to be) the severest detractors of the church, merciless critics of their erstwhile colleagues, remorseless chroniclers of their vices. Former priests' unsparing descriptions of clerical scandal, inertia, and ignorance evangelical leaders naturally encouraged and publicized. These, too, could be exaggerated or fabricated, but they stung because they hit close to the mark. If, in addition to apostatizing, these ex-priests were suspected of antifascist conviction, the government would, with the encouragement of the church, assign agents to spy on them. The Central State Archives for the fascist period are replete with reports on such men. So, too, we now know, are the Vatican Archive. One Vatican congregation tracked the movements and activities of ex-priests who had converted to one of the evangelical confessions.[99] Rumors whispered about their participation in the antifascist resistance often turned out to be more than idle speculation.

Youth and students were almost everywhere enticed to convert by educational and recreational opportunities as well as by "circles" of generalized assistance for students, involving the provision of food, clothing, supplies, and cash.[100] An employee of the national rail system in Naples publicly distributed "conversionary" literature, particularly to students taking the Circumvesuviana.[101] Institutions offering instruction in foreign language, almost always English, were found in Turin, Pisa, Rome, and elsewhere.[102] Special concentration on students and youth by evangelicals and construction of institutions and costly buildings to engage them are widely attested in Protestant as well as Catholic sources. Focus on youth was also a cause for alarm and, in cases, intolerance, both for the state and the church.

Through Europe, fascist movements had national rebirth—palingenesis—at the heart of their programs. For his part, Pius, too, was aiming for, if not the restoration of Christendom, a religious, spiritual, and moral renovation of Europe, Italy above all. In *Ubi arcano Dei* (1922) Pius lays out his dream: the Christian restoration of society in a Catholic sense. This vision leaves no place at all for Protestant Christianity. This is in part because Pius, like most Italian priests, was convinced that the secular and anticlerical problems that had so undermined Christian society had had their sources in the thoughts of the magisterial reformers. Regime and church sought a new society that shared many aims. Not for nothing has it been said that Italian Catholicism had "strong sympathy for fascism's 'spiritual and moral aspirations.'"[103]

Since the political as well as religious education of youth, who were the nucleus of a continuing confessional and fascist state, was a priority, both the totalistic systems of church and state would soon find evangelical propaganda a source of deep alarm. Both would move, sometimes in tandem, to suppress it. From a present-day cultural point of view, these ecclesiastical actions seem—and were certainly felt by their targets to be—heartless. It is therefore imperative to stress that, however foreign or repugnant to our cultural norms, the supernatural destiny of souls entrusted to their care, threatened by the unorthodox potential of Protestant-led instruction, was paramount to these prelates. This is not to deny that other, less honorable motives were also in play.

The reports give special attention to YMCAs. This preoccupation may be odd to twenty-first-century Westerners, who appreciate what is now a merely civic amenity. But for Catholic leaders, the YMCA's omnipresence, appeal, wealth, conversionary aims, and effectiveness aroused fury. These institutions came to be loathed by Vatican authorities and local bishops precisely because they were so alluring to a prized sector of the population: youth. In the eyes of a Catholic bishop in a large urban area of early-twentieth-century Italy, the Y was a Trojan horse. Crammed with militant Protestant proselytizers, it menaced the supernatural health of Catholic parishioners, especially the young (whom no admonition seemed capable of keeping out), right in the center city of his diocese. According to Selvaggiani, in Rome the institution "most pernicious to young souls" was the YMCA on Via Indipendenza. The number of those it had signed up exceeded twelve hundred, and Romans flocking to use its facilities were simply countless.

One of the curious genres of the polemical literature from this period is the *opusculum,* of which many were composed, written to warn the unwary of the evil intentions and seductive methods of the Y.[104] Not surprising: the Ys were founded by and staffed by Methodists, who notoriously used underhanded methods to convert the unwary. It was, again, anxiety over youth that supplied the energy for so much hostile writing against the Protestant personnel staffing the Ys. The staff were unprincipled and sneaky, a threat to the salvation of souls and, politically, to the continuity of the fascist regime.

Turin's Y was described as a "splendid palace." Aside from being equipped with facilities supporting "every kind of diversion," this Y was the one through which many Italian émigrés passed before their transatlantic journeys. Entering as impoverished Catholic peasants steeped in the traditions of Latin culture, they emerged transformed as converts: religiously, to Protestantism, and culturally, to the attractions of Anglo-Saxon plutocratic culture.[105] The values of Protestant and foreign cultures were said by Selvaggiani to be transmitted as well by a new, discouragingly potent form of Protestant propaganda: film, especially appealing to youth. "Many cinematographic films present a spirit and atmosphere revealing their true origins in the Protestant and foreign world."[106] Selvaggiani contends, quite plausibly, that among the distinguished guests giving lectures at the Rome Y is a group of Catholic modernists who were suspected of being sympathetic with Protestantism, especially German theological scholarship.[107] This was not the last time Catholic modernists were to be associated with evangelical groups in Italy. Here, as often, fear of conversion to Protestantism was associated with distress at the imposition of alien Anglo-Saxon cultural values as well as liberal (and heretical) theological ones.

DISORDER AND VIOLENCE

The arrival of Protestants into some communities could occasion deep tensions, existential threat, and sometimes violent resistance. Though not emphasized in these reports, this violence was occasioned not just by Protestant proselytizing but also by encouragement from priests, especially those associated with Catholic Action. Protestants in Benevento (Campania) gave scandal both "with their discussions and by the example of their lives."[108] Unfortunately, Sargolini furnishes no details on either issue. Conversations heard or attended on the absolute centrality and authority of the Bible, on the human invention of the Petrine office, the avarice of popes, or the idolatrous or neopagan character of Catholic devotional practice—all common Protestant themes—could have deeply disturbed him. These themes were the very bricks and mortar of Protestant conversionary literature and proselytizing and had long been. For the vast majority of unquestioning parishioners, the inherited faith of Roman Catholicism and the church, as then embodied in Italy, was quite simply the unique, divinely ordained institution through which humanity could be redeemed. As for the "example of their lives," Sargolini perhaps meant to indicate the practice of birth control or abortion, both of which Protestants were widely reported to have practiced.[109] Catholic polemicists also feared, not wrongly, that some Protestant missionaries had ceased to believe in some ancient and foundational doctrines of Catholicism, such as the divinity of Christ.

The sale of Bibles was a ubiquitously deployed means of conversion; it was reported by Sargolini to have occurred in most of the provinces of the country, including all of the South.[110] Much anti-Protestant literature attacked the "free interpretation" of the Bible, which, it was alleged, had caused the proliferation of a bewildering array of Protestant sects. Unguided reading had contributed to the calamitous, widespread sense of neutrality (indifferentismo) on the central issue of whether the Bible was divinely ordained, or offered a greater purchase on divine truth than the One, Holy, Roman, and Apostolic Church.

Protestant teaching practice could be more than disturbing; on occasion it was inflammatory, so much so that it was resisted, sometimes violently. In the northern town of Vittorio Veneto the repeatedly attempted distribution of Protestant Bibles was so offensive that it was "always resisted" (not very likely) by the lay population as well as the clerical.[111] Sargolini reports that "the work of penetration had been made very difficult in Castellammare di Stabia" in the commune of Naples because the Protestant population had been attacked, violently, by the Catholic.[112] The distribution of Protestant versions of the Bible, which differed from the Catholic in several significant respects, would become a source of deep irritation for prelates at the Vatican.[113]

Conversely, a book simply entitled *The Bible* (*Le Bibbie*) was not likely to be perceived by ordinary Catholics or local law enforcement as in any way harmful to its recipient. Nor, to the pain of Vatican prelates, was it known to most ordinary, superficially catechized Catholics, including most policemen, that the Catholic Bible differed in contents, translation, and interpretation from the Protestant. Nonetheless, in some communities, if detected, vendors of Protestant Bibles could be verbally abused by parishioners and sometimes physically attacked by a putatively outraged Catholic mob or individual.

In some cases community violence was not impeded by priests; indeed, priests themselves, infuriated by the sale of Protestant Bibles to susceptible Catholics, pounced on colporteurs with violence. In one case of physical assault the offender was a Jesuit priest, who was tried, convicted, and sentenced, much to the dismay of the Apostolic Nuncio; the legalistic Borgongini-Duca insisted that the Jesuit's violent reaction was legally justified and that his sentence therefore ought to be reversed.[114] In another case a Jesuit priest arranged for a group of Catholic men from Rome and in the vicinity of San Sebastiano to be prepared to assault British Wesleyans if they responded to a Jesuit mission intended to reconvert some of the community.[115] In any case, Catholic–Protestant tensions occasioned by sales of the Bible or propagandistic literature were one of the flashpoints in what Michael Ebner has called ordinary or quotidian violence in fascist Italy.[116]

Fascist police authorities could be sensitive not only to occasions of violence but even to the threat of disorder. If the governments of liberal Italy had been flexible in their treatment of popular demonstrations, the same can hardly be said of the fascist regime. A totalitarian regime can rarely tolerate public disorder. That absolute order was the ideal was known in every *Questura,* prefecture, and police headquarters in Italy, and the heads of all of these knew that their jobs depended on their ability to maintain it. In this context, as Rochat has pointed out, the simplest way to stop evangelical activity, above all, evangelical preaching, was to intervene to prevent public disorder. Indeed, there was a ritual quality to the way in which parish priests, bishops, and Vatican officials sounded the alarm of public disorder to shut down Protestant propaganda. One could not go so far as Rochat, who claims that a priest determined to rid the streets of evangelical preachers was, by complaining of public disorder, sure of success "nine times out of ten."[117] The endless stream of Vatican complaints about lax enforcement through the 1930s considerably weakens such a claim, for which no evidence is presented in any case. That said, such a complaint could be quite effective—especially if, as happened occasionally, it reached Mussolini. (One did in July 1932 from Padre Tabacco, the parish priest in Villa San Sebastiano, and from his bishop, Pio Bagnoli.) Mussolini and other authorities received direct appeals from evangelical communities as well.

When issues of culture, politics, and economics are considered, it remains true that what was central for many Catholic priests was divine religious truth and eternal salvation. If some profascist clerics worried about the stability of the government and some Catholic fascist officials about the church, some, including Pope Pius XI, anguished most about the threat to true religion. As the stakes were soteriological, they could not, for a priest, have been any higher. That is what made the arrival of Protestant missionaries, for Catholic priests like the pope, such a special danger. Whatever the hierarchy and structure of motives, genuine salvation for souls was central for many.

Perhaps this is why Pius XI rejoiced when, though it rarely occurred, once-Catholic Protestant ministers reconverted to Catholicism. Mistrorigo reports one instance that reminds one of the tiny number of medieval Cathars who reconverted to orthodoxy and then became zealous inquisitors.[118] According to information supplied by local law enforcement, one Antonio Mazzucca, a Protestant seminarian, "publicly abjured his heresy." Now, admirably, he makes "intense Catholic propaganda." Mistrorigo tracked him down, and the ex-seminarian provided him, as few others could, "precious information" on Protestant activities in the Province of Cosenza. Among the pieces of intelligence he passed along was the unhappy fact that "an evangelical renaissance" was under way there.[119] This information was acquired, then, by a tip from the local police. Carlo Zardi, a minister who presided over the Wesleyan Methodist church in the troubled town of San Sebastiano, also stunned his congregation and the Vatican by his sudden reconversion to Catholicism; his apparently sincere expression of contrition for having exposed countless souls to everlasting perdition drew much attention from Catholic writers, even outside the priestly polemicists at the Vatican, such as Igino Giordani. Aside from causing the pope to exult, cases like this made for powerful weapons in the war against Protestantism; Zardi's decision was held up and advertised as exemplary. He became the pope's poster child. In the end, nonetheless, few followed his example.

A source of frustration for the Vatican and for police officials was the inconsistent behavior of local law enforcement; this would remain a source of great irritation and anger through at least 1939. Generally, the more distant geographically from Rome, the greater the distance between the law and its enforcement. Local authorities, especially in the years immediately following the passage of the permitted cults legislation, acted largely autonomously in determining their views, if any, of Protestants in their jurisdictions. Some understood their task to be to respond to the protests of Catholic laymen or clergymen and to act on behalf of the presumed wishes of the church. Much of what Mistrorigo came to know was provided to him by local police.[120] Catholics in Gorizia (bordering Slovenia), for example, protested the establishment of the Centro di Propaganda; it was closed "by order of the authorities."[121] Here community tensions were resolved by effective law enforcement suppression from above. But local legal authorities treated Protestant communities erratically. Many were ignorant and, in some cases, defiant of national governmental or ecclesiastical policy formed in distant Rome. If in Gorizia police complied with the wishes of angry Catholics, in the Province of Pola, parties *di benificenza* thrown by evangelical missionaries were held with the aid of the police and governmental authorities.[122]

Very rarely, local ecclesiastical authorities, held up as exemplary by Sargolini, were credited with successful resistance. "The enlightened resistance of our bishop" in Gerace Superiore (Calabria), Sargolini reports, had succeeded in "impeding the spread of Protestantism."[123] As Vatican prelates fully recognized, effective resistance like this was rare among clergy, particularly diocesan priests, especially in the South. This Calabrian bishop thus stands out as a then-rare exception to regular clerical indolence toward, indifference to, or even ignorance of the existence and dimensions of a Protestant problem. The poverty-stricken, homeless,[124] poorly educated, idle (when not carnal), and thus irrelevant priest was not simply the product of legend or of fiction, like Carlo Levi's *Christ Stopped at Eboli.*[125] It was a neuralgic problem for the Catholic church. As was the case with reconversion, episcopal resisters were recognized as martial-saints and their conduct paradigms for imitation.

There seems to be some correlation between dioceses recognized by the Vatican as having indolent clergy and the success of evangelical missionaries. Mistrorigo blames the provincial clergy in Calabria for Protestant effectiveness in that region. Evangelicals there had been attracted by the "preaching of the Gospel and with the most beautiful songs." The peasant laborers had heard only "the Gospel of the priests." Now they "think they have found among heretics the true religion" (la vera religione).[126] That is, many were powerfully drawn into Protestant *sale* (halls or large rooms) by genuine religious motives and spiritual deprivation; not all were recruited by the promise of relief from material impoverishment or bodily hunger. At least that was not the sole motivation: not with all. The 1930 "Vulture earthquake," which devastated many southern provinces, drew out humiliating contrasts between Protestant energy and Catholic clerical lethargy.[127] That catastrophe revealed evangelical sympathy for human misery, which compared unfavorably to apparent priestly indifference. After the earthquake struck, the Baptist pastor remained to "care for the infirm," while, according to Mistrorigo, a sympathetic observer, "the priests slipped off." In gratitude, either the mayor of Rapolla or the local prefect (Mistrorigo is unsure which) sent the pastor gratis to other Italian towns to help, and the mayor "thanked him publicly."[128]

As Rochat has observed, bishops rarely took independent initiative against evangelical groups.[129] The Calabrian bishop silhouetted here by Sargolini thus stands in stark contrast to the broader landscape of priestly torpor, to which he stood as an extremely rare exception in the South. Sargolini was aware of just how rare. In one case, no less a figure than the archbishop of Potenza was present while, astonishingly, a meditation session was being led by a Protestant pastor. The latter was also giving instruction of another, unspecified sort to parish priests. With his automobile, another Protestant minister visited two archiepiscopal sees, those in San Severina (Le Marche) and Cotrone (Calabria), with whose ordinaries he had scheduled appointments.[130] If *archbishops* were socializing with or, even worse, learning from Protestant pastors, what could be expected of a lowly diocesan priest?

One instance of Catholic popular resistance, supported both by agents of the national government and of the Vatican, is reported. Early in the winter of 1931 the parish council of Torre dei Passeri, in the Abruzzo region of Italy, consisting of three laymen and the clerical representative for Catholic Action, met urgently. Having gathered the opinions of its members, the president of the council wrote a letter to the Vatican that found its way to the Apostolic Nunciature on 2 February 1931. The council had met to deplore the "insane work of several malcontents" who had submitted a petition signed by the "youth of the town." An invitation extended to a Protestant pastor to establish an evangelical community the following Sunday occasioned their urgency. The other objectives of the "malcontents" were clear to the parish council; they encompassed the political and religious indistinguishably. Increasingly ardent Protestant propaganda was aimed at stripping the populace of all "patriotic feeling . . . to inspire hatred of our institutions, and to fight against the faith of our fathers, the glory of Italy in the world." Given this description, it is certain that Protestants there (as everywhere in Italy) were, or were suspected of being, hostile to fascism. The evidence of spy and police reports, not to mention the testimony of many evangelicals itself, suggests that many, in fact, were. Still, the president of the church council may have spoken more truthfully than he knew when characterizing the rebel Catholics as malcontents. Protestant piety seemed especially appealing to those unhappy with the quality of local Catholic religious life. This was, with some individuals and in some communities, a decisive factor in the effectiveness of evangelical propaganda.

The parish council, along with "all right-thinking people" in the town, wrote a response. The Protestant community had not yet been established. In order to "avoid internal struggles so damaging to public life," and because it would "offend against the profound religious feelings of this town," perhaps the formation of an evangelical church could be impeded? "We beseech you," the council president writes, using the rhetoric of infection historically used to characterize heresy, to act so that "such evil does not germinate" in his small town.[131]

The entire case was finally forwarded to the government, likely because of the whiff of antifascist sentiment. No evidence seems to exist that reveals the outcome of the struggle between the proevangelicals and the fascist pro-Catholic factions of the community. Yet Sargolini's report illustrates very explicitly how the evangelical message could appeal to a segment of the community, occasion division and the establishment of factions, and result in appeals to the Vatican or the national government.

Cynical use of the law was not the preserve of state officials or of governmental lawyers. Indeed, even, or especially, good cardinals and archbishops—that is, ones hostile to evangelicals—seem, in many cases willingly, to have ignored the existence or the implications of the laws on admitted cults. Perhaps some simply could not abide, morally or psychologically, those tolerated by national law. Living out of time, rather like medieval bishops, they demanded suppression of the very denominations whose toleration had so recently been enshrined in law. Protestantism had become analogous to what in the Roman empire became known as a *religio licita:* a permitted religion. Despite this, anti-Protestant ordinaries would pursue and persecute the permitted confessions, often by appeal to the law, while ignoring the recently promulgated law on tolerance. Even when not opposed to Mussolini's government, they were made out to be. Pressure would intensify in the mid- and late 1930s: the Abyssinian misadventure, the advent of war, and putative links with Jewish Italians would cause them to be classified as enemies of the state.

On occasion Protestants could grow overconfident in their newfound status and in the law that granted them full liberty in discussion of matters religious. When they were understood to have provocatively broken the law, especially the articles of the Concordat setting limits to discussion of religious subjects, they could be charged and punished. All of this the Adventist journalist Giovanni Lippolis would learn in late 1931 to his dismay. Lippolis, who had spent most of his life in Puglia, was the evangelical owner of a periodical, the *Herald of the Truth,* published in Florence, where he was living when a dispute broke out in articles he had not only published but written.[132] Already suspected of antifascist preaching and proselytizing, he was found guilty by a tribunal in Florence of insulting the pope. He was sentenced to seventy-five days in jail and ordered not to write while cooling his heels in the *casellario giudiziaro.*[133] Lippolis appealed, but the tribunal's verdict was upheld by the court of appeals in Cassazione.[134]

An occasion of euphoria for Pacelli, Pizzardo, and the Apostolic Nuncio—a battle won in a war that, demoralizingly, they had been losing for years—the sentencing was a sobering outcome for Protestant writers and propagandists. Freedom of religious expression was, in fact, not "completely free," as the 1929 legislation had it. It could in fact be hemmed in and trumped by the articles of the Lateran Accords, which had declared Roman Catholicism to be the Religion of the State and the person of the pope to be inviolable. That said, other battles, almost epic in scope and duration, lasted for years and ended with ambiguous and disappointing outcomes. On no other town was so much anti-Protestant energy concentrated, with such unsatisfactory results, than tiny Villa San Sebastiano.

CHAPTER 5

A Stubborn Problem

VILLA SAN SEBASTIANO REVISITED (1931–39)

The history of the conversion to British Methodism of the peasants of Villa San Sebastiano, and of episcopal and papally directed efforts to resist defections or apostasy from the Roman church during the 1930s, has been examined by some of the foremost historians of evangelical Christianity in Italy. In his study of the evangelical churches during the fascist period Giorgio Rochat supplies a fine (if not entirely unbiased) account of the bitter hostility that prevailed in the 1930s between evangelicals and Catholic clergy, including both diocesan priests and powerful prelates connected with the Vatican. Eventually, hostility in the quiet mountain village in Aquila would boil over into open religious warfare and, finally, spill over into schism.[1]

While Rochat based his account on archival materials, it was even more squarely founded on a lengthy microstudy published by A. R. Leone in 1972.[2] Though praised by Rochat, that important article is not as well known as it should be. Leone, deeply sympathetic to the evangelical community of the Villa, portrayed the defection of some 250 villagers to the Methodist church as having been motivated by both religious grievance and economic-social adversity. On the one hand it was, he argued, a revolt against the sterilities of the "wholly exterior" character of traditional Catholicism as well as against clerical and papal hegemony.[3] At the same time, Leone, who was not untouched by Marxist theory, framed the story as a social and economic contest, even a revolution, by the poverty-stricken and fatalistic. They were, in embracing Protestant Christianity, resisting the repressive Catholic landowners and economic stakeholders of the Marsica.[4] While not untrue, that is a small part of the villagers' motivation, which, if overstressed, can eclipse the significance of their powerful religious motivations.

Topographically and socioeconomically the Villa itself was divided into two unequal portions: an internal locale (as Leone calls it) comprehending all the hydrographic basin of Lake Fucino, and an external perimeter, which had only indirect access to the critical agricultural resources supplied by the lake. In socioeconomic and demographic terms, this second part was populated by around thirteen hundred citizens, with problems then neuralgic in central-meridional Italy. After the fall of the Kingdom of Naples (1860), the property of the Torlonia House was split among lawyers, professionals, and wealthy farmers.[5] In the early twentieth century new proprietors acquired and leased out land in twenty-five-acre parcels at hunger wages, or what we would call starvation wages.[6] The exploitation continued, "with the sole difference," Leone concludes, "that the single old landlord was replaced with many new ones."[7] When the religiosocial rebellion was launched, it was led, Leone argued, by americani. Having returned from America, they were putatively shocked by what they found back home (putatively because Leone cites no sources for this view and because it so nearly mirrors his own). Changes wrought by the Industrial Revolution, including a more critical view of traditional religion, had begun to have their effects in the North of Italy. In the South, by contrast, Catholic dogma continued to legitimate "anachronistic social relations and power, to the harm of the humble classes."[8]

In Leone's view, the peasants, now in an "objectively revolutionary situation," attempted a religious solution to their problem. It was, additionally, an attempt at justice for a traditionally fatalistic population, distrustful of real possibilities for improvement of its lot as well as chary of the reliability and will of government. Into this complex economic and social matrix "the Methodist movement inserted itself."[9] Before the Methodists of Avezzano sent a pastor, however, the dreams of the villagers were temporarily realized when, in 1929, an exceptionally popular ex-Redemptorist priest, sympathetic to their utter destitution, was appointed by Pio Bagnoli (1859–1945), bishop of Avezzano (1910–45).[10] The villagers' dreams were shattered when Bagnoli dismissed the priest the following year. Furious, many in the community, newly emboldened (so Leone argued) by converted americani, called on the

British Methodists to send a pastor to the Villa. The villagers' frustration and anger with the local Catholic ordinary, above all his dismissal of a much-loved parish priest, helped give rise to the Villa's incipient evangelical community.

That much of the history remains true. But the *sources* of the villagers' anger could not have been divined by Leone and, indeed, by anyone until very recently. Unavailable before the studies of Leone, Rochat, and Giorgio Spini's posthumously published account, the recently released Vatican archival documents confirm and enrich details of both the religious rebellion and the fearsome anti-Protestant campaign that ensued.[11] They shed light especially on the complex sources of anger with the local bishop and thus on the origins of the Villa's remarkable evangelical community.

PADRE BERNARDINO AND THE BISHOP

The ecclesiastical tribulations of the Villa began with the death in April 1927 of the parish priest, P. Giuseppe D'Andrea, not unimportantly part of an old extended family in Avezzano. Bishop Bagnoli puzzled and then irritated the community when he left the village without a permanent priest for two years. Finally, in 1929, he provisionally appointed Padre Bernardino, an ex-Redemptorist, to the post.[12] As they conflict in important respects, Protestant and Catholic sources leave some features of his character and ministry opaque or incompatible, but much is still clear. To begin with, the villagers, especially the majority of his flock, who worked as day laborers or farmers, idolized him. They saluted him for not asking for money from the impoverished faithful for liturgical services—a tacit critique of the practices of the south Italian presbyterate of the day.

Padre Bernardino also impressed with his effective preaching as well as his deep commitment to the economic and social improvement—even survival—of his destitute flock (possibly a mark of his Redemptorist training).[13] Many of his parishioners still lived in stables with their mules and pigs.[14] For these, he built small houses (*cassette*). Fatefully, he erected them on land belonging to the church without troubling Bishop Bagnoli for permission to do so. Furious with this abuse of episcopal authority, Bishop Bagnoli resolved to remove him. Only the intervention of Domenico Amicucci, the Catholic mayor of Tagliacozzo, persuaded Bagnoli to wait for a more suitable moment.[15] With the encouragement of Amicucci, Fr. Bernardino—for reasons unknown to Leone or any interpreter—built a kindergarten, to be staffed by sisters, who were in some sense his followers and had preceded him to the Villa. Incensed, the bishop deprived him of his charge and in November 1930 expelled him from the parish.[16] Rochat claims that Bernardino's activism was not appreciated by the bishop, but Bagnoli's motivations, and his dissatisfaction with Padre Bernardino, were considerably more complicated than that.[17]

Was the bishop motivated by jealousy? The usurpation of his episcopal power? It is hard to say. According to Bagnoli, Fr. Bernardino had given "proof of minimal reliability," insofar as he had considered "neither the laws [of the church] nor of obedience" and had disposed "the patrimony of the church as he pleased, all with the utmost independence of any authority."[18] He accused Padre Bernardino of sleeping in the same shacks as the nuns who accompanied him to the Villa. He had led or, minimally, participated in secular gatherings that stretched far into the evening. Young women or girls were said to have attended; the bishop implies that these social occasions were marred by sexual impropriety, a far-fetched charge that would later be dismissed by villagers as a pretext for Padre Bernardino's removal. Whatever the truth of the charges, the bishop had dismissed a priest of whom many in the community were quite fond.[19]

Now infuriated, the community rebelled against the bishop. Rochat describes the revolt, with some exaggeration, as a "massive popular mobilization in [Padre Bernardino's] favor."[20] Thirty letters arrived in Bagnoli's office. These expressed deep admiration for Padre Bernardino and demanded that he be recognized as the community's established parish priest (*parocco titolare*). Bagnoli brushed off the villagers, but they refused, now, to be disdained.[21] Leone rightly suggests that the evangelical community may thus have had accidental or casual origins, occasioned by Bagnoli's surprising decision to remove Fr. Bernardino. Yet he also entertains the possibility that the Villa's americani—who had been converted to the reformed churches while in the United States and achieved a critical perspective on the social and economic conditions of their native country—nourished, on their return, a secret hope of resuscitating their communities socially and economically, even of attaining revolutionary aspirations. The Sturm und Drang over Fr. Bernardino provided the newly converted the opportunity to resist the traditional and (in Leone's view) repressive Catholicism of which they had, by then, become radically critical.[22] While helpful in some respects, Leone's interpretive framework imputes to the villagers Marxist aspirations that did not, in fact, actuate them—at least not wholly.

In January 1931, soon after Padre Bernardino's dismissal, some one hundred families signed a letter addressed to leaders of the Wesleyan Methodist church in Rome, asking it to send a preacher. The families were led, according to the traditional account, not by a local worthy but by a *paesano,* Emilio Gargano. A repatriated Italian, Gargano had converted in the United States before returning to his hometown. It may be, as Leone suggests, that most of the population hoped that the letter would pressure Bagnoli to reinstall Fr. Bernardino. If so, their hopes were dashed with the appointment of Fr. Alfonso Tabacco as the parish priest of the Villa in January 1931. In the same month, the Methodist leadership in Rome, in response to the community's letter, sent two ministers to the Villa, Emanuele Sbaffi and Dante Seta. Fatefully, Seta was an ex-priest from the diocese of Parma; his ecclesiastical status would haunt him and shorten his years in San Sebastiano.[23] It was Seta's status, in part, that tinged the schism with such vitriol. Once a Catholic priest, Seta would soon appear on the radar of the Sacred Congregation of the Council, which would, as part of the anti-Protestant campaign organized from the Vatican, compile a thick archive in the 1930s on apostate priests.[24] Together, the two ministers officiated at an evangelical worship ceremony in a field.[25] No fewer than eight hundred people attended the ceremony—more than half the population of the community of fifteen hundred.[26]

Soon appointed the permanent pastor of the Methodist congregation, Seta presided over a community that, over the course of the year 1931, achieved numerical equilibrium at the sum of roughly 250 faithful. The almost-immediate return to the Villa's Catholic parish of some 70 percent of the 800 villagers attending the evangelical service strongly suggests that their calling of the Protestant pastors was, in fact, intended to pressure Bagnoli into recalling Fr. Bernardino to the parish. Still, many did *not* return; they willingly joined the evangelical congregation. It was thus that the Villa had become part of the "Methodist diaspora" in meridional Italy, one of ten small communities in Abruzzo alone. In the lyrical words of Giorgio Spini, "The earth of the yokel of Ignazio Silone and of *Fontamara,* pressed hard by the burden of labor, of hunger, seemed to move: the humble had dared to take The Book in their callous hands and to seek there the Truth for themselves."[27] Like Leone, Spini frames the conversion of the Villa in terms of an organized rebellion against the traditional, repressive religious forces of Italian Catholicism. Whatever his motives, Bishop Bagnoli's decision to remove the popular Bernardino from the parish caused an ecclesial rupture in territory for which the seeds of schism had long been germinating.

AN UNCIVIL WAR

Bishop Bagnoli had sown the whirlwind; now he would reap it. No one could have guessed, then, that a schism between Catholic and evangelical Italy would afflict the tiny, remote mountain community with something like a severe, decade-long civil war based on religious difference and contempt for—or, in the view of Bagnoli and Vatican prelates, disobedience to—the local ordinary. Acrimony precipitated by the bishop was thus a major factor in the establishment of an evangelical community in the Villa. But it was not the only factor. The 250 evangelicals who remained in Seta's Methodist community did so for reasons that can only be judged principally religious. They had found something in the *religious* message of Seta—something for which Padre Bernardino had perhaps prepared the soil—that they embraced as a captivating form of the Christian message. It nourished their souls in a way emphatically not satisfied by the insipid gruel served up indifferently by the Italian presbyterate.

For his part, Bagnoli was initially persuaded that the insurrection was temporary; he reposed his confidence in the traditional fatalism of the peasant masses. Then a delegation from the Villa purchased land in Tagliacozzo (San Sebastiano was a small part of the commune) on which to build a church. Underwritten by funds furnished by the president of the British Wesleyans, the transaction jolted Bagnoli from that complacent view. It also motivated the bishop to launch a campaign against the Methodist community, a movement soon given accelerant by Roman prelates. One Protestant commentator framed the campaign in the rhetorically suggestive terms of a harsh crusade of reconquest.[28] All Protestant sources and historians agree that the reaction of the Catholic church was merciless and, in its tactics, coldhearted, even fiendish. Among other things, Bagnoli ordered Catholic *padroni* not to renew the leases of land worked by impoverished evangelical peasants. Spini writes that the "reaction of conservative forces" to the establishment of the evangelical community was "truly vehement." He concludes, severely: this was "a campaign of hatred and terror."[29]

Intriguingly, local governmental authorities, who were of course Catholic, refused to participate in the campaign. Indeed, they seemed curiously sympathetic to the evangelical project. The construction of the temple would be supported, for example, by the Catholic mayor of Tagliacozzo, Domenico Amicucci, for reasons that—until the recent release of relevant documents at the Vatican Archive—no historian could possibly have divined.[30] Indignant, Bagnoli, Borgongini-Duca, and Tacchi Venturi all angrily endeavored to have Amicucci removed. Tacchi Venturi met personally with Amicucci; even Cardinal Gasparri also tried to intervene, though more indirectly—a sign of how seriously the Villa's story was being followed at the highest echelons of the Vatican. The Methodist attempt to construct a temple would, with inspiration from the Vatican, be resisted with increasing tenacity by Bagnoli. Even so, the Vatican would receive word from several sources that Bishop Bagnoli was tolerant of Protestants and even promoted and favored them. This was very far from true, though no historian writing before 2006 could possibly know why writers of such missives reported the falsehood.

The bishop first ordered the local Questura to examine a list of 400 signatures gathered to petition for the construction of a temple. The list was reduced to 150 on two grounds. The first was the question—required by the culti ammessi laws—whether there existed a permanent nucleus of faithful. Only if there was could they get permission (*nulla osta*) for construction of the temple. Second, the bishop had engineers question the seismic suitability of the planned temple—this in the wake of a deadly earthquake, whose memory was still fresh in a region devastated by it. The dull reaction to the establishment of a Methodist community in the tiny Villa and the attempt to build a Protestant temple of worship there troubled the most powerful leaders of the church in Rome. In fact, the establishment of the evangelical church in the Villa demoralized Pope Pius XI, who would bring all his powers to bear on returning the converted to Catholicism. Catholic prelates are said to have regarded the situation in the Villa as "extremely grave."[31] They felt that the Vatican had to recruit powerful and able allies, from both church and the fascist state, to quell the religious uprising.

In the end, the personnel staffing the Catholic counteroffensive at the Villa came to include, among others at the Vatican, Secretary of State Pietro Gasparri, Giulio Serafini (prefect of the powerful Congregation of the Consistory), and, above all, Monsignor (later Cardinal) F. Borgongini-Duca, the new Italian nuncio, who had avidly studied the culti ammessi laws and, with demonic energy, led the anti-Protestant charge. He did this in part by successfully cultivating relations with the powerful undersecretary of the interior, Buffarini.[32] The campaign also included the editors of *OR.* Indeed, one historian has said that articles published in the newspaper in 1931–34 demonstrated nothing less than a "keen and constant interest" in the events of Villa San Sebastiano.[33] Catholic prelates, including Tacchi Venturi, Gasparri, and the Apostolic Nuncio, also involved themselves. In turn, these Vatican prelates enlisted powerful secular and political leaders like Director General of Cults Montecchi, Undersecretary Suvich, Chief of Police Arturo Bocchini, Minister of Justice Alfredo Rocco, and local ministers of OVRA—even Mussolini himself. As the term "reconquest" suggests, all intended to return the evangelical community to the Catholic church and away from the "heretical sect" that had ensnared them—and, in the eyes of the pope, had endangered their salvation. Catholic intentions were certainly, as in the Reconquista in eleventh-century Spain or in the Crusades, to take back land "belonging" to the church, then unjustly occupied by a small but zealous—and foreign—infidel army of fanatics.

In the face of this challenge Tacchi Venturi was initially entrusted by the Vatican with resolving the problem of San Sebastiano. Already by January 1932 Tacchi Venturi was characteristically proclaiming to the pope, to Mussolini, and to the undersecretary of the interior's Arpinati—quite wrongly as it turns out—that, because of action he had taken, the stubborn problem of Villa San Sebastiano had been resolved. After gathering data from several sources, Tacchi Venturi met with the mayor of Tagliacozzo, to whom he presented the evidence he had acquired. He also met with the prefect of Aquila. Having encouraged the mayor to cleanse the Protestants from the landscape of his jurisdiction in the Abruzzo, he begged the prefect to monitor the "pernicious propaganda" of the Wesleyans. Little else is known about the nature of the intervention; only that, in the view of Arpinati, it had succeeded. "In the Villa [San Sebastiano]," the undersecretary reports, "there remains no more even the shadow of a Protestant."[34] The Jesuit was then able to write to Pacelli that they were allowed to hope that (in Arpinati's tender phrase), "the germ of heretical infection [*sparso*] in the region has been entirely destroyed."[35]

This was far from true. In fact, the number of evangelicals had remained steady at around 260. Despite all the efforts of Bagnoli, the police authorities refused a direct, repressive intervention (except in the case of the question of opening the temple), a refusal that left Bagnoli bitter.[36] They preferred to leave to the clergy the responsibility of a counteroffensive. In the early stages of the dispute, the lack of cooperation from local fascist authorities mystified, then infuriated Catholic prelates involved in the campaign of suppression. Most were unaware of the deep-seated and intense hostility toward Bishop Bagnoli, rancor and resentment that simmered just beneath the surface and thus, temporarily, blinded many at the Vatican to the motivations of the major local actors, Protestant and Catholic, in the Villa. Within two years all would awaken to these realities.

BORGONGINI AND THE BISHOP

Meanwhile, another, even more distressing (because ecclesiastical) parochial circumstance came to light to Catholic authorities: the untrustworthiness, in multiple respects, of the bishop of Marsi. Borgongini had uncovered several odd allegations against the bishop. Far from campaigning against the local Wesleyans, Bagnoli had, allegedly, protected them. This was not at all true, but local Catholics, for reasons discussed below, believed it—or represented it as being true. Second, his clergy were said not to trust him. Borgongini concludes, in a report to Pacelli,

> Let me finally say to Your Eminence, with whom I open my soul candidly, as I believe to be required *coram Deo:*[37] after having followed the various phases of the sad defection [to Protestantism] of San Sebastiano, and after having treated with the various civil authorities, including the Head of Government, I am convinced, based on various meetings with the venerable Bishop Monsignor Bagnoli, that he is a man not equal to the situation; he is unable to satisfy what seems to me the urgent duty of his post. . . . With this I do not wish to detract from the merits acquired by the venerable Prelate in his twenty-four years of governing the diocese of Marsi; but I believe that the sad situation that has occurred under him can be easily resolved by another bishop.[38]

In a letter of acknowledgment written two days later, Pacelli thanked the nuncio for this last recommendation and mentioned in addition that he had (as the nuncio requested) passed it along to Cardinal Rossi of the Sacred Congregation of the Council, which oversaw the appointment and performance of bishops.[39] It would not be long before others at the Vatican would begin to doubt the suitability, even the sanity, of Bagnoli. All these elements mingled to upset what, from the Vatican, had seemed a stable socioreligious environment. Now it was a field of conflict, with no certain outcome and, indeed, with warnings portending a long struggle with the ever more confident Protestant minority of the Villa.

Like the pope, Borgongini regarded the Villa as an omen of what might happen to all Italy. Mussolini, as I have noted, assured Borgongini that, as there were so few evangelicals in Italy, he ought to worry less about them. To this the nuncio objected, in March 1931, "citing," as he reports, "the cases of Abruzzi and especially Villa San Sebastiano."[40] The date is not unimportant. In 1931 Italy, like much of the rest of the West, was still in the throes of a profound economic crisis, including the calamity of unemployment. In addition, the conflict with the regime over Catholic Action did not dispose the government to come to the aid of anti-Protestant polemicists. In 1931 the situation, religiously speaking, seemed to those connected to the Vatican to be bad, even dire. In view of the advances then being made by the Protestants, Catholic prelates from Pope Pius down the hierarchy were on their heels. The Protestants were in the ascendancy, and Catholicism did not have the full support of the state. This was especially true in San Sebastiano, where the mayor seemed to be working with the bishop on behalf of the Protestants in the Villa, though for obscure motivations.

In late October 1931 Borgongini recorded in a memo that the situation in San Sebastiano was worsening. There, during the hour dedicated to religious instruction, the "so-called Protestants" (here adopting the language of Pius XI to describe non-Catholic Christians), in this case British Methodists (*vesleiani*), were the cause of the problem. At the hour dedicated for religious instruction Protestant boys left school to go to the Methodist pastor, who was alleged to carry on proselytizing outside the school and to Catholics. Learning this, Borgongini became so angry he made the distant trip to Aquila, where he confronted the pastor. The first thing he did, according to his own testimony, was to explain the intent (*mente*) of the law on admitted cults, for which he predictably carried the text of the laws and read certain points out loud to Seta, then the Methodist pastor, emphasizing what the laws permitted and what they prohibited. He demanded that Seta stop proselytizing, or at least cease to use money or tempting offers of work, to bribe those of good faith. Nor was Seta to vend or distribute gratis published propaganda to the gullible peasants of the Abruzzi. The Methodist pastor was warned, finally, to stop taking advantage of the poverty of the local clergy.[41]

The director of cults fully agreed with the nuncio, who had written him, but he was just then confronting pressure from abroad—he meant from the embassies of Britain, especially—which was extraordinary. This was certainly true. In an undated pro memoria intended for Borgongini, Pizzardo noted that the English ambassador to Italy had "personally brought up the question with His Excellency Mussolini."[42] Now deeply alarmed, Borgongini, representing the situation as precarious, complained to Pacelli that the Italian government simply "could not approve the opening of a Wesleyan temple in Abruzzo," where "300 apostates had been created two years ago."[43] It was at this point that Borgongini "spoke to the good Father Crivelli on the necessity of preparing expediently, in order to give to the Government, an objective report based upon the published data on the Protestant sects." The result was the nuncio's anonymously issued, privately but widely circulated *Protestant Proselytism in Italy.*[44]

Borgongini had tangled, in Seta, with a Methodist minister who by no means was prepared to surrender to Borgongini's demands nor to admit the nuncio's interpretation of the law on admitted cults. To Borgongini's claim that the law on admitted cults did not allow him to proselytize, Seta replied: "Logic would suggest that the law would require an article that said, 'proselytism against Catholicism is prohibited.'" Yet there was, he pointedly asserted, no such law. Borgongini tried to respond by asserting that Italian law did not allow for antifascist propaganda, and therefore "it does the same [that is, forbid] for anti-Catholic propaganda." The Methodist minister was not impressed by this logic. Borgongini feared that the minister had bribed the local mayor (*podestà*) and perhaps even the prefect of Aquila. Seta had not done so; yet Borgongini rightly sensed that the fascist authorities, at this early stage, supported the Methodist community, though he could not imagine why. Meanwhile, the minister had started building a temple, though the government had not yet approved the project. Borgongini concludes his pro memoria lugubriously, commenting on the building of the church that "the construction goes on unrelentingly, day and night."[45]

From the point of view of Catholic participants in the dispute, this was a low point in the war against Protestant proselytizing in San Sebastiano. Here one sees themes common in the archival literature in the early 1930s. Protestant pastors were defiant in the face of Catholic resistance. The hated Methodists, backed by wealthy Anglo-Saxons and the British government, induced poor and simple Catholics to convert with promises of money or work or pressed pamphlets on them they were not equipped to interpret. The alliance of evangelicals and despised (and defiant) ex-priests, especially among the militant Methodists, galled. The local clergy were destitute; some converted to one of the Protestant sects out of sheer economic desperation. Catholic prelates and Protestant ministers could not agree on the meaning and implications of the law on admitted cults, and some Protestant ministers were willing and fully able to dispute the meaning of the law with an Eminence from the Vatican. The Wesleyans did not fear interference from local law enforcement, some of whom appeared to sympathize with them. Methodists began building their temple without fear of governmental opposition. Indeed, in this case the Wesleyan minister threatened Borgongini: both America and Britain would object, he threatened, if a new law prohibiting Protestant proselytizing were enacted. "Apostate priest" Seta, loathed by diocesan and Roman priests, himself was self-possessed, poised, and fully confident that he had the backing of two powerful Anglo-Saxon countries. Circumstances could not then have seemed much worse to the Vatican. With little confidence, it would, first, encourage the local ordinary to bring the fight to the Protestants. For its part the Vatican would harness its own resources in uninhibited fashion.

The bishop launched a literary campaign by appealing to the fascist authorities, beginning with a letter written personally to Mussolini.[46] Bagnoli, who had persuaded himself that the rebellion was temporary, was confident that appeals to Il Duce and to the prefect of Aquila would reduce the region to ecclesial order. So, too, were the editors of *OR*, who, as Spini observes, regarded the situation in a small mountain village with irrational gravity, as if it were a case of the "church standing or falling" (*stantis aut cadentis ecclesiae*).[47] Having launched a series of articles replete with "unbelievable insults and vulgarities"[48] entitled *Nella Nona Bolgia*—in *Inferno* 28 Dante populates the ninth *bolgia* with sowers of discord and schism—*OR* in one article written in early 1931 threatened: "The competent authorities have been informed and certainly arm themselves out of respect for the Religion of the State and for public order."[49] This threat, which its authors believed would unnerve the Methodists, was to prove empty; the fascist authorities, as I have noted already, initially refused to cooperate with representatives of the Religion of the State.

An ex-priest—by then the enemy non plus ultra of the clerical caste—Seta, for the three years he was pastor (1931–34), was a special target of *OR*'s writers. It was said that Seta had led licentious games with the young, gave himself over to illicit pleasures, and conducted parodies of the mass: all fabrications. He was, in addition, a socialist: hardly surprising for an apostate priest. Other articles questioned the sexual morality of the young women who attended the evangelical meetings—rather like the charges against Mastroianni; both sets of charges were likely bogus. Meanwhile, Bagnoli denounced Seta to Mussolini as a procurator of an abortion for a woman in his diocese—this after the decaying body of a dead rabbit was discovered by two boys in a field.[50]

If these charges may be doubted, and if Mussolini ignored the local bishop, Seta would soon incur misery all too real. His own words, to the delight of his clerical enemies, would engulf him in controversy not only with the church but also, fatefully, with the fascist state. They would also end his ministry in the Villa. In October 1932 Seta was accused of having defined Italy as an uncivil country, a land of mission, "like Africa"—precisely the sort of charge which had incensed Tacchi Venturi. In fact, in one of his sermons Seta had declared that, at the time, *fascist* Italy was an uncivil country; it was his congregation's job to civilize it. This comment was reported to the prefect of Aquila. Seta wrote the prefect, insisting on his patriotism, his love for country, and his practice of praying for Italy. It was this love that had led him to speak as he had. Besides, as evangelicals they had little political power, and so he preached a strict separation of church and state. *OR* took the opportunity to stigmatize all the evangelicals as communists (*rossi*).[51] Seta, it was alleged, had had a rich socialist past. Given the reaction, a frustrated Seta left the Villa on 7 June 1934 to take another pastorate in Padua.[52] The smear campaign undertaken remorselessly by the leading daily of the Vatican had been effective.

Still, despite Tacchi Venturi's smug promises, the British Wesleyans had not ceded the field of San Sebastiano. To the contrary, they had expressed grievances about their treatment at the hands of Italian law enforcement to the British government. Later, Borgongini learned from the director general of the Ministry of Cults that he had been deluged by "a continuous flow of letters" from the governmental and religious authorities in England. In addition, a Wesleyan bishop, livid with news of the harshness of the Catholic campaign of suppression, crossed the Channel and made for Rome, where he went "expressly to further the cause of the Protestants."[53]

Trouble came from authorities closer to home, too. Though not particularly sympathetic to the evangelicals, the prefect of Aquila was disturbed by the "excessive clamor" of the Catholic counteroffensive, which he thought was counterproductive. Second, none of the police authorities appreciated the campaign of *OR*. To the ears of those in the Questura, the criticism of the Methodists sounded like an imperfectly concealed critique of *their* work. It seemed to be for these reasons that the prefect defended the mayor; he also recommended more prudence to the Catholic authorities. Bagnoli complained at the time, after failing to persuade the mayor to block the construction of the Methodist temple, that the political and civil authorities were habitually favoring evangelical over Catholic clerics and enabling Protestant propaganda. He was, he claimed, a victim of reprisals and *vendette.* Bagnoli's complaint should have been taken to mean that he was not, in fact, sympathetic to the Wesleyans; yet for mysterious reasons he was rumored to be.

It was in 1931, too, that Bishop Bagnoli invited four learned Jesuits to conduct Catholic preaching missions (twenty-four in that year alone). Bagnoli conspired with a Jesuit more cultured, if less powerful or well-known, than his slightly younger contemporary, Tacchi Venturi. A well-recognized and even prize-winning composer of Latin poetry, a gifted writer of hymns who would in 1942 become the official hymnographer of the Congregation of Rites, Fr. Vittorio Genovesi (1887–1967) quietly bent his singular talents—as Camillo Crivelli and other Jesuits would theirs—to the resistance of the evangelical invasion. He wrote a short pamphlet entitled *Against the Errors of the Protestants,* anchoring each of his arguments in a scriptural text designed to vanquish Biblicist evangelicals on their own ground.[54] He also wrote polemical poems. One, unimaginatively entitled, "Chi sono gli heretici," urges its auditors to flee the false prophets of the day, who were wolves in sheep's clothing, traitors to their country and consciences, and, with this couplet, concludes its friendly counsel:

> Neppure dite loro: "buon giorno!"
> Chè l'uomo eretico è un pervertito.[55]

Fr. Genovesi also collaborated with Bagnoli to bring the local Wesleyan community into potential conflict with Catholic men imported from Rome and the surrounding villages for the occasion, as this letter from May of 1931 suggests:

> Rome, 27 May 1931
>
> Finally [Genovesi writes to Bagnoli] I have succeeded in deferring my trip to Venice after the Solemnity of Corpus Domini. . . . I believe that's a minor miracle, and I presume that the work we wish to complete will be to the glory of God.
>
> Your Excellency will have the goodness, if you wish that I come, to send me an appropriate letter of invitation, so that I might justify my presence in Villa S. Sebastiano. Otherwise [the Methodists] will have a pretext for saying that I have gone in order to provoke disorder. If you do not wish to send me the letter, could you have it sent to me from the parish priest? In any case, it is necessary that I have the invitation from an ecclesiastical authority.

> On that day, twenty men will come from Rome. It will be necessary to have a good number also from Avezzano and Tagliacozzo. It is important that it be an imposing mass of men. Your Excellency should see whether it is convenient on that day to make a procession of the Most Holy Sacrament through the village. . . .
>
> The tactic we will use will be this: I will preach in the morning on the Eucharist without any hint of polemic. If they provoke us, I will respond with another sermon in the evening. The Catholic men will be on the streets and will hear them insult our religion; they will react. In the contrary case, they will stay at their posts. . . . If the Protestants provoke us, we will summon the Questura, to send them away and warn them. For now, it is necessary that nothing be known.[56]

This was not the first time that Bagnoli had attempted to bait the evangelicals of the Villa into violence. Throughout the early 1930s the bishop had often provoked the evangelicals in the town piazza. This made the evangelicals subversive in the eyes of the fascist authorities, who were preoccupied with maintaining order.[57] Critical to the effectiveness of the anti-Protestant campaign, the evolving attitude of the local government would slowly change the fortunes of the Methodists in the Villa.

Given that Genovesi had come to provoke the evangelicals into insult or violence, for which they would then be punished by the authorities, it cannot be surprising to learn that he and the three Jesuits he brought with him were, to say the least, unwelcome by the evangelical community, which they attempted to split. Uninvited, they entered the homes of the major evangelical families to convince their members to abandon the false religion. Assisted by other Catholics, they forced a woman to repudiate the evangelical faith. They baptized two evangelical babies, it was alleged, by having one parent's debt forgiven by a Catholic creditor—here using venal tactics of which they accused Methodist missionaries. They were said to have encouraged wives of the Methodists not to have relations with their husbands. At the conclusion of the "grand mission," *OR* reported, on the basis of accounts supplied it by Jesuit Tacchi Venturi, that the heresy of the mountains in Abruzzo had been nearly entirely extirpated.[58]

This was not true. British diplomats and Methodist leaders in Rome were demanding permission from the Italian government to erect a Methodist temple in Villa San Sebastiano. Frustrated, Borgongini resolved to go to the top of the national government. He saw Mussolini. On the "unfortunate dispute concerning Villa San Sebastiano," the nuncio divulges that Wesleyan proselytism had again begun with the system of so-called private meetings, which Borgongini thought illegal. In order to be kept on, the nuncio complained, construction workers were required to declare in writing that they had converted to the Wesleyan sect—perhaps true, perhaps an attempt to smear the Methodists.[59]

THE FORTUNES OF THE WESLEYAN COMMUNITY

The temple was eventually completed, but Borgongini expressed the hope that he could secure a governmental decree keeping it from being opened, as the British Methodists had launched "a real aggression against the good faith of the [Catholic] population." In it he argued that, "against the established laws of Public Security and the other laws regarding admitted cults, Protestants are perpetrating in Abruzzi a real spiritual aggression." He attached a copy of his letter, which he humbly asked Pacelli "in your high wisdom to send to [Rafaelle] Cardinal Rossi." To Mussolini he reported that the Wesleyan sect was active among "the tranquil populations of Abruzzo" that "have no need of being evangelized by ministers of the English *chiesuole.*" In his letter to Pacelli, the nuncio goes on to explain that recently he had "sent a new and long note to the Honorable Mussolini." He had thoughtfully furnished Il Duce with a verbose interpretation of all the laws on admitted cults, repeating ad nauseam his familiar arguments and concluding finally by imploring Mussolini to consider this "most grave case." Mussolini did not respond. Sounding rather like the paranoid Tacchi Venturi, Borgongini would soon write Pacelli a letter that might have interested Mussolini more: aside from being objectionably British, the Methodist ministers "have the smell of being spies."[60] Borgongini thus makes them guilty of espionage as well as of having communist sympathies.

In the end, permission to open the temple was denied to the evangelicals, especially after the crisis of Catholic Action had passed. The coordinated attempts of Bagnoli and Genovesi, along with Tabacco, had provoked disorders and incidents. These were then brought to the attention of the government and blamed on the evangelicals. The complaints made by Borgongini and others that the Methodists had violated the permitted cults laws were not decisive, though the charge that the Wesleyans were foreigners, or spies, may have made them more suspicious. In any event, the local government, which had once used the evangelical project for its purposes, turned against it, especially as its

Catholic enemies represented it as fanatical and subversive. In the end, the fascist authorities concluded that the temple had to remain closed to maintain public order.[61] In the wake of this decision, the evangelical community began to use a subterranean space in the temple in the hopes of going unnoticed.

Soon grave dangers would come from actions of the Methodist community's pastors, who would complete the temporary ruin of the Methodist community. One of these, Carlo Zardi, shocked his congregation by converting to Catholicism.[62] His defection prompted the return to Catholicism of a large segment of the Wesleyan group. Another, Salvatore Scivales, intensified tensions internal to the Methodist church. He absconded at night. The tensions he left unresolved included the very serious charge that the Methodists were subversive and fanatical. The charge of subversion seems to have originated in the antipatriotic and antifascist words Seta had pronounced in October 1931. Anti-Protestant campaigners would emphasize these themes, and their repetition in letters and editorials in *OR* would make them, finally, heard and believed. In the eyes of the fascist authorities, so preoccupied with the maintenance of order, the mere charge of subversion was effective. They closed down the church.

These actions led to the near extinction of the community. When Francesco Cacciapuoti, sent by the Methodist hierarchy, reopened the church in March 1937, it had a dwindling congregation. After initial success, Cacciapuoti ran into trouble in October 1939, on the commemoration of the fallen in the fascist "revolution." The pastor's refusal to participate—a reversal of the liberal-era evangelical tendency to celebrate on days celebrating the Italian government and as ostentatiously as possible—led to local fascist hostility, and he was sent into confinement. The entry of Italy into the Second World War coincided with the end of Cacciapuoti's pastorate and the near disappearance of the evangelical community from the Marsica.[63]

Six years later the Methodist temple would finally be opened in the most improbable circumstances. German troops billeted in the vacant temple in 1943. When they left, it was restored by the Nazis to the community for the purposes for which it was originally designed.[64]

RECENTLY RELEASED VATICAN DOCUMENTS: NEW PERSPECTIVES

Thoroughly dispirited with the news from Abruzzo, in the form of letters from Catholic parishioners in San Sebastiano and even personal visits to the

Vatican by at least one parishioner, Pius XI himself finally intervened—this at a time when the tide had already turned against the Methodists. In February 1936 he summoned Emanuele Coranati, OSB, to the Vatican. Coranati was an old friend of Pius XI as well as a deeply respected abbot of the Benedictine monastery of St. John the Evangelist in Parma.[65] According to Coranati's testimony, he was asked in a personal audience with the frustrated Pius XI on 7 February 1936 "to construct a most accurate picture regarding the religious situation of the Parish of Villa San Sebastiano."[66] In uncovering the facts, communal relations, and tensions in San Sebastiano, Coranati's newly released report is critical in unlocking some of the mysteries of San Sebastiano, particularly why the Catholic mayor and the bishop both were represented as being favorable to the Protestants.

In the conclusion to his report, the abbot quite confidently states: "The establishment of Protestantism in the Villa did not originate in a crisis of faith, but was a popular revolt against the bishop, nourished by rancor."[67] This is true but incomplete. To whose rancor was the abbot referring? Who was angry with whom? And for what reasons? In this case, the answer lies deep in the hidden history and angers among and between community members, between now-Protestant and Catholic, wealthy and peasant, parishioner and bishop.

The first thing that strikes one in the abbot's account is that the rancor originated not from below, from poor peasants, but from above, that is, from powerful Catholic families, especially the Amicucci and Conti, the leading politicians and *petit*-élite of the Villa. Deeply aggrieved at some of the bishop's transgressions against members of their families, they publicized and reported on them to authorities in the Vatican. In a vendetta culture, they threatened to avenge the shame the bishop had caused them, and, to some extent, they succeeded. They did so by representing the anti-Protestant Bagnoli as a sympathizer with the Protestants. The Catholic mayor Amicucci *did,* in fact, favor the Protestants in civil and political matters, but his brief and insincere conversion was a way of avenging a profoundly personal hurt for which Amicucci thought the bishop responsible. At the same time, he joined forces with the Conti, who had its own grievances with the bishop. Together, the two families conspired against the bishop in a campaign of mudslinging; they made Bagnoli seem to the Vatican unsympathetic to the anti-Protestant campaign.[68] Though nothing could be further from the truth, confusion sown in the 1930s came to be reflected, very naturally, in all historical writing. The abbot's report, a brilliant piece of sleuthing and sharp judgment, clarifies the families' motivation and representation. These have much to do, again, with vengeance in a vendetta culture.

The abbot confirms that community rancor deepened with Bagnoli's dismissal of Fr. Bernardino. However, he gives a very different picture of Padre Bernardino than is contained in the Methodist sources used by Leone and, indeed, makes Fr. Bernardino's dismissal seem not only warranted but obligatory. Yet, because he depended on clerical sources tied to Bagnoli, he gets much wrong. According to those whom the abbot interviewed, Fr. Bernardino immediately began conducting himself in odd fashion. He attended or held functions, of mixed religious and secular character, until late at night. When he did, girls sang upon a stage "in indecent clothing, accompanied by cinematic screenings." He established an institute for Catholic nuns who had come to their profession without any novitiate and thus without any preparation for the intensities of the religious life. Some of these charges may have been exaggerated or simply fabricated. Still, having been made aware of the priest's behavior, the bishop "warned him, threatened him fruitlessly, and finally removed him."[69] Here the bishop's behavior was, in the abbot's view, beyond reproach; indeed, it corresponded precisely to the requirements of Canon Law, not to mention the canons of common sense—that is, *if* the charges he gathered against Fr. Bernardino had any basis in fact. They did not.

As the abbot reports, Bernardino's affability and social energy made him an "idol of the people."[70] When they discovered Bernardino had been removed, powerful local Catholic families joined those sympathetic with Father Bernardino—but for their own reasons: "as a vendetta" to "call upon the Protestants," whose Wesleyan sect they joined—but only briefly and as an expression of dissatisfaction with Bishop Bagnoli. No mention is even made of Gargano, the converted, recently returned immigrant credited by Leone with having started the Methodist community as a protest against repressive Catholic powers. Once the initial wave of anger passed, Bagnoli did not react except by attempting to calm the community, including the newly converted Methodists. This may be the source of some of the false allegations that he was sympathetic to the Protestants, which were heard immediately.

The portion of the community that had remained Catholic stated, insincerely, that "the bishop had no desire to struggle against Protestantism." This was not fair; it was not true. The statement does indicate that some, at least, in the Catholic community were anxious to *portray* him as pro-Protestant to the Catholic authorities in Rome.[71] But who? And why? The abbot reports that the teacher of the elementary class, Maestro Filippo Conti, had from time to time written to Rome to accuse the bishop of negligence and incompetence *di fronte ai protestanti.* "While conducting this inquest," the abbot writes, "certain things regarding the religious situation in Villa San Sebastiano were brought to light," not least of which was disillusionment with the bishop among his diocesan priests as well as "certain complaints periodically made against the bishop" by ordinary parishioners. Unfortunately, almost nothing is known about the nature of the diocesan priests' complaints, much less than we do about those of the local worthies. Conti imagined himself as a local *defensor fidei.* While this was in some sense risible, what he revealed was in no sense funny to Abbot Coranati. Among other things, Conti accused both Bagnoli and the parish priest of negligence and incompetence in the face of the Protestant threat.[72] Conti's charges, however, were not motivated by interest in the presence of the Protestants in the Villa—whom he joined temporarily and insincerely and for his own purposes—but by other, darker motives, above all, revenge for an insult from the bishop and a wound that Conti had long allowed to fester.

Indeed, the abbot informs the pope that Filippo Conti was motivated by pressures common to traditional honor-and-shame cultures. Conti was the nephew of Giuseppe D'Andrea, the former parish priest of the Villa, and Fr. Bernardino's predecessor. Before dying, this priest gave 6,000 lire for the propagation of the faith and contributed 30,000 lire to Bagnoli to help with priestly vocations. After his uncle's death, Conti accused Bishop Bagnoli of extorting from Fr. Giuseppe the aforementioned sums and came to describe the scandalous circumstances in which the extortion occurred. While D'Andrea was confessing to Bagnoli, the bishop—"in order to win the benevolence of Padre D'Andrea," whom he knew to be affluent—performed an "act of self-humbling and self-interested trust" (in the abbot's words) and "obtained the generous donation!"[73] In other words, he withheld absolution until Fr. D'Andrea had made a promise of a significant gift. That would have constituted a gross violation of the etiquette of the confessional and indeed a violation of Canon Law.[74] Furious with the unbecoming and indeed coercive actions of Bishop Bagnoli, Conti made one of several angry trips to the Holy See, without any profitable result.

This was a turning point. Conti's frustration with the bishop deepened in the face of what appeared to be indifference from the Vatican. "From this point," the abbot states, Conti nourished "a most lively resentment against the bishop, compounded with hate." Conti made no mystery of this resentment. He spoke of it with the abbot, "retailing for me," Coranati reports, "unsavory details regarding the Bishop." He spoke of it with two monks of Coranati's abbey who had accompanied their abbot to the Villa. The abbot concludes: "I cry when I hear [Conti] when he is inebriated, which is often." Conti was sober enough, nonetheless, to form a group whose members were, for different reasons, hostile to the bishop. These came to include the mayor of Tagliacozzo, Amicucci and his brothers, and "certain priests in Avezzano." That Bagnoli had alienated priests from the diocese as well as laymen Coranati repeated several times.[75] Though almost everything else alleged about Bishop Bagnoli by the Villa's powerful Catholic families was simply untrue, this one credible allegation—regarding the extortion—was not only serious; it made the other, incredible ones more plausible.

The abbot makes clear why the Amicucci also felt such ill will toward the bishop. On the occasion of the apparent suicide of one of the Amicucci brothers, the family asked for a religious funeral for their dead sibling. The bishop refused to allow it.[76] Technically, the bishop was correct, but pastorally, one may say, his behavior was insensitive. In any event, "friendly persons intervened," assuring the priest and bishop that the so-called suicide had been an accidental death; so the funeral was permitted. Still, as the abbot reports, "this was considered by the Amicucci a personal offense," and Bagnoli adds, ominously, that the brothers "have not forgotten."[77] By this point, needless to say, there was bad blood between the Amicucci and the bishop. This episode cemented the Amicucci with the Conti families in their deep antipathy to Bagnoli.

The resentment was further deepened by the supposed refusal by officials of the Commune of Tagliacozzo to issue licenses to the small businessmen of the Villa—apparently on religious grounds. Small Catholic merchants were enraged when officials issued licenses to Protestant businessmen. The abbot reports that, for unknown reasons, the bishop was believed to have supported the Protestant petitions for the license. This was untrue. Here one of the Amicucci, Domenico, in his capacity as mayor of Tagliacozzo, used his position to grant licenses to Protestant petitioners. The Catholic mayor was motivated to do so out of anger with the bishop and to strengthen the charge that Bagnoli was philo-Protestant. This Bagnoli vigorously, and with some justice, denied.[78] Be that as it may, the reasons for the rage felt in Catholic circles at the fascist mayor's favorable treatment of the Villa's Methodists now come into sharp focus.

The abbot's report continues. After the earthquake, Conti's brother, Amerigo, a medical doctor, proposed that the citizens of the Villa be housed in the *cassette* built by Fr. Bernardino. Coranati reports: "Many Catholic families seem to have been denied barracks erected after the earthquake." He notes that Amicucci was mayor of Tagliacozzo and asks, rhetorically, "A coincidence?" It was not. The Catholic Amicucci granted licenses and gave housing to Protestant seekers as a way of frustrating Bagnoli and of tarring him with the charge of preferring Protestants in the distribution of social and economic goods. The charges continued. A dispute over a loan of 80,000 lire led to "strong resentment" of the bishop among several business leaders, as a consequence of which Bagnoli developed a reputation of being, on top of everything else, a usurer. The business leaders were, the abbot reports, in league with the political and administrative authorities of Avezzano, and all collaborated in seeing that Amicucci's orders, driven by hostility for the bishop, would be executed.[79]

For these reasons, Coranati says, the citizens of the Villa had "periodically written to Rome regarding the motives that actuate the bishop." Eventually, the community was so frustrated that "they raised their voice publicly to the Holy Father." On 26 December 1935 Maestro Conti traveled to Rome. Somehow, Conti obtained an audience with Borgongini-Duca, to whom he complained about Bagnoli's "acquiescence" to Protestantism.[80] What Borgongini did not know, and never perceived, was that Conti only *represented* Bagnoli as pro-Protestant. The surviving letters of the bishop prove that he campaigned vigorously against the establishment of the evangelical church as well as the founding and opening of the Methodist temple. The abbot is clear on the motivations of the Conti and Amicucci families: the charge of philo-Protestantism was an effective theme designed "to conceal the reasons that truly motivate them and serve as the pretext for public protestation and even for making their voice heard by the Holy Father."[81]

Hostility to Bagnoli had religious as well as social and economic sources. Frustrated, among other things, with the quality of religious life in the parish, the Catholic community appealed to the bishop. Previously, members of the Jesuit order had exercised what the abbot describes as "a popular ministry" in the Villa—a more different view of the Jesuit mission from that of the evangelicals one can hardly imagine—and some parishioners began to agitate for their return. The community approached the parish priest and even began to gather signatures for a petition asking for the return of the Jesuits. The bishop refused. Instead, he simultaneously criticized the Jesuit fathers *and,* now, the "struggle against the Protestants." According to community members interviewed by the abbot, the bishop's "only mode of responding to the Protestant threat was to argue it was a matter of past history." This was more or less true. After a period of fighting all evangelical initiative, Bagnoli concluded that it was best to take an irenic approach. The alliance of those hostile to the bishops criticized this decision, arguing that the Catholic community ought to act aggressively, as in the past. They complained, again, that Bagnoli was ineffective in resisting the Protestant incursion.[82]

On 26 December 1935 Conti, still angry that his uncle had been extorted without compensation or action against Bagnoli, again went to Rome. He got another audience with Borgongini-Duca, to whom he denounced the acquiescence of the bishop and even his clergy to the evangelicals. Now enraged, Borgongini replied, "If the Bishop and the parish priest do not struggle against the Protestants, I will remove them both from their posts." He also ordered both Bagnoli and the parish priest to write to Buffarini.[83] Having returned to the Villa from the Vatican to complain about Bagnoli, Sig. Conti loudly warned the parish priest (Abbot Coranati puts the warning in caps and underlines it):

> FROM THE MOMENT THAT THE JESUITS DO NOT RETURN AND I AM DENIED SATISFACTION, I WILL TAKE MY REVENGE [*MI VENDICO*], AND I WILL PUBLICIZE THE QUESTION OF THE MONEY [EXTORTED FROM MY UNCLE]. IF I AM NOT GIVEN IMMEDIATE SATISFACTION, I WILL PUBLISH ARTICLES IN THE PROTESTANT NEWSPAPERS.[84]

According to the abbot, Conti was not exactly taciturn about the issue of extortion.

On another occasion, loudly complaining about the bishop, Conti roared in public,

> PERHAPS I SHOULD HAVE TOLD ALL FROM THE MOMENT THE BISHOP TREATED ME IN THIS WAY.[85]

Several weeks later Bishop Bagnoli was with Coranati. Bagnoli explained to the abbot that, after the initial and vigorous efforts of the anti-Protestant campaign, he had come to conclude that the better mode of resisting the evangelicals was by living a Christian life, in liturgy and in the example of his life. When the first moment of agitation had passed, the bishop, considering that the schism was motivated by rancor and not a crisis of faith, "thought that he could not hold the village in turmoil indefinitely and therefore resorted to sweetness and charity." How? He operated "through persuasion and the development of an intense religious and especially Eucharistic action."[86]

But Conti remained unhappy. He continued to denounce the bishop loudly and publicly for his inertia in the anti-Protestant campaign. Having reached this point in his report, the abbot comes to his conclusion. "The Amicucci and the Conti took up the cause of Padre Bernardino . . . and, as a vendetta against the bishop, called upon the Protestants."[87] In both Protestant and Catholic sources, disappointment with Bagnoli ignited a tinderbox.

It is from one of the bishop's letters that we learn how the Protestant problem in San Sebastiano was, from the viewpoint of the Vatican, finally solved. Evidently, a mission recently undertaken in San Sebastiano—to which Coranati had made brief, cryptic reference in his report—had been effective. A mission in this case means something like the Jesuit mission previously undertaken in the Villa or what in American evangelical circles is communicated by the term "revival." In the Catholic case, a group of priests, usually trusted, learned, and members of a religious order, is invited into a community. Their charge is to revitalize it religiously. In San Sebastiano, perhaps at the suggestion of Abbot Conti, Benedictines had been brought in to preach against the local Methodists and on behalf of their own church. According to Bishop Bagnoli, "The preaching of the Benedictine fathers" had had "optimal results." The adepts of the Wesleyan church, according to the abbot, began to return in large numbers to the Catholic church.[88] In fact, the desertion was so complete that the Wesleyan church soon had a population that was exiguous in number. The Catholic sources say nothing about other reasons—like pressure from the fascist government—for the diminution of the evangelical population, though these were obviously effective, if only temporarily. Much of the narrative regarding the effect of the Benedictines was corroborated by the new parish priest of San Sebastiano, Giovanni Bellarini, who wrote to Pacelli on 24 February 1936. The Benedictine monks had brought to the Villa "the noble odor of holiness."[89] This, the parish priest argued, not entirely convincingly, was decisive in returning the apostates to the Catholic church. At this point, the ex-Catholic minister of the Methodist church, Carlo Zardi, had been instructed to leave the Villa. Apparently, he had begun to start new Protestant communities in Aquila.[90]

If so, Zardi's actions could only have magnified the shock sent through the curial offices by his next reported choice. On 23 August 1936 Zardi had, startlingly, reconverted to Catholicism.[91] One year later he wrote to Pacelli. A remarkable, poignant document (it was at least regarded as such by those who read it at the time, including the pope), it is wholly sincere, suffused with remorse, and fixed on making amends for deeds he now regarded as sinfully ruinous of souls. "I am the ex-evangelical pastor of the Villa San Sebastiano," he begins his letter to Pacelli. He reports that he has returned to the one true church, which has brought him joy. Yet a frightening "revelation" had been given him of countless souls that his own conduct had imperiled: "The joy of my return has not made me forget the brothers whom I voluntarily separated [from the Roman Catholic church], and I wish, with all the ardor of my soul, to give them that which I myself have received." As a means of reestablishing right relations with the church, of relieving an overburdened conscience, and of saving endangered souls, he made a proposal to Pacelli. Could he establish a "House for Prodigals" for those who, as he had, strayed and rejected the "sacred deposit of our faith"? He describes conversations he had had with priests and bishops, who had encouraged him in this endeavor.[92] Pacelli responded, thanking Zardi for his letter (in which Pacelli had underlined in blue pencil the word "revelation"), expressing his pleasure with Zardi's "noble sentiments" and apostolic work. He informed Zardi that he had spoken with Monsignor Sargolini, then the assistant general for Catholic Action, who was looking at the possibility of implementing Zardi's plan.[93] A letter from Fr. Ottaviano Ghigliotti, a Benedictine who had participated in the missions to San Sebastiano, reported that he had become friendly with Zardi and his family, which had fallen into dire economic straits.[94] Serious economic and genuine religious motives seem to have suggested this plan to Zardi.[95]

In another letter Pacelli reported that the news of Zardi's conversion had reached and even enlivened the pope. "The Holy Father," he divulged to the secretary of the Sacred Congregation of the Council, "is directly interested" in the case of Zardi. The anti-Protestant polemicist Igino Giordani was also in touch with Pacelli; he had taken an interest in Zardi. So, too, had the director of Catholic Action, Ciriaci.[96] Why the pope or these other luminaries in Italian Catholicism took such interest in Zardi is not known. Perhaps the pope was genuinely moved by his reconversion. Also plausible is the possibility that Zardi could now be exploited by the pope as a powerful symbol of right, self-correcting behavior for wayward Protestants. One of their own, and a famous pastor at that, had seen the light and put himself back on the one true path to salvation, which, as Zardi himself now proclaimed, went only through Rome.[97] What more powerful example of correct—that is to say, obedient—behavior, in an Italy so vulnerable to Protestant penetration, was available to the pope? Months later it was the pope and the curia who were shocked.

Zardi had left Rome. Long suspected of being actuated by economic motives, he had taken another Protestant pastorate. That was alarming enough. But another enemy of the church would soon enter the picture.

Nothing else is heard about San Sebastiano for two years. What we do hear is an utterly odd coda that occurred long after the events just narrated. In a handwritten letter to the office of the secretary of state written on 19 January 1939 Borgongini reports that, in a recent meeting with Buffarini, he had made several complaints against Farinacci. He had been told that Farinacci had written to Mussolini "on behalf of the Protestants." More specifically, Farinacci had asked for the temple at the Villa San Sebastiano, long closed, to be reopened. Buffarini assured the nuncio that the temple was never reopened, but "he did not explain the interest of Farinacci in acting on behalf of the Protestants." He had learned from other sources that Farinacci had been inspired to such an action by a "certain Sig. Pantaleo, a Protestant."[98]

Farinacci was by no means a Protestant. Yet, as is well-known, he had always loathed Catholicism. Like Mussolini and other early fascist leaders, he was profoundly anticlerical. He was certainly among the anticlerical fascists who did not celebrate the Conciliazione. Farinacci was motivated to assist the evangelicals of the Villa out of deeply felt anti-Catholic and anticlerical hostility. In fact, Farinacci's actions illustrate a central theme: it was often fascist officials acting in bad faith who assisted the evangelicals in any way. Farinacci aided them in a moment of vengeance, as had the Conti and Amicucci. It was just at this moment that Farinacci, criticized by the church, chose to defend the Racial Laws by pointing out in his newspaper that nothing in them required Jews to be treated more harshly than they had by popes over the centuries.[99] The strange story of San Sebastiano thus ended with one last attempt, by a despiser of Catholicism and its clerics, to reestablish Protestantism in the Villa and, at the same time, to demoralize the Vatican and quiet potential criticism of the new antisemitic program.[100] Perhaps it is fitting that the archfascist Farinacci's hopes were realized by troops loyal to Hitler, and that these two uncultured despisers of Christianity succeeded in establishing, finally, a lasting Methodist community in Villa San Sebastiano.

Both Methodist and Catholic sources lead us to conclude that the establishment of an evangelical community was rooted in profound disappointment with Bishop Bagnoli. In Leone's view, the conversion to evangelical Christianity was motivated from below. An americano who had converted in the United States and wished to convert his fellow Italians had spearheaded the effort to establish an evangelical community in Villa San Sebastiano. It was he who was first in touch with leaders of the Methodist church. By contrast, Abbot Coranati's account suggests that the conversion was stoked from above, namely, by the leading Catholic families of the Villa, who had other reasons to be disappointed with the bishop. The abbot may well be right that the schism began in rancor; but that rancor had complex sources. For the nascent evangelical community, encouraged by evangelical emigrants, conversion was motivated chiefly by Bagnoli's dismissal of the popular Padre Bernardino. On the other hand, we hear almost nothing in the local Methodist sources—on which Leone, Rochat, and Spini all had to rely—about the Amicucci or Conti families' anger over his dismissal.

Motivations for conversion unmentioned in the Methodist sources are emphasized in the Catholic. Bellarini, for example, reports that the Protestants took advantage of his parishioners' extreme poverty to convert them away from Catholicism. According to Bellarini, Methodist proselytes said, "You see that the priests do not care about you. The Catholics will leave you to die. Come with us, and we will help you."[101] Bellarini is a credible source. His picture of local economic misery is convincing; it corresponds to what we know of hundreds of similar parishes in early-twentieth-century meridional Italy. Although not emphasized by Abbot Coranati, the punishing poverty experienced by the parishioners of San Sebastiano surely made some, regardless of their opinions (if any) of the local bishop, more receptive to Protestant proselytizing. Leone contemptuously dismisses the notion that the Methodists had won dollar converts, but there is simply an unignorable mountain of evidence to suggest that both British and American Methodists generated converts from the destitute by the provision of subsidies and other social services, including child and medical care. (Historians and anthropologists alike can tell you: this is how it has always been done.) The number of converts brought to evangelical Christianity by money rather than by zeal can never be determined with precision. The numbers were almost certainly underestimated by evangelicals and overestimated by Catholics. In any case, the newly available sources furnish interesting data here, data that tend to fit uneasily with the Methodist sources.

The embryonic evangelical community in Villa San Sebastiano felt the wrath of Bagnoli, whom they regarded as a hateful, implacable inquisitor hostile to evangelical Christianity. He did everything in his power, it seems, to block permission for the construction, then the opening, of the evangelical temple. The leading Catholic and fascist authorities regarded Bagnoli as weak and inert in the face of the Protestant menace. Many of the Catholic sources that do not originate in the episcopal offices of Avezzano (that is, those not written by Bagnoli or one of his parish priests), and above all those written by Abbot Coranati, reflect this view as well. Why? Because the leading Catholic families in the Villa depicted Bagnoli as such.

What about the reconversion to Catholicism of Carlo Zardi? Was *it* genuine, as Zardi's letters and his correspondence with luminaries like Igino Giordani, seem to indicate? Or was it opportunistic? Was Zardi, as Leone has it, manipulated by the Catholic clergy of Avezzano into reconverting? If not, why do we hear, in secular sources from the 1940s, that Zardi had resumed his evangelical ministry? The sources indicate more than once that Zardi was impecunious. At a more philosophical level, we might ask what "conversion" meant in meridional Italy in the fascist period. Zardi's motivations may remain always unclear. But the varied motives of the stakeholders in the Villa—which included prelates at the Vatican—will not.

All were motivated by rancor with the bishop, some because of his treatment of Father Bernardino. These latter tended to be poor peasants who were also motivated by anger with their Catholic *padroni.* It was these who made up the majority of those who stayed to form the impermanent community of Wesleyans. The Methodist missionaries intended to liberate Italy from clerical denomination, false religion, and, possibly, their Catholic social and economic overlords. Borgongini and other Vatican prelates were motivated by anti-Protestant animus as well as obedience to the pope. That animus may have included fear or suspicion of the Anglo-Saxons. What did they intend, other than to deconvert the new Protestants? Were they cultural imperialists? Did they want to subvert the fascist regime? Were they spies? This we, to a large extent, already knew. The Vatican's archival documents richly reveal mysteries surrounding Bishop Bagnoli's supposed acquiescence to the Protestants; the Catholic mayor's habits of preferring Protestants to Catholics for civic favors and his reasons for doing so; and, finally, the Conti family's motivations for complaining to the Vatican about the bishop. Those motivations were tied, as Abbot Coranati rightly observed, to rancor. Catholic defections to Methodism were just that: temporary absences, insincere expressions of interest in Methodist Christianity, which they used as an instrument to bring down a bishop whom they had other reasons, unrelated to religion, to despise. After the mission of the Benedictines, these Catholics, too, saw the Methodists as foreigners and heretics—ones they had been willing to exploit to avenge themselves against a bishop's blunders.

The complex history of Villa San Sebastiano illustrates how intractable for the Vatican the Protestant problem was. The pope and the most powerful clerics at the Vatican struggled for more than a decade against the British Wesleyans there. They brought literary and physical violence to bear. No tact was untried. Yet circumstances were well beyond their control. Some converts harbored resentment for the church, based on socioeconomic as well as religious motives. The local authorities defied the national law for reasons unknown to the bishop and to Borgongini. No single figure hurt the Catholic cause as much as Bishop Bagnoli. Their prize convert left the church for a second time and again took a pastoral position in an evangelical denomination. Even Farinacci improbably played a role in frustrating Catholic aims. Despite the immense energy and resources allotted; despite the visceral hatred they harbored for the Methodists; despite the violence they brought to bear—the evangelical community survived, if barely.

CHAPTER 6

The Apostolic Nuncio and the "Free Discussion" Clause (1934–35)

Over the course of the 1930s Borgongini-Duca flooded high-ranking officials in the Vatican and state government with letters regarding the meaning of the laws governing the religious activity of permitted cults. In the nuncio's immodest view, these letters had been highly effective. Mussolini, he said, had accepted in full the theses he had sustained. Buffarini, he claimed, had accepted "my view" about the character of apostates. The government did not disagree with "my theses" regarding the Laws of Public Security and evangelical propaganda.[1] These theses came to have three ever more repressive components. First, insofar as Protestant ministers were propagandizing and attempting to recruit converts, they were, in Borgongini's view, breaking the law. While Protestant worship was lawful, Protestant proselytizing was, he argued, illegal; it was not encompassed within the meaning of "discussion," which Law 1159 (1929) had made "wholly free."

Second, over time Buffarini's views came under the influence of the fascist legal code assembled by Minister of Justice Alfredo Rocco (1875–1935). Rocco intended to compose a new code that would secure not just the safety of the state but its political interests. Profoundly imbued with authoritarian ideology, the code dramatically reduced the rights of suspects and expanded the scope of police activity; collective interests wholly eclipsed individual rights. The code explicitly allowed police to stop meetings deemed any sort of threat to the continuity of the fascist state. In relation to my topic, it allowed police to shut down religious meetings thought to be suspicious—those held for the purposes of proselytizing, for example. Crucially, this was the case even if such meetings were held in private homes. For the purposes of the law, propagandizing transformed a private meeting into a matter of public interest, because framed as a potential threat to the nation; this opened the way for the intervention of the officials of public security. Under the growing influence of the so-called Rocco Code, promulgated in 1931, Borgongini came to call for police authorities to act upon the view that propaganda was illegal. He urged them to invade homes, violate privacy, disrupt prayer and worship, all on the suspicion that proselytizing might be occurring. Ultimately, he came to conclude that, as antifascist propaganda was prohibited, anti-Catholic propaganda, as he defined it, must be interdicted as well—and that the mere presentiment of anti-Catholic speech justified its swift suppression. The code legally made a private meeting public and opened the way for police questioning, harassment, raids, and arrests, even if based on subjective belief—a hunch. In 1934 this law, initially deemed unconstitutional, became the basis upon which the regime forbade and shut down private meetings.

Finally, Borgongini interpreted to his advantage a public statement of Mussolini's on the cohesive power of religion: he warned that Protestant recruitment efforts were an assault not just on Catholicism but also on the fascist government, which had legally made Catholicism the Religion of the State. In Borgongini's view, this made proselytizing not just an offense against the Catholic population but a treasonable act—a crime against the state. Although intended to command the attention of Mussolini, Borgongini's inflationary rhetoric never did so. However, it did persuade the powerful undersecretary, Buffarini; he would criminalize Pentecostalism at least partly on the basis of Borgongini's arguments, which he heard in person, many times, and in full. This was an act for which the nuncio would not credit Buffarini; instead, he declared that it was he who had "abolished Pentecostalism in all of Italy." Although Borgongini would soon learn to his regret that he had done no such thing and that the Pentecostal sect had not vanished, the rhetorical overkill reveals much about Borgongini's intentions, his insecurities, and, above all, his perception of his influence on Buffarini.

Borgongini's initial, less repressive views originated in reflection on the articles of the Concordat and the laws that clarified the status of religious minorities. As discussed above, the relevant legal clause for the permitted denominations was Article 5 of the implementing legislation: "There is complete freedom of discussion as far as religious matters are concerned" (*La discussione in materia religiosa è pienamente libera*). Catholic and Protestant leaders repeatedly clashed over the meaning of this ostensibly clear legal article. Protestants had habitually declared that the Concordat amounted to the "Magna Carta of religious liberty in Italy."[2] In practice, as we have seen, it was hardly that. Under pressure from Catholic authorities like Borgongini-Duca, police authorities would spy on, harass, detain, or even incarcerate members of evangelical circles, especially those thought to be (or just said to be) some sort of danger to public order or to the maintenance of the regime. Still, Borgongini's heavy-handed tactics did not always work, though it was seldom that the law actually protected evangelical communities from them. In the end, what typically won communities, especially the Pentecostals, religious liberty was the ignorance, sometimes willing, or indolence of local governmental authorities, their inconsistency in applying the laws, and the willingness of evangelicals to defy both.

JUSTIFYING VIOLENCE? BIBLE DISTRIBUTION AND THE LAW

In some cases Borgongini applied the admitted cults laws to vendors of Bibles. That is not surprising. However, vendors of Protestant Bibles were vulnerable, if the Bibles were discovered to be Protestant, to crowd hostility and even violence. Indeed, in one case a Jesuit priest was brought before judicial authorities for assaulting a purveyor of Protestant Bibles in Soriano nel Cimino, a small town perhaps ten miles east of Viterbo, within whose province it lay. The case is interesting, among other reasons, because the archival documents contain several different accounts, some Protestant, of the incident. Not surprisingly, the accounts do not agree; one of those written by a Catholic narrator goes so far as to omit the fact that one Father Scorza, S.J., had been charged with assault. What is clear is that Borgongini argued that the Jesuit's violence was justified on the basis of the permitted cults legislation, and that he recruited Buffarini in an attempt to exonerate the Jesuit and to tighten application of laws governing the sales of Bibles.

Two anonymous memoranda—one from a Jesuit convent identifying itself as having been composed at the community of Gesuiti degli Astalla/Ostalla 6, another from an unnamed individual who must have been a Jesuit—set the context, though not an utterly unbiased one.[3] According to this report, several americani had recently committed a series of scams (collectively called *truffe all'Americana*), selling Protestant Bibles on the pretext that they were permitted and approved by the Catholic church. During the previous June a book fair had been held at the Basilica of Maxentius in Rome. When it was discovered that some Catholics had been deceived into purchasing Protestant Bibles, indignant and sometimes violent reactions occurred—or were said to have occurred. The anonymous Jesuit referred his reader to two newspaper articles in which the incident had been reported.[4] He also claims that, when confronted, Protestants sometimes claimed that the laws on permitted cults had been changed to allow the sale of non-Catholic books.[5] These were charges repeated in the Catholic sources and were likely true, as Protestant complaints tended to focus on harm done to a vendor of Protestant literature rather than on the veracity of the charge of fraudulent sale. The incident described here fits neatly, in this respect, into this framework.

All documents—in this case, the anonymous memoranda, a letter from Borgongini to the director of cults, a letter from Buffarini to Borgongini, one newspaper article from a Catholic daily and one from the Baptist *Il Testimonio,* and, finally, a letter from the nuncio to Pacelli—agree on the following facts. A street vendor named Alfonso Maini, from Viareggio, claimed in 1934 to have been directed by Mussolini himself to sell Catholic Bibles and art. To the immense dismay of Borgongini-Duca, it was (again) not within the capacity of most ordinary Catholics, who were ordinarily poorly catechized, if at all, to distinguish Catholic from Protestant Bibles. Indeed, he acknowledges that many Catholics did not even know that the two had different contents. Undoubtedly traumatizing the nuncio, Buffarini bluntly admitted that he had found himself in difficulty, as "the Bible is the Bible, and it is neither Protestant nor Catholic."[6] In this case a thirteen-year-old girl named Anna Sapori, evidently well-educated, was the first to discover that the vendor Maini had swindled the crowd.[7] At this point, one who had purchased the Bible asked that his money be restored. The vendor refused. Soon municipal guards arrived. After a brief interrogation they discovered that the vendor had been sent not by Mussolini but by the Società Biblica Brittanica. This biblical society was later said by Borgongini-Duca to have been composed of "ex-priests and malefactors." Maini was selling books obviously not approved by the Catholic church. The crowd, enraged at having been victims of fraud—and at the hands of a Protestant foreigner no less—began to demand the wholesale restitution of their money. Soon, what began as a tiny protest against commercial fraud quickly turned into a tumult, with the crowd supposedly chanting, "Viva Mussolini—Viva L'Italia—Vive Soriano Fedele a la Re, All'Italia, Al Papa!"[8] Perhaps needless to say, this account has been fabricated; it reflects not social reality but a Catholic religio-political agenda, above all, hostility to evangelicals. Be that as it may, the transition from a small, commercial, apolitical protest to a raucous, dangerous, profascist, and pro-Catholic tumult was said to have occurred quite rapidly. This was evidently a crowd composed of "good Catholics and good Fascists." The second anonymous Jesuit memorandum concludes by suggesting the incident was begun because of "interference from foreigners."[9]

At this point, the moment at which Father Scorza, S.J., enters the picture, accounts differ quite dramatically. According to the near-hagiographical account that appeared in the friendly and influential Catholic newspaper *L'Avvenire d'Italia* (12 January 1934) and in both Jesuit memoranda, Father Scorza's main aim was to compose the crowd and restore calm among the defrauded Catholics. The author of the second Jesuit pro memoria remarks of the danger: "Popular indignation was very great, as was the threat [to the vendor]." Generously, Father Scorza himself restored money to those who had lost it. The crowd, evidently not completely calmed by this gesture, then started a bonfire into which they threw the Protestant Bibles, along with, the Jesuit improbably claims, "pornographic books and journals," which, he need not have observed, were "prohibited by the Holy Church."[10]

A very different picture emerges from the second account. Later, at a distance of months, the Società Biblica Brittanica took the case to the procurator of Viterbo and charged Scorza with assault. Why? The Jesuit author of the anonymous memorandum had concluded, apparently in an effort to sanitize the record, that "no violence was done" to the vendor. Indeed, Padre Scorza had saved him from physical harm.[11] Neither the Jesuit nor the Catholic press revealed all. As the Baptist newspaper *Il Testimonio* accurately reported, Fr. Scorza, far from pacifying the crowd, violently attacked Maini and, if anything, intensified the furor. According to the newspaper account, the Jesuit priest stood accused of "violence and commercial damage."

For this violent attack Scorza was brought before the penal tribunal of Viterbo. At his trial, the lawyer for the Jesuit maintained that the vendor, via the sale of his books, was making Protestant propaganda. In Scorza's mind, so his attorney argued, this constituted a provocation and a violation of the law. Invoking the decree of 24 June 1929—the Law on Permitted Cults, which gave permitted denominations rights, but with restrictions—he maintained that the sale of Protestant Bibles was tantamount to the "making of Protestant propaganda," which constituted an incitement against which it was lawful to respond. The tribunal was not persuaded. It sentenced Father Scorza to fifteen days of *reclusione* (a sort of temporary clerical disbarment).[12] Here the law punished a Catholic offender.

Outraged, Borgongini leapt to the Jesuit's defense. He never denied that Scorza had committed the assault of which he was convicted. It was on other grounds that he defended the Jesuit and, in the process, used the case to escalate his campaign against Protestant propaganda and proselytism. As was typical of the determined Borgongini, he wrote, involved, or conversed with Pacelli, two directors general of the Affairs of Cults, Buffarini, the minister for press and propaganda, and Pizzardo. In his mind, Scorza should have been acquitted, having been given legal protection by the law, which was, he maintains, violated by Maini and other Protestants. The nuncio also complained about the dubious and biased source (thinking here of the account supplied by *Il Testimonio*) of the story, which he believed had convinced the tribunal to convict the Jesuit.[13]

Borgongini began by writing, on 22 March 1935, to Pacelli. Surely unnecessarily, he reminded him that Mussolini had stated that to "injure the religious unity of the state was a crime against the nation." Borgongini then proceeds to argue that Scorza was convicted largely on the basis of an article that had appeared in a Baptist journal, which could not be expected to have reported objectively on the incident. He also insists that the laws on permitted cults distinguish clearly between freedom of religious speech and aggression against the Catholic faith, which is how he interpreted the sale of Protestant Bibles. He reports that the director general of cults was in full agreement with his theses, which he adds with his customary modesty, "are plainly in conformity with the law."[14] "In any case," the nuncio proceeds, "it has been verified" (Borgongini does not say by whom) that the tribunal's sentence was interpreted "in a contrary sense"—contrary, it seems, to Borgongini's interpretation of the law.[15] According to the ever-troublesome law for permitted cults, Protestants were allowed *libertà di esercizio* (again reminding Pacelli of a law with which he was all too familiar) but not the freedom to proselytize; and so the sale of Protestant Bibles clearly violated this restriction. Borgongini seems to imply that this violation excused or perhaps justified a violent attack on the Protestant vendor; in any case the only aggression he mentions is that borne by "the Catholic religion." All the Protestants involved in the case were said to be apostates, malefactors, uneducated (*incolti*), and, of course, foreigners; Borgongini suggests that their social status made them, not the Jesuit, guilty of aggression.[16]

The nuncio then moved his campaign to the office of the Ministry of Cults. As late as February 1936 the nuncio, still angry, wrote to Montecchi. "Allow me to bring to your enlightened attention," Borgongini wrote, "a case, which recurs often, of the diffusion of Protestant bibles in the midst of our people, without any exterior sign that would allow one to avoid the deception of innocent Catholics." Protestant vendors sell their editions with the equivocal title of "Holy Bible." Borgongini continues: "It is known to Your Excellency that these Bibles differ from our Catholic editions." These Protestant editions vended on the street are either "mutilated or tendentiously translated to disseminate error and to combat the truth of the Catholic faith." Regrettably, "the greater part of Catholics is not capable of distinguishing the Protestant edition from the Catholic." These insincere methods (*metodi poco sinceri*) of propaganda have given rise to many regrettable incidents. He closes by asking the minister to take his report into "sympathetic consideration."[17]

In response to the report of the trial of Father Scorza, the nuncio sent Pizzardo a transcription of the report in *Il Testimonio.* The article reviewed the laws on permitted cults. At the bottom of the attachment, the nuncio left a handwritten note (for "the Minister," that is, Buffarini) about his own response to the legal discussion in the article: "I ask you to read the attached opusculum, *Il proselitismo dei protestanti in Italia.*" He also sent Pacelli a copy of the pamphlet.[18] Over time the case had morphed from a defense of Scorza to a defense of Borgongini's thinking on the law.

Shortly after a conversation with Buffarini, the nuncio received a letter from the undersecretary of state on 3 April 1936. He had met with the minister for publication and propaganda regarding the diffusion of Bibles that carry no exterior sign indicating if the edition is Catholic or Protestant. He was pleased to report to the nuncio that the minister of propaganda "was interested in examining the possibility of not allowing any longer the publication and dissemination in the Kingdom of Bibles that are not clearly marked on the frontispiece which church has published them."[19] Developments seemed to be going Borgongini's way.

The nuncio's momentum was halted somewhat by a decree issued by Guido Beer, the prefect of Catania, a city on Sicily's east coast and one of the largest in all of Italy.[20] He had learned of Prefect Beer's decree from Pizzardo, who wrote to him on 28 February, with an attachment of Beer's 11 January

1937 circular.[21] Beer's decree started off promisingly enough: "The publication and diffusion in the Kingdom of Bibles without a frontispiece clearly indicating the Church or curia by which they have been published is not allowed." However, it then went on: "Exceptions are made for the Società Bibbie [*sic*] Brittanica," the organization that had sent the hated Maini, "which is authorized to publish Bibles with one of the following titles." (Borgongini would soon reveal why this exception had been allowed.) Beer then listed the versions he had authorized.[22] On the prefect's decision to authorize the publication and diffusion of these two Protestant Bibles, Pizzardo simply says, "You will wish to consider judging if and how one can act."[23] This seems to invite Borgongini to quit.

Naturally, Borgongini acted, writing a letter on 10 March 1937 to Pacelli, a response to Beer's circular regarding the diffusion of Protestant Bibles. Borgongini generously retailed for Pacelli the steps he had previously taken regarding the "grave abuse of the diffusion of Protestant bibles, which threatens the good faith of Catholic readers." Borgongini was able to enlighten the interior minister to the differences, by describing "notable mutilations and deformations of the text" made by Protestants as well as "heretical and tendentious prefaces and comments." He also insisted that the Società Biblica Brittanica, as an "interconfessional society," could not distribute a Bible that bore on its frontispiece the name of any single denomination. Having reviewed the facts of the case, the nuncio goes on to insist that clergy ought to ensure that government norms not be ignored by Protestant Bible vendors and remind their flocks not to accept the Bibles of the various Protestant sects. Borgongini concludes his letter to Pacelli by suggesting that perhaps *Civiltà Cattolica* or *OR* could write an article along these lines.[24] In his letter acknowledging receipt of this letter, Pizzardo thanks the nuncio for the steps he has taken and assures him that his suggestion regarding an article on the subject by the Vatican or Jesuits has been appreciated by Pope Pius XI.[25]

Sure enough, on 10 April 1937 *OR* published an article entitled "Honesty [*Sincerità*] in the Sale of Bibles." It begins by making many of the points already stressed by the nuncio (who, indeed, may have written the article) and goes on to assert that Protestant propaganda occurs in Italy by the sale of Bibles. It then imagines a hypothetical scene of a street vendor attempting to put a Protestant Bible under a pair of unsuspecting Catholic eyes. In this imagined scene, the author puts the actual words of Buffarini into the mouth of the imaginary Protestant vendor: "The Bible is the Bible; it is neither Protestant nor Catholic." This, the article states, is the most common, deceitful, and insidious mode of selling Bibles not approved by the church, recalling that at the Book Fair held in Rome in 1933 Bibles were sold that were said to be "accepted by all the churches." If challenged, a Protestant vendor would argue that different editions of *The Divine Comedy* were all by Dante. If confronted more vigorously, they would assert their legal right to "liberty of cult." This was a liberty, according to *OR,* that consisted primarily in deceiving the people and luring Catholics with good faith to buy anti-Catholic books. Therefore, the article concludes, what is at issue is not a matter of civil or legal rights but of civil obligations, above all, the obligation of honesty. The article concludes by alerting Catholics to editions of the Bible that Prefect Beer had exempted from the general rule. In short, the article reads as if written by Borgongini himself, whose opinions undoubtedly reached the editors of *OR* through Pizzardo or Pacelli.[26]

HOW FREE IS DISCUSSIONE LIBERA? *THE CASE OF FRANCESCO GIANCASPERO*

A second good example of Borgongini's modus operandi with alleged violations of the law by evangelicals comes from Bari in 1931. At the end of that year Antonio Melomo, the bishop of Monopoli (1927–40), wrote to Giuseppe Bruno, then secretary of the Sacred Congregation, from his episcopal see on the Adriatic.[27] Monopoli lay some twenty-five miles southeast of Bari, the capital of the province of Puglia, which had been heavily evangelized by many Protestant denominations, including American Methodists. A powerful bishop profoundly opposed to evangelical proselytizing, Melomo would correspond not only with Borgongini on the matter but also with Serafini and even Pope Pius XI. He was to complain repeatedly about the audacity of the Pentecostals from Rome. His letters reveal, as clearly as any, the central role Borgongini played in the anti-Protestant campaign. When Melomo was anxious that action be taken against evangelicals in his diocese, he would write directly to Borgongini rather than to Serafini or to the pope. He enlisted Borgongini particularly when the very powerful leader of the Pentecostals in Rome, Ettore Strappaveccia (1886–1957), seemed immune to his episcopal interventions.[28]

In this case the bishop had learned in December 1931 of meetings of Pentecostals taking place in Monopoli, he thought clandestinely. Suspecting them of being communist, subversive proselytes, apostate Catholics who criticized the pope (if true, this would have been a direct violation of Article 8 of the

Concordat) as well as antifascist, he denounced them to the police. On the evening of 18 October 1931 Pentecostals living in Monopoli were visited by their pastor, Francesco Giancaspero, a man from Triggiano, a small town in the southern part of the province of Bari. The meeting was held in the private house of one of the coreligionists. While they were in conversation there, two representatives of local law enforcement shut down the meeting. They declared the entire group under arrest. All were released except Giancaspero. He was detained and then incarcerated for political crimes.[29] What was the legal justification for this harsh action? The raid occurred on the basis of a mere suspicion. Moreover, if, as Pentecostal leaders would argue, the group had gathered only for the legal activities of prayer and worship, was the police action not a violation of freedoms guaranteed by the Concordat and its implementing legislation?

The leader of the Roman Pentecostal community, Strappaveccia, certainly thought so. After Giancaspero's arrest he lodged a complaint based on an interpretation of the admitted cults law. The wealthy owner of a construction company, Strappaveccia had converted to Pentecostalism after attending meetings in Rome. In 1923 he was elected pastor of the community that met in Rome at Via Adige 20, a space in his own villa. Of the six or so Pentecostals who applied to the Ministry of the Interior to be recognized as preachers, he was the only one to have obtained such permission, which came on 3 June 1931. For this reason he was regarded as the first legal representative of the Pentecostal movement. In that capacity he wrote on 29 May 1931 to Mussolini himself, complaining of harassment and the "sudden cessation" of harmless worship services being held in private homes of evangelical citizens. These citizens, he insisted, "had gathered peacefully for acts of worship and prayer."[30] Clearly he was a man familiar with the law and persuaded that it had not been broken and that the Pentecostal community was innocent of all relevant charges. Beyond that he was a man who had the ear of Mussolini as well as other powerful governmental officials and Anglo-Saxon ambassadors.

Strappaveccia wrote to the prefect of Bari on 25 November 1931. Identifying himself as the pastor of the Christian community—"so-called Pentecostals"—on Via Adige in Rome, he insists that the Pentecostals in Bari were in a private house "praying to God and discussing the Holy Gospel." As the meeting was about to break up the police appeared. Demonstrating exact knowledge of the pertinent law, Strappaveccia states, "I do not understand how these [police] actions do not constitute a violation of the law," which says, "Discussion in matters religious is wholly free." He goes on to inform the prefect of Bari that he had transmitted a circular to all Italian prefects asking them to leave all admitted cults alone—a remarkably bold and confident act. In addition, he had written to the minister of justice about the Giancaspero case, in the hopes that such cases "not be repeated or increased," as they put a "negative light [*cattiva luce*] on modern civilization" and "on the good name of our Italy."[31] With those last words the Pentecostal leader implicitly claimed full recognition of his coreligionists as Italian citizens and of himself as a loyal national, implicitly contradicting the bishop's assertions that his coreligionists were seditious. In Strappaveccia's view, the actions taken in Monopoli, encouraged by its bishop and resulting in a legal trial, had obviously violated the right to freedom of religious discussion explicitly enshrined in Italian law.

Almost needless to say, Catholic hierarchs interpreted the law quite differently. Because the word "permitted" or "admitted" (*ammessi*) might be interpreted to allow a wide field of legitimate, licensed religious activity, which might include propagandizing, Borgongini concentrated on what, precisely, the word "discussion" allowed and proscribed. Never does the nuncio deny that the law authorized Protestant sects to conduct worship. Worship, for Borgongini, implied the acts of prayer, practice, and ritual traditional to the sect in question, dedicated expressly for the purpose of religious devotion—and for no other motive. By law Protestants must, he reiterated, limit their activities to "worshiping with their own adepts." As Protestants would recognize, this was a strict definition of what field of religious activity the law authorized, especially for those evangelical denominations—all of them, in fact—for whom conversionary activities were a sacred obligation. As Borgongini's strict construction of the law implies, any religious activity that did not fall within the domain of "worship" (*culto*) logically fell outside of it. In a letter to Pacelli he maintains, as he consistently would, that "propaganda" fell outside the field of the "strictly religious."[32] By definition, then—by Borgongini's definition—proselytizing and propaganda fell outside the law: they were, in his view, constitutionally illegal activities. As such, they should be prosecuted.

Protestants like Strappaveccia objected, arguing that the category "discussion" included the right to exchange views about religion so long as such speech included no "offenses and public insults" to "the person of the Supreme Pontiff" (as Article 8 of the Lateran Treaty put it). So conducted, religious discussion could not, ipso facto, be construed as insulting or offensive to the pope. This was a view with which neither Mussolini nor his government seemed initially unsympathetic. Indeed, Law 1159, the statute that elevated the status of Protestant sects from "tolerated" to "admitted," was encouraged in both construction and passage by Mussolini himself and appears to have expanded the field of licit religious activity. So did Mussolini's comments on the law: cults once tolerated that were now admitted ought not to be persecuted or suppressed.

Thus, much depended, both legally and practically, on what "religious discussion" meant. Borgongini was again ready to hem in Protestant propaganda by means of precise and narrow definition. What was *discussione in materia religiosa?* In a letter to Buffarini, Borgongini declares, "Discussion is a scientific debate based on intellectual arguments among well-educated people and is not proselytizing based on money, favors, or promises made to the poor, or . . . to the ignorant and . . . those made desperate by poverty or by the sufferings of hidden and embarrassing secrets. What the Protestants do among the poor is not 'discussion.'"[33]

Here, Borgongini relies almost verbatim upon the words of Paolo Boselli (1838–1932), then a senator in the Italian parliament. He had served previously as prime minister for a brief time, until the disaster at Caporetto brought his government down.[34] In 1929 Boselli was made president of the Central Commission of the Senate that examined the Lateran Accords. As rapporteur, Boselli submitted a report on 18 June 1929 which attempted to address, among other things, what "freedom of discussion in matters of religion" meant in practice. He supplied a definition that could not have been more agreeable to the pope or his nuncio, who would soon distinguish between edifying conversation conducted in private and proselytizing speech conducted in public. The former was legally permissible; the latter, they decreed, not. In addition, Protestant churches could not be established in "integrally Catholic zones" or among the uneducated—this latter category would have constituted much of Italy, and churches were in fact erected for and usually by the presumed uneducated in scores of Italian cities. In his writing over the 1930s Borgongini would compulsively cite this report.[35]

With typical polemical emphasis on the material poverty and vulnerability of Catholic targets for conversion, Borgongini suggests that Protestant speech was not even a form of persuasion but of baiting and bagging the economically and intellectually susceptible. Beyond that, Borgongini and others maintained that, in fact, Protestant propaganda *had* offended against the pope in precisely the way the Lateran Treaty had made illegal. Given what we know about Protestant attitudes toward the papacy in the late nineteenth and early twentieth centuries—from both the literature produced by Protestants and hundreds of archival reports from agents of the government as well as the church, all alleging antipapal aspersion—this was surely true. (And would be even if only a small percentage of the archival documents are completely accurate.)[36] Whatever his intent, Boselli implied that public propaganda was not permissible because it could occasion a public disturbance or trouble Catholics. In that sense public propaganda could be viewed, legally, as something like a misdemeanor offense. But Borgongini took Boselli's legal prohibition much, much further. In effect, he wanted misdemeanors to be treated as felonies, with legal penalties corresponding to the gravity of the crimes.

That, perhaps, is why Borgongini concludes his definition of *discussione* by dwelling on the first article of the Lateran Pacts. If Catholicism was indeed the Religion of the State, then attempting to draw the faithful away by proselytizing was more than just an assault on the Catholic religion. Borgongini expands the scope of the law proscribing offenses against the pope. For him the law encompassed any kind of offense against the Roman *church,* including attempts to lure its members away. This was a grievous crime against the *state* as well as an offense against the church. Surely an extravagant, legally dubious charge, it made Protestant missionaries, even without additional transgression, enemies of the state. Their proselytizing was, amazingly, "a crime against the nation."[37]

Giancaspero's case was further complicated by the new Italian Penal Code, which, after six years of work, took effect in July 1931, just months before the incident in Bari. Conceived in the wake of the attempted murder of Mussolini in October 1926, its composition was overseen by Rocco. Mussolini had hoped to wield the code as an instrument to repress dissent. It certainly helped him to do so. The legal historian Paul Garfinkel has said that the law "captured the very essence of fascist Italy." Profoundly imbued with authoritarian ideology, the code aimed, in Rocco's blunt words, "to make Italy fascist." One way it did this was by dramatically reducing the rights of suspects. Based on Rocco's conviction that individuals made up only a transient component of the political body, the code expanded the scope of police activity and the power of the state in general.[38] Borgongini commonly invoked Article 18 of the new code of the laws concerning public security (Testo Unico delle Leggi di Pubblica Sicurezza, or TULPS), which had to do with the right of the state to take measures to protect public safety, including prohibiting or dissolving religious assembly and criminalizing dangerous groups. Public safety laws like this are customarily enacted in Western law to protect the safety of the individual. This one was crafted to protect the state from a putatively dangerous individual or troublesome minority group.[39] On its authority, police were encouraged to stop meetings they judged any sort of threat to the fascist state or alleged to be suspicious—held for the purposes of proselytizing, for example. This was the case even or especially if such meetings were held, as they often were, in private homes. In view of the new law, propagandizing transformed the private sphere, made private meetings a matter of public interest, and opened them to public scrutiny. The law required that a religious minister recognized by the state be present at all private meetings. As Rochat has pointed out, a private meeting could be viewed with "suspicion and annoyance," which made it easy for police authorities to establish the public character of these meetings and "submit them to authorizations, supervision and prohibitions."[40] The Protestant legal historian Giorgio Peyrot would write against this and other repressive laws, still on the books long after Mussolini's fall, indeed for much of the 1950s.[41] On the basis of this new law, the Pentecostal church member Giancaspero was charged and then put on trial.[42]

Over time Buffarini's views came more closely to mirror the repressive measures licensed by the Rocco code. Under its influence, Borgongini encouraged, even demanded, that police authorities invade homes, violate privacy, and disrupt prayer and worship. He particularly enjoined prefects, as local heads of police, to enforce these laws—all on a slight suspicion that proselytizing *might* be occurring in an evangelical home. Ultimately, Borgongini came to conclude that antifascist and anti-Catholic propaganda were all but indistinguishable. In March 1938 Borgongini commented on governmental seizure of a pamphlet put out by the Salvation Army, entitled *Gesù Cristo Ritornerà*. Both he and Buffarini (he reports) agreed that "if the brochure could be dangerous for the Catholic Faith, it was deadly for the State."[43] Just as antifascist propaganda was prohibited, so anti-Catholic propaganda, as Borgongini defined it, must be proscribed as well, and the mere presentiment of anti-Catholic speech justified its swift suppression.

"According to Article 18 of the Texts of the Laws on Public Security," Borgongini declares, meetings held by Protestants even for purposes of worship (*a scopo di culto*) "are not of a private character, but public."[44] Here the influence of the Rocco code on Borgongini's thinking and actions is clear; it would extend into other dimensions of evangelical religious activity as well. Writing to Pacelli in March 1934, Borgongini contends that Protestant activities, which he once tolerated so long as they were held in private places, had become illegal after the Rocco code. Borgongini was likely suspicious that activities occurring in Protestant *sale* were not in fact *a scopo di culto,* but from his vantage, far more nefarious. Borgongini would suggest that meetings became private or public "in view of their intent."[45]

In the war against the Protestants, Borgongini would also repeatedly manipulate Mussolini's pronouncement that religion could be a "potent force for sustaining national unity." Retrospectively, Mussolini's declaration—repeated several times, from 1922 at the earliest to the Second Quinquennial Assembly of the Regime (18 March 1934) on religion and national unity at the latest—gave a valuable hostage to fortune. Little could Mussolini have known how anti-Protestant polemicists would manipulate his words. Writing on Mussolini's proclamation that "religious unity is one of the great strengths of a people," on the day after the proclamation Borgongini comments, "Compromising or even simply injuring [religious unity] is to commit a crime of *lèse-nation.* Therefore, Protestants may not perform works of injury against the Catholic Church. . . . Evangelical proselytism . . . is an unacceptable assault against the Religion of the State."[46] The Lateran Pacts had criminalized injury to the papacy; Borgongini so construes Mussolini's comment as to extend that injury to make proselytizing a libelous offense.[47] That is astonishing but hardly more so than Borgongini's suggestion that *he* had persuaded Mussolini that Protestant propaganda should be so construed: "With such words," Borgongini crows in familiar language, "it seems to me that he has accepted in full the ideas I have sustained in our correspondence and meeting these past few months."[48] Knaves have power, fools gold. Precious to Borgongini was the belief that Mussolini treasured and learned from him.

PROSELITISMO PROTESTANTE IN ITALIA

In the archives of the Italian Nunciature there is an opusculum entitled *Il Proselitismo Protestante in Italia.*[49] Indeed, an entire thick folder is dedicated to it, containing correspondence about the completion, release, intent, and reception of the pamphlet.[50] The booklet is undated and anonymous; neither its author nor its publisher is even named, and even its intended audience is not obvious. Nonetheless, the nuncio's own archives contain evidence that allows us to address all these mysteries. The evidence allows us to date the opusculum quite accurately, identify its publisher, and, most important, ascertain who wrote it and why.[51]

The author was Borgongini-Duca himself. Borgongini had, he says, been helped in the statistical part of the pamphlet by "the exceptional Father Crivelli, S.J.," suggesting that Borgongini had prepared most of the written text (the majority of the pamphlet). Father Crivelli was among the most prolific authors of handbooks on Protestants, having composed works on evangelicals in Italy, Latin America, and the Christian East.[52] Only a limited number of copies of Borgongini's pamphlet had been made, as the published document was intended not for public but for clerical and governmental consumption.[53] On 13 May 1934 the nuncio, in an audience with the pope, had given two copies of the text to the Holy Father. Pius XI, "in his high wisdom believed it opportune to send two copies to the Sacred Congregation of the Council, as it treats materials within its range of competence"—as Serafini, better than anyone, would have known. With his letter Borgongini had included a copy to Serafini. He had also sent a copy to the minister of external affairs and given one "personally to the Secretary of State for the Interior, for his Dicastery, and for His Excellency, the Head of Government."[54] In a letter written to Pacelli in March 1935, Borgongini, after meeting with the director general of cults on another matter, reports having left several copies "of the opusculum against the Protestants" for the minister of justice. Similarly, in a letter sent to Mons. Francesco Cammarota (1874–1935), bishop of Capaccio Vallo (1917–35), who had complained about Protestant activity in his diocese in the province of Salerno, Borgongini wrote, "I will send you, under separate cover, an opusculum I have redacted and that I beg you to keep confidential."[55] A handwritten note at the bottom of his letter to the secretary of state suggests he also sent a copy to Pacelli. Given the dates of the two letters, *Il Proselitismo Protestante in Italia* must have been published in late 1934 or early 1935. Several letters from the Vatican publishing office complained to Borgongini about late payment, proof that the Typographia Vaticana published the pamphlet.[56] Most important, the contents of the pamphlet indicate that it was a vade mecum intended to alert priests in Italy to the range, dangers, and legal violations of Protestant proselytism as well as means for resisting the perceived threat to the church.

Almost the entire first half of the pamphlet, intended to impress the recipient with the ubiquity of the Protestant danger, is dedicated to listing every evangelical church or center in the country of Italy, which Borgongini, with Crivelli's help, numbers at 785. These are centers not of simple worship but in the majority of cases, at least according to Borgongini, "real and active proselytism." The nuncio then explains how proselytism was allowed to take root in Italy. Needless to say, it had nothing to do with defects in Italian Catholicism. The first cause, in the eyes of the profascist nuncio, was the liberal tolerance of the "anticlerical politics that ruled in Italy before the advent of fascism." Second, the law on admitted cults, which was "welcomed by all the Protestant press, Italian and foreign," had been hailed "as a great victory of their ideas in Italy and have signaled a renewal of proselytism, all to the damage of the Catholic Church." The nuncio informs the priest-reader, who is presumed not to know, that this allows Protestants to practice their worship and establish their schools, "just as Jews have their synagogues, schools and rabbinical seminaries." Finally, Protestant propaganda could flourish in Italy because of the failure of the legislature to adopt measures to impede it. "Five years of experience," concludes the nuncio, "have demonstrated the deficiency of the laws in this respect." Having credited fascist politics in his first point with ending an era of tolerance, here he ends by blaming it for tolerating the liberal sins associated with prior political regimes.

Borgongini then passes on to a discussion of "the dangers of Protestant proselytism." For the most part, he rehearses the problems discussed in depth by Tacchi Venturi and others who wrote against *il pericolo Protestante,* including the pope. In one polemic on Protestants, which appears to have been written by Selvaggiani, for example, the author poses the following catechetical-style question and response:

> Q. What do Protestants believe?
> A. Whatever they wish.[57]

The nuncio agreed. He went on: Protestant sects are antihierarchical, which allows every individual, no matter his capacity, to interpret divine revelation; he is therefore free to form his creed for himself, solely by reading the Bible. This principle is the "foundation of every democratic error, from liberalism to socialism and anarchy." Protestants also deny the divinity of Christ. For this denial the Protestant sects have no convincing defense "because they do not have a doctrinal or hierarchical authority." All the Protestant sects allow divorce. Many also admit birth control, as the Anglican bishops did at the Lambeth Conference. "The other Protestant sects did not hesitate to imitate the Anglican confession, [such as] the Methodist Episcopal Church. All Protestant sects intended to assault the Catholic church "and seek to destroy the papacy." Somehow, they fail to see that "the Bishop of Rome is the Pontiff of all the Church, in all the world." This Petrine privilege, which has lasted two millennia, "magnifies even more the shining glory of the Eternal City and therefore of Italy, the target of all their blows." Yet Protestants are blind to the ecclesiastical centrality and glory of Rome. Instead, they trot out the tired "old sayings of the first Lutherans, like 'the pope is the Antichrist.'" That is why the Protestant sects are, without exception, motivated by "the struggle against Rome."[58] According to Borgongini, the Waldensians—"a venerable church," he sarcastically calls them—argue that it is honorable for every Christian to assist in propagating the gospel in Italy, so the nation can liberate itself from the iniquities of Babylon (*affinchè questa Nazione possa liberarsi presto dai mali di Babilonia*). In this way, the prophecy contained in the words of Christ, "the Light will shine in darkness," will be fulfilled.[59] The Baptists contend, Borgongini goes on, that "the religion of the Italians is nothing other than a hodgepodge [*miscuglio*] of earthly politics and pagan idolatry." This continual denigration of Italy and its religion has had a deleterious effect. Referring to Zardi, Borgongini points out that a Wesleyan Protestant from San Sebastiano—who, "like many in that village," returned to the Catholic faith after converting—testified to the impact of his short-lived Methodism on his patriotism. Borgongini quotes from the erstwhile Protestant: "It is certain that from the discourses I heard in those gatherings, I lost all esteem and love for my country, which would be enveloped in the shadows of ignorance and superstition," while the "true light would be found only in the hazy skies of England and the United States."[60]

By 1934 Borgongini-Duca had begun to petition both secular and sacred authorities for reports and testimonies regarding sects he regarded as most menacing to Catholicism. Several testimonies of Italian clerics—including bishops but especially parish priests in Rome—regarding Pentecostal activity in their dioceses are now preserved in the archives of the Nunciature.[61] Among the reports submitted to the nuncio was one composed by Commendatore Carlo Costantini. Costantini was among the elite *Bussolanti.* A very high ecclesiastical honor, this is not a name but a title given to certain members of the papal household. They were divided into participants (Costantini fell into this category) and supernumeraries. As a member of the *famiglia pontificiana,* he would go on to support Borgongini in the suppression of the Pentecostal sect.[62]

Costantini requested testimonies from quite a number of priests in Rome, on the dubious basis of which he crafted his report. Witnesses from the parish priest of the Church of the Addolorata in S. Bonosa testified that the Pentecostal proselytes active near his parish use money and promises of jobs for each one who matriculates to their sect. The priest testifies: "I know of a father of a family to whom they [Pentecostal proselytes] had promised 1,000 lire and 500 lire to each of his children" if "they immediately joined the sect. To others they promised various amounts of money."[63]

Borgongini goes on to detail the ways in which the Protestant sects violate the law. While "permitted," the sects are not permitted to proselytize to the harm of Catholicism. Proselytism endangered the religious unity of Italy, an important ingredient in national unity. The Royal Decree says clearly that "the faithful of each cult can have a proper temple or oratory." Therefore, it is evident that the temple, according to the law, is designed for adepts of the evangelical churches—and not to attract Catholics. The law had established, in response to a request to open a temple, the legal obligation "of proving it necessary to satisfy effective religious needs of important nuclei of faithful." In addition, the Royal Decree (Article 20) established that evangelical leaders must make known the precise denomination of the admitted cult, to avoid confusion and abuses; this is not only for the information of the government but also and especially for the public (a law honored only in the breach). On the rooms of the cult one must write not simply the generic title—for example, "evangelical *sala*" or "Christian *sala*"—as that can induce poorly instructed persons to error, especially in the countryside, but the complete title, like *sala evangelica wesleiana*. "The church founded by Our Lord Jesus Christ is one only; therefore, as proven by the Gospel, the name of *Church* can only appear on a Catholic Church."

Borgongini would strengthen these views of the legal status and character of Protestant proselytes, then communicate to fascist officials who had the power to suppress, as one would do with several sects in 1935.

CHAPTER 7

Resistance, Respite—and Retreat (1935)

Sometime in 1935 or 1936 the Sacred Congregation of the Council compiled a document entitled *Proselitismo Protestante in Italia.*[1] Although this pamphlet had the same title as that written by Borgongini-Duca, its purpose and tone were much different from those of the one put out by the Apostolic Nuncio. The aim of the document was to assess the impact of defensive actions taken by the Catholic church over the course of four years. It is divided into twenty chapters, one for each province of the country, and it evaluates every parish in every diocese in the country. By the date of its publication, the anti-Protestant campaign had begun, from the point of view of the Sacred Congregation, to show impressive, encouraging results. In general, the author of the pamphlet is, while occasionally cautious, pleased and at times upbeat. The document is valuable not only as an accurate portrayal of the situation of Protestant communities in Italy, showing which were losing numbers (*in diminuzione*) and which few were gaining (*in aumento*). It also opens a window into what means of resistance to Protestantism were used and with what effectiveness. The document gives a glimpse as well into which provinces seemed quiet and which still had active proselytizing; and, finally, which social groups were being especially aggressively recruited. Many modes of resistance were adopted, according to recommendations put out by Borgongini and others at the Vatican. Cumulatively, they had, if ephemerally, quite a devastating effect on Protestant presence and proselytizing in Italy. At the same time, as this news, heartening to the Sacred Congregation, was being received, disheartening reports on popular ignorance, priestly poverty, and priestly defections were arriving at the Vatican. This reflected a pattern that persisted throughout the 1930s: cheering news was rarely unmixed with reports that demoralized many Vatican clerics and dejected the pope.

The crisis of Catholic Action having passed, the compilers of the report were, without question, most pleased with the impressive achievements of Catholic Action. This gratified Pope Pius. As is well known, the negotiations pertaining to the Lateran Accords and the history of the three years that ensued were dominated by conflict over Catholic Action. Though organized primarily for "recreational and educational activities having a religious purpose," Catholic Action was a willing and indeed eager instrument of the pope. De Felice probably went too far in suggesting that Catholic Action had imagined that its own ruling class would become successors to the fascist leaders.[2] Nonetheless, there is no doubt but that Pius's vision of the Catholic restoration of Italy included the revival of Catholic influence in the domains of public morality, education, youth, labor, and, as Scoppola has put it, helping the pope to Catholicize and clericalize the fascist regime.[3] In the 1930s this meant that the Christian army that Catholic Action imagined itself to be would be used as a bulwark against Protestant penetration—in the same way that Italian politicians would use it, after the war, against the threat of communism.

Catholic Action is credited with having been effective from north to south. It was present in the traditionally strong Waldensian provinces and active in every southern province where American and British denominations were strong: Puglia, Campania, Basilicata, Calabria, Sardinia, and Sicily. In Lombardy it was credited with an "optimal contribution" to the anti-Protestant effort. Generally speaking, where Catholic Action was strong, Protestant denominations were said to be in dimunizione. In the few places where it was numerically weak, absent, or not mentioned, as in Etruria (Tuscany), Protestant groups still flourished and proselytizing activity went on virtually unimpeded.

Catholic Action undertook a number of efforts to improve in those activities at which Protestants excelled. New churches, Catholic schools, and kindergartens were opened in Spezia and Teramo (Abbruzzi), as well as in ever-problematic San Sebastiano—one kindergarten was established by Pope Pius XI where Protestants had already built their own. The opening of a Catholic orphanage in Portici (Campania) was said to be in direct opposition to one the Protestants had already established. (This was happy news, as Portici was so problematic it had recently been brought to the attention of the pope.)[4] Several new *salone* for youth, erected explicitly *in contrapposizione* to compete with Protestant institutions like the YMCA, were opened in, among other places, Cremona, one of the cities where Methodists were said to be still on the rise. Athletic and social institutions had been established in Abbruzzi, which also drew potential converts away from the YMCA. New parishes were established in Grosetto and a new chapel in (again) the areas "most threatened" by Protestants. In general, one might say that by 1935 the Vatican had a very clear idea of those dioceses it considered most threatened, and it naturally concentrated the full array of its forces in these areas.

Not surprisingly, the Sacred Congregation gave much credit to the initiative of bishops and their attempts to improve parochial clergy. In the Annual Conference of the Episcopate of the Ordinaries of Piedmont on 25 September 1935, parish priests were invited for special instruction concerning Protestant propaganda and Italian legislation on the admitted cults. In Ventimiglia the bishop led the successful effort to close a nondenominational school with several Catholic pupils at San Remo, which was regarded as a victory. A Waldensian school was closed by the civil authorities in Agrigento, Sicily.

In Genoa a pastoral letter of the archbishop condemning "the errors of the Protestants" had been circulated. Anti-Protestant instruction in the seminaries, for which bishops were responsible, had been effective, it was said, in many provinces. Most important, extraordinary courses were given in preaching in Campania, Basilicata, Salerno, Puglia, and the Veneto, among other places. This again suggests that in practical domains where Catholicism had failed, as in preaching, Protestants had succeeded; the field was only retaken when Catholic preaching came up to snuff.

The bishop of Zara (Veneto) had succeeded in repressing Protestants in his diocese because he had insisted on involving Public Security. The police forces, so often frustrating to the Vatican for their indolence, indifference, and ignorance, were credited with impeding an attempt by Adventists to hold a national congress in the Piedmont. New attempts at Protestant propaganda in Asti were repressed by Public Security. The report credits law enforcement for Benevento no longer being a "center of the first class" and enforcing the decree outlawing the Pentecostals. Increased vigilance of the Waldensian Center in Sardinia was noted.

International and regional conferences and congresses were also held to be effective. Several Eucharistic Congresses, in which clergy and laity gather to celebrate the "real presence," were said to strengthen anti-Protestant feeling (the Reformers, with the notable exception of Luther, generally rejected the doctrine of the real presence, and even Luther rejected the specifically Catholic and Aristotelian doctrine of transubstantiation). In Aosta a Eucharistic Congress was held to memorialize and celebrate the expulsion from that city of Calvin, who rejected the notion of real presence. The wide diffusion of publications against the errors of the Protestants was also cited as a major factor. Finally, the efforts of many religious orders, especially in dioceses most threatened by Protestantism, like Marsi and cities in Sicily, garnered enthusiastic credit from Rome.

As a result of these efforts, by 1935 most of the Anglo-American sects and institutions found most irritating by the Vatican were said (wrongly) to have disappeared or to be in diminuzione. The YMCA in Turin, which Tacchi Venturi regarded as an institution that erased the Italian cultural identities of citizens about to immigrate to North America, was reported to be in decline. Methodist, Adventist, and Baptist sects were reported to be on the decrease almost everywhere in Italy. In many places, such as the Piedmont, "attempts at penetration had failed." Venice had ceased to be a "center of the first class," as had many other capital cities of the provinces. While the Waldensians had "revived their activity" and Adventists had "made attempts at penetration," Romagna had ceased to be fertile field for proselytizing, in part because of the success of an anti-Protestant congress there organized by the Third Order Dominicans, a lay organization. A document from a different source suggests that the Third Order Franciscans had constructed a national plan of "intense action" against Protestant propaganda in Italy.[5] Similarly, Methodists and Baptists were said to be in dimunizione in Emilia, and a Protestant school had been closed in Parma. Giving one a good sense of how small these Protestant communities could be, the evangelical community in Reggio Emilia had "stabilized in number at eight persons," which was credited to the intensification of activity by Catholic Action, the construction of new churches, and assistance by religious orders in the "most threatened locales." While some attempts had been made at penetrating Foligno, Umbria had never been strong in the number of Protestant converts; "almost no change" had occurred in the province in the years covered by the report. Similarly, Protestant Bibles and other literature had been distributed in the Marches, "but generally there was no variation or success." Only Pesaro is mentioned as an exception. In Lazio, Catholic Action and "extraordinary preaching" impeded Baptists from reviving their activity. In Tivoli, the report bluntly states, "there are no more Protestants." In Gaeta (Campania) almost all evangelicals disappeared after their pastor, like Zardi in Villa San Sebastiano, abruptly abjured Protestantism and reconverted to Catholicism. In Montecassino, home to the historic abbey founded by Benedict, the Methodists had given up preaching altogether. This was credited, not surprisingly, to the assistance given to the anti-Protestant campaign by the Benedictines of Monte Cassino, who, as we have seen, were similarly effective in Villa San Sebastiano.

Without question, Etruria (Tuscany) was the province where Protestant propaganda was least impeded by Catholic resistance, and Florence the city in Tuscany where the Methodists, the YMCA, and others remained active and successful. Publications and Bibles were distributed by several sects in Fiesole, and in Livorno both the Waldensians and Methodists augmented numbers by the persuasive power of published materials. The "outlawed Pentecostals" had attempted to reconstitute themselves in Grosetto and Aresso under the name of "evangelicals" and "continue their propaganda." While resistance in Basilicata and Salernitano was said to be in general improved, Rapolla, Matera, and Salerna all remained "centers of the first class." By contrast, the Calvinists—it is not clear which group is meant—and Methodists had largely disappeared by the time the report was composed. There again "religious orders in the most threatened parishes" were credited for the disappearance of the Protestants, as they were, too, in Piazza Armerina, a most threatened area.

Where proselytism succeeded, it was often with the young, particularly students and soldiers. In Liguria Waldensian propaganda had intensified in Genoa, while in Spezia the Baptists, otherwise on the decline, were also propagandizing. Missionaries were targeting students, as were evangelicals in Bergamo. In those places in Lombardy where evangelicals had "restarted their activity" (perhaps Pentecostals), they had targeted soldiers. The Salvation Army in Lombardy made students and soldiers the special object of their efforts, as had other Protestants in Brescia. Still active in the military city of Spezia were Protestants attempting to convert soldiers. In 1935 Bishop Costantini wrote to Pizzardo to alert him to the presence of propagandists among soldiers leaving for the war in Ethiopia. (Other Vatican archival documents suggest that evangelical missionaries followed the soldiers to Africa.) Pizzardo then warned Borgongini-Duca.[6] On 24 May 1935 Borgongini wrote to Pacelli regarding the meeting he had had at the Ministry of the Interior. The minister of war was made aware of the problem, as was the prefect of Spezia, who was advised to see that "the aggression"—that is, by Protestants against the Catholic Italian soldiers preparing to invade Abyssinia—be made to cease.[7] A year later military authorities in Piacenza were alerted by the local bishop that Protestants were attempting to propagandize soldiers at the arsenal in the city.[8]

When we survey this wide array of activity we see that Catholic resistance sometimes succeeded because it emphasized elements of the Catholic tradition—but often because they competed successfully with Protestants on what had historically been their own ground. For example, Eucharistic Congresses were clearly Catholic in origin and nature, and they strengthened Catholic devotion to a cherished belief, to practice rooted in antiquity, and to the institutional church. Again, one cannot overemphasize the role of the learned and zealous religious orders in rejuvenating religious life in communities that had been Protestantized. On the other hand, the opening of athletic and social institutions, efforts at improving preaching, and more energetic diffusion of publications were all inspired by Protestant gains made by these means. Here Catholics succeeded because they did better or at least as well as the evangelicals. In all cases, the young were targeted by both confessions. All of these activities, in turn, were successful because Vatican authorities had acquired very precise information on every city in every province in the country.

In 1936 it may have seemed to prelates at the Roman curia that their vigorous campaign, which stretched out over more than five years, was on the brink of success. The events of the next years were to disappoint those expectations. Had this report been published just a year later, the tone would likely have been quite different; indeed, it would have resembled the much more lugubrious report submitted two years later by the same council, which came to conclusions opposite to those expressed here. By then, Pentecostal communities, which had been outlawed, had begun to reconstitute themselves in large numbers and caused alarm at the Vatican and anger at the undersecretary of the interior. Vatican analysis suggested that many of the gains made by all evangelical communities could be attributed to a variety of seemingly intractable problems with the education, character, and economic life of the parish priest.

POPULAR AND PRIESTLY POVERTY, INDIFFERENCE, AND IGNORANCE

In a document analyzing the causes of Protestant success Selvaggiano remarks that the "religious indifference of the people" is "one of the greatest coefficients to the progress of the Protestants." He goes on to observe that this problem is easily dealt with: it can be defeated with, among other things, catechisms.[9] The experience of the railwayman and of numberless parish priests suggests otherwise. Despite efforts at educating and invigorating the laity, priests often found themselves defeated by popular ignorance, or worse. In the course of the controversy at San Sebastiano the local priest, Padre Bellarini, gives a wholly convincing account of the religious illiteracy and apathy of many in his diocese. Most of his parishioners are "extremely ignorant" of the "elements of our faith." This is not their fault, he says, as they had never received any religious instruction. At the time he wrote his letter Bellarini had been parish priest for only four months. During that time he had poured his energies into giving religious instruction. On Sunday afternoons he gave instruction to adults. Children he taught twice a week during the days. To all he emphasized the importance of "frequently receiving the Holy Sacraments." (Failure to take Communion or to confess, though required annually since 1215, had been a problem for eight centuries; in this respect, as in others, little had changed in rural Italy since the Middle Ages.)[10] Nonetheless, adults almost completely ignored his Sunday afternoon sessions.[11] Here the problem does not seem to be ignorance; it is much more profound than that.

A similar story is told by Michele Paolone, the parish priest at San Giacomo degli Schiavini, in the diocese of Larino and Termoli (fishing villages on the Adriatic Coast in Campobasso), whose bishop verified to Pizzardo that Paolone's account "reflected the truth."[12] In a letter of unknown date, probably spring or summer 1934, the parish priest writes to the secretary of state. In the course of his letter, whose central purpose is to inform the Roman authorities of Waldensian proselytizing in his diocese, he describes not only the extreme poverty of his parishioners (not to mention his own) but also the shocking lack, despite his efforts, of basic catechetical instruction. His parish consists, the priest says, of roughly "one-thousand souls." About 30 women, he says, regularly attend Mass on Sundays. Some 160 had converted to Waldensianism. Bernacchia, the priest's bishop, confirms that, in general, the priests of his diocese have been demoralized because "their zeal bears no fruit."[13] Even the teachers do not attend church. With one exception, none of them teaches the catechism in school; basic instruction in the rudiments of the faith was almost entirely lacking in this small parish. Some nominal parishioners aged 20–25 had not yet been baptized. The elementary schools the parish priest describes as one of the sources of the de-Christianization of the village. In these, they do little more than "perform obscenities" and "sing pornographic songs" (by which Paolone likely means irreverent, blasphemous, or otherwise vulgar performances).

In order to encourage the poor who have left the Catholic church (*fuorviati*) to return and to retain the "barely Catholic" majority, he had hopefully launched a program of "deep Christian education." Unfortunately, he concludes, "the fruits have been minimal." In these dismal respects, this parish was almost entirely representative of the region in the 1930s. Paolone's parish reflects the dire conditions which the railwayman and many others divulged in documents received in that decade by the Vatican.

Elsewhere, Marchetti seems to recognize that the problem goes deeper than poor or nonexistent teaching. Aside from the indolence of poor priests and the dejection of conscientious ones, the profound modern problems of apathy and even hostility to religion seem to have overwhelmed the capacity of any Catholic cleric to thwart or even impede them. This he seems not to perceive. To be sure, Marchetti goes on to remark that "there is no lack of information on the religious indifference of the people." This, he says, must be "resisted with all means possible. . . . Especially by greater intelligence and participation of the people in the sacred Liturgy; a better developed worship of the Eucharist and of the Sacred Heart, the celebration with solemnity and devotions of first communions, with parents and relatives taking part; the establishment of Catholic Action and especially of Gioventù Cattolica."[14] Given reports from parish priests, this proposal borders on the naïve. To return to Larino and Termoli, in Paolone's parish, heretics, that is, converts to evangelical Protestantism, outnumbered faithful practitioners of Catholicism, who were, notably, all female, by a ratio of 5 to 1. There was worse. The remainder of the village was largely indifferent, even averse, to *any* kind of religion. Indeed, the majority was atheist and immoral. Ignorance was one thing; indifference another. Remedies for the latter—deep-seated and tied to the profound changes in culture described by the railwayman—were, as now, not obvious then.

PRIESTLY INDOLENCE AND SACERDOTAL SCANDAL

"The personal prestige of the parish priest," Selvaggiano states, was critical to neutralizing the Protestant invasion. He "must be among the faithful, esteemed, pious, affable, and solicitous of [his parishioners'] spiritual and temporal well-being." Yet, along with popular ignorance, according to Selvaggiano the "scandalous life of priests" was the greatest *coefficiente* of Protestant progress. Unfortunately, evidence of indolence and scandal was abundant.

Complaints about Catholic clergy, especially in the South, had begun to be heard already in Restoration-era Italy (1815–48). Critics poured scorn on clergy for intellectual incompetence, spiritual indifference, and moral depravity—and clerics would continue to be denounced for many of the same failings throughout the fascist period. Occasionally that criticism was bent inward, and the Italian church denounced itself for essentially dooming diocesan priests to destitution by failure to provide rectories (or "canonical houses") or minimally sufficient annual stipends. The result? The creation of a class of the transient priest, who would drift to Rome from the South, for economic reasons—that is, in the hopes of lashing his mast to a stable church. In this respect, the movement of priests reflects the broader movement of the lower orders moving northward for work at the same time.

For just such reasons many secular priests, for whom the supply was then much greater than demand, were serving no parish at all. Quite a few took positions as private chaplains to the affluent. Others served the children of middle- and upper-class parents as private tutors. Still others were uninvolved in religion or education; they used their (sometimes minimal) skills in literacy to manage estates. In these conditions, the religious practices of common folk slipped out of control of the priesthood, especially in the South, and parishioners resorted to practices most educated clerics then judged superstitious or magical in the hopes of reversing their fortunes. Archival reports suggest these were still being practiced into the fascist period. While oversupply was the root economic cause of these problems, Catholic officials deplored the poor educational fare ladled out in seminaries, the seriousness and energy of clergy, and the conditions in which preparation for ministry took place. Students often lived outside seminaries, usually with their parents, missing out on aspects of theological education like formation and community the hierarchy thought crucial. Some students enrolled simply because secondary education was inexpensive. Deeply frustrated, Pius IX (r. 1846–78) would publish two new encyclicals on priestly discipline (he had already published two) in 1858.[15] *Cum nuper,* issued in January 1858, practically blames a recent earthquake on the failings of the priesthood, particularly sexual immorality and religious ignorance.

In October 1934 Bishop Costantini wrote to Serafini at the same time the prefect of the Sacred Congregation of the Council was receiving a largely optimistic report. Adventists had recently intensified their propaganda in Montemarcello and in the Piano di Ameglia. More recently, a house for cures at the Gulf of Spezia had opened; it had been occupied in the most recent summer by children from the region and from Tuscany, of whom several were converted and baptized in an Adventist church.[16] What had facilitated the diffusion of Protestantism? The bishop trots out some of the usual complaints: the Adventists had deceptive tactics; were wealthy and had the means to attract young converts, of whom there were many in La Spezia. But he focuses on other factors: the "lack of zeal of parish priests" as well as the "scandalous sexual misconduct by priests." These exasperated Serafini. It seemed as if many of his troops had no appetite for ordinary priestly duties, much less war.

Because of a "certain Olympian security" that the Protestants will accomplish nothing, "nothing has been concluded"—that is to say, the diocesan priests had done nothing to resist Adventist missionizing. Costantini contrasts their lack of zeal with evangelical energy. Protestant propaganda goes on tenaciously. It is precise, well-organized. "Since 1927," he complains, "I have insistently recommended to the parish priest of Pegazzano, Borata, that he open an *asilo* and give religious instruction to those abandoned people." "A bit was done" but "because of lack of zeal and initiative on the part of the parish priest, all has died out." The Adventists, Costantini concludes, immediately afterward opened an *asilo* and it "remains there still."

The bishop goes on: "I exhorted the parish priest to search for a locale to open a chapel and do some practical things." They were *in corso,* when the Adventist leader Arrigo Pullen "immediately bought up land for an Institute a few meters from the place I indicated." The contract had been signed, and immediately work began on the construction. In Sestri Levante there were several churches but all in the hills, while the valley, relatively well-populated and far from the parish, is without a church and religious ministry. The Protestants took advantage and "immediately made adepts among the peasants, and their work continues." The converted peasants "become fanatics." What they believe dogmatically is "shocking." Result? More than one hundred Adventists "have begun to administer baptisms."

When the railwayman wrote the Vatican in 1934, nothing weakened Protestantism's crusading zeal or impeded its success, least of all the Catholic clergy and laity. In his eyes, in fact, that clergy was simply deplorable. Some strange magic or "mysterious force" seems to have made the Italian priesthood, particularly in the parishes, sluggish, inert. Rather than resist the demands of the age, especially the impulse to gratify one's profane appetites, the clergy, then the laity, seem to have succumbed to them. The result? A "religious cooling" of "our people," that is, of the Catholic populace: a peculiar, almost inexplicable indifference, especially on the part of men, to matters religious. In their torpor, ordinary parishioners mirrored the inertia of the secular clergy.

Time, meanwhile, had marched on. Many of the clergy were aged; fifteen years had passed since any young man from Ariano had felt called to the secular priesthood. Ominously, youth were failing to replenish the local diocesan clergy. When a young man fit for the priesthood surfaced—a rare occurrence—he was snapped up, educated, then put to work by one of the learned religious orders, never to return to the bleak, religiously dry haunts of Ariano. The lack of youthful enthusiasm di Lorenzo attributes in part to changing cultural norms. Yet he also laments the loss of any organized Catholic Action for a town, then, of twenty-five thousand citizens. (Its population has barely changed over the past eighty years.) The young have no place, he complains, "where they can gather to be taught religious morality."

Overwhelmed by the lure of unnamed but powerful profane attractions, fathers had lost power—or will—in their own homes. No longer could they impede their children's fascination with the seductions of a new age. This unfortunate development di Lorenzo also lays at the door of a detached, indifferent, all-but-absent local clergy. Both clergy and laity were, it seemed, unable to retard the progress of the evangelical campaign or frustrate the forms of culture of which Protestant missionaries were symbols or actual carriers. To some Catholic thinkers, Protestant missionaries brought threats to the traditional religious culture of Italy and indeed to all the Latin world: a liberal attitude toward denomination, creed, or confession. This attitude represented an indifferentismo, or latitudinarianism, that had been condemned many times by Catholic thinkers in the nineteenth and twentieth centuries, including by the author of the *Syllabus of Errors*.[17] Some Protestant leaders were participants in the burgeoning ecumenical movement, which popes would soon contemptuously dismiss; and some evangelical thinkers maintained that certain affinities linked Christianity, especially as reflected in the ancient church depicted in Acts, and communism—the latter of which had also been condemned in the *Syllabus*.

The Protestant clergy had humiliated the local Catholic priesthood, "who [had been made] impotent" by their competitors' youth, vitality, and determination. In di Lorenzo's years in Ariano the Protestants had opened two rooms for meetings, one, brazenly, in the Catholic cathedral parish of Via Annunziata. They scoured the impoverished countryside in cars for recruits.

Dynamic, convinced, optimistic, they were somehow immune to the prevailing anomie that had crushed the spirit of Catholic clergy and laity alike. Protestants "roam[ed] throughout all regions and the farmhouses." These youthful Brits and Americans captured because they captivated youth, whom they especially targeted; if they succeeded, that would simply mean, demographically, that Italian Catholicism, already enfeebled, would perish rapidly rather than slowly. The railwayman could not perceive all the motivations of the Anglo-Saxon invaders. These evangelical missionaries were propelled powerfully forward by intoxicating religious motivations characteristic of evangelical Christianity since the mid- and late nineteenth century and, often, powerful apocalyptic, millennial, and messianic expectation. These visions catapulted American and British missionaries to Italy, where they expected to confront and overcome the Antichrist and his minions and to defeat Babylon—apocalyptic code for vanquishing the corrupt Roman church and its wicked leader.

Preying on (or, as the railwayman puts it, abusing) the loneliness of those surrounding Ariano, these missionaries, dynamic, forceful, seemingly indefatigable, "completely outshine the work of our clergy." This was especially true in the realm of worship. Irregular, dry, and paltry, Catholic cult was already attended fitfully, if at all, by many of the railwayman's countrymen. When missionaries told these simple people that Catholic worship was, in addition, a form of idol worship—or a form of priestcraft or even of paganism—they found an audience ready to receive their message. Theirs was a message, a gospel, very different and in many cases more appealing, meaningful, and difficult to resist than the one vended by unenthusiastic local clergy. It also represented a way for some, now emboldened, to defy the social complex of clergy and landowners associated with a church increasingly seen as a repressive social force.

Like many devout Catholics, the railwayman imputes blame for the current religious deficiencies in part to the laws passed in June 1929, which granted to evangelical communities not just toleration but full recognition as culti ammessi and full freedom in discussion of matters religious. The Protestants, he says, exploit the freedoms granted them by the state, perverting the ignorant peasants by enabling them "falsely to understand the Bible." This they use to criticize the clergy and Catholicism (religione). For the most part, however, the railwayman trains his critical eye not on the deviousness of the Protestants but on the utter collapse of Catholic infrastructure in buildings and personnel. For example, the summer before writing to the Vatican the railwayman had accompanied a priest for a few days to inspect an area of roughly thirty square kilometers. In that entire zone there was not so much as a rural chapel. Could it be any surprise that the forty families of farmers there had "fallen to Protestantism"? The railwayman estimates that roughly two-thirds of the countryside had converted, a quotient that astonished him.

This, then, is the railwayman's catalogue of a sickly institution's symptoms: clerical inertia and powerlessness, caused in part by a secular age, in part by surrender to prevailing cultural norms; the vanishing influence of Catholic Action (which would have required an energetic parish priest to keep it from becoming moribund); the power and mysterious allure of cultural fads and commodities, and the loss of traditional habits, mores, and values, which fathers and family were powerless to preserve—especially when abandoned by the secular clergy; and indifference and indifferentismo. In sharp contrast to these qualities stood the agility of the Protestant missionaries, their youth, energy, acuity, and deep conviction. Both the church and the fascist regime were deeply jealous of the allegiance of their youth. Both feared that their age and susceptibility would make it easier to convert Italians of the same age cohort; and both dreaded that they would offer Anglo-Saxon forms of cultural attractions and institutions of recreation (above all, the YMCA) that might induce them to convert. This is the last of the many symptoms of cultural and religious illness that persuaded di Lorenzo that Ariano, like many other southern towns, was experiencing something sinister. Indeed, the religious infirmity then being exploited by Protestant missionaries had, in the railwayman's mind, become chronic. It looked as if evangelical Christianity, around Ariano, had vanquished the traditional religion of Italy.

Yet di Lorenzo was hardly ready to surrender. Indeed, he proposed to Pizzardo and the pope a cure, one with deep roots in the history of medieval and early modern Christianity. In centuries when the clergy had seemed slack or supine—parochial life listless, the institutional church corrupted by secular norms, parts of Christendom overrun by dissenters or heretics—new monastic and religious orders had emerged to rejuvenate the apathetic, engage the indifferent, and renew the church. In the Middle Ages the Cistercians and Franciscans famously played such a role; the Society of Jesus, or Jesuits, originated as the classical Counter-Reformation retort to the Protestant Reformation in the sixteenth century. To address this profound problem, the railwayman proposes a remedy: to create a new (specifically male) religious order. By contrast to the local clergy, the new religious order, supplied by young men from Ariano, would be "strong, hardworking, and holy." This would, he hopes, "create a new trend," namely, vigorous resistance to the "miserable bad habit" that makes both clerical and lay soldiers of Christ indolent and even iniquitous. So dynamic and attractive would the new order be that they would, in due course, replace "the old carcasses that make up the local clergy." The railwayman's proposal is to reenact modes of reform that had, in the past, reanimated the heavy spirits of the faithful. This instinct ran deep in the Catholic imagination. Indeed, when attempting to repel the Protestant enemy, the church prepared something like an ecclesiastical Operation Overlord of itinerant priest-monk-preachers to rout the Anglo-Saxon enemy from the sacred land of Italy.[18] However Catholic di Lorenzo's planned remedy is, it is impossible to miss that the railwayman is essentially proposing to imitate the zeal, conviction, and power of the Protestant conquerors of Ariano and its countryside.

PRIESTLY POVERTY

There is another "grave danger that I will not hide from you," Costantini wrote, in the aforementioned letter: priestly sexual misconduct. In one of the parishes in the mountains, Torpiano, a parish priest encountered a young student leaving the Protestant Collegio of Spezia. The young maestra is "intelligent and fanatical for the religion in which she has been educated." The priest left his parish and married her. The substitution of a *parrocco bravo* did nothing to impede the scandal from spreading. On top of everything, the collapse of two banks, a very common occurrence in the years the bishop wrote, impoverished the region. He himself is without means. Indeed, he cannot now afford to pay for a villa that was intended to be his new episcopal lodging. Costantini plaintively concludes: "Ecco lo stato doloroso delle mie Diocesi!"[19]

Reports by local parish priests emphasize the extreme poverty of their parishioners. In addition, poverty is a chronic problem they themselves had, somehow, to manage. Poverty was so severe for many that they drifted away from their parishes for principally economic reasons. Serafini recognized that many of these would become resentful ex-priests. A letter written by Bellarini, the parish priest of San Sebastiano, is telling.[20] In the course of his correspondence Padre Bellarini gives a sobering glimpse into his own economic struggles, which were pressing, and that of his parishioners, which were frightful. His parish consisted of perhaps two thousand or so members, most of them farmers or shepherds. Sometime in the mid-1930s (the letter is undated, but it was probably written 1934–36), Bellarini wrote the pope himself: "In my parish," he complains, there are many "extremely poor" families who "struggle with extreme misery." The parish priest had himself taken out loans—not for himself but to aid his destitute parishioners. Unable to incur any further debt, he wrote to ask for financial help for his congregation, which he received. In a letter later written to Pacelli thanking him for financial help, Bellarini mentions that he had recently paid 500 lire (that is to say, roughly one-third of his annual stipend) for the electrical expenses of his parish rectory, but he had not been reimbursed. He lives, he says, quite believably, "in the most squalid misery." A member of the Poor Servants of Divine Providence, a religious congregation founded in 1907 in Calabria, often called the Calabrians,[21] he says, remarkably, "Still, for a religious, it is fitting to experience the practical effects of poverty" so as to know intimately what his parishioners daily endure.[22] In an age when Vatican authorities complained about the chronic indolence and indifference of the parochial clergy, the obviously genuine and generous Bellarini emerges as a shining exception to the discouraging rule.[23]

In fact, things could be worse. Paolone, the parish priest of San Giacomo degli Schiavini, gives a picture of presbyteral poverty that makes his plight seem more dire than Bellarini's. It was so bad that Oddo Bernacchia, his bishop, deeply troubled, implored the Vatican authorities to come to his aid. To begin with, there was no rectory (*casa canonica*) for him to live in. Forced to lease out a tiny apartment, Paolone paid the rent of 76 lire per month. A recent tax on rentals subtracted 9 lire monthly from that amount. Unable to pay the rent on his meager annual stipend, Fr. Paolone had been threatened with eviction by the owner of his small apartment. As there were no other buildings in the paese that he could rent, he concludes, "I do not know where I will be able to sleep."[24] Fully sympathetic with the desperate plight of his parish priests, his bishop asked Pizzardo how a parish priest like Paolone could live on his annual stipend, then 1,500 lire per year.[25]

A letter from Massimo Rinaldi, the bishop of Rieti to Pizzardo, illustrates starkly how deplorable (in the bishop's words), even unbearable, extreme poverty could make local parish life for clergy.[26] Indeed, it could render impossible the conduct of any sort of religious life at all. One such case occurred in the parish of Torano, in Rinaldi's diocese. First of all, Torano had been targeted, successfully, by Wesleyan missionaries from Villa San Sebastiano. Yet the bishop underscores to Pizzardo that the situation in Torano is "more grave materially" than morally or religiously.[27] Several parish priests in his diocese, including the one who staffed the parish in Torano, had left their positions. They did so, the bishop states, simply "to improve their [economic] conditions"—the decisive factor in the departure of priests from their cures. "Apostate priests" were, first of all, poor priests; they "apostatized" for reasons of unbearable hardship. In short, they were economic apostates.

The bishop had employed a rotating circle of Franciscan and diocesan priests to attempt to establish some sort of regular mass on Sundays. Hardly critical of these priests, the bishop adds that they were men of good will who were also morally impeccable. Yet these defections left several parishes vacant. Intolerable living conditions drove them away. For lack of funds the parish church had been so poorly maintained that it was now nearly destroyed. As in other parishes, no rectory was ever built—the conditio sine qua non for subsistence living for a priest. The bishop hoped to appoint a permanent parish priest whom he knows to have grown up in Torano. His mother was still alive and living in the *casa paterna,* so the priest, the bishop says, could live with his mother. A priest in a poor diocese often lived with his mother until she died or he left the priesthood.

A shortage of qualified parish priests coming from seminary or another parish made appointment difficult as well. Yet, the bishop confesses, even if there were not a scarcity of qualified priests, he would hesitate to appoint one—that is, unless the priest were in addition a simple ascetic content, like a medieval eremite, with an insalubrious anchor-hold and a roof badly in need of repair. (The mention of medieval ascetics and collapsing churches inevitably calls to mind that medieval penitent Francesco da Bernardone—in this, as in several other ways, little had changed in parochial Italy in seven centuries.) Several vacant churches were in such danger of collapse that the civil authorities had closed them down as risks to public health. Bishop Costantini had one year spent the relatively modest sum of 10,000 lire of diocesan funds to make only the most urgent repairs to churches in his dioceses. In one letter he begged Pizzardo "to notify the Holy Father of my need for financial assistance—again."[28] Few bishops are known to have contemplated conversion to evangelical Christianity. One wonders, nonetheless, if any observed with some envy the abundance of American dollars in the wallets of evangelical clergy.

APOSTATE PRIESTS

The final paragraph of Article 5 of the Concordat reads: "Apostate or suspended priests may not be employed or continued in employment as teachers in any office or post that brings them into direct contact with the public."

Only with some appreciation of the treatment of apostate priests in the decades before fascism can one grasp the significance of an article that, on its face, is severe and even punitive. It would be important to know, for example, that the percentage of priests defecting from the Italian Catholic church was much higher in the late nineteenth and early twentieth centuries than in other European states. In the anticlerical decades between the establishment of the kingdom and the ratification of the Lateran Pacts, apostate priests were embraced in the universities, where the prospect of a clerical appointment was nearly inconceivable. Officials in the state's primary and secondary schools were, if anything, encouraged or already predisposed to select a former priest. The result? Apostate priests were extremely well represented—indeed, overrepresented—in the educational sector of the country. One Italian writer estimated in 1929 that more than one thousand ex-priests were teaching in state schools or universities.[29]

Vatican officials objected strenuously to the appointment of apostate priests. They did so on several grounds. First, and most importantly, the appointment of an apostate priest, especially if a convert to Protestantism, represented a possible threat to the Catholic faith of students in his charge: the now-Protestant educator might pour scorn on his onetime clerical colleagues or he might attempt to Protestantize his students. Second, the state had, it seemed, reneged on its pledge to make religious instruction—Catholic catechesis—the "basis and apex" of national education. Finally, such an appointment was a breach of the Lateran Pacts. Representatives of church and state, including Pope Pius XI and Mussolini, tangled over the question whether Article 5 could be retrospectively applied. The pope insisted that the relevant article, the language "*continued* in employment," and the entire intention of the Concordat suggested retrospective application, while Mussolini repeatedly stressed that they did not. Many apostate priests had served in the military, supported Mussolini's grand plans for empire, and were members of the National Union of Fascist Teachers. Mussolini was initially sympathetic, at least in theory, to these loyal to him. He also recognized that the poorly compensated teachers had not struck "during the dark period of Bolshevik strike-mania." Nonetheless, Mussolini's commitment to apostate priests weakened over time. Under steadfast pressure from the Vatican, fascist officials quietly but steadily moved ex-priests from the schools and universities to other positions in the government. This was a hill on which Mussolini was not prepared to die or even, as in the case of Catholic Action, an issue on which to precipitate a crisis. Perceiving that the pope and the Vatican in general would not easily surrender, he discreetly relented. The alleged or real antifascist sentiment of some Protestant ministers and churches, on which the regime began to spy, may have led Mussolini to withdraw his support. The cultivation of youth was for him, as it was for the Vatican, a matter on which he would not compromise. It may be that even the possibility of antifascist ex-priests influencing the minds of the young was a factor in his change.

EX-FILES: STALKING APOSTATE PRIESTS

The tracking of priests who had left their sacerdotal posts, especially if they then married or became Protestant ministers, or both, was pursued at the Vatican with uncompromising intensity. Why? There are many reasons, but one is theological. Priests who had left their posts were identified not as Protestant pastors or ex-priests but as *apostate* priests. This has to do with technicalities in the theology of ordination, according to which a priest receives, in the ordination ceremony, a special, immutable character on his soul. No matter his state of life—be he non-Catholic, married, or a Protestant minister—in the eyes of the church, once ordained, he never ceases to be a priest. Technically, he can become an apostate priest only if he converts or marries.[30] Very foreign in non-Catholic eyes, this was a theological principle given its imprimatur by Augustine in the fifth century and was thus, as well as for other reasons, a nonnegotiable one. But it was not for principle that Vatican congregations kept files on recusant priests. Bad feeling and fear—dread of criticism and panic about accurate representation of the dark realities of diocesan life—were the motives that actuated the Vatican authorities.

The Sacred Congregation of the Council was especially dedicated to tracking the activity of apostate or ex-priests. Its archives have preserved many files on individual ex-priests; in fact, some merited several folders from different years. In 1932 Monsignor Giuseppe Bruno, the secretary of the council, had asked the Jesuit Crivelli to draw up a document that listed all of the ex-priests active in Protestant pastorates in Italy. On 4 January 1933 Crivelli presented the completed work, which listed all the now-Protestant ministers, once Catholic priests, by geographical region. All, Crivelli said, in what was by then a familiar argument, had taken advantage of the allowed denominations law to insist that their "multiple sects [were] equal to the Religion of the State. *Some were not only Protestant ministers but active propagandists.*" Others were subversive and "against the State."[31] Others were reported by diocesan ordinaries to be regarded by the local Catholic population "with indifference."[32]

In cases that made their way to Borgongini, the nuncio usually insisted, on legal grounds, that the priest be removed. This was the case even when an ex-priest had received official governmental recognition and in no way was engaged in seditious activity. Paride Fava appeared on the radar screen of the Sacred Congregation of the Council; it had been alerted by the Pontifical Congregation for the Preservation of the Faith and the Provision of New Churches in Rome.[33] Eventually, the case made its way to the Apostolic Nuncio. Fava was often paired with another apostate priest, Dante Seta, both of whom, according to Crivelli's blacklist, worked in churches in Parma and Abruzzo. Borgongini pairs them as well: before leaving for Parma, Seta had faced down Borgongini in San Sebastiano, and the nuncio had not forgotten. Borgongini suggests that they were particularly dangerous, as they appeared to work together. Be that as it may, the nuncio acknowledges that Fava had received governmental recognition by royal decree as a Protestant pastor in Abruzzo. Yet, he insists, this was only because the General Directorate in Rome "was unaware of the status of the candidate as an ex-priest." In addition, his appointment was "a violation of the Fifth Article of the Concordat."[34] Therefore, his approval "must be revoked." This was a case, in the nuncio's view, that again involved lack of coordination between a local minister and the national government or, more precisely, of local ignorance of the Concordat's laws—an unrelieved frustration. Borgongini concludes his letter by reminding Bruno that he had repeatedly complained about the inconveniences caused by provincial ministers because they were unaware of the meaning of the law. The interpretation of the law by a provincial governmental minister should thus be trumped by what, in Borgongini's view, is its recognized national meaning, and local approval ignored by central governmental officials. In this case we learn from Bruno's response to the Apostolic Nuncio roughly one month later that ecclesiastical pressure had caused Fava's approval as a minister to Methodist congregations to be reviewed by the governmental authorities.[35] Two months later Fava's approved status was revoked.[36]

Occasionally, one of the prefects of the council would write directly to the secretary of state about a particularly troublesome apostate priest. Indeed, in June of 1935 Serafini wrote to Pacelli regarding one Lorenzo Palmieri. (Palmieri earned a folder all to himself in the archives of Serafini's congregation.)[37] Formerly a priest in the diocese of Sant'Angelo in Lombardy, Palmieri was, as Crivelli had noted on his 1933 blacklist, minister of the Baptist congregation of Gioia del Colle in Bari (which Tinti had discussed, as noted above). Ordained in 1901, he had exercised his priestly ministry until 1907. In that year, according to Serafini, he fatefully, and fatally, became friendly with a Protestant minister and "passed into heresy." Sometime in the 1920s he had obtained official governmental recognition. Yet, Serafini goes on, he remains an "occasion of grave worry and scandal." This is not only because his "condition" as a priest is known. It is not only because he is living with a woman in a civil union. Most gravely, he is known as the author of pamphlets written against the church and, crucially, against the pope. If Serafini was right about the latter allegation, Palmieri would have violated Article 10 of the Concordat. Yet what really concerns Serafini is the first point of scandal. Accordingly, he asks Pacelli if—since one cannot now take away his official recognition by the state—he can somehow provoke his transfer to another locale, where his history as a former priest is unknown.[38]

Pacelli passed the case on to Borgongini-Duca.[39] The Apostolic Nuncio reports that he met with the director of cults. He did not ask for a transfer, just a revocation of Palmieri's governmental recognition. Yet he expanded his argument to include all apostate ex-priests, "of whom there are not a few." He proposed that the laws on admitted cults be applied retroactively to these priests, many of whom had received governmental approval before the Concordat. Again, the Apostolic Nuncio argues that Article 5 of the Concordat prohibited ex-priests from holding any office in which they would be in immediate contact with the public. The minister, Borgongini adds, typically, felt "the force of this reasoning," though Montecchi was hesitant. The nuncio therefore left the office asking for the official revocation of the royal decree not only for Palmieri but also for Nesterini. The last we hear of the case is that Montecchi wished first to consult with the government's lawyers, presumably in order to see if the retroactive application of the permitted cults laws was legal.[40] The request for a retroactive application of the law opens a window into the mind of the Borgongini-Duca. For the Apostolic Nuncio, the end of eliminating Protestants from Italian soil and ex-priests from their pastoral posts justified any means, even those clearly immoral as well as *contra legem*. In any case, though the pastor in question was alleged to be an anti-ecclesiastical and even antipapal propagandist, and these would be the only legal grounds on which he could be transferred, Serafini's major preoccupation is with his status as an erstwhile diocesan priest. His defection could humiliate the Catholic church and might encourage others to imagine following his example. As prefect of the Sacred Congregation of the Council, Serafini's anxieties revolve not around insult to the pope but the damage an apostate priest might do to still-faithful priests.

Montecchi, in the aftermath of the case, did confer with state counsel, who gave a response to Borgongini's question that would contradict everything the nuncio had ever said about the application of Article 5 of the Concordat to the situation of ex-priests. The state counsel's legal ruling was revealed to Borgongini when the case of Antonio Fegatelli, an ex-priest serving as a minister in Rapolla, was sent to him by Pizzardo. Born in Città di Castello in 1881, Fegatelli was sent to seminary in Cortona. He was ordained in November 1907, after which he became parish priest of Cagnano. He was reported to have comported himself well for a time. Then he fell in love with a young woman in the parish. With her, he left for Rome in 1924, where he converted to Protestantism. He was called to the evangelical church in Rapolla in 1933. The bishop of Rapolla reports to Serafini that his presence there did not give scandal to the Catholic faithful, though he did tell his own congregation that he had lived in error for many years. The case made its way to the office of the secretary of state, which then, as was customary, handed it over to the Apostolic Nuncio.[41]

Borgongini-Duca sent Buffarini a letter about the case, retailing his usual arguments about how such an appointment was a violation of the fifth article of the Concordat, and (despite the contradictory testimony of the local bishop) argued that his misconduct scandalized the citizens of Rapolla and, moreover, was not unknown to the government before he received his approval.[42] He then met with Montecchi in private. What he was to learn there was to stun him. Montecchi informed him that the state counsel had knocked the legs out from under his argument regarding Article 5 of the Concordat: the office of minister was not a governmental office and therefore did not fall under Article 5 of the Concordat.

Astonished, the nuncio quickly made an appointment with Buffarini. The undersecretary did not attempt to argue with the legal thinking of the state counsel. Fegatelli had licitly acquired his approval from the governmental ministry; it could not be retroactively revoked. Not surprisingly, though, this did not defeat Buffarini. Indeed, he promised Borgongini on the spot that an ex-priest would never again receive approval for evangelical ministry. Perhaps needless to say, his plans for blocking such approval were given in confidence, as they were wholly devious and illegal.

To the nuncio's delight, Buffarini suggested that he would compose a questionnaire. It would have to be completed by any applicant seeking approval for Protestant ministry. One of the questions would ask "expressly if the candidate has ever belonged to other cults." In this manner, the nominating sect would be obliged to say whether it was putting forward an apostate priest or not. If the candidate responded affirmatively, the ministry would refuse the nomination. Instead, it would use its "discretionary powers," which did not make it obligatory to give a rationale for action, to deny approval. In the case of Fegatelli, he continued, he could not revoke the ministerial decree. However, he would send instructions from the minister of cults, directing the agents of Public Security, characteristically, "to make life impossible for him." On 30 June 1936 Borgongini sent a report of his meeting with Buffarini to Pacelli, along with the letter he had sent to Buffarini regarding Fegatelli.[43] It appeared as if Borgongini's arguments on the basis of the fifth article of the Concordat lay in ruins.

Or so it seemed in March 1938, when Pacelli wrote to Serafini. He wanted the assurances given orally by Buffarini that no ex-priest would be approved by the government. He thanked Serafini for keeping him informed about the further steps suggested by the Apostolic Nuncio.[44] Buffarini, having met with Montecchi, was told that such assurances could not be put in writing but that, nevertheless, applications from ex-priests would be rejected on the basis of responses to the question proposed by Buffarini.[45] The battle over the interpretation of Article 5 had been lost.[46] Yet the war over governmental approval—at the national level—had nonetheless been won.

National law, however, was all too often, in the view of bishops, a dead letter. The familiarity of local officials with the law and their willingness to enforce it meant everything. Again, diocesan bishops, such as Luigi Drago, bishop of Tarquinia and Civitavecchia, found themselves frustrated. He wrote Pacelli.[47] Ex-priest Pietro Nesterini had established two *sale* in which around two hundred Baptists met frequently. Their pastors had started an intense oral propaganda and publication campaign among the troops of the Central Military Schools among the students and the workers of the port. Three years later the number of his adepts had not disappeared or even diminished in size.[48] The national law did not bother him at all.

Another ex-priest, Daniele Battisti, had become pastor of the Baptist Sect at Paganico Sabino, roughly thirty-five miles northeast of Rome.[49] Battisti seemed very dangerous to Serafini; he wrote Pacelli, "This congregation is interested in the sectarian activity of the apostate D. Battisti, Baptist Pastor." He was considered a special threat because he was now serving as a Protestant pastor in the town, astonishingly, "where he was once parish priest!" Could the secretariat provide any direction?[50]

Pizzardo immediately involved Borgongini. The nuncio reports that he had interested the director general of cults. Nonetheless, despite unspecified measures taken against Battisti, the "scandal unfortunately remains, and recent events, which are said to be prodigious"—he means evangelical propaganda—have been verified in the same locale. These demand, at least for a measure of public order, the "removal [*allontanamento*] of the apostate." The nuncio expresses his hope that Battisti will be removed but can promise no more.[51] Bitterly, Borgongini insists, as he had many times before, that "one cannot concede the Royal Decree of approval to an ex-priest named to a non-Catholic ministry, because such a decree constitutes him as a public official and puts him at the immediate service of the public."[52] As usual, Borgongini was a *vox clamantis in deserto.* It was a voice to which local officials were often, as in this case, deaf. Serafini's mood as well as Borgongini's would darken over the months they attempted, without success, to suppress the Pentecostal cult.

CHAPTER 8

Borgongini and the Pentecostal Repression (1934–35)

By the early 1930s reports from various dioceses in Italy, particularly from the southern provinces, were beginning to trickle into Borgongini's office. The trickle soon became a flood. In 1932 Borgongini received a report regarding Roman Pentecostals, typical of the sort that was by then engulfing the Roman curia. In it, Melomo, the aforementioned bishop of Monopoli, reports that a number of Pentecostals had traveled from their subterranean seat on Via Adige 20 to his diocese on a propaganda mission. Three Pentecostals, all from the lower classes, he specifies, had attempted to infiltrate his diocese and to make proselytes at a public meeting. Melomo reveals that they succeeded in gaining no converts in this case.[1] Yet dangers loomed.

The bishop was not too humble to indicate how his efforts had, in part, stymied them. "These three foreigners," he reports, "I have attempted to resist in every way." As a result of the bishop's efforts, all three were arrested, convicted, and sentenced for holding illegal public meetings. Nonetheless, in Melomo's view, other Pentecostals in the region remained dangerous: first, they profited from the ignorance of the small population of the countryside and, above all, from the "misery of unemployment." However grievous for peasants, economic anguish established optimal conditions for their conversion. Like other Protestant proselytes, the Pentecostals, "well-funded Americans," were attempting to make converts through gifts of cash or offers of employment. Second, having been convicted of holding public meetings, the three foreigners had now entered a formal application to the Ministry of Cults to build a church (*chiesa*—one of the few times in the entire archival record on this topic that a Protestant church is dignified with that noun) in the bishop's episcopal city. This pattern of Pentecostal behavior was by no means remarkable. Resisted by governmental, legal, and episcopal authorities, the Pentecostals were pressing on to undertake a project that was, in the bishop's eyes, impertinent.[2]

Melomo in fact did resist the Pentecostals in every way he could. Familiar with the local authorities, he visited the prefect of the province and other governmental officials. Using a well-worn argument, he contended that the establishment of a Pentecostal church would offend against the religious sensibilities of the entirely Catholic population, who were (he asserts dubiously) "profoundly devoted to Mary."[3] The establishment of a Pentecostal church would thus "constitute the gravest offense to the sentiment of the whole Catholic population" of the diocese. More ominously, he warned them, a church would provoke angry reactions; these would result in "unanimous protest" and "immense disturbance" to the order and peace of the town. Partly through Melomo's intervention, he had persuaded the local authorities to oppose the "audacious" request of the "sectarian heretics."[4] The episcopal appeal to law and order was again effective.

Melomo reveals that he had already spoken with Cardinal Serafini and even the pope about Pentecostal propaganda in his diocese. But about the "latest effrontery," the petition to build a church in Monopoli, Melomo is particularly distressed, given the power of Strappaveccia. Melomo was well aware—indignantly aware—of the stature and power of Strappaveccia, the minister who presided over the Pentecostal cellar, as the bishop calls the Pentecostal sala, on Via Adige. He knows that the reputation and status in Rome of the chief minister (*capo ministro*) in the city are such that he can "easily open doors in the Ministries of Interior and Justice and at the English and American Embassies." For that reason the bishop of Monopoli asks Borgongini to intervene with his acquaintances in government: "I have already mentioned to the Holy Father and to the Most Eminent Cardinal Serafini everything I have already done. But regarding this latest insolence—requesting permission to build and open a Pentecostal Church—I have not apprised our superiors. Rather, I thought it better immediately and directly to be in touch with you so that I might beg you to intercede forcefully, either directly or indirectly, at the Ministry of Justice to make sure it rejects the permission so *illegally and audaciously* requested."[5] This is a remarkable request. It demonstrates that even a prominent bishop, one who had the ear of the pope and of Cardinal Serafini, would, when Italian governmental power had to be brought to bear, go directly to Borgongini with his request. The bishop could be sure that Borgongini, as remorseless as he, shared his view of Pentecostal insolence. He could be sure, too, that Borgongini would intercede with powerful fascist officials to defy Strappaveccia and the Anglo-Saxon governments, not to mention Italian officials, who championed him.[6]

Determined to eradicate the Pentecostals, Borgongini invited several of his sympathizers to spy on the sect, then to supply him with reports on Pentecostal activity. None did this with such enthusiasm or such a flair for literary embellishment and invention as Carlo Costantini. The nuncio was able to use Costantini's largely fabricated reports to convince Buffarini, who needed little convincing, that the government should criminalize the sect, as it soon did. Buffarini intended to eradicate the sect; Borgongini soon claimed credit for having done so. He relished this rare success in the brief interval within which it became apparent, to his dismay, that this boast, like so many others, was empty. The Pentecostals had not been eradicated.

COMMENDATORE COSTANTINI'S FABLES

Borgongini did indeed respond vigorously—even with overkill. He requested a report on the Pentecostal groups in Rome from Commendatore Carlo Costantini, whom he had used before, soliciting a report that would so blacken the reputation of the Roman Pentecostals as to criminalize their activity. This would bring their troublesome propaganda to an end; or so Borgongini thought. In December 1934 Costantini, after extensive, anonymous "site visits," submitted to Borgongini a lengthy report on the history and roots of Pentecostalism in Rome.[7] The report is something on the order of seven thousand words, augmented by no fewer than ten attachments, largely narratives from local priests, animated by Costantini as well as genuinely unsympathetic to Pentecostal adepts, proselytes, or halls (*sale*) in their parishes.

In the cover letter to his nearly fact-free report, Costantini asserts that the facts plainly suggest that the extravagant and even fatal actions of the Pentecostals in Rome constitute a threat to "the Religion of the State, to the peace, and to the physical health of families." Borgongini-Duca could hardly have been more pleased with this conclusion had he written it himself (he might have). Costantini emphasized what he perceived to be the pathological properties of Pentecostal ritual, the threat the sect posed to Catholicism, and the harm done to the integrity of Catholic families, some of whom it divided by religious affiliation.

The impact of the report was, to say the least, profound. Replete with lurid details, most of them embellished if not fabricated, it decisively confirmed Borgongini's worst suspicions, or, to put it perhaps more truly, responded to his dearest hopes, about the Pentecostal community; it is not impossible that Borgongini tacitly or openly asked for such a report. In any case, Costantini surely knew what Borgongini sought. Because Borgongini then brought it to Buffarini, the report would ultimately bring grave legal harm to communities of the Assemblies of God. Indeed, it would result in the criminalization of the Italian Pentecostal communities.

Anticipating just this sequence of events, Costantini submitted his report to Borgongini, certain that "Your Excellency will wish to denounce [the Pentecostals'] fatal works to the civil authorities, vigilant executors of the orders of the Head of Government." Costantini assured Borgongini that Mussolini had agreed with him on the seriousness of the Pentecostal: it needed to be neutralized. He declared that Il Duce "wishe[d], from the depths of his heart, that neither the peace of families nor the physical health of our race [*stirpe*] be disturbed in any way, and that the Religion of the State not be offended with impunity." The threat to the Italian "race" would not only become the very grounds on which Buffarini would, the following year, make the sect illegal in Italy; it would become the grounds on which the regime would establish legal isolation and death as a prelude to the physical death of Italy's tiny Jewish population. It was this report, commissioned and submitted by Borgongini, that played the decisive role in moving Buffarini to issue his infamous decree in April 1935.[8]

Because of the way he had gathered "evidence," Costantini's report had special authority with Borgongini. According to his own account, Costantini on several occasions attended meetings of the Pentecostals in Rome. "I have myself attended their meetings many times," he wrote, and "have taken personal account of their fatal works," whose intent was "to strip from the heart of Italians the glorious Faith of their fathers, to sow discord in families, and to compromise seriously the physical health that comes to those attracted to their pathological propaganda."[9] The de-Catholicizing, rupturing, or pauperizing of families were grave accusations. Whether true or not, and in how many cases, is another question—one, unfortunately, that can hardly be addressed in any meaningful way, given the number and nature of the extant sources. But it is certain that in many or most cases, the charges were fabricated and thus false.

Costantini's presence as an observer was noticed, and it sometimes changed the character of the Pentecostal meeting. On one occasion several elders were "keeping an eye" on him. On these occasions, when the pastor suspected espionage, he was, Costantini declares, less likely to "slander the Catholic church." In addition, the "convulsions and juddering movements occur[ed] less frequently."[10] Despite this, so much objectionable religious activity occurred and putatively caused such grave physical, psychological, familial, and religious harm that his anomalous presence there only made his charges *more* serious. What, his readers are meant to wonder, occurs when a skeptical Catholic from the papal court is *not* present?

A PUBLIC HEALTH HAZARD

The report begins with a brief, not entirely accurate history of the Pentecostal movement in the United States. Costantini quickly, and for good reason, begins by discussing its origins. Begun by "Charles H. Perham" [*sic*], the movement grew out of a "Bible school" in Topeka, Kansas. Costantini then focuses on the character of Parham himself in an attempt to demonstrate that the sickness of the Pentecostal movement derived from the depraved character of its founder. Parham had been accused of a *brutto peccato,* an unnatural sin. For this, Costantini claims, he had been imprisoned and then exiled by the state of Texas.[11] Catholics hostile to the strange new sect would claim that other Pentecostal leaders were also pedophiles or homosexuals. Michael Ebner has noted that homosexuality was considered antifascist conduct. Indeed, thousands of those identified as pederasts or homosexuals were persecuted, hundreds by rustication to small villages or confinement on small islands. As Ebner puts it, "In the eyes of authorities, homosexual men, particularly prostitutes and flamboyantly effeminate men, belonged to the category of 'dregs' that the Fascist regime sought to eliminate from public spaces." The effeminate pederast was the "antimodel" of the new fascist man.[12] The association of a sect hated for its religious practices with a homosexual founder and pastors was to magnify in the fascist imagination the harm they might cause.

Costantini also underscores, not insignificantly, the very recent origins of Pentecostalism. This was meaningful to Roman Catholic observers. As I noted earlier, antiquity was a mark of authenticity in religion, novelty a sign of inauthenticity, or worse. Indeed, one of the first comments Costantini makes about the movement pertains to the novelty (*novità*) of its worship.[13]

Passing from origin to nomenclature, Costantini observes that, in Italy, members of the sect are known as *pentecostali* or *pentecostisti* or, more pejoratively, tremblers (*tremolanti*).[14] At a meeting held on an early November evening in 1934, in the Pentecostal sala at Via Conte Verde, some 250 adepts were present. Young and old were represented. Some 30 children were there. Six infants were in their mothers' arms. Workers and peasants attended in great numbers. One priest reports that those in need were overrepresented; another that the poorest families in his parish were drawn in. Propaganda was frequently heard at residences inhabited by families in need. Also present was a soldier, who testified that he had previously been a great sinner, which he now realized, having seen "the true light of God."[15] In short, the social and occupational classes represented were not remarkable. In some cases pressure to convert was said to originate not only from material need but badgering from converted employers and friends.[16] If true, such coaxing, involving as it often did poor or impoverished families, would have been especially challenging to resist.

Costantini represented Pentecostals as a threat to the bodily and mental health of the Italian people. This conclusion, reached by psychiatrists, fascist ministers, and cardinals of the curia and ultimately made the foundation of the law outlawing the sect, was occasionally anticipated by priests reporting to Costantini. One reports "damage to health" and "serious illness."[17] Naturally, that raises the question: did priests feel any pressure or expectation to report physical or psychic harm? Were they prompted to report what the authorities wanted to hear? As some priests did not witness Pentecostal services but merely reported on the testimony of others, the response to these questions seems obvious.

Pentecostals were, above all, a menace to the "integrity of the Religion of the State."[18] The parish priest of San Saturnino Martire, Father Giulio Battisti, wrote to Costantini that propaganda was "carried on diligently at the Via Chiana Market," around which Pentecostal residences had by then clustered. The preaching was filled with anticlerical and anti-Catholic invective. Padre Battisti reported an instance of something like Pentecostal iconoclasm. One family, with the vigor characteristic of the newly converted, threw out the windows "with imprecations" sacred paintings removed from the walls of their home. "They burned all the sacred images they could find," he reveals.

Battisti claims that Strappaveccia always used offensive language against the Catholic church and the hierarchy, a claim not otherwise heard in the records except in those produced by Costantini. Lay Catholics he supposedly ridiculed as neopagans, priests as devils. Pentecostals made propaganda assiduously in the nearby Via Chiana Market, always with vehement and explicit invectives against the Catholic church and clergy.[19]

Costantini himself was present at Via Adige 20 when Strappaveccia, the pastor, supposedly ridiculed or slandered the Catholic church. In a sermon on a text from the Gospel of Matthew, the pastor attacked the Catholics with "great bravado." Catholics, Strappaveccia responded, were neopagans and idolaters; this was a common charge, one made not only by Pentecostals. Strappaveccia dismissed Saints Peter and Paul as two "unlettered idiots." If the Catholic church was a perverse deformation of the church founded by Christ, it was the fault, in large part, of these two apostles: one a Judean fisherman, the other, by his own admission and the witness of others, a vicious persecutor of the earliest and most genuine followers of Christ.[20] Here, the general evangelical desire to ground belief and practice in the New Testament stands in stark tension with the special place of these two apostles, especially Peter, in the foundation stories of the Catholic church and above all in the conviction that all popes were successors to Peter as first bishop of Rome. It also conflicts, incredibly, with the Pentecostal aim to found its cult and practice exclusively on the New Testament.

The "strangeness" of Pentecostal worship, for Costantini, consists in the "morbid phenomena" it induces. Some present become agitated and excited. Slowly, all are dragged into a morose state of mind characterized by tremors and violent shocks, above all abrupt and unnatural, even—Costantini anticipates even the campiest of supernatural horror films—"circular" movements of the head.[21] After his first visit to Via Conte Verde, Costantini records the following: "An 'Elder Brother' . . . was screaming like a madman. Uttering incoherent cries, he spoke his words in great haste, as if not taking a breath; and from time to time he animated them with a crescendo of a suggestive voice, screaming as if possessed by the same spirit. . . . Almost all present were sobbing and shook their heads and shoulders convulsively."[22] At the end of every service he attended, Costantini saw repeated "the same paroxysmal scene," with strong, tremulous excitement bordering on collective hysteria.[23] Battisti indicates that the "nervous frenzy" resembled a shared episode of epilepsy. The parish priest also reports that he himself had witnessed, though he does not mention in what context, a young woman from the Pentecostal congregation fall to the ground.[24] This was an effective charge, as both fascist and ecclesiastical authorities were hypersensitive to allegations that the young were put in danger by Pentecostal ritual.

Conversions and the pressure on entire families to convert could lead to intense propaganda, said by some of Costantini's spies to be felt as harassment; in some cases, familial violence was borne of the frustration with constant cajolery. When a porter of a condominium on Via Chiana gave his name to the Pentecostal sect, he was, at least as represented by Fr. Battisti, besieged by incessant propaganda. Even when direct propaganda ceased, he was allegedly harassed by post for a long time.[25] In one case a family had been living "serenely" until the father was converted by "a Pentecostal fanatic." Wishing but failing to convert his family, above all his wife, he grew so angry with her that he struck her violently. He was then arrested.[26] This—familial tension spilling over to furious, sometimes murderous passion—is a common motif in the clerically produced anti-Pentecostal literature. Another priest reports that disaster befell families, particularly children, whose fanatical mother or father forced them to convert.[27] The author of the report, a parish priest, emphasizes the grave threat to children; again, one must ask: was this a topos the authorities hoped to find? and which parochial authorities were only too ready to supply? Here Pentecostals fall into a pattern well established by the time of Costantini's report. All Protestant sects incited social and familial tensions and jeopardized the well-being of the young.

It was not only clerics who alleged this. Relying in part on the testimony of physicians, Costantini contends that Pentecostal rituals were quite dangerous to a convert's mental and physical health, especially to youth—even to those not participating but merely observing. The charge of harm was critical: it was because of the putative danger to the Italian race that the Pentecostals would, within one year, be outlawed by governmental decree. As early as the summer of 1928 Bocchini had called upon a distinguished psychiatrist, Osvaldo Zacchi, to furnish him a medical report on the physical and psychological effects of Pentecostal worship.[28] In February 1934 Costantini called upon him to do the same. Late in that same month Zacchi wrote Costantini a letter recording his impressions after personally attending an evening meeting at Via Adige 20. Zacchi obligingly evokes a tableau of collective hysteria, induced by the suggestion of a sinister pastor. What should truly worry, the physician writes, is the impact that such spectacles can exercise on the psyche of adolescents, "especially among adolescents who may have hereditary defects of a neuropathic character."[29] Again, this was a theme larded with the mysterious jargon of psychiatric medicine, likely to play on both fascist and Catholic fears. Both were jealous for the allegiance of their young. Any threat to that loyalty was likely to be met with resistance.

Pentecostal propaganda and even meetings sometimes occasioned violence. Often enough the Pentecostals would meet resistance, especially in Rome, from young men associated with Catholic Action, which regarded itself as a papal shock corps charged by the pope himself with resisting the Protestant menace. One report, from a Professor Moresi, depicts the clandestine meetings Pentecostal propagandists would hold on the Appian Way (Pentecostal communities, as in this case, would often establish themselves on the periphery of Rome or in the suburbs). On two Sundays in a row, men of Catholic Action interrupted Pentecostal services and put a stop to audible prayer. On a third Sunday, a large number of young men from Catholic Action invaded the same room and scattered them.[30] Costantini depicts the essence and especially the intentions of the leaders of Pentecostal ritual, which he portrays in cynical terms. The entire performance and in particular the agitations of the body were cunningly orchestrated by the pastor and elders of the congregation. Fanatics of the sect were seated strategically so that if neophytes were present they could rise and make way for the newcomers. Their bodily movements were induced by the elder brethren, who skillfully manipulated those present into a state of religious frenzy. Costantini concludes, of the intentions of the elders, "The aim was clear: to influence those present."[31]

About the adherents themselves, Costantini leaves no doubt at all: they are fanatics, plain and simple. Their bodily zeal is excessive and perverse, sinister if not satanic. The leaders of the sect, who are depicted as particularly outré, are less interested in leading prayer than in accumulating adepts. They choreograph and manage the proceedings and manipulate potential recruits. Their charisma looms so large in the proceedings that Pentecostal worship borders on a cult of personality. During the "long, monotonous vociferation of uncertain tongues, paroxysmal screaming and nervous frenzy," their adherents' muscles contracted so unnaturally that some swooned and fainted. One priest, the pastor of the basilican church of St. Agnes on Via Nomenantana (very near the fourth-century Constantinian church of Santa Costanza), reports that a "zealous pseudo-apostle" lured away one of his parishioners, who was now "terribly shaken in the nervous system." The psychic damage to the young who performed in or even witnessed Pentecostal ritual was profound. Their hands shook "as if they were old paralytics." The newly converted young would habitually become stupefied or entranced, rags in the hands of the master.[32]

In order to be approved by the Italian state, Costantini asserts, the Pentecostals had concealed from the governmental authorities the "dangerous oddities of their doctrine" and "worse, the ruinous road to mental and physical health" constructed in their cult—which is indeed "the essence of their deadly teaching." Now, Costantini plans to reveal everything he knows about the "dangerous work Pentecostals do in Italy."[33] His way of doing so was particularly effective, as he drew liberally from critical Protestant sources. In fact, his "report" was a tissue of the fabulous and the pirated. In a Protestant pamphlet entitled *Exposure of the Modern Movement of Tongues,* it is stated that the "fruits of the Pentecostal movement are: free love, immorality, spiritism, hypnotism, false healings and madness."[34] The Protestant magazine *Christian Witness* accused Pentecostal practice of being licentious. Then as now, politics, including religious politics, made strange bedfellows. Hardly all Protestant denominations approved of their Pentecostal brethren, and Costantini, otherwise so suspicious of their propagandistic literature, was delighted to recruit evangelicals to the Catholic anti-Pentecostal campaign. Harnessing evangelical sources to criticize an evangelical sect proved to be quite effective.

Costantini embellishes these claims with stories he had heard from Catholic parishioners and priests. A Catholic mother, a "distinguished woman" of the Via Addolorata parish in Rome, reported to her priest that her son had recently visited a Pentecostal meeting.[35] One evening he secretly invited a Pentecostal pastor to their home and indeed into his bedroom. Suddenly (*improvvisamente*) the young boy's mother opened the bedroom door. She was appalled to see her son being sodomized or, as the text puts it, "She was terrified to see her son the victim of the carnal outpourings of the Pentecostal pastor." The parish priest to whom she reported the supposed incident encouraged her to denounce the shameful fact to the authorities. Fearing that the papers would publish the story and that the "most honorable name" of her family would be ruined, she declined to do so. Lest the reader miss the point of this little story, Costantini concludes: "That shepherd was guilty of the same vile sin of the Pentecostalist founder, Charles H. Parham."[36]

Needless to say, the picture Costantini paints is shaped by his own hostile agenda. The Pentecostal meeting is presented less as a prayer session than as a cynical opportunity for recruitment. Costantini does not even entertain the idea that the bodily expression of religiosity is authentic; it is simply deranged or even a bluff. The sect is a cult in the modern, pejorative sense of that word. For Costantini, this was a form of perverse, unordered, bizarre, and even deviant devotional practice. Pentecostal beliefs and practices are at best strange, at worst pernicious to the psychological and even physical health of all present.

BORGONGINI AND BUFFARINI

By the time Buffarini issued his infamous decree in 1935, which criminalized the practice of Pentecostalism, he and the Apostolic Nuncio had become a fearsome and sometimes fiendish duo. Borgongini-Duca would, by then, complain about a Protestant nuisance, then (sometimes none too subtly) hint that the Protestant irritation ought to be legally interpreted and practically managed. The undersecretary of the interior, encouraged by Borgongini, would, ordinarily, ruthlessly quell the aggravating party.

It had not always been this way. To the contrary, in some instances the two initially disagreed on cases involving Protestant propaganda. As late as 1934 Borgongini would challenge Buffarini on his interpretation of the law, particularly regarding propaganda. Composing his vade mecum *Protestant Proselytism in Italy* may have sharpened the nuncio's own severe interpretation of the law. Certainly it shaped Buffarini's thought and action. Aside from being given to Mussolini and Buffarini, Borgongini's pamphlet had also been distributed to the pope, to the secretary of state, to powerful cardinals like Giulio Serafini, prefect of the Sacred Congregation of the Council, to other congregations, and to many bishops. As a consequence, many of the most powerful prelates in Italy came to construe the laws as they had been interpreted by Borgongini, whose views eventually became normative. In circular fashion, complaints from cardinals, bishops, and priests from around Italy then began to land on the desk of the Apostolic Nuncio in the very legal idiom Borgongini himself had encouraged. The use of the nuncio's language by so much of the Italian episcopate not only satisfied Borgongini; it credentialed him in his discussions with Buffarini.

By 1935 Borgongini had brought the powerful minister of the interior around. This was crucial. Once Buffarini accepted the nuncio's strict interpretation of the laws on admitted cults, he remorselessly issued orders that implemented Borgongini's legal views. As Zanini has observed, "It remains a very interesting fact that Borgongini Duca was always informed ahead of time about the measures the Ministry of the Interior was about to take."[37] There is good reason for this. The Apostolic Nuncio, having cultivated Buffarini in person and in correspondence, sent many of the prelatical complaints he received to Buffarini. Scholars of Hitler have shown that Nazi racial policy seemed to radicalize each time Himmler visited Hitler.[38] Analogously, Buffarini's increasingly harsh legal measures correspond to the pattern of missives received or meetings had with the Apostolic Nuncio. This pattern is punctuated by the infamous Buffarini Decree (written by Bocchini) by which Pentecostalism was criminalized in 1935. After Buffarini and the Apostolic Nuncio had agreed to the action, but before the decree was issued, the latter would boast (in a letter only recently made available at the Vatican Archive) that *he*—Borgongini—had suppressed the practice of Pentecostalism in all of Italy. In fact, the infamous Buffarini Decree was, in large measure, as much an expression of the dogged will of the Apostolic Nuncio (and, by extension, the Roman curia) as it was the desire of the undersecretary of the interior.

Buffarini succeeded Leandro Arpinati as secretary of the Interior Ministry only in May 1933. By that time Borgongini had already taught in the College for the Propaganda of the Faith. He had also tangled with no less a figure than Ernesto Buonaiuti, viewed by many Catholics as a heretical modernist; the two had argued about Augustine's doctrine of original sin.[39] It was in this dispute with Buonaiuti that characteristics eventually associated with Borgongini's conduct in the campaign against the Protestants came to light: an appreciation for univocal, established Catholic interpretations; distaste and even contempt for deviation from them; inflexibility in discourse; and a capacity, from sheer stubbornness and obedience to inherited doctrine, to wear down opponents. These characteristics would serve him well as the Vatican's anti-Protestant generalissimo during the fascist period. So, too, would the experience he had in the office of the Congregation for Extraordinary Ecclesiastical Affairs, and his participation in the negotiations that led to the signing of the Lateran Accords.

After the pacts were signed Borgongini was made Apostolic Nuncio. Throughout the fascist period he would defend fearsomely—using often extreme means, from which the Vatican would occasionally dissociate itself—what he took to be the interests of the church. By the time Buffarini took his position as undersecretary of state, Borgongini had been point man for the Vatican on "the Protestant problem" for four years. He had dealt with complaints from dioceses around the peninsula on the issue of Protestant propaganda and had been asked by the pope and Pacelli on numerous occasions to respond to a particular episcopal request for guidance or assistance. Above all, he had reflected for years on the application, meaning, and implications of the permitted cults laws. He had had the opportunity to insist to religious and governmental ministers, single-mindedly, intransigently always, on his interpretation of the laws.

In February 1934 it had come to the nuncio's attention that the Free Christian Church in Siena had been proselytizing peasants in small villages in the area. Borgongini immediately asked Buffarini to see if there was any way the government could stop the propaganda. On 10 February Buffarini replied, outlining actions he had taken. The prefect of Florence, with whom Buffarini had consulted, reported that he was unable to stop "the alarming proselytism" because "such propaganda was confined to the strictly religious field."[40] At this point Buffarini accepted the view, shared by the prefect of Florence (and the overwhelming majority of his peers) that propaganda was activity permitted by Italian law.

Incensed, the Apostolic Nuncio set up a meeting with Buffarini. They met on 13 February in his office. Borgongini had brought a prepared text with him, presumably reflecting the position he took in *Protestant Proselytism in Italy.* He had Buffarini read the relevant text in its entirety, in which he concluded that while "the law had guaranteed free exercise of cult . . . the Italian laws do not authorize . . . proselytism." With typical self-satisfaction Borgongini reports to Pacelli of Buffarini's view on the free exercise of cult: "It seemed to me that he was persuaded and impressed with it."[41] Citing Boselli and the relevant laws of 1929–30, he argues that propaganda did not fall "in the strictly religious field" and indeed was an aggression against the Catholic faith. He then instructs Buffarini to ensure that the laws, as explained, would be observed and enforced and that the proper interpretation of the laws, Borgongini's own, be brought to the attention of the authorities in Florence and Siena.[42] Buffarini, however, like his superior, Mussolini, thought that Borgongini had exaggerated the dimensions of the problem. The Ministry of the Interior had, he said, conducted an inquest and concluded that only some eighty Italian centers of Protestantism existed in all of Italy. Borgongini presumed to correct him again. He, too, had conducted an inquest (he was referring to the work done by Crivelli), and the number of Protestant centers was an order of magnitude larger. Admitting that he had counted only two large cities, Buffarini conceded the argument to Borgongini.[43]

Borgongini suggested that Buffarini phone the prefect of Aquila to clear out the Protestant centers of Villa San Sebastiano and Cerchio. Buffarini agreed.[44] For Borgongini, it was an extraordinary hour. He brought Buffarini to his view of the meaning and implications of the law, corrected him on the extent of propaganda in Italy, and, amazingly, suggested a course of action to which the powerful and sometimes ruthless undersecretary of the interior instantly agreed. As Borgongini attempted to justify further why the fascist government should react according to his view of the laws, Buffarini stopped him. "Your Excellency," Buffarini assured him. "You are right. We will respond to you." He then added, ominously ("in these exact words," Borgongini says), "But we will do more than respond to you."[45] Given what we know about the events of April 1935, it is difficult to read this as anything but a sinister assurance that Buffarini's future response to Borgongini's requests would be more than verbal.

"I HAVE SUCCEEDED IN ABOLISHING THE PENTECOSTAL CULT IN ALL OF ITALY"

Borgongini summarizes, so he says, a document he received from Costantini. Actually, he solicited it. Based on the fact of their "well-known criminal violence," Costantini "*came to suspect,* based on the details of the Report," that a murder in Pescara had been committed by "a Pentecostal Protestant."[46] The report is, again, fabulous, highly constructed, self-contradictory, folkloristic. It also arrived on a curious date: 1 April 1935. Borgongini had been looking for one final persuasive document to convince Buffarini to move legally against the Pentecostals. This was that document.

Basing his "findings" on a newspaper story, a police statement, and a letter from a parish priest, which he then recombines with vivid imaginative power, Costantini reports that in Villanova, a village in the province of Pescara (Abruzzo), a man who appeared to be a Pentecostalist had violently murdered his Catholic wife. The report in the *Giornale d'Italia* (26 February 1935) stated only the following: Luigi Torricelli, aged fifty-five, a farmer from the village of Villanova in Pescara, around six thirty in the evening on 25 February 1935 murdered his wife, aged forty-nine. He had struck her with a hammer and shot her four times. After absconding with his ten-year-old daughter on a bicycle, he was stopped, arrested, and charged with homicide. Torricelli had once been imprisoned for life. (He was later amnestied.) The newspaper article does not state with certainty what his motive for murder was but concludes that Torricelli had long since converted to Protestantism. Since then—a leitmotif in the anti-Pentecostal literature—the couple had quarreled continuously. Torricelli had demanded that the couple's daughter be "educated in the new religion." Her mother refused.[47]

According to the parish priest of Villanova, Padre Giuseppe Rossi, Torricelli, on the evening before murdering his wife, had had a long conversation with a peasant from the nearby village of Spoltore. Named Gino, the visitor from Spoltore was known locally by his nickname, Puzzabaffi (smelly moustache). Puzzabaffi (we are helpfully reminded by Padre Rossi that he was *brutto d'aspetto*) presided over evangelical meetings held in a farmhouse in Spoltore. His freakish physical appearance and ugliness—a folkloristic touch that Costantini belabors—make him seem particularly sinister. For reasons I will discuss presently, Padre Rossi's claim that strange activities "peculiar to the so-called Pentecostals" occurred there is dubious. Puzzabaffi, the priest goes on, had recently been spotted roaming tiny villages in the countryside. This description corresponds to what we know about the religious landscape of Pescara. It was a land where free-form itinerant evangelism was common. Evangelists often had no credentials from any church or church body or from the state; no one recognized them officially as ministers; and they were supported by no organization. Puzzabaffi was such a minister. Bible in hand, "he gave an interpretation all his own." This point was absolutely true, even understated—one of the few wholly reliable of Costantini's otherwise mostly untrue remarks. According to Costantini, Puzzabaffi preached

1. The end of the world would occur in the year 1935. All ought to stop cultivating the land, as it was now useless.
2. Jehovah [*Jeova*] had forbidden murder, so that, if conscripted, one must refuse to participate in military service.
3. Jehovah had forbidden one man to submit to another, for he would then become a slave. The king, the pope, and Mussolini were the Three Beasts of Italy, and they "must be gotten rid of."
4. The Lord alone [that is, not Mary, or any of the saints] exists in Heaven. He alone must be obeyed. One must not worship saints, who do not exist, and therefore must burn all images of them. [Costantini then adds that he also teaches specifically about the spouse of Torricelli]:
5. The wife [of Torricelli] represents Satan, so that, if she were to refuse to accept the new teaching, it would be necessary to "tie her hands and feet and stick a red-hot iron in her mouth up to her throat."[48]

There is much that demands reflection here. First, his teachings strongly suggest that Puzzabaffi was not a Pentecostalist; he appears to be a Jehovah's Witness (the Witnesses were and still are well represented in Pescara). Not only does he prefer the use of *Jeova* to *Dio.* His teachings are full of apocalyptic warnings and imagery that, though hardly absent from Pentecostal discourse, were typical of Jehovah's Witnesses in fascist Italy. Moreover, the Witnesses were pacifists and conscientious objectors; Torricelli had been convicted of desertion. He was not the only one. Italian authorities were well aware of the Witnesses' refusal to take up arms and their many requests for exemption from military service. That they would not participate in the military made them special targets of the regime as the Ethiopian War began.[49] They certainly were represented by Catholic and fascist authorities, not untruly, as being opposed to Mussolini, to fascism, and to Catholicism.

Much less likely to be true is the reported claim that the three beasts of Italy—the dictator, his regime, and the church—had to be gotten rid of. After all, this would require the sort of violence to which the Witnesses were profoundly opposed. The same objection may be made to the fifth point, which recommends a kind of violence so baroque that it appears to be entirely fabricated. In fact, Costantini *had* embroidered a tissue of fables and falsehoods, all intended so to blacken the reputation of Italian Pentecostals as to make them a grave and imminent danger to the state.

Costantini's tale continues. According to Padre Rossi, the evening of 25 February was not the first time that Puzzabaffi and Torricelli had met. Whenever Puzzabaffi came to visit Torricelli, he always hectored him. Puzzabaffi insisted that Torricelli compel his wife to do what he ordered: burn the household saints. According to Costantini, Torricelli directed her to do so many other odd things that the poor wife was too embarrassed to repeat what he had said to her sister after her husband had vented (*sfogava*). Through 25 February the most Torricelli had done was vent. Yet his was, apparently, a terrible anger.

The following morning the couple argued. As if following the program laid out by Puzzabaffi, the husband filled a ditch with all the images of saints they had in the house. From here the story becomes positively lurid and incredible. Furious that his wife would neither convert nor allow their daughter to do so, Torricelli attempted to cut off his wife's finger; he wanted to take back her wedding ring. Torricelli then supposedly picked up an axe and smashed his wife in the head. Her eyes "shot out of their sockets" before she fell into a "lake of blood." His wife prone, Torricelli shot her four times. Then, "in coldest blood," he nonchalantly recharged his weapon. As there were no witnesses to the shooting, Torricelli's nonchalance, among other things, seems entirely manufactured. The murderer then put his ten-year-old daughter on a bicycle and left before authorities arrested him. Later Puzzabaffi, too, was arrested.[50]

The protagonist of this story is probably a pacifist by religious conviction. The saga is so farcical, so thoroughly soaked in blood, that it reads as if feverishly concocted by Quentin Tarantino. The modern reader may also find the testimony of witnesses darkly comic in its resemblance to the postmortems televised after mass shootings in present-day America. The sister of the victim and all the murderer's relatives agreed. Torricelli had been a "tranquil, hardworking man, affectionate toward his wife, one who went to church regularly." Then he converted: "*From the moment he had contact with the Protestants,*" his relatives state, "he *totally* changed."[51]

Costantini continues. The tension introduced into marriage and family life by Pentecostal propaganda was hardly confined to the small towns mentioned here: "It is obvious that this last episode reveals a system and a teaching which, though it happened in Pescara, occurs in numerous other villages in Italy." The unremitting discord between husbands and wives, brothers and sisters had spread among small evangelical communities so comprehensively that it was now "the order of the day."[52] In fact, the abduction of children by evangelical parents had occurred "in many other villages," including the ever-neuralgic Villa San Sebastiano. Even after the arrest of Puzzabaffi, his nefarious influence "ramified out, deeply." A parish priest near Castellana reported that one Giuseppe Nevicone constantly quarreled with his wife in an attempt to induce her to become evangelical. On one occasion, he attempted (as Puzzabaffi would have recommended) "to burn her tongue." Hearing her cries, her neighbors rushed to the scene and prevented the husband from mutilating his wife.[53] How could Italy tolerate such violence against women and children?

Just days before the Buffarini Decree was issued, this was precisely the sort of question that Borgongini wanted asked. Costantini delivered a narrative that required a reader to ask it. On the list of teachings imputed to Puzzabaffi, Borgongini concludes, likely thinking of the demand that Mussolini and fascism be "gotten rid of": "As is obvious, this is Bolshevism." That may not be obvious to all, but Borgongini warns, if "the Authorities did not take energetic measures immediately," these villages "will be overcome with revolutionary furor."[54] Later in Costantini's account we learn that Tommaso Ricci, a construction worker in Pescara, came under Puzzabaffi's influence and converted to evangelical Christianity. Like all of Puzzabaffi's acolytes, Ricci too, according to Borgongini, had ideas that were "decidedly unpatriotic and have the whiff of Bolshevism." Indeed, Ricci had once proclaimed, about the future of communists in Italy: "We will come, as in Russia!" (for which "antifascist and subversive ideas" he was imprisoned). Puzzabaffi himself is represented as declaring that communists in Russia had achieved their aim, "but we hope to do so here soon."[55] In Red-baiting and mythmaking, Senator McCarthy had little on Costantini.

Costantini's catalogue of charges is methodically, if ludicrously, comprehensive. Torricelli and the Pentecostal pastor are

Antifascist
Bible Bangers
Bloodthirsty
Bolsheviks
Deserters
False Prophets
Iconoclasts
Ignoramuses
Murderers
Pacifists
Perverters of the Young
Pope Haters
Proselytes
Unpatriotic
Wife Batterers
(And brutto d'aspetto—Ugly)

Inspecting this all-inclusive list of enormities, one may doubt whether *anything* about Costantini's tale is true. It is quite overdone. Witnesses are not mentioned, only commentators on Torricelli's character. Why so wide-ranging a list of iniquities? Hoping to persuade Buffarini of Pentecostal danger, the nuncio got (and likely solicited) from Costantini a comprehensive indictment that could not fail to shame them. Was such criminality worthy of anything but legal suppression? Borgongini himself answers this rhetorical question: "It is therefore certain that the Government, aware of these facts, will take appropriate steps to free Italy from those who abuse the freedom of the Cults admitted by the State to undermine that union of minds and hearts, which, under the aegis of the Catholic Religion and of the Regime, arouses the admiration of foreigners and forms the greatness of our Homeland."[56] The regime would have found any combination of these crimes injurious either to physical health or to the sensibilities of Catholics. Costantini supplied a "hermeneutical" or constructed Pentecostal—constructed so as to bring down Italian Pentecostalism.[57] He did so two months before Buffarini issued his "Circular" criminalizing the sect.

On 9 April, the day he would issue his infamous decree, Buffarini wrote to Borgongini, indicating he had received his letter and the "report of Professor Constantine on the heinous crime committed in Villanova by an affiliate of the Pentecostal sect." He goes on: "I would like to inform you that the activity of the sect has been under close scrutiny, on the basis of which measures adopted are *in the course of being executed.*"[58] Borgongini then excitedly writes Pacelli:

> I am honored to communicate to Your Reverend Eminence that at a meeting, which I attended yesterday at the Ministry of the Interior, I was informed of the successful suppression of the sect of the Pentecostals all over Italy. The Ministry has given orders for this suppression with a circular sent to all the Prefects of the Kingdom. I was also told that all the Prefects have acknowledged receipt of the circular. It also reported the centers or stations of the existing sects in the various provinces have been rapidly disbanded. Finally, I was informed that the appeal from the head of the Pentecostals of Rome [Strappaveccia], directed to His Excellency Mussolini, was rejected; the instruction regarding the act of dissolution, depending as it does on the discretionary powers of the Minister, is incontrovertible. . . . I attach here a copy of the report of His Excellency the Honorable Buffarini.[59]

In a letter written on 18 March 1935 to Pacelli, Borgongini reports to the secretary of state that he "had been informed that the Prefect had issued a decree for the closure of the sala of the Pentecostals on via Adige in Rome and had ordered the Questura to enforce it." He adds that Bocchini and the director general of cults both supported the decree and had taken measures to see that it was adopted. "Therefore," the nuncio concludes, "there is every reason to believe that the closure decreed will soon be a fait accompli." In a letter written to Luigi Cardinal Lavitrano concerning Adventists in his episcopal city of Palermo, Borgongini-Duca urges Lavitrano to be in contact with Buffarini. Why? Because, Borgongini boasts, it was with such direct requests that "*I* have been able to abolish the Pentecostal cult in all of Italy" (*sono riuscito ad abolire il culto pentecostale in tutta Italia*).[60] Borgongini was not wrong to suggest that it was he who had had a major influence on the policy of suppression associated for almost a century now with the name of Buffarini.

To the dismay of the nuncio and the pope, however, he was quite wrong about one claim: the Pentecostal cult had not been abolished. Like other proselytizing groups, they would soon reconstitute themselves under the generic name of "Protestants" or "evangelicals."

CHAPTER 9

Stalemate (1936–39)

Sensing that Protestant proselytizing was not diminishing, despite all efforts, Pope Pius himself ordered Serafini to compile another report. Soon, the head of the Sacred Congregation of the Council commissioned reports from bishops, priests, and other trusted Catholics in cities and towns where "major proselytizing in Italy" was believed to be occurring. The reports of all but two of the ordinaries from Italy and Sicily arrived on the desk of Serafini, most of them in the middle to late months of 1936. The prefect subsequently submitted a report very briefly summarizing conditions in situ from the men who knew them best: the diocesan bishops.[1] After the pope read it, the report would be forwarded to Borgongini.

Despite the brevity of the report, it painted a most discouraging picture. Most of the bishops reported that Protestant propaganda was intense or intensifying. Some reports were even worse. The bishop of Cremona reported that the sectarian activity of the Protestant pastor was accompanied by "ardent Socialist-Bolshevik propaganda." In La Spezia an evangelical orphanage welcomed sixty children, all of them from apostate Catholic families. Slavic Protestants, allegedly communist, began settling in Gorizia, in northern Italy. (Opposition to *slavo-communismo,* as Bartolini has pointed out, united many Italians, including nonfascists.)[2] In Foggia the Waldensians were said to be helped by a wealthy Swiss family; they were bringing students into the fold by financial subsidies. Waldensians in Taranto were a "troubling and quite radical organization" with a very active and able pastor, one Bertini di Torre Pellice. He uses "most deceptive methods." In Bologna, Adventists continuously made incursions, where "they are attempting definitively to establish their community." In December 1935, for example, Pizzardo received news that Pentecostals in Brindisi had resumed their propaganda. He sent the case to Borgongini, who had an assistant take the case to a functionary in the Ministry of the Interior, Senator Mormino. The minister reported, improbably, that the Pentecostals were attempting to proselytize local Catholics with séances. Mormino also promised to alert the local authorities in Brindisi.[3] Many letters arrived at the Vatican to inform the disappointed cardinals there that the Pentecostals had reconstituted themselves under the broad name of evangelicals. The bishop of Grosetto wrote Giuseppe Bruno in February 1936 to say that Public Security had attempted to shut down Pentecostal activity, but that they had "camouflaged themselves under the name of *evangelici* and so are unfortunately able to continue their deleterious work."[4] Bruno passed on the letter to Pacelli, asking him to do what he could to eliminate the problem.[5] Borgongini finally had the director general of cults intervene. The nuncio reported, too optimistically, that "the *subdole insidie* of the adepts had been foiled as a result."[6] The Pentecostal community, it appeared, had been scattered but not extinguished by the papal nuncio and Buffarini.

When the pope read the completed report in 1937, it deeply demoralized and puzzled him. He could not imagine how fruitfully to address so recalcitrant a problem; even pondering it troubled him greatly. In a state of near despair, the pope ordered Pacelli to send the entire lengthy file, roughly one hundred folio pages, to his nuncio. Borgongini's response to Pius XI could not have elevated his mood. Evangelicals were still active. The Pentecostals had reconstituted themselves. Governmental institutions were not consistently cooperating; many officials were still not enforcing the law. In short, despite Borgongini's assurances, almost nothing had changed since the start of the evangelical campaign.

The file consisted mostly of thirteen highly detailed reports on regional conditions from diocesan bishops. In his letter to Borgongini-Duca, written in March 1937, Pizzardo told the nuncio why the file was being sent to him: "His Holiness, sadly impressed by a situation so troubling [*cosi preoccupante*], has expressed the desire that the entire *incarto* be sent to you, so that you may treat the question in a mode more effective than will be possible for him."[7] Perhaps the most enlightening of the reports was written by Amedeo Ghetti, a delegate from the Congregation for the Preservation of the Faith and a parish priest at a church in the center of Bologna; he was also an official at the archiepiscopal curia of Bologna.[8] Borgongini would later state: "The report of Rev. Amedeo Ghetti, Delegate of the Preservation of the Faith in this city, is very well documented." Though he was part of an episcopal curia, his was the only report not written by a bishop. This, perhaps, is what makes it so unusually revealing. It is a microstudy of the diocesan dynamics of clergy, Catholic parishioners, Protestant proselytes, converts, and law enforcement by someone who was not too busy to write a clear, comprehensive report on local conditions. How, the Sacred Congregation of the Council wished to know, were the laws of permitted cults curtailing or conditioning Protestant activity? Ultimately, the reports addressed to the council would make their way to Borgongini.

In this case, a whole series of obstacles frustrated local authorities, both ecclesiastical and legal, from permanently effecting Borgongini's essentially legal vision from the Vatican at the local or regional level. As is almost always the case, a lawmaker envisages one thing, however clear; it is another thing for law enforcement to implement the specific provisions, or even to understand what they seem to require.

It is clear from his report that Ghetti, at least, was fully familiar with Borgongini's thoughts on the interpretation of the culti ammessi laws.[9] Indeed, he finds the local Protestants in more or less continuous violation of them. "This sect," he begins, "profits from too elastic an application of the observance of the article of the laws of the Concordat regarding permitted cults."[10] In this case, the troublesome sect for the Catholic and police authorities was a congregation of Adventists. They were, Ghetti pointedly notes, all of "foreign origin: Swiss, Anglo-Saxon, American."[11] Like other such sects, they took advantage of the religious ignorance and the economic distress of many families "with cunning [*subdoli*] and not always sincere methods." They held meetings without the permission of authorities, sold religious materials in private homes, persuaded the ignorant to believe that the books, fascicles, and reviews they distributed were written by Catholic missionary orders;[12] and, finally, they bribed the poor with subsidies and benefits.[13] It was thus that many souls had been drawn from "the purity of the Catholic faith."[14]

Protestant denominations were thin on the ground in Emilia-Romagna during the fascist period. Although Italy was the first European nation in which Adventists had attempted to missionize (arriving in Torre Pellice in 1864, where the large population of Waldensians welcomed them), their number was never large. At the time of the Geneva Conference (1909), Adventists numbered only 44 members in all of Italy, of whom 26 were still in Torre Pellice.[15] In 1910 they established themselves in Florence; it would remain an important center for the denomination. By the end of the Great War the Adventists had spread both north to Genoa and Pisa and south to Bari and other towns. Still, in 1920, they had managed to establish just 7 communities and numbered just 120 members. After a publishing house called the Herald of Truth (after which the sect's Italian newspaper, *L'Araldo dell Verità,* would be named) was established in 1926—its publications would trouble the Catholic community several times in the decade after its establishment—an Italian Union Mission was organized in 1928. The sect then grew relatively rapidly. Shortly before the report was submitted, membership increased to near 600, and the sum of churches to 25. The Jesuit Crivelli reported that, in the fascist era, growth among the Adventists was consistent, if not sensational.[16]

Ghetti wrote his report at about the same time Crivelli finished his book. Ghetti covers the diocese of Bologna during the period from 30 April 1936 to July 1937, which is to say, rather late in the anti-Protestant campaign. He begins by saying that, of the "sects of foreign origin" now active in Italy, only the Adventists were propagandizing actively in Bologna. In the apocalyptic vision of the Adventists, the Catholic church and the papacy were the seven-headed beast from the sea (Apocalypse 13:1–10). Despite the existence of a moderate wing, most evangelical activity was directed by those quite hostile to Rome. That antagonism was reciprocated by Ghetti, who supplies many details about the leadership, proselytizing, and fate of the Adventists in his diocese over the course of more than a year.

Ghetti focuses on the relationship of Adventist activity to the Law on Permitted Cults, which would have pleased Borgongini-Duca. But he reveals, among other things, that the civil authorities, still at this late date, were ignorant of the law or interpreted it erroneously. For how severely evangelical sects were persecuted during the fascist era, and how their suffering has been rightly underscored by Protestant historians, it bears repeating that Vatican authorities were profoundly frustrated throughout the entire decade with the ignorance or indolence of police authorities.

Further, even when interpreted correctly—that is to say, as the nuncio would have seen it—by law enforcement, Adventists defied the law or claimed that it had been revised to their advantage. On occasions in which Adventists were disciplined by law officers, decisions were reversed. The religious innocence of the parishioners, whom the sectarians had exploited with "deceitful arts" (*arti subdole*), could have pleased no one at the Vatican. It is little wonder the pope was so discouraged by the report. As Ghetti proceeds, he makes clear that the real difficulty is not flexibility in application of the law per se or even the deceit of the Adventists but the governmental authorities' ignorance of the law. Local police authorities, Ghetti reports, had difficulty in interpreting the laws of the Concordat, presumably including the implementing legislation of June 1930; it would be "a great providence" if civil authorities could supply more precise orders on their observance.[17] The police authorities in Bologna had, to that point, interpreted the laws in favor of the Protestant cults and "to our disadvantage." Little could have frustrated Borgongini more at this late date. For example, the local parish priest had on several occasions alerted the Carabinieri Reali to Protestant infractions, especially proselytizing. When interrogated, however, the accused "invoke certain articles of the law, which they interpret in their favor." This threw the governmental officials into a state of indecision and inhibition: "The authorities, especially in the small towns, do not know for certain if anti-Catholic propaganda is forbidden or not." In such cases, a zealous parish priest with clarity on the law, Ghetti observes, could "clear up the confusion." In the relatively populous town of Via Scipione del Ferro, under intense Adventist propaganda, spread from a sala established in 1934, many citizens were converted to Adventism only to be reconverted to Catholicism. "[Yet] in some small towns, such nasty propaganda continues, unfortunately," as the Adventist pastor Lippolis had already made "several victims of his error" and continued to hold at least weekly visits and conversations in their homes. Again, this was in 1937.

Ghetti proceeds to catalogue the number of laws that Lippolis and his fellow Adventists had broken in order to proselytize. First, according to the law decreed by the Ministry of the Interior, a nucleus of baptized faithful of a particular cult had to be proven to exist in order to establish an oratory. Yet no such nucleus existed before the arrival of Lippolis. Thus the oratory had been opened "purely to propagandize" and, thus, "in contradiction to the law."[18] Ghetti reports that, on these grounds alone, he felt empowered to appeal, successfully, to the Questura of Bologna to have the Adventist oratory closed. For the moment, the local Catholic diocese had beaten back the Protestant threat. Yet its triumph was ephemeral. Ghetti complained to the authorities that, while Adventist worship was permitted, the Adventist sala was being used for purposes of propaganda and proselytism. Despite "ample reports sent to the Prefecture on 17 May 1935," the "oratory was newly opened" in May of 1936, "and even currently functions as such." Startlingly, it was opened after intervention on its behalf by the Ministry of the Interior. This was at the very moment that the same ministry was, at Borgongini's direction, suppressing the Pentecostals of Calatabiano.[19]

Frustrated, Ghetti then met with his archbishop, who counseled him to report that evangelical meetings were being held every Friday evening at Via Scipione del Ferro 11 (several miles east of Ghetti's church) in the home of a recent convert named Landuzzi. Unauthorized proselytizing occurred there, which, as Borgongini had insisted, made activities occurring in a private residence a matter of public interest and therefore open to police intervention. Ghetti had persuaded the questor of Bologna to intervene. The subsequent Friday the questor sent a functionary along with the Carabinieri to make an arrest. Somehow, the pastor was alerted or had suspected there would soon be trouble. The police discovered that he had recently returned to the Adventist seat in Florence. He did not appear for any of the Friday meetings in the subsequent month (December 1936). However, in January he began returning. One Friday evening the Questura finally located him in the Adventist sala "in the very act of catechizing several persons." "Frightened and embarrassed," Ghetti reports, he defended himself by asserting he was not propagandizing but only "conversing with sympathetic Adventists." The policeman was not persuaded. He threatened arrest to those sympathetic to the pastor if they held another meeting, then sent them home.[20]

The authorities invited the pastor, Lippolis, to present himself the following day at the Questura in Bologna. On that day Lippolis was ordered to desist from his propaganda. He agreed to do so. Ghetti reports that the Catholic population of the quarter of Bologna in which Lippolis's congregation was seated was pleased that Lippolis would "no longer disturb them by making Protestant propaganda." Yet Lippolis shortly began to make furtive visits from Florence to the houses of neophytes and continued to make converts. A couple he had converted, elementary school teachers, were said to be propagandizing in the schools. Once the Adventist oratory was reopened, Lippolis was almost continuously in Bologna, "making works of proselytism everywhere" in the city. He also went into the provinces. For example, on a weekly basis he traveled to Castel San Pietro, a town with more than six thousand inhabitants. He went to family homes, where he "catechize[d] his false doctrine."

After a complaint from Ghetti to the police authorities in Bologna, the Questura sent a number of the Carabinieri along with a governmental official to the casa Landuzzi, where Lippolis frequently visited: he had already returned to the Adventist headquarters in Florence. On another occasion he was caught at the Landuzzi residence; he explained that he was not propagandizing, merely conversing. Not believing him, the police functionary collected Protestant Bibles and publications, threatened to arrest all present, and then invited the pastor to present himself again the following day at the Questura. To Ghetti's dismay, his followers in the neighborhood persuaded the authorities that Lippolis would no longer disturb the peace by propagandizing.[21]

"Now," Ghetti laments, "it seems as if nothing practical can be done at the Questura for the closure of the oratory." By the time of his return, Lippolis had been officially recognized by the Ministry of Cults as an Adventist pastor, and, according to information Ghetti got from the Questura, the oratory was opened with the authority of a government decree. But the Questura told Ghetti more: they were still keeping an eye on Lippolis. This was not for his propaganda but because he was suspected of being antifascist.[22] This was an offense against the state about which no policeman could have been in doubt. Still, Borgongini, learning of Lippolis, was frustrated that Public Security was generally either ignorant of the law or lax in its application, as when offenses against the church, which were also crimes against the state, went unpunished.

He was even more exasperated that the authors of several reports—bishops and archbishops—were also, and more culpably, ignorant of the law. Evidence for this consists of the marginal notations Borgongini made in the full reports of some of the bishops. For example, Archbishop Carlo Margotti of Gorizia (1934–51) wrote to Serafini that meetings run by a pastor from Trieste had occurred in his diocese. A list of the places they met was given to Public Security. The archbishop goes on: "But these do not seem to require intervention because these meetings are entirely private." The nuncio underlined the words *del tutto privata* and, in the column, wrote in red pencil, "No."[23] Evidently the good archbishop was unaware of the nuncio's views on the character of private meetings. Once the entire document, of which Ghetti's report is the largest part, was finished and the pope absorbed its findings, Pius XI asked Tacchi Venturi to bring it to the attention of Mussolini. In March of 1937 the Jesuit intermediary reported that he would be happy to do so. The last we hear from Tacchi Venturi is that he had not yet been able to agree on a date with Il Duce.[24]

Having finished the report, one assistant to the pope, Monsignor Giovanni Pizzocolo, was disheartened. He trains his criticism not on diocesan priests or on the ignorance of the laity but on the confusion, indifference, ignorance, and indolence of the Italian bishops. While some bishops affirmed that in their dioceses there was no Protestant propaganda, others lamented that, to the contrary, such propaganda was quite strong. Some bishops lament clerics who are not well-formed or zealous. Others complain that they lack Catholic Action and other institutions to combat Protestant propaganda. Some bishops deplore the ignorance of the people as one of the principal causes that favor propaganda. True, Pizzocolo says, but what have the bishops done for religious instruction, for example, by Christian teaching on holidays? The Sacred Congregation is perplexed at certain reports. For example, in one report it is said that there are at most a dozen Protestants, while another source says there are 2 pastors, 3 deacons, and 250 Wesleyan Methodists in a single diocese. In another report, assurance is given because Protestants diffuse books, hold conferences, sell newspapers; at the same time, the bishop wishes to remind the Congregation that their propaganda is innocuous. Some ordinaries use the generic word "Protestant" without determining the particular species of the sect; their reports demonstrate that they do not know "which sect works diabolically among their own flocks!" It seems necessary that the Holy See, yet again, must "instruct the bishops to help in the great work of combating proselytizing." The regular religious—that is to say, priests and brothers in religious orders, like Jesuits and Benedictines—are well-motivated in this regard, but they are waiting "with holy impatience" for the help of the local ordinaries. Some bishops say it is impossible or too difficult to combat Protestant propaganda. Others are perpetual pilgrims. Some seem to travel so much that they can be found "in every diocese except their own." Absenteeism, a chronic problem among the European episcopate for centuries, naturally made it impossible to monitor Protestant activity. Even worse, it made the task seem unimportant, trivial.

As for the pope, "His Holiness was sadly impressed by a situation so troubling" (*così preoccupante*).[25] This was said about the pope in 1937. The very words were used to describe his mood as early as 1929–31. Little or nothing had changed, the pope thought, despite the efforts of Borgongini and of the fascist regime at repression. Pizzocolo draws his jeremiad to its conclusion. The "treasure of our faith," he laments, could not be protected from "the Antichrists of our Day."[26]

Epilogue

Evangelical Christianity seemed to have appealed primarily to those who had emigrated, converted in America, and then returned to Italy. Needless to say, religion can function in multiple and often contradictory ways in immigrant contexts. That acknowledged, in the Italian neighborhoods in New York and Chicago, it seems that Italian Protestantism offered immigrants the three traditional benefits of refuge, resources, and respect. Evangelical churches helped mediate between the immigrants and their new cultures. Without question, they put much more effort than American Catholic churches into welcoming migrants from the homeland. For some converts, the experience of conversion was not simply about friendship, assimilation, or economic interest. It was also a genuine religious experience. There are no statistics on these matters and likely never will be. It seems logical to assume that those for whom conversion was an authentic and deeply felt religious experience were among the ones most active on their return home, and their families and communities the most likely to hear the message of a converted americano or an American missionary.

When the pope and Mussolini met in February 1932, the dictator responded to Pius XI's concern over plans for evangelical missionizing by pointing out that Protestants constituted only a tiny minority of the population. This was quite true. Statistically speaking, they were almost insignificant, a minuscule minority. In a country of 42 million, Protestants amounted to some 135,000 individuals, of whom tens of thousands were foreigners. In subsequent meetings with the pope's representatives, Mussolini expressed surprise and sometimes irritation at the persistence of papal complaints about Protestant proselytizing. Had the pope not absorbed the statistical facts communicated so clearly in their February 1932 meeting? How could Pius fail to perceive that the Protestants were not the bogeymen he had allowed his imagination to make them out to be?

Mussolini's response, while demographically accurate, failed to quiet or even to address the pope's fears. Indeed, the pope would soon complain regularly that neither Mussolini nor his government had taken appropriate measures against the grave threat—a threat to Italy's political as well as religious integrity—posed by Protestant presence and propaganda in Italy. The pope interpreted this as a failure to honor promises that Mussolini had made to Gasparri, in negotiations regarding the Concordat, to restore ecclesiastical influence and primacy in Italy.[1] The laws on culti ammessi he interpreted as another broken promise. These treacheries, in Pius's view, had undermined the clear juridical meaning of the Concordat. They gave license to Protestants to live with legal protection in Italy. Worse, they ruinously allowed evangelical sects to attempt to convert Catholics—this in a land where Roman Catholicism had been promoted to the status of Religion of the State.

At the end of the 1930s the pope was still anguishing over a problem that, despite his efforts and those of thousands of clerics he authorized to address the issue, some of whom did so obsessively, proved intractable. How was it that Mussolini, with whom by now he was thoroughly disillusioned for several reasons, had never grasped the gravity of the problem?[2] The Protestant threat was more than an irritant. It was a complication that, in Pius's view, and despite the enormous resources and energy the church had committed to defeating it, still plagued the church and the country. The country was historically, culturally, and even legally defined by its relationship to Roman Catholicism. How, then, could the enormity of evangelical preaching on sacred Italian soil be permitted to endure? And how long would it linger to torment him and frustrate his vision for Catholic Italy?

The reality or dimensions of a threat can be established only when measured against a vision whose realization it may frustrate or scupper. Evangelical missionaries had their own grand visions not only for the Protestantization but, for some, the defascitization of the Italian state. Yet they never endangered Mussolini's dreams for the country, in large part for the reasons

Mussolini had specified to the pope. Demographically, they were simply too small to constitute any real political threat. Some groups were pacifist; none had armies. The few that tried to organize political resistance were surveilled by the police and often enough incarcerated, confined, or otherwise contained. Demographic realities counted for Mussolini. Since they did not seriously threaten the fascist state, he could not imagine why they so worried the pope.

Yet Mussolini was only one, albeit the most powerful, of fascist actors in Italy. One truth revealed by the anti-Protestant campaign is how little unified the fascist government was about eliminating the Protestant threat. Aside from the demographic issue with which he constantly responded to the pope and Borgongini, Mussolini remained anticlerical and, in addition, had every reason not to antagonize historically Protestant countries, especially Britain. Nor did he wish to be seen, by other fascists, especially the most anticlerical, as having surrendered wholly to the demands of the church. Some of the most anticlerical fascists, like Farinacci, actually used the anti-Protestant campaign to frustrate the Catholic church and support Protestant expansion. As in Villa San Sebastiano, he supported the Methodist cause as a way to thwart Catholic attempts to suppress the Wesleyans. Some local fascist officials favored Protestants to make local Catholic priests and bishops look foolish or incompetent, others to achieve vengeance for some slight. Others never achieved clarity on the law, while still others had links of friendship or employment which made it awkward for them to enforce the law.

Some few fascist officials, like De Vecchi, attempted to buttress the anti-Protestant campaign, at least in part, because they were sincere Catholics. Buffarini Guidi's motivations were entirely more sinister. His suppression of Pentecostals and Jehovah's Witnesses should be understood in relation to his support for the persecution of Jews. Protestants and Jews were simply outside the fold of those to whom fascist Italy, in his mind, owed any protection. Both domestic events, like the publication of the Racial Laws, and foreign ones, like the Ethiopian War and Italy's increasing subsequent international isolation, reinforced his exclusivist instincts. All this is to say that one reason the anti-Protestant campaign failed is that it never had the consistent support of fascist leaders nor consistent enforcement of the laws by its lower ranks.

The laws over which the Protestants rejoiced legitimated the activities that so anguished Pius XI. If Mussolini hearkened back to the glorious Roman Empire for inspiration, the pope looked back, romantically, to some ahistorical vision of medieval Christendom on which Italy might model itself.

As we have seen, he hoped to restore a society organized around Roman Catholicism and its moral principles. If the evangelical invaders had hoped to restore Christianity to its apostolic model, Pius XI, in *Ubi arcano Dei* (1922), expressed hope for a very different kind of restoration: the reestablishment of society in a Catholic sense, that is, of Christendom (*Christianitas*). Christendom, for Pius or for any Catholic cleric, had no room for serious religious dissenters—heretics, as they were still called in the fascist period in Italy. The only religious minority tolerated in medieval Christendom—with strict limitations, to be sure—was the tiny community of European Jews. Unless dissenters recanted, heretics had no rights in Christendom. Heterodoxy, which might spread and destroy the souls of many, was too dangerous to tolerate. The medieval inquisition came into being in an attempt to convert heretics back to orthodoxy. If heretics refused to repent, inquisitors would then impose a penance, which could be quite heavy. It was a religiously homogenous society that Pius XI hoped, at least in Italy, to restore in the twentieth century. The existence, spread, and growth of Protestantism therefore threatened this essentially medieval dream. Were Protestantism permitted to expand, that expansion would render such a restoration impossible. Mussolini's nonchalance thus appalled and embittered Pius. The pope was attempting to establish a much different sort of society than Mussolini had imagined, and as a sacred society it eclipsed in importance the political order the fascists were attempting to create. Mussolini thought, not unjustifiably, that he had restored the Catholic church to a place of influence and primacy. If Il Duce wanted ethnic purity, the pope yearned for an order of religious purity; this is what he meant by "primacy." To achieve this sort of religious homogeneity, however, would have required Mussolini to function like a medieval lord cooperating with the church, intent on carrying out medieval-like inquisitorial decrees. To say the least, Mussolini had no intention of doing so—at least not against Protestants. With the failure of Pius's vision of society, the dream of restoring Christendom, even on a small scale, finally passed from the European bloodstream.

The failure to rout Protestants from Catholic Italy marked the end of another chapter in Italian history as well. Many Catholic princes and kings in the sixteenth through the nineteenth centuries avidly persecuted Protestant dissenters. In Italy, the history of the Waldensian church, at least until 1861, was a history of martyrdom and persecution. Again, the anticlerical Mussolini could not have imagined that he would be asked to play any part in cleansing Italy of non-Catholics. It simply would not have occurred to him, nor would he have ever agreed to such a program. Though Pius may not have wished Mussolini to take murderous measures against the Protestant minority, he certainly was operating within a worldview of Christendom in which the head of state would wish to see his realm united religiously—and, even more, would honor a pope's desires to make it so. From this historical perspective, then, the anti-Protestant campaign can be viewed, from one point of view, as the last gasp of the Counter-Reformation. Pentecostals and other evangelicals would face discrimination into the Christian Democratic period in Italy.[3] But never again would Italian Protestants face a campaign of repression organized from the Vatican as an expression of papal will to eradicate confessional pluralism and establish a society unpolluted, religiously at least, by heresy or dissent.

For evangelical proselytes the end of the fascist period may have marked the end of a fearsome campaign of repression. Yet it also marked the failure of their own ambitious program for Italy. Their aspirations to convert all the country's Catholics to Protestantism and away from paganism and papolatry were, given "Italy's" history, culture, and government, perhaps even more fantastic than the pope's determination to establish a confessional Catholic state. Small communities of Protestants still exist in Italy. However, weighed against their founders' hopes of Protestantizing Italy, of bringing down the Roman Catholic church, and of seeing popery and priestcraft disappear from Italy, they, too, landed far short of the mark they set for themselves. They aimed not just for the survival of a tiny remnant but for much, much more: the establishment of a large Italian evangelical church and, they hoped, the disappearance of a deeply corrupted form of Christianity, which they intended for Protestant Christianity to supplant. Today, they survive as a tiny remnant in Italy. So, the anti-Protestant campaign, after so much sound and fury, had not made Catholic Italy *Evangelischenrein.* Nor had evangelical missionaries transformed the religious world of historically Catholic Italy.

Appendixes

Appendix 1
Thomas Molloy, Bishop of Brooklyn, to Amaleto Cicognani, Apostolic Delegate to US (Washington, DC)

Molloy indicates that the List of Heresies was written by an émigré, S. L. Testa from Basilicata, in his youthful years. He entered Broome St. Tabernacle, "the oldest proselytizing Italian center in America . . . [was] promised a free education and after preparatory studies sent to Union Theological Seminary, ordained . . . [and] opened an Italian mission. . . . [He] employed L'Araldo Italiano of New York as a medium of public writing addressed to Italian émigrés . . . for a time [he was] . . . 'extraordinarily successful in proselytizing Italians.'"

Molloy indicates: "He endeavored to engage ex-priests to distribute bibles and tracts among Italians on a commission basis but was no [*sic*] very successful."[1]
I have translated Testa's text from the Italian.

List of Heresies
Adopted and Perpetuated by the Roman Catholic Church in the Course of 1600 Years[2]

CAUTION—These dates are in many cases approximate. Many of these heresies were prevalent in various places in the Church long before; but only when a council officially adopted them and the pope proclaimed them as dogmas of the faith were they required to be believed by Catholics. In the Reform of the 16th Century, these heresies were repudiated as not constituting part of the Religion of Christ as taught in the New Testament.

A.D.

1. Among all the human inventions practiced by the Roman Church and contrary to the Gospel, the most ancient are prayers for the dead and the sign of the Cross. Both were invented around 300 years after Christ (see the Caution) 310

2. Wax candles were introduced into the churches around the year 320

3. Veneration of dead saints and of angels, around the year 375

4. Daily celebration of the Mass was adopted in 394

5. The adoration of Mary as "Mother of God" began in 431

6. Priests began to dress differently from the laity in 500

7. The doctrine of Purgatory was first taught in 593

8. The Latin language as the language of worship was imposed by Pope Gregory I in the year 600 after Christ 600
The Word of God instead teaches that one should pray and preach in the language of the people. (See 1 Corinthians 14:19)

9. According to the Gospel, prayers must be directed to God alone. In the primitive Church there were never prayers addressed to Mary or the Saints. Such a practice originated 600 years after Christ 600
(See Matthew 11:28; Luke 1:46; Acts 10:25–26; 14:14–18)

10. The papacy is of human origin. The title of Pope was first given in 610
by the Emperor Phocas to the Bishop of Rome. . . . Jesus left no one Head of the Church, being himself the immortal Head of the Church. (See Luke 22:24–26; Ephesians . . . Colossians . . . 1 Corinthians 3:11)

11. The kissing of the feet of the pope began in the year 709
The pagan emperors made one kiss their feet. The Gospels condemn such Practices. (Read Acts 10:25 . . . Apoc. 22:8–9)

12. The temporal power of the papacy began in the year . . . 750
When Pepin usurper of the throne of France, ordered by Pope Stephen II to make war against the Lombard, usurped the throne of France; he confiscated

and gave the cities and the area surrounding Rome to the Pope. Jesus absolutely prohibited this. (See Matthew 20:25–26; and John 18:38)

13. The adoration of the Cross, of images and of relics began in 788
by order of Empress Irene of Constantinople, who first gouged out the eyes of her own son Constantine VI, and then called a Council of the Church at the request of the pope of Rome at that time. In the Bible such a practice is called idolatry, and is severely condemned. (See Exodus 20:4–5; Deut. 27:15; Ps. 115; Jeremiah 10:1–5)

14. Holy Water, because blessed by the priest, was invented in the year 850

15. The veneration of St. Joseph began in the year 890

16. Baptism of bells[3] was invented by Pope John XIV in 965

17. The canonization of saints, the first by Pope John XV, in 995
All believers in Christ are called saints in the Bible. (See Romans 1:7 . . . etc.)

18. Lent and the Friday fast were imposed by the Catholic Church in 998
998 years after Christ by popes interested in the buying and selling of fish
This has no precedent in the Gospel.

19. The Mass as a sacrifice was developed and made obligatory in the eleventh century. The Gospel teaches that the sacrifice was offered only once for all, and does not have to be repeated, except only as a commemoration of the Last Supper. (See 1 Timothy 3:2–5; Matthew 8:14)

20. Priestly celibacy was decreed by Pope Gregory VII in 1079
The Gospel however teaches that the ministers of God may have wives and children. St. Peter was married. (See 1 Tim . . . Matthew 8:14)

21. The crown of the Rosary[4] was introduced by Peter the Hermit
in the year 1090
This was copied from the Mohammedans. It is . . . a pagan practice and is severely condemned by Christ. (See Matthew 6:5–13)

22. The Inquisition against heretics was established by the Council
of Verona in 1184

23. The sale of Indulgences began in . . . 1190
The Gospel condemns such diabolical traffic . . . it gave rise to the Protestant Reform in 1517

24. The dogma of Transubstantiation was decreed by Pope Innocent III in 1215
With this doctrine, the priest pretends first to create Jesus Christ every day and then to eat him alive. The Gospel condemns similar absurdities. (See Luke 22:19; John 6:35; 1 Cor. 12:26)

25. Auricular confession of sins made to the ear of the priest was established by Pope Innocent III at the Lateran Council in the year 1215
The Gospel commands us to confess our sins directly to God and to those whom we have offended. (See Psalm 51:35; Luke 7:48; John 1:8–9)

26. The adoration of the host was sanctioned by Pope Honorius III 1220
In this way, the Roman church adores a god made of human hands. Such a practice is the height of idolatry and is absolutely contrary to the spirit of the Gospel. (See John 4:24)

27. The Bible is prohibited to the people and put on the Index of Prohibited Books at the Council of Toledo in the year 1229
Jesus says that the Scriptures should be read by all. (John 5:39; 2 Timothy 3:15–17)

28. In the year 1414 after Christ, the Roman Church prohibited the Gospel to the faithful at communion. The Gospel commands us to celebrate Communion with bread and wine 1914 [*sic*]

[29 is missing in the original.]

30. The doctrine of Purgatory was considered a dogma at the Council of Florence 1439
In the Gospel there is not even a word that touches upon the purgatory of the priests. The blood of Christ is the sole purification of our sins. (See John 1:9 . . .)

31. The doctrine of the Seven Sacraments was proclaimed in 1539
The Gospel teaches that Jesus Christ instituted two sacraments alone: Baptism and the Holy Supper. (See Matthew 28:19–20; 26–28)

32. The Hail Mary, the second part of which[5] was added in 1508
Was completed 50 years afterward and finally approved by Pope Sixtus V at the end of the sixteenth century, that is, after the Reform.

33. The Council of Trent, in the year 1545 after Christ, declared that Tradition retains an authority equal to that of the Bible 1545
By "tradition" they mean human teachings. The Pharisees believed the same things and were reproved bitterly by Christ, because with the tradition of men, the Word of God is in vain.

34. The Apocryphal books were added to the Bible also at the Council of Trent also in the Year 1546 after Christ. Such books are not recognized as canonical by the Jews 1546
(See Apocalypse 22:8–9)

35. The Creed of Pius IV[6] was imposed in the year 1560 after Christ
True Christians heed only the Gospel and the Apostles' Creed.

36. The Immaculate Conception of Mary was proclaimed dogma by Pius IX in 1854
The Gospel, however, teaches that all men, except Christ, are sinners and Mary herself had need of the Savior. (See Luke 1:30, 46–47; Romans 3:23, 5:12; Psalm 51:5)

37. In the year 1870 after Christ Pope Pius IX established the dogma of Papal infallibility. This is the height of blasphemy and a sign of apostasy and of the Antichrist predicted by St. Paul (see [2] Thessalonians 2:2–12; Apocalypse 13:5–8) 1870

38. Pius X condemns together with "Modernism" all the discoveries of civilization that do not please the Pope 1907

39. In 1930 Pius XI condemned public schools 1930

40. In 1931 the same Pius XI confirmed the doctrine that Mary is the Mother of God, which was first invented at the Council of Ephesus in 431 1931
This is a heresy, contrary to the words of Mary herself. (See Luke 1:46–49)

CONCLUSION

What will the next invention be? The Roman Church says that it never changes, and also that it has developed no doctrine contrary to the Bible, but practices rites and ceremonies taken from paganism.

Note. Cardinal Newman, in his work, *On the Development of Christian Doctrine,* says that temples, incense, lamps, candles, votive offerings, holy water days and seasons of special devotion, processions, blessings of fields, priestly vestments, the tonsure, images . . . are all of pagan origin (p. 359)

The "Document of Origins" above, or chronological list of human inventions, destroys the pride of priests that their religion is that taught by Christ and that the popes are the faithful custodians of it. The real religion of Christ, however, is not found in Romanism, but in the Gospel.

BROTHERS! The word of God commands us to leave behind Babylon.

Listen: "Then I heard another voice from heaven saying, 'Come out of her, my people, lest you take part in her sins, lest you share in her plagues'" (Apocalypse 18:4). All true Christians prefer to be faithful to the religion of Christ as taught in the New Testament and reject human inventions, paying heed to the warning of St. Paul, who says: "But even if we or an angel from heaven should preach a gospel other than the one we preached to you, let them be anathema" (Galatians 1:8).

The price of this leaflet is 5 cents per copy; $3 for 100 copies, posted. It is also published in English. Corrections are accepted.

For this and other religious and instructive books, order from the
SCRIPTURE TRUTH SOCIETY, Rev. S.L. TESTA, Director
2156 Homecrest Ave., Brooklyn, NY[7]

Appendix 2
Activities of Various Protestant Sects and Societies (ARSI)

A typical survey of evangelical worship centers in Italy.[8]

SITUAZIONE DEGLI ENTI DI CULTO EVANGELICO IN ITALIA

TAVOLA VALDESE—già riconosciuta in personalità giuridica per sé e per le sue parrocchie.
Fu legalmente riconosciuta nelle Valli Valdesi dal Duca Emanuele Filiberto col trattato di Cavour del 5 Giugno 1861—dal Duca Vittorio Amedeo II con l'editto con l'editto del 23 maggio 1694 ed emancipata dal re Carlo Alberto con le patenti del 17 febbraio 1848.
La Chiesa Valdese è composta da 9 membri—un moderatore, un vice moderatore—quattro Pastori e tre membri laici eletti annualmente dal Sinido.
Le parrocchie, congregazioni ed opere dipendenti dalla Tavola Valdese Italiana con sede in Torre Pellice, dove ogni anni si riunisce il Sinodo, sono:
I° Parrocchie delle Valli Valdesi
Angrogna—Bibbio Pellice—Luserna—S. Giov. Massello—Perrero—Pinerolo—Pomaretto—Prali—Pramollo—Prarostino—Riclaretto—Rodetto—Rorà—S. Germano Chisone—Torre Pellice—Villar Pellice.

II° Congregazioni fuori dalle Ville Valdesi
Abbazia—Aosta—Bari—Benevento—Biella—Bordighera—Borrello—Brescia—Brindisi—Caltanissetta—Casale Monferrato—Castelvenere—Catania—

Chieti—Como-Coazze—Corato—Courmayeur [f. 23]—Cuneo—Felonica Po—Firenze-due—Napoli—Nizza—Orsara di Puglia—Pachino—Palermo—Pescolanciano—Piani di Vallecrosia (Istituto Femminile Valdese)—Piedicavallo—Pisa—Reggio Calabria—Riesi—Rio Marina—Roma (due)—Sampierdarena—S. Giacomo degli Schiavoni—S. remo—Schiavi d'Abruzzo—Siena—Siracusa—Susa—Taranto—Torino—Trieste—Venezia—Verona—Vittoria.

III° Ufficio di presidenza
Pastore: Costabel—Moderatore
Pastore: Rostan—Segretario

IV° Scuola di Teologia
Roma, Via Pietro Cossa 42

Proff. Rostagno—Comba—e Longo
Liceo Ginnasio Pareggiato—Torre Pellice
Preside Dr. Jahier
Scuola latina—Pomaretto
Casa editrice—Claudiana Firenze
Convitto Maschile—Torre Pellice
Convitto Maschile—Pomaretto
Convitto Femminile—Torre Pellice
Istituto Femminile Valdese—Vallecrosia
Orfanotrofio femminile—Torre Pellice
Orfanotrofio maschile (Ist. Gould) firenze
Ospedali Valdesi—Torre Pellice—Pomaretto—Torino
Casa delle Diaconesse—Pomaretto
Rifugio per incurabili Re Alberto—Luserna S. Giov. [f. 24]
Asilo per vecchi—Luserna S. Giov.
Asilo per vecchio—S. Germano Chisone
Scuole elementari oltre a quelle delle Valli Valdesi:
Carema—Dovadola—Grotte—Pachino—Palermo—Riesi—Rio Marina—Salle—Sanremo—Vallecrosia—Vittoria.

GIORNALI SETTIMANALI
La Luce (Roma)
l'Echo des Vallées (in francese) a Torre Pellice
Bollettino della Società di Storia Valdese (Torre Pellice)
L'amico dei fanciulli (per i bambini)—a Roma

RIVISTE MENSILI
Fede e Vita (S. Remo)

CHIESE EVANGELICHE DIPENDENTI DA ENTI MORALI

I° Per la cura delle anime di stranieri residenti in Italia.
In lingua inglese (anglicana e o calviniste presbiteriane)—Roma (due anglicane e una presbiteriana)—Venezia (una ed una)—Torino (anglicana)—Bellagio (anglicana)—Milano (anglicana)—Bologna (anglicana)—Genova (una ed una)—Alassio (presbiteriana)—Siena (anglicana)—S. Remo (anglicana)—Rapallo (anglicana)—Bordighera (presbiteriana)—Firenze (due anglicane e una presbiteriana)—Livorno (anglicana)—Viareggio (anglicana)—Napoli (una ed una)—Palermo (anglicana)—Taormina (anglicana). [f. 25]

In lingua tedesca (luterane)
Roma—Trieste (due)—Trento—Milano—Venezia—Gries (Bolzano)—Merano—Genova—Bologna—Livorno—Firenze—Napoli—Gardone—S. Remo—Bordigera—Nervi—Capri.

In lingua francese (riformate—calviniste)
Napoli—Firenze—Genova—Milano

II° Per la cura di anime di italiani
Chiesa Battista (con sede centrale a in Richmond—Virginia—U.S.A.)
Chiesa Metodista Episcopale (con sede centrale in New York)
Chiesa Metodista Weslegana (con sede centrale in Londra)

La Chiesa battista, con sede principale in Roma, Piazza in Lucina 25, ha le seguenti congregazioni:
In Roma: 4 chiese—la casa editrice Bilichinis (che pubblica i giornali: Bilychinis—il Testimonio ed il Seminatore)—l'Orfanotrofio G.B. Taylor a Monte Mario—la Scuola Teologica Battista.
Altre chiese o congregazioni:
A Torino: S. Antonino di Susa—Mompantero—Meana—Vayes—Avigliana—Genova—Chiavari—Sampiederna—Pordenone—Milano—Varese—Ferrara—Firenze—Ascoli Piceno—Civitavecchia—Grosseto—S. Benedetto dei Marsi—Isola Liri—Formia—Spigno—Saturnia—Paganico Sabino—Avellino—Bisaccia—Macchiavalfortore (Campobasso)—S. Elia—Ripabottoni—S. Gregorio Magno (Salerno)—Napoli—Boscoreale—Bari—Calitri—Altamura—Cersonino—

Barletta—Gioia del Colle—[f. 26]—Gravina di Puglia—Mzera—Miglionico—Messina—Lentini—Floridia—Cagliari—Iglesias—Tunisi.
Chiesa battista autonoma della SPEZIA con scuola elementare ed orfanotrofio femminile.

Chiesa Metodista Episcopale—Sede Via Firenze 38—Roma
Congregazioni:
Albanella (Salerno) . Alessandria—Altino (Chieti)—Bari—Basilea—Bassignana (Alessandria)—Bologna—Calosso d'Asti—Catanzaro—Firenze—Foggia—Genova—Sestri—Ginevra—Gorizia—Lanciano—Losanna—Milano—Modena—Modica—Mottola (Lecce)—Napoli—Newchatel—Palombaro (Chieti)—Perano—Perugia—Pisa—Pistoia—Pola—Portici (Napoli) dov'è una Casa Meterna [sic]—Pozzello (Siracusa)—Pozzuoli—Reggio Calabria—Renens—Vallorbe—*Roma* (chiesa a v. XX Settembre—Chiesa a v. Firenze—Scuola teologica—Casa editrice "La Speranza" che stampa: L'Evangelista (settimanale); Vita gioconda (per i fanciulli)—Istituto Internazionale Grandon a Via Savoia—Collegio Monte Mario—Via Trionfale 61)
S. Marzano Oliveto—(Alessandria)—Savona—Scicli (Siracusa)—Sondrio—Terni—Torino—Trento—Trieste—Udine—Venezia—Venosa—Vevey—Zurigo.

Chiesa italiana Weslegana—Sede Roma Via della Scrofa.
Opera di Ponte S. Angelo
Scuola Teologica in via di Villa Madama 4
Altra chiesa al Quadraro. [f. 27]
Aquila—Giulianova—Pescosansonesco—Torre dei Passeri—Castiglione—Cologna—Rosburgo—Mutignano—Sulmona—S. Jona-Beffi—Ofena—Loreto Aprutino—Popoli—Cagnano—Amiterno—Firenze—Spezia—Carrara—Milano—Gallarate—Rho—Melzo—Ramello—Pallanza—Laveno—Baveno—Arona—Omegna—Mont'Offano—Quarna—Gravellona—Pettenesco—Orta—Cireggio—Casale—Ramate Cattugno—Omavasso—Aontronapiana—Luino—Domodossola—Varzo—Viganello—Premosello—Villadossola—Trontano—Cadoglia—Cuzzago—Vagna—Vagogna—Cimvamulesa—Seppiana—Formezza—S. Maria—Re—Toceno—Novara—Vercelli—Magenta—Olgiate—S. Bernardino—Crevola—Lucarno—Rimasco—Morea—Mogliano—Mantegna—Fara Novarese—Carpignano—Ghemme—Rocca Pietra—Vintebbio—Seravalle—Borgosesia—Quarona—Cavaglia—Civiasco—Marailo—Cervarolo—Vocca—Balmuccia—Scopa—Cerva e Folecchio—Cremona—Croce S. Spirito—Soresina—Piacenza—Fiorenzuola—padova—Rovigo—Colalzo—Vicenza-Treviso—Schio—Arsiero—Montecchio Precalcino—Montebelluna—

Caereno S. Marco—Seghe di Velo—Parma—Reggio Emilia—Mezzano Inferiore—Vicobellignano—Casalmaggiore—Rivarolo del Re—Napoli—Salerno—Fratte—Eboli—Cappelle—S. Pietro—Nocera Inferiore—S. Cesario—Battipaglia—Laviano—S. Maria Capua Vetere—S. Prisco—Capua—Caserta—Curti—Falciano—Alvignano—S. Tamarro—Centurano—Casapulla—Potenza—Rapolla—Caposche—Calabritto—Valva—Santanunna—Quaglietta—Cagliano . Palermo—Cosenza—Marsala—Palazzo Adriano—Prizzi—Filaga—Alessandria della Bocca—Corleone.
L'organo dei Metodisti Weslegani è la rivista mensile "Il Risveglio" che si pubblica in Roma. [f. 28]
Esistono pure in Italia, autorizzate, associazioni di carattere non chiesastico ma religioso e filantropico. Esse sono:
L'ESERCITO DELLA SALVEZZA, autorizzato con decreto 1° febbraio 1923—Ha a Roma un albergo popolare a S. Lorenzo—A Torino una casa di riabilitazione per donne—a Napoli un asilo infantile, un posto per i bassifondi, una casa estiva,—a Faeto un asilo infantile, un doposcuola con annessa cappella.
Il suo giornale è: "Il Grido di Guerra" (Firenze)

L'ASSOCIAZIONE CRISTIANA DELLA GIOVANE e
L'ASSOCIAZIONE CRISTIANA DEI GIOVANI
che hanno una rivista mensile: "Gioventù Cristiana" (Roma)
(Piazza indipendenza Sede)

LA CASA DELLE DIACONESSE LUTERANE
LA SOCIETA' BIBLICA BRITANNICA che pubblica e vende la Bibbia.

Gli evangelisti di tutti i paesi fanno capo a dei grandi organismi mondiali di carattere federativo che, mentre lasciano ad ogni chiesa la sua autonomia, le uniscono tutte per gli ideali comuni.

Vi sono pure delle Congregazioni evangeliche autonome come:
la Chiesa di Cristo del Vomero (Napoli)
la Chiesa Cristiana Libera Italiana
le Congregazioni dei Fratelli, dei Pentecostali, degli Avventisti.

la *Chiesa cristiana libera italiana* ha assunto il nome di Chiesa Evangelica Italiana, ed ha sede in FIRENZE e congregazioni a ROMA, Palermo, Bologna,—Imola—Reggio Emilia—Livorno—Pisa [f. 29]—Marina di Carrara—Campiglia Marittima e Piombino.
Ha un giornale mensile "La Vedetta Cristiana"

Le *Congregazioni dei Fratelli* pubblicano due giornaletti: "Il Cristiano" (Alessandria) e "L'Ebeneger" (Firenze). Hanno un Orfanotrofio evangelico Comandi (Firenze).

Libri che si possono consultare:

PER LA STORIA VALDESE:
Storia dei Valdesi—di C. Comba.

PER I BATTISTI
I Battisti del Dr. Whittinghill
Cenni storici e dottrinali sui Cristiasni Battisti: di A. Fasulo.

PER I METODISTI EPISCOPALI e WESLEGANI:
Breve storia del Metodismo—di Pizzott
Storia della Chiesa Met. Episc. di F. Dardi
Cenni storici della Ch. Met. Ep., di F. Dardi
Del Metodismo episcopale, di C.M. Ferreri
La Chiesa Met. Episc. d'Italia—Cenni storici—C.M. Ferreri" [f. 30—END OF DOCUMENT].

Appendix 3
Transcription of "Law Regarding Permitted Cults" by Gabriele Pugliatti

A set of suggestions (one of scores) sent to Pius XI on how Catholics might react to the freedoms granted to Protestants by the culti ammessi *laws.*[9]

CODICE DEI CULTI

I. La Religione Cattolica, Apostolica Romana non è soltanto la Religione dominante; ma la Religione scelta e professata dallo Stato della presente Italia Imperiale. La Religione Cattolica Apostolica Romana, non può essere offesa con propaganda contraria. Il farlo è reato.
Qualunque religione estranea alla Cattolica può solo limitarsi all'esercizio della propra, in coloro che già vi appartengono; ma non all'offesa e menomazione della R. C. A. R. che è la Religione dell'Italia Imperiale. [f. 172r]

II. Quella Chiesa protestante in cui fossero sorprese stampe contrarie alla R.C.A.R., verrebbe chiusa. I Pastori possono parlare di ciò che vogliono circa il Vangelo; ma guai ad erigere paragoni con le credenze della Chiesa Cattolica.

III. Come è proibito lo strozzinaggio [= usura, ndt] in Italia, tuttochè [= sebbene, ndt] sia esercitato di libera volontà da parte dello strozzino e di chi prende denaro da lui, così è proibito lo strozzinaggio spirituale.

Così chi, portando prove dicesse di esser stato costretto alla religione protestante per fame, o promessa di posti; il pastore ne sarebbe responsabile [f. 172r] con reato di strozzinaggio spirituale e condannato al confino.
Lo stato dell'Italia Imperiale non à [sic] bisogno che i propri figli calpestino la loro fede per un boccone di pane. Lo stato provvede contro la disoccupazione a chi ne segue le norme necessarie.

IV. Come i rinnegati della Patria sono inviati al confino così è proibito in Italia l'esercizio di pastori a coloro che risultassero di essere stati prima sacerdoti cattolici. Non tanto per lo scandalo dei fedeli cattolici; quanto perché non è lecito apprendere [f. 173r] le armi della verità e sapienza cattolica e commerciarle nella religione protestante contro i stessi cattolici.
Religione e Patria in Italia furono difese col sangue, non furono vendute e non saranno vendute da rinnegati.
Data l'inferiorità di coltura religiosa protestante è indispensabile per costoro il prete apostata per la propaganda acattolica. Ma in Italia non debbono esservi rinnegati, ne della Patria ne di Cristo.
Perché chi oggi vende Cristo domani venderà la Patria. [f. 173v]

V. La tolleranza dei Culti riguarda le religioni che non si rendono intollerabili. Essa tolleranza è vincolata alle seguenti norme:

1. Proibizione di attaccare a voce o per iscritto la religione dello Stato.
2. Proibizione di far proseliti con mezzi disonesti come lo strozzinaggio spirituale.
3. Proibizione di fa proseliti in coloro che sono già cattolici.

La ragione di questa seconda proibizione viene dal diritto della Conciliazione.
Il leale governo Fascista à [sic] conciliato la Chiesa e lo Stato non per una manovra [f. 174r] puramente politica; ma per geniale ed indovinata interpretazione degli Italiani fascisti e cattolici. L'antica romana lealtà di Fabrizio e di Camillo è risorta dopo 2000 anni nel fascismo.
Lo Stato non permetterà che le file dei Suoi militi, pur ascoltando la Messa Cattolica, pur presentando le armi alla Eucarestia, siano tutti protestanti.
Il Diritto della Conciliazione, (quella Conciliazione che à [sic] reso ammirato il mondo) non può essere menomato. [f. 174v]
Esso è stato uno spirituale sposalizio tra Chiesa ed Italia.
Non si può offendere la sposa senza offendere il consorte.

Questo è Santità, uno schema che dovrebbe essere propugnato con massima efficacia e con trattative pacifiche nelle quali il pro e contro sarebbe bilanciato senza fretta.

Certo l'Italia non ci guadagna niente a tenere i protestanti; ma ci perde moltissimo a lasciare scuotere [f. 175r] l'unità del principio religioso sul quale è poggiato nientemeno che la Corona Monarchica.
V.S. m'insegna che dove in Europa non si poggia il ginocchio a terra davanti a Dio, non s'inchina la fronte davanti al Re.
E la religione protestante è fatta di opinioni personali più che di una sola fede (tante teste, tante fedi). Così mi scriveva un pastore protestante, ex prete che aveva portato il dubbio e lo scompiglio in una famiglia cattolica (qui a Napoli) e che rimasto da me battuto in disputa per iscritto, andò a ricorrere al Procuratore del Re "per mettermi a posto." [f. 175v]
Naturalmente l'ò [sic] coperto di ridicolo; ma intanto lo spirito aggressivo protestante dimostra come costoro approfittano della tolleranza dei Culti per renderli intollerabili.

Quello che potrebbero dire o pensare le nazioni protestanti non riguarda noi cattolici.
1° perché la legge colpirebbe i protestanti Italiani e i commercianti apostati.
2° perché è l'epoca in cui la nazione di ogni popolo pensa al proprio benessere [f. 176r] anche più del giusto.
Ce ne dà un bell'esempio (bello per modo di dire) l'Inghilterra con la proibizione della lingua Italiana nel pubblico insegnamento.
Davanti ad una sola ombra di proprio tornaconto in pregiudizio, sembra che non esista più altro.
E Malta lo sa.
L'utile e la salvezza non solo spirituali di quasi 50 milioni d'Italiani, vale perfino più del destino dei centomila cattolici in Inghilterra o in Germania.
Eppoi la ragione politica [f. 176v] oggi è così rispettata che non offende più nessuno.
Il colore di un tal codice non è affatto il bando ai protestanti; ma "una misura di sicurezza contro il commercio degli apostati prezzolati che si vogliono arricchire ai danni di un popolo generoso e leale come l'Italiano."
Vuol dire che gli apostati, o gli affaristi della Massoneria sceglieranno un altra maschera: quella protestante s'è fatta vecchia. [f. 177r]

I.
Questo codice dimostrerà il massimo accordo religioso-politico di un Italia saldissima che non può esser più aggredita ne dall'aperto antifascismo ne dall'ipocrita infiltrazione religiosa[10] (ancorché venga da maestre elementari protestanti che possono esser sempre sostituite a parità di merito con quelle cattoliche che spesso da molto tempo aspettano il posto)

II.
La massima lealtà del governo che nella Conciliazione à [sic] realizzato il sincero sentimento del popolo Italiano. Ed ancorché la Conciliazione non tratti il protestantesimo,

pure il decoro di Italia Cattolica ed una di [f. 177v] di pensiero e di azione vuole, esige nell'opinione ormai pubblica un provvedimento. Come si è ragionevolmente soppressa una malintesa libertà di stampa calunniosa ed infetta,
Come si è assai lodevolmente levato l'abuso e gli abusi di certe elezioni d'altri tempi, si potrà non dico togliere ma rendere razionale e decorosa la tolleranza dei Culti.
E l'Italia ne guadagnerà in prestigio presso i Cattolici ed anche non Cattolici degli altri Stati. [f. 178r]
Si dirà: E' uno Stato che non permette gli abusi ed i lucri ciarlataneschi.

Appendix 4
Per La lotta contro il protestantesimo

A document of unknown date and authorship (though internal evidence supplies several clues).[11] *The author proposes a commission be established by the Sacred Congregation of the Council to oversee the "struggle against Protestantism." Given that proposal and the prominent role allotted to bishops, the author was likely a cleric in the council. The document is valuable not because of its originality but because its proposals were heard ubiquitously in such documents. A transcription.*

DIREZIONE

Essa può essere affidata ad una *Commissione* avente questi scopi:
1°—Tenere aggiornata una statistica delle sette protestanti che operano in Italia, delle loro Chiese, Istituti ed Opere o iniziative, luoghi in cui sono.
2°—Studiare la loro storia, i loro errori, la vita dei loro ministri, i loro mezzi di propaganda.
3°—Raccogliere i libri, riviste, foglietti diffusi dai Protestanti nei diversi luoghi a scopo di propaganda e controbatterli con gli stessi mezzi da diffondersi nei medesimi luoghi per mezzo del Clero e dell'A.C. Vi sono già alcune buone pubblicazioni, come quelle di Igino Giordani.
4°—Interessare dei giuristi e esporre in senso a noi favorevole la legge 24 Giugno 1929 N. 1159, in computazione[12] [sic] dei due libri di Davide Jahier (Le condizioni giuridiche delle Chiese evangeliche) e di Mario Piacentini sulla detta legge. E inoltre e preparare memoriali per denunziare coloro che fungono da ministri senza aver fatto

almeno due anni di studio in un Seminario Teologico protestante, e i maestri che fanno proselitismo in iscuola[13] [*sic*].

5°—Proporre alle Competenti autorità di ordinare ai Vescovi una sufficiente preparazione del Clero alla lotta contro le sette moderne, richiamando la loro attenzione sulla realtà e gravità del pericolo e alle circostanze che nelle loro Diocesi lo favoriscono (discordie, scandali, inerzia del Clero ecc.)

6°—Compilare e trasmettere ai Vescovi un elenco di tutti i Collegi, Asili, scuole, ricoveri, luoghi di ritrovi per bagni, sport, ballo ecc. tenuti dai Protestanti, perché ne mettano in guardia il popolo.

7°—Mettere a disposizione dei Vescovi dei sacerdoti preparati a tenere conferenze ai Chierici in Seminario e in adunanze di giornate, settimane, ritiri, o altri Convegni di sacerdoti intorno alle sette della rispettiva diocesi e al modo di combatterle, all'occorrenza, anche al popolo.

8°—Eccitare i Vescovi a costituire nella loro Diocesi, se infestata da Protestanti, l'Opera della Preservazione della Fede.

9°—Invitare le direzioni dei collegi cattolici, maschili e Femminili, a mettere in guardia gli alunni contro l'invadenza protestante nei loro paesi, illuminarli e spronarli alla difesa.

10°—Preparare alcune domande e risposte da inserirsi nel catechismo per istruire il popolo sul Protestantesimo almeno in genere.

Questa Commissione dovrebbe essere costituita dalla S.C. del Concilio.

ESECUZIONE

Nell'esecuzione della lotta, oltre ai Vescovi, possono essere di aiuto:

I°—*Gli Assistenti e Vice Assistenti Generali e loro Aiutanti di A.C.* i quali, recandosi nelle Diocesi, per adunanze di Associazioni o di Clero possono parlare anche del pericolo protestante sia alle Associazioni, sia al Clero, sia al popolo. Inoltre possono parlarne sulla loro stampa e introdurre tale tema nelle gare regionali e nazionali. Inoltre dare le direttive per la collaborazione dei soci di A.C.

II°—Altrettanto possono essere incaricati di fare i Propagandisti delle Opere Missionarie Pontificie, tanto più che i Protestanti ebbero l'imprudenza di raccogliere offerte per sé tra i cattolici nella Giornata Missionaria.

III°—I gregarii di A.C. possono:

a) scovare i Protestanti e avvisare il Parroco di ciò che fanno—

b) visitare le famiglie appena sanno che vi passò il protestante, raccogliere le stampe da lui segnalate e sostituirle con stampe nostre—

c) avvisare le Conferenze di S. Vincenzo[14] dei soccorsi distribuiti dai Protestanti, perché tentino di sostituirsi presso le Famiglie bisognose—

d) prestarsi ad insegnare il catechismo dove manca il sacerdote—

e) avvicinare le persone cadute nell'eresia e in procinto di cadervi, specialmente a causa di matrimoni misti.
f) Cercare impiego ai convertiti ecc.
g) In qualche caso far un po' di cagnare[15] per dar modo alle Autorità di Pubblica sicurezza di proibire la vendita in pubblico mercato di libri protestanti, o almeno farlo conoscere al popolo ignorante."

Appendix 5
The Pope's Circular

A document composed, probably in 1934, by Selvaggiani, typical of the period identifying dangers of Protestant propaganda and remedies. A transcription of a published document.

Pro-memoria. Brevi cenni sul pericolo protestante in Italia e sui mezzi per respingerlo: Osservazioni generali tratte dai documenti ricevuti.[16]

INDICE

I. *Pericolo da parte dei Protestanti*

a) Ministri e loro ausiliari.
Ministri protestanti nazionali e stranieri.
Sacerdoti apostati.
Rimpatriati dall'America. Salariati dalle Sette.
Maestri di scuola.
Evangelisti e Colportori

b) *Mezzi adoperati dai Protestanti*
Filantropia.
Educazione.

Evangelismo.
Stampa protestante.
Bibbie protestanti.

c) *Circostanze favorevoli alla propaganda protestante*
Discordie e scandali.
Congiunti.
Penuria di Clero.

II. *Difficoltà da parte del clero*
Ignoranza delle Sette.
Disprezzo e troppo timore.
Negligenza.

III. *Difficoltà da parte del popolo*
Indifferenza religiosa.
Ignoranza religiosa. [f. 3r]

I PROTESTANTI IN ITALIA

PARTE PRIMA

I. *Sette e Società Protestanti che lavorano in Italia*

I. Sette che fanno propaganda intensa.
II. Sette di propaganda attiva ma non intensa.
III. Sette che fanno nessuna o poca propaganda.
IV. Sette o Chiese italiane di vita languida.
V. Società Bibliche.
VI. Società filantropica.
VII. Società di giovani.
VIII. Società di pubblicazioni.

II. *Mezzi adoperati dai Protestanti per la loro propaganda*

I. Scelta di luoghi.
II. Scelta di persone.
III. Scelta di occasioni.
IV. Opere di educazione.
V. Opere filantropiche.
VI. Opere sportive.

VII. Culto.
VIII. Con on le Autorità civili.
IX. Mezzi buoni ma con fine di far proseliti.
X. Bibbie.
XI. Stampa.

III. *Rimedi.*

I. Rimedio proposto dal Santo Padre.
II. Rimedi urgenti.
III. Rimedi adoperati o suggeriti.
IV. Rimedi già proposti nell'altra Memoria

IV. *Chiese di lingua straniera. Città dove esistono cappelle della Chiesa Evangelica Italiana*

PARTE SECONDA

Regioni Conciliari nelle quali è *divisa l'Italia*
Di ognuna di queste Regioni si espongono:
I. Sette e Società protestanti nelle singole diocesi.
II. Centri principali.
III. Resistenza.
IV. Rimedi

Appendix 6
A "Vast and Arduous Program": l'Unione Missionaria del Clero

The detailed plans of the Missionary Union of the Clergy to neutralize the Protestant danger are analyzed below. I have been able to discover no evidence that the plan was ever implemented. It may be that the archives of Pius XII, when opened, will enable other scholars to add to the story I begin here.

The Missionary Union conceived their task in martial terms, specifically as a defensive battle in a war of aggression started by the Protestants. In a letter to Serafini, Ruggero Bovelli (1875–1954), Archbishop of Ferrara (1929–1954) says that the Union, in which he would take one of two leading roles, "must cooperate in the battle we must necessarily take on against the dangerous Protestant invasion of so many parts of our Italy."[17] Three months later, in a letter to Giuseppe Bruno (1875–1954), Secretary (1930–1949) and later Prefect (1949) of Congregation of the Council, he would describe the work of the Missionary Union of the Clergy as an "urgent battle."[18] In the archives of the Sacred Congregation of the Council, there is much evidence to suggest that Pius approved *in massima* proposals submitted by both religious orders and diocesan priests designed to resist the proselytizing of the Protestants.[19] Religious orders, including the Franciscan Capuchins, Jesuits, Third Order Franciscans (that is, laymen), Salesians, Redemptorists, and Passionists, all volunteered to participate in the "Schiera volante dei Missionari per la difesa della Fede contro la propaganda dei Protestanti in Italia."[20] Bruno prepared a *pro memoria* on the organization, preparation, preaching, and expected results of the campaign, which was explained to the

Council of Bishops and to the Superior Generals of the religious orders as "the idea of the Holy Father."[21] This was not quite true. In fact, one document explicitly says it was the idea of Camillo Crivelli, S.J.[22] Regardless, virtually every document in the folder indicates either that the pope conceived the idea, or enthusiastically supported it, or that the Mission was undertaken (as were the medieval crusades) only by his express authority and oversight. This campaign against the infidel, like the crusades against the infidel in the twelfth century, required the clarion call of St. Peter.

The missionaries were urged to prepare for their work by studying the history, doctrine, and organization of those sects that are most active in propagandizing in Italy: namely, the Waldensians, Baptists, American and British Methodists, and Adventists. This was the study Crivelli was especially likely to recommend, and on which he was expert, as he produced more than one vade mecum on the Protestant sects. There are some "special sects," such as the Brethren (*Darbiti*) and the Pentecostals, which require concentrated study on them alone, "above all their doctrines." Several centers across the peninsula would be set up for courses of two or three weeks. The Gregoranium had indicated its willingness to organize such courses in Rome, which would be taught by the Missiological Faculty. In fact, the Gregoranium followed up in 1934 by publishing a program for seminarians regarding the different doctrines, sects, and societies of Protestantism.[23] The program also recommended training in recognizing Protestants of "good faith, bad faith and apostates." It is a surprise to find that the faculty of the Pontifical University recognized Protestants of good faith, until we read that those of good faith include those who convert to Catholicism or at least have imbued distinctively Catholic ideas. Those of bad faith—no surprise here—attempt to convert Catholics to Protestantism.[24]

Based on the apostolic model, the priests would be sent into dioceses in pairs.[25] In their preaching, the missionaries ought "principally to explain the truth of the Catholic Faith," and they should "avoid every sort of exaggeration against the Protestants." Again this language, seemingly irenic, comes as a surprise. However, the recommendation was not motivated by fear of insulting Protestants, but by fear that Protestants would exploit "every error of exaggeration of the Catholic priests for their propaganda." The missionaries, specifically, should concentrate on the points most disputed by the Protestants: the *Sommo Pontefice,* the sacraments of Confession and Eucharist, the necessity of good works for justification, the error of free interpretation of scripture, the necessity of an infallible magisterium, and so on. The consequences of such errors (multiplicity of sects, religious anarchy) ought to be emphasized, especially as contrasted with the beauty of Catholic unity and of its doctrine. Not only should the preaching be clear and well-prepared. It should be at the same time "full of holy zeal, fervor and enthusiasm," but always taking care to avoid every word that could offend Protestants *di buona fide.*

Another, altogether different kind of preparatory document is preserved in the archives of the SCC. Entitled "Confidential Considerations on the Protestant Danger in Italy," it is mostly a standard vade mecum on the reasons for the peril, including the *culti ammessi* laws. Nothing in it is, by the standards of the day, exceptional or exceptionable; reading it, one finds nothing that seems sensitive or worthy of being treated *riservatissime.* The appendix to this document, however, is altogether extraordinary. Prepared by the Canadian government, it is entitled *Religious Denominations by Racial Origins: 1931.* The vade mecum in this folder indicates that the appendix may aid priests and perhaps civil authorities to distinguish between sects that go under the ambiguous name "Evangelical." The first page of the Canadian document begins by noting that in a previous bulletin regarding the 1931 census, "the religious beliefs shown for persons in some racial groups were so contrary to accepted opinions" as to have caused renewed inquiry. "For example," the document goes on, "in certain localities the number of persons of Jewish origin credited to a Christian denomination were so large as to demand rigid inquiry." Confronting problems that would confound the Nazi authorities after the passage of the 1935 Nuremberg Laws, the Canadian document concludes: "In some instances . . . it would appear that the mother was of a different origin from the father; the children were given the racial origin of the father but the religious belief of the mother."[26] The inclusion of this document in the folder, which is marked confidential for what are now all-too-obvious reasons, seems to suggest that some involved in the Mission were convinced that the anti-Catholic campaign would be enhanced by knowing everything possible about the local sect, including, presumably, its "racial origins." The "racial origins" of the *culti ammessi* was not a common theme in the polemical literature of the period; this document is quite exceptional. However, it is, in retrospect, ominous for non-Catholic religious communities in Italy that it was thought important to establish the racial origins of such communities.[27]

Once the missions are completed, Catholic Action should continue its work. A similarly extensive program was drawn up by Bruno at the request of Bovelli,[28] who took a leading role in the organization of the program, in the letter to Serafini mentioned above, which suggests that Catholic Action, "which must be the most effective collaborators with the clergy," should be involved, by prayer, good example, and enlightened work, from the start.[29] Catechetical centers should be organized, above all in villages where there is no priest. Publications prepared by the Society for the Preservation of the Faith ought be distributed as well, again without exaggeration. University students should be well prepared, then, to give conferences for youth.

Having received these instructions and prior approval from Bruno, all of the superior generals wrote back to the secretary, indicating which of their priests had been sent to which Italian province. Many bishops indicated their willingness to cooperate with the missionaries. Ultimately, a national office was established (on the Via di Propaganda), letterhead was made, a periodical founded,[30] and a national director of the Missionary Union, Monsignor Adelfo Ciarappa, appointed.[31] He would eventually write a small manual on the Missionary Union.[32] Ciarappa was among those who was persuaded that, though priests would take the lead in the missionary endeavor, their work would be critically augmented by "the faithful of Catholic Action."[33] At the same time, Archbishop of Ferrara Bovelli took on a distinct role as "President" of the Union.[34] He seems to have been *primus inter pares* of the priests who formed the Council for the Missionary Union.

Whoever conceived the idea, there is no doubt at all that, once hatched, it was enthusiastically supported by the pope. Indeed, Pius gave it his "apostolic blessing" and expressed his feelings of care and compassion for the manifestation of such zeal and the conception of so fine an idea. Their objective, he said, was no less urgent than "the defense of the Faith, especially in their own country, whose integrity and stability the Protestant invasion has menaced."[35] To the National Council of the Missionary Union, with Bovelli acting as president, Pius gave a particular audience in the late spring of 1934 in which he warmly encouraged the project. He must have been gratified to have been informed by Bovelli that fully forty-four thousand priests had signed up to fight the Protestants "with the arms of prayer, of example, of word, publication and any other means Your Holiness would wish to suggest, to smash the insidious *tesa* to the Catholic Faith in our Country."[36] Among the publications intended for distribution was the Apostolic Nuncio's pamphlet on Protestant proselytism in Italy, which seems to have found its way into the archives of nearly every archive at the Vatican.[37] Perhaps we ought not be surprised to find the nuncio's *Proselytism in Italy* among the documents on the Mission, which has a note on the frontispiece that it was "presented by the Nunziature."[38]

How well did the Missionary Union campaign work? Bovelli wrote in September 1935 to Serafini about a meeting to be held in Bari on "The Current State of the Infidel and Catholic World." The heretical propaganda of the various Protestant sects and the means of Catholic defense was to be the theme of a special report given by Prof. Giordani, editor of the review *Fides*. Over three hundred priests from every part of Italy, and much of the episcopate in Puglia, had already committed to attending. Bovelli wrote to ask Serafini for a "word of encouragement" to "renew the zeal of the defense of their faith."[39] It is hard to know what to make of this document. One possibility, though, is that just months after the beginning of the missionary movement, the initial zeal of the priests involved was already in need of renewal.

There is no evidence of this grand plan ever having been carried out. Perhaps war (1935) or other national priorities inhibited its implementation. The question of what happened to this plan is one that I encourage other researchers to take up.

Appendix 7
List of Apostate Priests Who Have Taken on Protestant Pastorates, by Region

An early list of apostate priests from the statistical leader of the anti-Protestant campaign to the Sacred Congregation of the Council that closely tracked ex-priests.[40] *A translation.*

Crivelli to Bruno, List of Apostate Priests_31 dic 1932 (ASV, Sacra Congregazione del Concilio, Sezione Catechista—*Protestanti*)

b. 1 fasc. 1933
A. List of Apostate Priests Who Have Taken on Protestant Pastorates by Region (4 January 1933). From Camillo Crivelli, S.J., to Mons. Giuseppe Bruno, Secretary of the Sacra Congregazione del Concilio (31 December 1932).

I have the honor of presenting to your Excellency the work you asked of me:
1) Those who can be demonstrated to have united the Protestants with subversive elements and those against the state; 2) those who are Protestant propagandists;
3) *how their activity has intensified after the Concordat, by abusing the term "culti ammessi,"* pretending that it makes their multiple sects equal to the Religion of the State.

1. Piedmont: One does not hear talk of apostate priests.
2. Lombardi: Diocese of Milan. One hears of two ex-priests now Protestant pastors.
3. Liguria: One does not hear talk of apostate priests.

4. Veneto: Diocese of Padua. One hears of the apostate priest VERRI.
5. Emilia: Diocese of Parma. One hears talk of an S.P. from the diocese of Sarzana. Note: Among the documents from the Diocese of Parma is information on two ex-priests, Dante SETA and Paride FAVA.
6. Romagna: non si parla.
7. Etruria: Grosseto: Pietro NESTERINI and there is information on him. Prato: Ex-Augustinian.
8. Umbria: Spoleto: ex-p who is a propagandist. Riet. An apostate priest.
9. Marche: Montalto and Ripatransone. Ex-p BRIGLIADORI.
10. Lazio: Civitavecchia: NESTERINI. Sora: Baptist Minister.
11. Abruzzi: Marsi: SETA and FAVA.
12. Campania: Nola: ex-frate apostate.
13. Beneventana: Avellino: ex-frate Agostino BIAGI.
14. Salernitana e della Basilicata: none.
15. Puglie: Bari: Lorenzo PALMIERI from the Diocese of Avellino. Trani: three ex-ps in the village of Corato.
16. Calabrie: Reggio: Freancesco PUGLIESE. Documentation on him from the Diocese of Nicotera.
17. Sicily: non si parla.
18. Sardinia: non si parla.

Appendix 8
Agenda for Meeting between Tacchi Venturi and Mussolini

A pro memoria written after Tacchi Venturi met with Mussolini, in a year when he was still principally charged with the problem of Villa San Sebastiano, which he apparently brought up on this occasion (see point 5 below).

Udienza del 19 dicembre 1931

1. Ambasciata del S. Padre circa l'udienza
2. Communicazione della relazione circa il moto di Barletta dei 9 e 10 nov[embre] inviato da ? [word unclear] Arc. Leo
3. La premilitare non si aduna alle 10, ma alle 9 ancora vige la circolare del Comando Gen[era]le della Milizia. Qui assistenza religiosa Avanguardisti. L'istruzione farla nelle Scuole Ricci si oppone
4. Interessare il Governatore di Roma perché venga sistemata P[ort]a Pia
5. Protestanti di Villa S. Sebastiano. Necessità di stroncare il movimento capitanato dall'America
6. Pascarella
7. On. Negrini; fargli ridare la tessera
8. Note Bianchi Villa per l'agricoltura in Brescia
9. Caso del fiumano Arturo Aurelio analogo a quella del Negrini
10. Ing. Palazzo
11. Benedetti

Lotteria per la nuova chiesa di S. Teresa ai quartieri Sebastiani. Di Benedetto Generale. Com. Cesta Stefan

Abbreviations

ARCHIVAL SOURCES

ACDF	Archivio della Congregazione per la Dottrina della Fede, Vatican
ACS	Archivio Centrale dello Stato, Rome
AESI	Segretaria di Stato, Affari Ecclesiastici Straordinari, Italia
AGMF–AIG1	Archivio Generale del Movimento dei Focolari (AGMF)
	Archivio Igino Giordani, parte 1 (AIG1)
ANI	Archivio Nunziatura Italia
ARSI	Archivum Romanum Societas Iesu, Rome
ASMAE	Archivio Storico, Ministero degli Affari Esteri, Rome
ASV	Archivio Segreto Vaticano

PUBLISHED DIPLOMATIC DOCUMENTS

DDI	Documenti Diplomatici Italiani

OTHER ABBREVIATIONS

CC	*Civiltà Cattolica*
OR	*L'Osservatore Romano*

Notes

Translations are mine unless otherwise indicated.

INTRODUCTION

1. Di Lorenzo to Pizzardo manuscript letter (AESI pos. 795, fasc. 395, ff. 65r–66v [1934]). No monthly date is indicated. For a brief biographical summary of Borgongini, a key figure in this study, see Guasco 2013b.
2. A devastating and humiliating defeat suffered by the Italians to the Austro-Hungarian army, one which took much of the year 1917 to fight. Mussolini described the failure of the Socialist General Strike in 1922 as a "Socialist Caporetto." See Nolte 1969, p. 274. Many more examples could be adduced. One author treats it in a book tellingly entitled *More Military Blunders* (Regan 2004, pp. 130–45). It and its aftermath have been treated in several literary works, none more famous in English than Hemingway's *A Farewell to Arms.*
3. For this history, especially that of Anglo-American evangelical churches, which I will take up in greater detail in chapter 1, see especially Spini 1971; Maselli 1978; and Chiarini 1999.
4. See Kertzer 2006 on "prisoners of the Vatican" and, more recently, Kertzer 2018 on Pius IX and his reaction to unification and the loss of the papal states as well as much more, much of it new, in this fine biography and study of a fascinating piece of Italian national history.
5. Denzinger 1967, pp. 795–97 (nos. 2890–92). *Quanta Cura* can be found in Latin and Italian at the Vatican website: https://w2.vatican.va/content/pius-ix/la/documents/

encyclica-quanta-cura-8-decembris-1864.html; and in English at https://www.papalencyclicals.net/pius09/p9quanta.htm.

6. See *CC* 70/2 (1919): 231–33; and Pollard 2014, p. 116, for brief discussion. The numbers from the Jesuit writers at *CC* must be taken with caution. See also Giordani 1930, pp. 9–10, for statistics, equally to be taken with critical care. See Crivelli 1952 for a typical introduction to Protestant sects, intended expressly for the education of Catholic parish priests.
7. Pollard 2005, p. 54.
8. See Tacchi Venturi (1927) below; and Cardinal C. Dalmazio Minoretti (archbishop of Genoa), *Il Pericolo Protestante* (Genoa: Buona Stampa, 1935). Can be found in AESI pos. 795, fasc. 397, f. 30. Rochat 1990, pp. 37–38, notes, correctly, that the Catholic press grew more alarmist after 1930 and the passage of the *culti ammessi* laws.
9. And Canadian Catholics as well. See the Jesuit polemic *La Y.M.C.A. aux États-Unis, au Canada: l'antidote,* by Édouard Lecompte, S.J. (1856–1929) (Montréal: L'Œuvre des tracts, 1920). The YMCA was regarded, not wrongly, as the principal institutional structure for international Protestant proselytizing and was present in many of the major cities of Italy. It was also the subject of many scores of polemical pamphlets and of secret reports to ecclesiastical authorities, which listed cities and addresses where YMCAs were present.
10. Pollard 2005, p. 211.
11. Pacelli to Borgongini-Duca (ASV, ANI b. 49, fasc. 2, f. 360 [25 March 1938]). The letter was motivated by a missive received by Pacelli, sent 16 March 1938, from Giovanni Costantini (1880–1956), bishop of Luni (1929–56). The Questor of Spezia had notified the ordinary that the secretary of the Evangelical Mission for Spezia, secretary of Evangelical Mission for Puglia and Naples, had visited evangelical communities in Naples, Barletta, Bari, Taranto, Altamura, Matera, Castelnuovo, and other minor centers and had been "triumphantly received"—this despite his having expressed "offensive opinions regarding the current economic state of the Regime"—which caused the Questura of Spezia to intervene and spy on the British evangelical leader Wilfred Gottard. Pacelli suggests that Borgongini be in touch with the appropriate governmental officials, advice the nuncio hardly needed in 1938, by which time he had collaborated with Buffarini, the undersecretary of state, in the suppression of Pentecostal communities in Italy. Bishop Costantini sent the letter to "Your Eminence [Pacelli], so that you might have as complete a picture as possible of the activities of the Protestants" (ASV, ANI b. 49, fasc. 2, f. 362 [6 March 1938]). Borgongini-Duca responded to Pacelli, reporting that he had alerted the Interior Ministry to the presence of Gottard, who had made a lengthy trip, "even though the discourse that he gave in Spezia was given with anti-Fascist expressions" (ASV, ANI b. 49, fasc. 2, f. 365 [26 March 1938]). Among the many treatments to address the views of the Vatican toward *le leggi raz-ziali,* see Sale 2009, esp. pp. 72–102, for the views of Pope Pius XI.
12. "Osservazioni" in "Circa la relazioni degli Ordini sul proselitismo protestante" (ASV, SCC, SC b. 1, fasc. 1936 [1 August 1936]). The Sacred Congregation of the Council and its powerful prefect, Giulio Cardinal Serafini (1867–1938), would take leadership on the issue of Protestant proselytes (especially that of "apostate priests").

13. Scoppola 1973, pp. 331–32.
14. Rochat 1990; Spini 2007.
15. I have transcribed or translated seven types of documents in the appendixes to this book.
16. In June 2015 Pope Francis would ask the Waldensians for forgiveness, citing the "non-Christian and inhumane" treatment they had received at the hand of the Roman church, an apology that was not accepted by all. See *National Catholic Reporter* (22 June 2015).

CHAPTER 1. THE EVANGELICAL CONFESSIONS IN ITALY

1. "Secularization theory," "secularization," "secularizing": all these words are notoriously fraught; about each so much literature now exists that no one scholar can control it all. Here I simply mean the process by which the sacred or religious came to be distinguished from several phenomena and domains of human activity (especially the political) they once dominated and from which they have been marginalized (as, e.g., in the "separation of church and state"); by which religion has been made a private or strictly compartmentalized concern or, explicitly at least, a nonpolitical matter. As is well-known, debate about the cogency of this way of describing societal transformations in modernity is ongoing. See Latourette 1959, chapter 22, for a brief overview of Protestantism in Spain and Portugal, along with Italy.
2. Casanova has powerfully argued, in ways applicable to nineteenth- and twentieth-century Italy, that populations can become subjectively secular even as traditional religious institutions and cultures, in this case the Roman Catholic, retain their power and role in public and political life. See Casanova 1994, esp. pp. 112–17, 173–76, and 288–305, where Roman Catholicism is discussed in extenso. By "subjectively secular," I simply mean the ways in which Catholic prelates and popes felt, as a *matter of history*, that individuals, groups, or nations had become less religious in experience, practice, or belief, a tendency that may be reflected in the increasing inability of traditional social, cultural, and religious structures to control or even influence public institutions. In Italy, secularization seems to have both reflected, and then intensified, anticlerical feeling as well as religious indifference. "At times" because, to the dismay of prosecularists, Catholicism, even popular, that is, superstitious, Catholicism to which Anglo-Saxon Protestants were most opposed and which political liberals were anxious to repress, has experienced several revivals in the past two centuries.
3. Keltie et al. 1903, p. 803. Of the sixty-two thousand evangelicals, twenty-two thousand were Waldensians, indigenous to Italy.
4. See Madigan 2015, pp. 191–97, esp. 191.
5. See Muston 1853, who used the term for the title of his history of the Waldensians.
6. See Cameron 1986, on which I depend heavily in this section, for early history of the Waldensians.
7. Much more could be said. As not all Reformed churches were inspired by Calvin, Calvinism, or the Reformation in Geneva, it is best, in specialized discourse, to avoid the term "Calvinist." Other elements of the Reformed churches adopted by the Italian

Waldensian church included a this-worldly form of asceticism, belief in the scriptural foundation only of baptism and the Lord's Supper as well as in the "third use of the law," the authority of the Augsburg Confession (1540), and much else of somewhat slighter significance.

8. On the hegemony of Geneva and of Italian visits to and from it, see Cameron 1986, pp. 157–84.
9. The full quote is as follows: "St. Pius V was stern and severe, as far as a heart burning and melted with divine love could be so. . . . Yet such energy and vigor as his were necessary for the times. He was a soldier of Christ in a time of insurrection and rebellion, when in a spiritual sense, martial law was proclaimed" (Anderson 1978, p. 46).
10. On persecution and martyrdom, see Cameron 1986, pp. 83–118.
11. Milton, Sonnet 18, in Kerrigan 2009, p. 155. The biblical allusion here is to Psalm 137:9.
12. The term "Alpine Ghetto" appeared after the collapse of the Savoy monarchy and the establishment of a provisional republican government in Torino. See Romagnani, "Italian Protestants," in Liedtke and Wenderhorst 1999, p. 148.
13. For a history of the Bible Society, see Maselli and Ghidelli 2004; and Ricca 2011, p. 110.
14. Spini 1998, pp. 41–42. "Misleadingly," as prostitution was not given legal recognition in Italy.
15. See Vinay 1961a and Freitag 2003 for a history of the Italian exiles.
16. For history of the seminar, see Vinay 1955.
17. See Molnár et al. 1989 for a comprehensive history.
18. See Ricca 2011, pp. 108–10.
19. The Barnabites, along with the Capuchins and Theatines, were the earliest new religious orders of the Counter-Reformation, preceding the Jesuits by more than a decade.
20. To get some flavor for Gavazzi's anti-Catholic and anti-sacerdotal rhetoric, see Gavazzi's *The Priest in Absolution* (1877).
21. Ricca 2011, p. 111.
22. See Kertzer 2018 for an absorbing account of these issues.
23. On Gavazzi, see Sylvain 1962 and Santini 1955, on whose accounts I rely heavily here.
24. Ricca 2011, p. 111.
25. On the Italian *Fratelli,* see Maselli 1978.
26. See discussion of Savonarola's importance to evangelicals in fascist Italy, below.
27. See Freitag 2003.
28. See Spini 1959 for an analysis of *ginevrismo;* see also Spini 1998, pp. 8, 115–18; and Nitti 2012, p. 184.
29. Vinay 1965, p. 331.
30. Heitzenrater 1989.
31. For Arminius and Arminianism, see White 1992; for early Methodism, see Heitzenrater 1989.
32. Above all, the British and Foreign Bible Society.

33. See Piggott 2002 for an analysis of Piggott's letters and ideas.
34. Ricca 2011, pp. 112–13.
35. See his account of Cavazzi's public argument against the traditional belief that Peter was first "pope of Rome," in Piggott, "Public Discussion between Catholics and Protestants in Rome," *Christian Advocate* 47, p. 97.
36. This emphasis was ubiquitous: "The Methodist missionary reports include plans to subvert Catholic influence among Amerindians, encourage democratic movements in South America, continue the work of the Reformation among German Catholic migrants, seize Corsica for the evangelical cause, and use British colonial influence to keep Catholicism in check in Bulgaria" (Hempton 2005, p. 165).
37. Hempton 2005, p. 165.
38. Stackpole 1894, p. 29.
39. *North American Review* 134 (1) (1911): 134.
40. Hempton 2005, p. 165.
41. Spini 1998, pp. 221–27.
42. Spini 2002, p. 226.
43. Ibid.
44. See discussion of opposition below.
45. Ricca 2011, p. 113.
46. See Maselli 2003 for a history of the Italian *battisti.*
47. See study of Clark's missionary work in Italy in Scaramuccia 1999.
48. Ricca 2011, pp. 113–14.
49. See discussion below.
50. For the Italian Baptist mission in La Spezia, see the recent sympathetic study by Stretti 2016; see Ricca 2011, pp. 113–14.
51. Rowe 2008, pp. 83–90, 105–29, 196–226.
52. On White (and Mary Baker Eddy), see the forthcoming double biography by my colleague David Holland.
53. See De Meo 1980 for a history of Adventists in Italy.
54. De Meo 1980, p. 85.
55. Rochat, pp. 19–20.
56. For the Christian Church, see Harrell 1966; and McAllister and Tucker 1975.
57. Hughes and Roberts 2000, p. 3.
58. Hughes and Roberts 2000, p. 61.
59. Campbell 1843, pp. 207–8.
60. Hedlund 1970, p. 107.
61. See Hattersley and Belamy 1999 for a biography of Booth and his wife, also a preacher; and Murdoch 1994 for the early history of the army.
62. See Armistead 1987 for a history of the *Esercito* in Italy.
63. Burgess and McGee 1988.
64. Anderson 1992, chap. 1.
65. Anderson 1979, chap. 1.
66. Anderson 1979, chaps. 1–4.

67. On Pentecostalism in Italy, see Womack and Toppi 1989; and Rochat 1999, pp. 22–23, 613–14.
68. As Zanini 2015 has recently emphasized.
69. The literature on Pentecostalism is vast. I have relied especially on Wacker 2001.
70. Holden 2012, p. 14. Oddly, there is a dearth of academic literature on the Witnesses. See Holden on growing movements in the world. Today, there are some 12.5 million followers worldwide. Stark and Iannaccone 1997, pp. 153–54.
71. Holden 2012, chap. 1.
72. Ricca 2011, p. 112.
73. For the early history of the Jehovah's Witnesses in Italy, see Besier and Stokłosa 2016, chap. 1; and Holden 2012. I have relied heavily on Holden's excellent and perhaps unique history for my own account.
74. Comba 1930, pp. 403–4.
75. All these points will be developed at length in the succeeding chapters.
76. Newman, ed. Svaglic 2016, pp. 133–35.
77. *Dominus Iesus* can be found at http://www.vatican.va/roman_curia/congregations/cfaith/documents/rc_con_cfaith_doc_20000806_dominus-iesus_en.html.
78. AESI pos. 795, fasc. 400 f, f. 47r–v. I have translated the entire pamphlet in Appendix 1.

CHAPTER 2. BEFORE THE CONCORDAT

1. See Kertzer 2014, p. 12, especially chapter 7 for an account of the attempted murder, Tacchi Venturi's evasions, and the suspicions of the police investigating the case.
2. As I learned in the autumn of 2015 at the Jesuit Archives in Rome.
3. A Colloquium in Italian History and Culture at the Center of European Studies has been named for Salvemini. He taught at Harvard 1934–48. An early and vigorous opponent of fascism, he engaged in literary polemic with Mussolini, who (characteristically) challenged him to a duel when Salvemini continued to criticize him and fascism.
4. ARSI, Fondo TV, b. 17, fasc. 446, ff. 14–17, con tre allegati (22 October 1926).
5. ARSI, Fondo TV, b. 17, fasc. 446, f. 15 (1 December 1926). Emphasis added. Here, too, while the dependence on Tinti is not verbatim, we see the influence of his ideas. See Tinti to Tacchi Venturi (ARSI, Fondo TV, b. 17, fasc. 446, f. 57 [12 January 1927]).
6. For further discussion and examples, see Perin 2010, pp. 147–48.
7. Tacchi Venturi 1927, p. 1 (ASV, ANI b. 49, fasc. 1, f. 6r).
8. Tacchi Venturi 1927, pp. 1, 6 (ASV, ANI b. 49, fasc. 1, f. 6r–6v).
9. Tacchi Venturi 1927, p. 9 (ASV, ANI b. 49, fasc. 1, f. 8r).
10. Relazione di alcuni intendimenti della opposizione internazionale anti-fascista ed anti-religiosa (ARSI, FONDO TV, b. 17, fasc. 446, ff. 21–23 [January 1927]).
11. My thanks to David Kertzer, who solved the mystery of his identity for me (private correspondence December 2015).
12. See Killinger 2010 for Salvemini's career and especially his antifascist activities.
13. See Polasky 1995 for a comprehensive treatment of his "democratic socialism." A British social reformer, Besant was a follower of the Russian-born mystic Helena Blavatsky

and a cofounder of the Theosophical Society. She was also an early advocate of birth control, a leader for Indian independence, and a theosophist educated by the Indian spiritual leader Jiddu Krisnamurti (1895–1986). Besant wrote and lectured extensively on Theosophy, mainly from Madras, though she would finally renounce the religious system in 1929. She, too, was also deeply involved in the antifascist movement; and she, too, was a socialist. There is little doubt that Salvemini was involved in an antifascist movement that was led or supported by socialists or those with socialist sympathies or connections.

14. Vandervelde was based in Brussels. It is of interest that the spy indicates that the support of international Freemasonry would, in part, originate there. That freemasonry was opposed to fascism is well known. This claim, then, is plausible. Tacchi Venturi himself wrote *ebrea* (Jewess) in parentheses above Signora Vandervelde's surname. This annotation is an expression both of Tacchi Venturi's deep antisemitism and of the general truth that European Jews were opposed to fascism. See Polasky 1995, pp. 45–50, for discussion.
15. For a discussion of the use by Tacchi Venturi, the general of the Jesuit Order, and others of threat of "the international conspiracy," see Kertzer 2014, pp. 229–70, 281, 443, 448.
16. Tinti 1926. Tinti would later bring out volumes on Italian Jewish animosity toward Bolshevized Eastern European Judaism, and then, in 1937, sexual education "for purity"—the latter a theme popular with Tacchi Venturi, the pope, and some sectors of the fascist regime. Much earlier (1897) he had brought out volumes on the authority of Public Security in Italy, of which he was an employee.
17. Compare Tinti's 1926 letter to Ciriaci (ARSI, Fondo TV, b. 17, fasc. 446, f. 1) with Tacchi Venturi's "Osservazioni" (ARSI, Fondo TV, b. 17, fasc. 446, f. 14).
18. Intriguingly, Tacchi Venturi heavily edits this letter as well. Again, he excises the salutatory section of the letter, gives the letter a new title, purges the sentences that are critical of the bureaucracies and ministries, crosses out the sentences in which Tinti mentions that he is putting the finishing touches on his "Studio" as well as, of course, the clauses "we will publish it [the 'Studio'] in the form of an article by you" and "mio opuscolo, 'Sionismo e cattolicismo'" (ARSI, Fondo TV, b. 17, fasc. 446, f. 59). Tacchi Venturi edits this letter, in other words, exactly the way in which he edited Tinti's letter to Ciriaci, which he then passed on to Gasparri. This would lead one to suspect that Tacchi Venturi used *this* letter, too, as the foundation for a private letter or even a publication. Other letters in the Fondo TV suggest the same conclusion. Yet I have not yet been able to find evidence that he did so.
19. See ARSI Fondo TV, b. 17, fasc. 446, f. 57.
20. ARSI Fondo TV, b. 17, fasc. 446, f. 59.
21. See Tinti 1926. As Kertzer has pointed out, the book was dedicated to Tacchi Venturi. The Jesuit made sure Mussolini, who was said to have appreciated receiving it, got a copy. See Kertzer 2014, pp. 122–23, 487 n. 6.
22. ". . . in ogni modo Lei lo modifichi, lo aggiusti" (Fondo TV, b. 22, fasc. 583, f. 1).
23. See ARSI Fondo TV, b. 22, fasc. 583, f. 10. The sixth page of Tinti's typescript is missing from the fascicolo.

24. See *Il Pericolo Protestante* (Bari: Scuola Tip. Salesiana, 1927), with an appendix on the Bible and its interpretation (pp. 17–22). A copy of the pamphlet has also been preserved in a busta on Protestant propaganda at ASV, ANI. b. 49, fasc. 1, ff. 3–15. The same publishing house produced a book entitled *Religione e Fascismo*—dedicated to "il Genio dell'amato Duce S. E. Mussolini," whom it praises for "la restaurazione dei valori religiosi Cattolici moralizzatrico." See ASV, ANI b. 49, fasc. 1, f. 15v.
25. Which the publishing house advertises as an "opuscolo di grande interesse contro il settarismo internazionale ebraico massonico bolsevico." This is also the theme of Tinti's "Studio" and, by extension, of Tacchi Venturi's *Il Pericolo Protestante.*
26. Via Dante Alighieri 150, Bari. See Tinti, "Studio" (ARSI, Fondo TV, b. 22, fasc. 583, ff. 5–6).
27. Tacchi Venturi 1927, p. 5 (ASV, ANI b. 49, fasc. 1, f. 6v).
28. Tacchi Venturi 1927, p. 6 (ASV, ANI b. 49, fasc. 1, f. 6v).
29. See Hanson 1988 for an excellent study of Arianism.
30. For the Catholic church, the definitive decree on the metaphysics of the incarnation was worked out at the Council of Chalcedon, to which indeed the pope, Leo the Great (440–61), made a critical linguistic contribution. See Denzinger 1854, p. 41, for the "Definition" in Greek and Latin. The Decree has always been authoritative for the Roman Catholic and Greek Orthodox churches as well as other Orthodox churches. However, like many ancient creeds it split churches it intended to unite, and those divisions have lasted to the present day. The Armenian, Coptic, and Ethiopian churches, to name just three, are among those that never accepted the Chalcedonian Definition.
31. Tinti, "Studio" (ARSI, Fondo TV, b. 22, fasc. 583, f. 6); Tacchi Venturi 1927, p. 6 (ASV, ANI b. 49, fasc. 1, f. 6v).
32. Tacchi Venturi 1927, p. 6 (ASV, ANI b. 49, fasc. 1, f. 6v).
33. Tinti, "Studio" (ARSI, Fondo TV, b. 22, fasc. 583, ff. 5–6); Tacchi Venturi 1927, p. 6 (ASV, ANI b. 1, fasc. 49, 6v). On this last point, some Catholic polemicists ridicule the American temperance movement. The *complete* prohibition, the tee*totalism:* this the Roman church could not accept or even comprehend. To practice or to preach complete abstinence was, after all, to deviate from the desirable Aristotelian mean. It was excessive, extreme. Taken to its logical conclusion, it even made consumption of Eucharistic wine illicit. What could be more absurdly *in*temperate? This was a theme popular among Catholic polemicists. In his pamphlet on the Protestant danger, Tacchi Venturi argued that there was a "dangerous Protestant tendency to religious and political extremism."
34. Tacchi Venturi 1927, p. 10 (ASV, ANI b. 49, fasc. 1, f. 8v).
35. Tinti, "Studio" (ARSI, Fondo Tacci Venturi, b. 22, fasc. 583, f. 9)
36. Tinti, "Studio" (ARSI, Fondo Tacci Venturi, b. 22, fasc. 583, f. 5).
37. See Kertzer 2014, p. 123, where he discusses Tinti's *Zionism and Catholicism,* for a nice description of each man's antisemitism.
38. See Kertzer 2007 throughout. An especially ugly example is on p. 123, where Kertzer quotes Giuseppe Oreglia, S.J. There, Oreglia associates Catholicism, Protestantism, even paganism, as religions, in contrast to Judaism, which is a race and a people.

39. See Kertzer 2014, pp. 231–32. An article from *CC* 1932 claimed that the Russian Revolution had been led not by native Russians but "Jewish intruders." (Jesuits could use outsiderhood whenever their polemics called for it.) It went on to assert, though Jews constituted only about 5 percent of the population, that roughly 80 percent of the highest 550 leaders of the Bolshevik regime were Jewish. This, as Kertzer points out, would become a pervasive theme in antisemitic literature in the 1930s and, then, a rationale for their extermination.
40. "Il giudaismo: fomentatore del protestantesimo" (*Difesa della Razza* 3/17, 5 July 1940). Thanks to David Kertzer for sending me a copy of this number.
41. See encyclical *Humanum genus,* entirely dedicated to the Freemasons, at http://w2.vatican.va/content/leo-xiii/en/encyclicals/documents/hf_l-xiii_enc_18840420_humanum-genus.html. The head of the main Italian Masonic Order, Adriano Lemmi, memorably dubbed the ending of the pope's temporal power in Italy "the most memorable event in world history" (Conti 2003, p. 359). The New Code of Canon Law (1917) declared Masons excommunicate.
42. See, e.g., Pollard 2014, p. 53. The stories that grew up around the German priest Gerlach are many and legendary. Aside from being convicted of espionage on behalf of the Austro-Hungarian Empire, he was said to be a sexual libertine. Gerlach came back into public view recently during the "Vatileaks" scandal, when Benedict XVI's private butler, Paolo Gabriele, took sensitive documents, many alleging corruption within the Vatican (especially its bank), and leaked them to the press. Gerlach's actions were said to have resulted in the sinking of two Italian warships in the First World War; Gabriele's, which the defendant insisted were morally motivated, in the humiliation of the Vatican. Many journalists saw Gerlach as a forerunner to Gabriele. See, e.g., "Pope Benedict's Butler Jailed for Stealing Pontiff's Private Letters," *The Guardian,* 7 October 2012; and an article on the "camiere segreto" in *La Stampa,* 30 September 2012.
43. See Conti 2003; and Mola 1993.
44. Tinti, "Studio" (ARSI, Fondo TV, b. 22, fasc. 583, f. 6]); Tacchi Venturi 1927, p. 6 (ASV, ANI b. 49, fasc. 1, f. 6v).
45. See Kertzer 2014, p. 148.
46. ASV, AESI pos. 855, fasc. 548, ff. 38r–39r. See Kertzer 2014, pp. 230–31, for an account.
47. ASV, AESI pos. 855, fasc. 548, f. 39.
48. Tinti to Tacchi Venturi (ARSI, Fondo TV, b. 17, fasc. 446, f. 18).
49. See Kertzer 2014, pp. 266–67, for an account of this meeting. The Vatican's long suspicion of Freemasonry may have influenced Tinti and Tacchi Venturi. This was a suspicion that Pius XI certainly shared. Indeed, after the Concordat was signed he demanded that Mussolini, in putting together his government, purge anyone thought to be a Mason. If he did, he would show, again, that he was a man "sent by Providence." See ibid., 151–52.
50. See Tacchi Venturi 1927, p. 8 (ASV, ANI b. 49, fasc. 1, f. 7v). While no evidence suggests Jewish individuals or groups were involved in the bloody Mexican Revolution, Tinti is not entirely incorrect about American motivations for intervention and especially about the way in which they viewed former Spanish colonies and Mexico. Anglo-Saxon Protestant Americans did view Catholic Latin Americans as inferior,

culturally backward, and dangerously misled by the Antichrist, the pope. There is no question but that many American Anglo-Protestants linked the supposed cultural and moral backwardness of Latin American (and European Latin) society to Catholicism. It is also true that Catholics were persecuted during the revolution. See Anderson 1998. Others saw the Protestant offensive as directed toward Catholic countries in general. Crivelli saw the British oppression of Ireland in such terms, as it had "reduced that Catholic population to a state worse than a pariah in India" (Crivelli 1931, p. 38).

51. Tinti, "Studio" (ARSI, Fondo TV, b. 22, fasc. 583, f. 8); Tacchi Venturi 1927, p. 9 (ASV, ANI b. 49, fasc. 1, f. 8). The bishop in question was Francis Clement Kelly (1870–1948), who was indeed bishop of Oklahoma. The state and diocese were coterminous until 1948, when Kelly became bishop of Oklahoma City and Tulsa in the same year he died.
52. Tinti, "Studio" (ARSI, Fondo TV, b. 22, fasc. 583, f. 7); Tacchi Venturi 1927, p. 8. (ASV, ANI b. 49, fasc. 1, f. 8).
53. Tacchi Venturi 1927, p. 8 (ASV, ANI b. 49, fasc. 1, f. 7v). The Jesuit claims that this had been reported in the *Corriere d'Italia* (16 December 1926).
54. Baldwin, 1990, p. 178.
55. Tacchi Venturi 1927, p. 8 (ASV, ANI, b. 49, fasc. 1, f. 7v).
56. Tacchi Venturi described the YMCA as "this deadly association" in a letter to Gasparri (Fondo TV, b. 17, fasc. 446, ff. 54–55 [1 September 1927]).
57. Indeed, one of the reports that the Jesuit relies on gives the addresses and brief descriptions of YMCAs in Bari, Bergamo, Bologna, Florence, Lucca, Modena, Rome, Turin, and Trent (the last of which, an informant asserts, is home to the Board of the Foreign Missions of the Methodist Episcopal Church). See ARSI, Fondo TV, b. 17, fasc. 446, f. 60.
58. See ARSI, Fondo TV, b. 17, fasc. 446, ff. 50–51.
59. *CC* 70/2 (1919): 231–33.
60. Tacchi Venturi 1927, p. 7 (ASV, ANI b. 49, fasc. 1, f. 7).
61. Tinti to Tacchi Venturi (ARSI, Fondo TV, b. 22, fasc. 583, f. 6).
62. ARSI, Fondo TV, b. 22, fasc. 583, f. 7; Tacchi Venturi 1927, p. 1 (ASV, ANI b. 49, fasc. 1, f. 6).
63. Tinti, "Studio" (ARSI, Fondo TV, b. 22, fasc. 583, f. 8); Tacchi Venturi 1927, p. 9 (ASV, ANI b. 49, fasc. 1, f. 8v).
64. Corroborated by Selvaggiani. The YMCA on Via Indipendenza is "decorasamente arredato con sale da gioco, da lettura, da corrispondenza; bagni, installazioni complete per esercizi ginnastici, conferenze e conversazioni di caratteri biblico" (ASV, ANI b. 49, fasc. 2, f. 56).
65. Tinti, "Studio" (ARSI, Fondo TV, b. 22, fasc. 583, f. 8)
66. Tinti, "Studio" (ARSI, Fondo TV, b. 22, fasc. 583, f. 9).
67. Tinti, "Studio" (ARSI, Fondo TV, b. 22, fasc. 583, f. 9).
68. Tinti, "Studio" (ARSI, Fondo TV, b. 22, fasc. 583, f. 9).
69. Tinti, "Studio" (ARSI, Fondo TV, b. 22, fasc. 583, f. 9).
70. Crivelli 1931, pp. 12–14.
71. Moore and Vaudagna 2003, p. 157.

72. Stackpole 1894, p. 29.
73. See Tinti, "Studio": "Questa dei metodisti dunque è la setta più pericolosa per noi Italiani" (ARSI, Fondo TV, b. 22, fasc. 583, f. 6).
74. Moore and Vaudagna 2003, p. 157.
75. Quoted in Copplestone 1949, pp. 318–21.
76. ASV, ANI b. 49, fasc. 2, f. 53.
77. *OR,* 22 October 1934.
78. See Tacchi Venturi 1927, p. 8 (ASV, ANI b. 49, fasc. 1, p. 8). In his "Studio," Tinti warned of the Methodist effort to establish a Protestant Vatican: "The attempt, as we have seen, failed, but the hope has never been lost" (ARSI Fondo TV, b. 22, fasc. 583, f. 11).
79. The Methodist church would soon attempt to acquire property on Castel Gandolfo.
80. Tacchi Venturi 1927 (ASV, ANI b. 49, fasc. 1, f. 7v).
81. On Conrad Hilton putting one of his hotels at the top of Monte Mario in the late 1950s, see *Forbes* 53 (June 1956): 72. The article on the plans to put up a hotel is entitled "Second Sack of Rome?" When Pope Pius XI mounts to the roof of the Vatican he sees, the reporter asserts, on Monte Mario a mile to the north, something which vexes him. It is the Collegio Internazionale, a Methodist institution. Of all Protestant denominations in Italy, the Methodists had made themselves most disturbing to the Holy See by aggressive evangelism. *Time* reported in 1930 on the pope's distress with Monte Mario and the actions he took against Protestant proselytizing: "Last week *L'Osservatore Romano,* Vatican newspaper, even accused them of trying to take advantage of last month's earthquake (*Time,* 4 Aug., 11 Aug.) to convert the bewildered populace." Other Italian papers hinted that this was the real reason that Prime Minister Mussolini had rejected earthquake aid from the Protestant-supported American Red Cross: "*L'Osservatore Romano* last week struck directly at the Methodists' Collegio Internazionale. Catholic students of the college have complained because the school required each to have a companion when he goes to mass." Observed *L'Osservatore Romano:* "In a college where receptions are given at which Protestant girls are present; where there are cinematic shows with the usual falsifications against the Papacy; where swimming is indulged in with ultra-modern conceptions on the question of surveillance, the excuse that the students have no one to accompany them to Mass seems secondary when it comes to fulfilling the act of devotion" (*Time,* 14 July 1930). Antipathy to Methodist (and to slightly less extent Baptist) activities in Italy inspired the pope's recent denunciation of Protestant proselytizing. The previous week he proceeded beyond mere denunciation. He organized a defensive–offensive body, the Pontifical Organization for Preservation of the Faith and for the Provision of New Churches in Rome. As president of this militant religious police His Holiness appointed newly hatted Francesco Cardinal Marchetti-Selvaggiani, 58, and instructed him to work in close co-operation with Basilio Cardinal Pompili, vicar-general of Rome. "Well-equipped is Cardinal Marchetti-Selvaggiani for his new assignment. Born in Rome he knows its neighborhoods and people better than most of his Cardinal colleagues. As secretary of the Congregation for the Propagation of the Faith the past seven years, he is an expert in this sort of proselytizing" ("Papal Offense-Defense," *Time* [18 August 1930]).

82. "The School on Monte Mario," *Christian Advocate* 96 (7 July 1921): 876.
83. Moore and Vaudagna 2003, p. 157. "Disapproval" is a kind but inaccurate word to describe a sensibility of contempt and revulsion.
84. Plans for the construction of a Protestant Vatican by the Methodists failed largely because the Roman government, under pressure from the Catholic population of the city, refused to issue the zoning and building permits. Under pressure that began in the pontificate of Pius X, the American bishops bought in 1925 twelve acres on the Janiculum Hill to construct a new North American College, in part to thwart a second effort by Protestants to purchase property overlooking the Vatican. See DiGiovanni 2013, pp. 8–9.
85. Moore and Vaudagna 2003, p. 157. See Moore's interesting observations regarding critical comments made by European Protestants, especially Methodists, regarding their European counterparts and the reaction of Protestant European church leaders, e.g.: "Every church that Americans funded in northern Europe represented an effort to spread the gospel of church disestablishment" (p. 158). The use of "funded" rather than "founded" is a telling and intentional distinction, one of which many European Christians, Protestant and Catholic, would have approved.
86. Tacchi Venturi 1927 (ASV, ANI b. 49, fasc. 1, f. 7).
87. "Udienze con Mussolini" (ARSI, Fondo TV, 46, cc.nn [10 May 1926]).
88. Dionino DeCarolis to Borgongini (ASV, ANI b. 49, fasc. 2, ff. 78–80 [11 February 1931]).
89. Alfredo Vitali, Aiutante di Studo della dataria to Borgongini (ASV, ANI b. 49, fasc. 2, ff. 88–89 [18 April 1931]; Parish Priest of Pontifical Church of S. Thomas of Villanova in Castel Gandolfo to Mons. G. MARAZZI, Bp. of Albano (ASV, ANI b. 49, fasc. 2, ff. 101r–101v. [26 April 1931]). This letter was forwarded on 30 April 1931 by the bishop of Albano to Borgongini (ASV, ANI b. 49, fasc. 2, ff. 99–100).
90. Because, as an essentially Protestant nation, the United States would have had no interest in intervening in a war that was, in Tinti's view (and in Tacchi Venturi's), aimed at Catholics and Catholicism.
91. Tinti had referred briefly to American plans for the "invasion of a small evangelical church in a small town in Puglia" (ARSI Fondo TV, b. 22, fasc. 583, f. 9).
92. "Brevi Cenni sul Pericolo Protestante in Italia e Sui Mezzi per Rispingerlo" (AESI pos. 795, fasc. 395, f. 6r). Like so many anti-Protestant polemics of the period, this was put out anonymously. However, a document in the Italian Nunciature's archives identifies the author as Selvaggiano. See ASV, ANI, b. 49, fasc. 2.
93. "Anonymous" to Tacchi Venturi (ARSI Fondo TV, b. 22, fasc. 583, fasc. 22, f. 20).
94. The letter reads as if sent by Tinti, and the signature, which is illegible, resembles his. However, it is probably not from Tinti, despite the striking commonalities in syntax, tonality, and preoccupation with foreigners and Masons. Tinti's sphere of influence was from Bari to Rome, not the North, and he was not, it seems, concerned with the Swiss. It is another, anonymous informant of Tacchi Venturi whose report the Jesuit edits and seems intent on using.
95. Precisely as a neutral, Switzerland was in fact a valuable territory from which all sides spied in both the First and Second World Wars. See Morton 2010; Garliński 1981.

The notion that the Swiss were spying on Italy in the interwar period seems quite far-fetched.

96. "Anonymous" to Tacchi Venturi (ARSI Fondo TV, b. 22, fasc. 583, ff. 20–23).
97. "Anonymous" to Tacchi Venturi (ARSI Fondo TV, b. 22, fasc. 583, f. 23).
98. Tinti to Tacchi Venturi (ARSI, Fondo TV, b. 17, fasc. 446, ff. 56–59).
99. As reported by Tinti, "Studio" (ARSI, Fondo TV, b. 22, fasc. 583, f. 9); Tacchi Venturi 1927, p. 10 (ASV, ANI b. 49, fasc. 1, f. 8v).
100. Tinti to Tacchi Venturi (ARSI, Fondo TV, b. 17, fasc. 446, f. 58).
101. Tinti reports, in addition, that some Protestant institutions were in the hands of international socialists from Amsterdam (ARSI, Fondo TV, b. 22, fasc. 583, f. 12); Tacchi Venturi 1927, p. 7 (ASV, ANI b. 49, fasc. 1, f. 7v), a point Tacchi Venturi repeats. See Tacchi Venturi 1927, p. 11 (ASV, ANI b. 49, fasc. 1, f. 9). Tacchi Venturi indicates that the two journals are *L'Impero* and *Il Tevere.*
102. See Tacchi Venturi 1927, p. 12 (ASV, ANI b. 49, fasc. 1, f. 9v).
103. Tinti to Tacchi Venturi (ARSI, Fondo TV, b. 22, fasc. 583, f. 1).
104. Though home to many great Greek thinkers and artists, this region of ancient Greece (now central Greece) became known for the dullness of its inhabitants, even, proverbially, for the stupidity of its citizens.
105. *"Papuasia"* in Tinti's Italian, where cannibalism and human sacrifice were practiced into the twentieth century.
106. ". . . qualsiasi Ottentottia da civilizzare," a region of southern Africa near the Cape of Good Hope, where an indigenous African population lived (ARSI, Fondo TV, b. 22, fasc. 583, f. 14).
107. Here, Tacchi Venturi's observations are based, by and large, on fact. Fought from 24 October to 3 November 1918, the battle at Vittorio Veneto, in the northeast of Italy, was indeed a decisive Italian victory. It concluded hostilities on the Italian front and led to the end of the First World War and thus to the disintegration of the Austro-Hungarian Empire, the *impero* to which Tinti refers here. See Gooch 2013, pp. 295–99, for an account of the battle and its significance.

CHAPTER 3. AFTER THE CONCORDAT

1. *OR* (12 February 1929).
2. See text of *Statuto Albertino* at https://www.quirinale.it/allegati_statici/costituzione/Statutoalbertino.pdf.
3. The article actually "reaffirms the principle consecrated in the first article" of the 1848 *Statuto Albertino* of the Kingdom of Italy: "L'Italia riconosce e riafferma il principio consacrato nell'articolo 1° dello Statuto del Regno 4 marzo 1848, pel quale la religione cattolica, apostolica e romana è la sola religione dello Stato." For a classic study, see D. Mack Smith 1997, especially section 3, for a history of the Albertine Statute.
4. For a classic study, see Mack Smith 1997.
5. D'Agostino 2004, p. 200.
6. I will refer to these, respectively, as "Law 1159" and the "implementing decree." Law 1159 was entitled "Disposizioni sull'Exercizio dei Culti Ammessi nello Stato." It may

be found in the *Gazzetta Ufficiale della Repubblica Italiana* 164 (16 July 1929). The implementing decree was entitled "Norme per l'attuazione della L. 24 giugno 1929, n. 1159 sui culti ammessi nello Stato." It may be found in the *Gazzetta Ufficiale della Repubblica Italiana* 87 (4 April 1930). An online edition of the 1159 laws in Italian may be found at http://www.edizionieuropee.it/LAW/HTML/39/zn74_01_003.html.

7. For the complete speech of Mussolini, see *O.O.* 21 (1951), 14. See general discussion of these laws in Rochat 1990, pp. 127–45.

8. For broad discussion of Law 1159 and the implementing decree, see Rochat 1990; for detailed legal discussion, see Piacentini 1934 and Giacchi 1934

9. See the statement of the Protestant jurist Mario Piacentini, "La legge 24 giugno 1929," in *Bilychnis* 35 (1929): "Questa legge è stata detta, giustamente, la Magna charta della libertà religiosa in Italia."

10. Jewish communities and the Waldensians did not require a law crafted especially for them, as both had legal capacity from 1861. There was a fourth level of legal status that came to include those cults not present in Italy at the time the laws were passed. Today, such a hierarchy still exists, and that fourth level (if we might call it that) would include Scientology and Islam as well as many "new religions." With 1.5 million followers, Islam is de facto the second largest religion in the country; it does not exist de jure. Italian Buddhists and Hindus both secured preliminary *intese* (in 2002 and 2007, respectively), but these have not been bureaucratically finalized. Catholic bishops have occasionally opposed recognition of the religious traditions just mentioned. I take this language of hierarchies from a legal analysis in Ferrari and Ferrari in Thayer 2016, pp. 409–28.

11. Or "Rocco Code," discussed below.

12. "L'arma potentissima della preghiera raccomandata del Santo Padre per respingere l'insidia protestante in Italia" (*OR,* 23 September 1934). As the title suggests, Pius XI recommended a "special apostolate of prayer" in the struggle against Protestantism in Italy ("nella lotto contro il protestantesimo in Italia"). This number of *OR* is preserved in the archives of the Sacred Congregation of the Council and was highlighted by a reader in red pencil. See folder entitled "L'Apostolato della preghiera nella lotta contro il protestantesimo in Italia—Parola del Santo Padre" (ASV, SCC, SC b. 1, fasc. 1934 [25 September 1934]).

13. The Italian word "propaganda" is not synonymous with the English word, which ordinarily implies disinformation, advocacy, or indoctrination. "Propaganda" is ordinarily translated into English as "propagation." When used in polemic, the Italian word can carry both meanings, but it usually simply means proselytizing, missionizing, or Christianizing in this context.

14. Clerico-fascists in Parliament vigorously opposed passage of the bill. Part of their argument against it included a critique of Protestant missionary methods. Igino Giordani, who wrote the clerico-fascist publication *La Rivolta Cattolica* (1925) as well as a long book on the Protestant menace (see Giordani 1930), also issued a protest, and Catholic Action, in its publications, its petitions to the papacy, and its deeds, would almost immediately spring into action against the newly permitted cults. I discuss Catholic Action in detail below in chapter 7.

15. On Pius IX's reaction to the Law of Guarantees, see Kertzer 2006, pp. 86–87, 195–97.
16. Article 28, for example, stated that "Bibles, missals, and prayer books may not be printed without the prior approval of the bishop." As a matter of fact, scores of bishops interpreted the pacts as giving them wide authority in their dioceses, and they complained in letters to the Holy See, to the Holy Office, to the Prefectures, to Mussolini, to Tacchi Venturi, and to others. Some even took drastic action, like shutting down Protestant churches and even Protestant schools in their dioceses.
17. The Rome correspondent for *The Times,* who was obviously sympathetic to the 24 June legislation, acutely observed, in an article all too accurately entitled "Historia Concordium, Historia Lachrymarum" ("The History of Concordats, A History of Tears"): "In agreeing to the Conciliation the Vatican had hoped to make Italy Catholic in the confessional sense of the term, to direct education in the public schools, both elementary and higher, and to put non-Catholic cults in a position of fundamental inferiority. These pretensions have been disallowed by Sig. Mussolini. So long as Sig. Mussolini remains Prime Minister, the non-Catholics can rest assured of impartiality" (*The Times* [8 January 1931]). In the event, the journalist was too optimistic. The article had been cut out of the paper by a concerned cleric and is now preserved in ASV, ANI, b. 49, fasc. 2, f. 42. In his classic and still valuable study of the church and state in fascist Italy, D. A. Binchy observed that *historia concordatum historia dolorum* is "almost a maxim of ecclesiastical history" (Binchy 1941, p. 668).
18. This is how Borgongini characterized Protestantism in a pro memoria following a meeting on how to handle the British Wesleyans at Villa San Sebastiano. Pro memoria by Borgongini-Duca after Audience with Rocco on Villa San Sebastiano (ASV, ANI b. 49, fasc. 2, f. 104 [20 October 1931]). On the stubborn problem of Villa San Sebastiano, see chaps. 4, 5.
19. The pamphlet is extracted from *Studia Sacra,* a monthly periodical of the clergy of Padua, published in 1920.
20. *Due Domande,* in ACDF (Materiae diversae, Rerum Variarum 1920), 7, p. 4. On Casciola's career, see Aronica 2003.
21. Casciola was in fact a modernist and friendly with most contemporary Italian modernists, including Buonaiuti. See *CC* 83 (1932/2): 515–32, entitled "Propaganda Protestante e Modernista," especially pp. 521–26, which talks at length of modernism as a heresy and which attacks Buonaiuti at length. Modernism was so denounced also because thought to have been influenced, as in fact it was, by German Protestant insights into the sources of the Pentateuch ("the documentary hypothesis") and the notion of developing revelation. A movement that began at the end of the nineteenth century, modernism attempted to interpret anew ancient Catholic teaching in view of the revolutionary historical and philosophical developments of the nineteenth century. Many of its members were notably unenthusiastic about the centralization of ecclesiastical authority in the person of the pope and the papal bureaucracy. The movement was heavily influenced by the insights of biblical scholars, who had demonstrated that Israelite religion had evolved over the millennia, that the Gospels and the evidence for modern biblical criticism lay, by and large, within the biblical materials themselves. For views like this, the French priest-scholar Alfred Loisy (1857–1940),

with whom the movement is often identified, was dismissed from his teaching position at the Institut Catholique in Paris in 1893. Loisy's studies on the sources of and differences among the Gospels were condemned by François Cardinal Richard, the archbishop of Paris. An English, Irish-born Jesuit, George Tyrrell (1869–1909), was also dismissed from his teaching post for challenging the decrees of the First Vatican Council (1869–70), including the teaching on papal infallibility. The books of these and other modernists were put on the Index, and two decrees, *Pascendi* (a papal encyclical: see http: //w2.vatican.va/content/pius-x/en/encyclicals/documents/hf_p-x_enc_19070908_pascendi-dominici-gregis.html) and *Lamentabili* (from the Holy Office: http: //w2.vatican.va/content/pius-x/en/encyclicals/documents/hf_p-x_enc_19070908_pascendi-dominici-gregis.html), condemned the movement, and the priest Umberto Benigni organized a circle of censors, known as Integralists, who reported to him suspect writings. (Among the fiercest opponents of modernism was Cardinal Merry del Val in his then role as secretary of state.) Nonetheless, the writings of Loisy and Tyrrell influenced many of the intellectual stars of the intellectual firmament, especially those advocating church reform, not least of which was Buonaiuti (1881–1946), who would be forbidden to teach in 1929 and then, in 1931, lose his chair for opposition to Italian fascism. See Jodock 2000 for a recent and extensive treatment. In an audience held with Mussolini on 7 February 1927, when Buonaiuti was teaching at the University of Rome, after his excommunication but before being forbidden to teach, Tacchi Venturi, who thought Buonaiuti would have been subject to the Concordat's ban on the employment of apostate or censored priests, would speak with Mussolini about stopping him from teaching (see ARSI, Fondo TV, 46, "Udienze con Mussolini" [7 February 1927]). He was often reported by enemies to have spoken in one or another Protestant venue, including in the YMCA in Rome.

22. Not to mention psychopathy. Gemelli, OFM (1878–1959), the profascist founder of the Catholic University of Milan and a psychiatrist, once opined that modernists were in need not of priestly ministrations but of psychiatric treatment like that administered to chronically unhappy deviants. Oddly, though he fiercely denounced and ridiculed modernism, this did not except him from cautiously accepting Darwin's theory of evolution. He was probably helped by the fact that, at the time of his acceptance, the church had yet to comment authoritatively on the theory, and, while encouraging Catholics to believe what they wished about Darwin, he admonished them to be ready to abjure their convictions if the theory were to be disapproved by official magisterial teaching. Catholic reaction to evolution was in part shaped by its adoption of Aristotle's ideas on species, which, being permanent, do not evolve. See Kohn 1988, p. 724. Gemelli's susceptibility to irrational theory, unbased in empirical study, may be judged in light of his approval, in a 1939 speech in Bologna, of the regime's recently passed racial laws and policies. "Like Hitler, when writing of such matters as Jewish usurers, Gemelli remains in the realm of pure myth." See Feinstein 2003, p. 243.

23. *CC* 65/4 (1914): 475–84, found in ACDF (M.D.R.V. 1920) 1920, 7. Two years earlier the same journal had published an article on the Baptist journal *Bilychnis* again linking the two: "Bilychnis: Una doppia lucerna di protestantesimo e di modernismo" (*CC* 63/2 [1912]). Also found in the folder of the archives of the Holy Office noted above,

which, oddly, contains much material on the YMCA. Founded in 1912, the journal ceased publication in 1932. It did indeed publish articles by many ex-priests, and it was, in fact, an organ for the expression of modernist scholarship. See Binchy 1941, p. 576.

24. Sometimes called the Pio-Benedictine Code (because begun under Pius X and promulgated by Pope Benedict XV), the first all-inclusive revision and codification of Western Canon Law, promulgated in 1917, remained in force until November 1983. It has been recognized as the greatest achievement in Canon Law since the compilation, in the twelfth century, of Gratian's *Decretum.* Largely because of ecumenical gains that popes of the early twentieth century would have found odious and owing to the reforming achievements of the Second Vatican Council, the code was abrogated after the promulgation of the 1983 code. For the translated *Code* and Commentary, see Peters 2001.
25. *Due Domande,* in ACDF (M.D.R.V. 1920) 1920, 7, p. 5.
26. Tacchi Venturi 1927, p. 14 (ASV, ANI b. 49, fasc. 1, f. 10v).
27. See *Ubi Primum* 13, where the pope traces the origin of indifferentism to Augustine's *De haeresibus,* written in 428–29 (http: //www.papalencyclicals.net/leo12/l12ubipr .htm).
28. For an extensive historical treatment of these issues, see Gabriel 2010.
29. *OR* (22 October 1934).
30. *OR* (22 October 1934), p. 6.
31. See especially *Mortalium Animos* 8–9. (http://w2.vatican.va/content/pius-xi/en/encyclicals/documents/hf_p-xi_enc_19280106_mortalium-animos.html). The encyclical was issued just three years after the Stockholm Conference of 1925 brought together Orthodox, Protestant, and Anglican Christians not long after the ecumenical patriarch of Constantinople Germanos (1835–1920) called, in 1920, for a fellowship of churches, rather like an ecclesiastical League of Nations.
32. The doctrine is often described as Augustinian, and it is, though another North African bishop, Cyprian of Carthage (200–258), used the famous Latin phrase *Extra ecclesiam nulla salvus* almost two centuries before Augustine, and many ancient Christian thinkers, Greek as well as Latin, used similar phrases. By the time of Mortalium Animos and in response to the fissiparous and latitudinarian potentialities of the ecumenical movement, the ancient Latin phrase had evolved to *Extra Ecclesiam Nullus Omnino Salvatur,* the key emendation being the addition of the intensifying adverb *omnino* ("by no means"). For a history of the development of the idea, see the polemically tinged volume by Müller 2007.
33. *Due Domande,* ACDF (M.D.R.V. 1920) 1920, 7, pp. 7–9.
34. Decree of the Holy Office, ACDF (M.D.R.V. 1920) 1920, p. 7.
35. *La peste della età nostra è il così detto laicismo.* See *Quas Primas* 24 (11 December 1925) at http://w2.vatican.va/content/pius-xi/it/encyclicals/documents/hf_p-xi_enc_11121925_quas-primas.html. The English translation of the encyclical renders *laicismo,* too narrowly, as "anticlericalism." Anticlericalism was an important element, but no more than a component of a much broader, vastly more complex areligious worldview.

36. Tacchi Venturi thus would have started his anti-Protestant campaign about the same time as he was appointed (1923) as the intermediary for Mussolini and Pius XI. See Kertzer 2014, esp. chapter 7.
37. Catholic polemicists, who did not recognize bishops outside the Catholic line of "apostolic succession," almost always put the word "bishop" (*vescovo*) in scornful quotation marks.
38. Burt's famous remark may be found in Copplestone (1973), vol. 4, p. 320.
39. Grandi to Borgongini-Duca (ASV, ANI b. 49, fasc. 2, ff. 11–12 [15 July 1930]).
40. "An Undesirable American Pilgrimage" (*La Tribuna,* 20 July 1930). Indeed, the dates are so close to being simultaneous, one wonders if the journalist did not somehow gain access to the pope's views, even his words. Allegato, Grandi to Borgongini-Duca (ASV, ANI b. 49, fasc. 2, f. 8).
41. For Catholic polemicists and diplomats, *cosidetto* was a favorite adjective of derision. The Methodist Episcopalian church, for example, had only "so-called" bishops.
42. Grandi to Borgongini-Duca (ASV, ANI b. 49, fasc. 2, ff. 11–12 [22 July 1930]).
43. Pizzardo to Borgongini-Duca (ASV, ANI b. 49, fasc. 2, f. 21 [15 February 1931]).
44. See ARSI, Fondo TV, b. 19, fasc. 474, ff. 8–9 (11 January 1927).
45. See Frugoni et al. 1991 for the latest biography on Arnold, particularly good on the critical use of the sources.
46. For a brilliant biography of the Dominican reformer including a subtle analysis of Savonarola's visions and prophecies, see Weinstein 2011. For a short analysis, see Madigan 2015, pp. 405–10.
47. See ARSI, Fondo TV, b. 19, fasc. 474, ff. 8–9 (11 January 1927).
48. Even before the death in 1226 of Francis of Assisi, two wings of the order he had founded could be distinguished. One wing was the conventuals, who wished to blunt the radicality of Francis's commitment to poverty so as to reconstruct the order along the lines suggested and in order to fulfill educational, pastoral, and inquisitorial tasks given it by the papacy. The other was the spirituals, who were determined to resist the modification downward by legal decrees issued by the papacy of Francis's original austere vision of the religious life. Eventually, four spirituals were burnt (May 1318) in the marketplace of Marseilles for heresy—in this case for refusing to obey certain demands laid down by Pope John XXII (1316–34). For a brief summary, see Madigan 2015, pp. 209, 253–56.
49. See Spinka 1968 for an authoritative biography and Kaminsky 2004 for a magisterial analysis of the Hussite Revolution. For a short treatment, see Madigan 2015, chap. 19. For an up-to-date and elegant analysis of the "great schism" (not to be confused with the schism between Eastern and Western Christianity, often, if problematically, dated to 1054), see Oakley 1991, pp. 55–68. A brief account may also be found in Madigan 2015, pp. 378–83.
50. See Eck, ed. F. L. Battles, 1976; and Cajetan, ed. J. Wicks, 1978, for a sampling of the anti-Lutheran polemic. These are the distant sources for the anti-Protestant polemic of Italy in the fascist period. Often the arguments used in the sixteenth century were simply replicated in the twentieth. Nowhere has this the importance of novelty in religion been more elegantly and convincingly demonstrated than in the impressively

erudite Feldman 1996; see especially the whole of chapter 6. Speaking of the authority antiquity could confer in the ancient world, Feldman has observed, "The general principle seems to have been that the older things were, the more divine and the more credible they were" (p. 177).

51. See Guerra 1992 for a recent analysis of the purposes of Justin's *First Apology*, where he attempts to make Christianity older than either Greek philosophy or the books of the Jewish Bible.

52. I have my doubts about the utility of the category "forerunners of the Reformation," not relevant for this study here. Yet see Obermann 2002, who uses those words as the title for an influential study.

53. Whatever the purposes of the pilgrimage, this was certainly not the first organized to visit important Protestant sites in Italy. As early as 1910 John Good had published a guidebook for Protestants entitled *Famous Places of the Reformed Churches: A Guidebook to Europe*. See Good 1910. While concentrating on the Swiss and German reformed churches, Good does dedicate a section of his book to Italy and especially to the Waldensians. These he calls, not surprisingly, "Protestants before the Reformation." See Cook 1910, p. 311. On the Waldensians, see the authoritative study by Cameron 2000.

54. "Nota d'Archivio" (ASV, ANI b. 2, fasc. 49, f. 14 [21 July 1930]): "Essere volunta del Santo Padre che il Governo Italiano, nella sua nota, non doveva attenenersi semplicemente ad indicare le misure prese restringere *lo scandalo del pellegrinaggio avengalico* [*sic*], ma bensi deplorare il pellegrinaggio stesso, come offensivo all cattolicità della Nazione."

55. Pizzardo to Borgongini. To which Pizzardo adds: "Si augura percio che lo zelo per una lodevole difesa dell'unità spirituale della Nazione sia rivolto colla conveniente energia contro la detta propaganda eretica e straniera" (ASV, ANI b. 49, fasc. 2, f. 21 [15 April 1931]).

56. He himself would be canonized, simultaneously, with John XXIII (1958–63) on 27 April 2014. Canonizing the great reforming pope of modernity, the Good Pope, who convoked the Second Vatican Council (1962–65) and whose pontificate marked a major transitional era in the history of the church, helped quiet unease at the alacrity with which a traditionalist pope like John Paul II was brought to sainthood. The latter was canonized so rapidly because his successor Benedict XVI (2005–resigned 2013) waived the mandatory—or at least customary—five-year interval before a prospective saint could be considered for beatification. In this way Pope Benedict ensured that a reformer would be canonized with a pope whose attitude toward the reforms of Vatican II were ambivalent. See the Vatican's web page about the dual canonizations at http: //www.vatican.va/special/canonizzazione-27042014/index_en.html. Accessed 15 October 2015. See the Apostolic Constitution for sanctification procedures, entitled *Divinus Perfectionis Magister*, issued by John Paul II in 1983 at http: //w2.vatican.va/content/john-paul-ii/en/apost_constitutions/documents/hf_jp-ii_apc_25011983_divinus-perfectionis-magister.html. See Woodward 1990 for a popular but competent study of Catholic saint making. The notion that miracles were a necessary, but not sufficient, cause for canonization goes back to the pontificate of Innocent III

(1198–1216). Canon Law currently states that two miracles have to be approved by the presiding pope in order for one beatified to be canonized. This requirement was waived in the case of John XXIII, and John Paul II almost had to be exempted before Floribeth Mora Diaz, from Costa Rica, who had a brain aneurysm from which she was not expected to recover, reported that she had prayed to John Paul while watching his beatification ceremony on television. She then had an audition during which, she reported, the pontiff ordered her not to be afraid and to get up (an echo of several New Testament pericopes). A subsequent brain scan was said to have revealed no scars. A Vatican medical commission concluded that the cure was scientifically inexplicable. See "Costa Rican 'Miracle' Woman Was Key to John Paul's Sainthood," *Reuters,* 24 April 2014.

57. See Robert Wistrich on Benedict's decision to beatify Pius XII: "Why Has Pope Benedict Chosen Now to Beatify Nazi-Era Pontiff?" *Haaretz,* 28 December 2009, at http://www.haaretz.com/jewish/2.209/why-has-pope-benedict-chosen-now-to-beatify-nazi-era-pontiff-1.1227.

58. See *OR,* 4–5 March 1935, where the article announcing the canonization was entitled "The Pope Celebrates the New Spring of the Church in Imperial Britain."

59. Though a man of irenic temperament, he feared that England would fall to the Lutheran cause, and he fervently participated in the examination of heterodox works, many of which eventually would be prohibited or burned. More would also defend traditional medieval devotional practices, like the veneration of saints and pilgrims, which virtually all the Protestant churches repudiated with something like pious repugnance. He would later write ardently against Lutheran doctrines concerning justification by faith, the metaphysics of divine presence in the Eucharist, the nature of the church, and the relationship between scripture and tradition—all issues on which the Lutheran and Catholic churches remained deeply divided in the early twentieth century, with each confession genuinely believing the other had utterly misinterpreted the meaning and message of Christianity and the teaching of its founder. See Ackroyd 1998 for a decidedly nonhagiographical biography of More.

60. See the fine biography of Fisher by Dowling 1999.

61. See Kertzer 2014 for a magisterial treatment of the relationship, which began with the pope supporting Mussolini. The pope's hope was that fascism would, after the establishment of democracy and the separation of church and state, restore a society, if not a confessional state, that was governed by the (essentially medieval) values of hierarchy and authority, guided and restrained by the norms of private and social conduct established by the church and given authoritative expression by the pope. The pope also hoped fascism would neutralize the threat to church interests posed by socialism and liberalism. Eventually, the pontiff, after exploding with anger on many occasions over a decade, would grow weary of Il Duce for many reasons, including his opposition to Catholic youth groups, his incomprehension of the Protestant menace, his self-deification, his deference to Hitler (whom he thought, angering Il Duce, Mussolini imitated in many ways), his statolatry and, finally, racism.

62. Borgongini to Pacelli (ASV, ANI pos. 23, fasc. 2, ff. 129r–130r [2 June 1930]).

63. Crivelli to Giuseppe Bruno (ASV, SCC, SC "Sacerdoti apostate e ministri protestanti," b. 1, fasc. 1933 [31 December 1932]).
64. Zanini 2015, p. 691. Zanini cites the letter from Crivelli to Bruno to support this argument. Zanini's argument is correct, but it is doubtful that this particular piece of evidence, which has to do with equality before the law and not the genesis of Protestant propaganda, supports it.
65. Documenti Diplomatici Italiani 7/9, p. 45, no. 112.
66. Rochat 1990, p. 40.
67. Rochat 1990, p. 42.
68. See Kertzer 2014, pp. 129–31.
69. Bocchini, "Circolare," ACS. G.1. Propaganda Evangelica (13 April 1927).
70. Bocchini, "Appunto," ACS. G.1. Propaganda Evangelica (27 June 1927). And in March 1928 he noted ten other prefects (ACS. G.1/Avventisti) of Adventist presence and earlier had warned of the presence of the Salvation Army as well.
71. ACS. G1. Pentecostali (19 January 1928). The document is not signed.
72. ACS. G1. Pentecostali. Statement on those Denounced by Catholics in Rome (9 October 1928).
73. See Kertzer 2014, pp. 222–23, for a full and recent account of the meeting.

CHAPTER 4. THE POPE'S ANGUISH

1. English text of *Non abbiamo bisogno* available at http: //w2.vatican.va/content/pius-xi/en/encyclicals/documents/hf_p-xi_enc_29061931_non-abbiamo-bisogno.html.
2. See Kertzer 2014, p. 223, for the pope's use of the term "Catholic totalitarianism": "The pope added that he could understand the principle of 'totalitarian Fascism,' but this could refer only to the material realm. There were also spiritual needs, he said, and for these what was needed was 'Catholic totalitarianism.'"
3. The Congregation still exists today, northeast of Vatican City, in the Piazza San Giovanni Laterano. The pontiff's decision to open the new congregation and his profound distress at the freedom of Protestants to proselytize was covered by the print media in America. *Time* reported: "Said His Holiness to his Cardinals: '[To counteract] the proselytizing Protestant effort which from 1870 onward has never ceased its work of corrosion and gain, but pursues it with increasing persistence,'" the number of Catholic parish churches in Rome and its suburbs must be increased. "'We could never have expected these forms of worship to receive such treatment as to seem not only tolerated in theory and admitted in practice, but favored as well in no small way, affording the opportunity of which this regrettable proselytism cannot fail to take advantage.'*" In an asterisked comment, the writer of this magazine, founded by the son of Protestant missionaries, noted, and implicitly criticized, the pontiff by observing: "*Of Italy's 43,000,000 population, at least 95% are Catholics, less than one-third of 1% Protestants" ("Condition of the Pope," *Time* [14 July 1930]).
4. Pizzardo to Borgongini-Duca (AESI pos. 795, fasc. 400, f. 9r [9 July 1937]).
5. *OR,* 6 June 1929. Less than three weeks later the new fascist ecclesiastical legislation gave Protestants "complete freedom of discussion as far as religious matters are

concerned," permitted freedom of worship and excused non-Catholic students from the requirement of religious education.

6. See, e.g., *OR,* "Propaganda Perniciosa" (24 March 1929), "Il Pericolo Protestante in Italia" (19 June 1929), "Propaganda Protestante" (22 October 1929).
7. Pro memoria by Borgongini-Duca. "Udienza del Santo Padre" (ASV, ANI b. 42, fasc. 2, f. 64 [15 March 1931]). The nuncio mentions that he had spoken with Minister of Justice Alfredo Rocco on 27 March, by which time Tacchi Venturi had already spoken to him. The Ministry of Justice was the governmental organ that, in the early 1930s, began to collaborate with Vatican officials, above all Borgongini-Duca, in suppressing Protestant activity. Born in Naples, Alfredo Rocco (1875–1935) was an early exponent of the theory of corporatism, later a central tenet of fascist ideology, to which Mussolini himself gave brief definition in his lengthy 1932 treatise, *The Doctrine of Fascism:* "Fascism is therefore opposed to Socialism to which unity within the State (which amalgamates classes into a single economic and ethical reality) is unknown, and which sees in history nothing but the class struggle. Fascism is likewise opposed to trade unionism as a class weapon. But when brought within the orbit of the State, Fascism recognizes the real needs which gave rise to socialism and trade unionism, giving them due weight in the guild or corporative system in which divergent interests are coordinated and harmonized in the unity of the State." Complete texts, with notes, available at http: //www.worldfuturefund.org/wffmaster/Reading/Germany/mussolini.htm. Rocco served as president of the Chamber of Deputies from May 1924 to June 1925 and was Mussolini's minister of justice—his department handled matters of the rights of and restrictions on the activities of permitted cults—in 1925–32. This is why both Borgongini and Tacchi Venturi had approached him. A professor of law before entering the government (and rector of La Sapienza, 1932–35), he had a hand in developing the Italian Criminal Code and the Code of Criminal Procedure. See Gentile 1996a, pp. 349–53, 377–85; and Gregor 2005, the entirety of the third chapter of which is dedicated to Rocco's contributions to fascist doctrine. A very brief selection from Rocco's "The Political Doctrine of Fascism," delivered in Perugià in 1926, useful for teaching, can be found at http: //www.d.umn.edu/~schilton/1610/Readings/1610.B+DReader.Rocco.PoliticalTheoryOfFascism.html.
8. Tacchi Venturi to Gasparri, 1 January 1927 (ARSI Fondo TV, b. 22, fasc. 583, f. 54).
9. Borgongini to Pacelli (ASV, ANI pos. 23, fasc. 5, ff. 15r–19r [18 March 1933]).
10. ASV, ANI b. 49, fasc. 2, f. 21r (15 February 1931). In discussing instances in which Catholic complaints to police led to investigations (they often did not), John Pollard remarks: "The Catholics naturally exploited the authorities' anxiety about the foreign links of those churches in their campaign of harassment against the Protestants" (Pollard 1985b, p. 111). That may be quite true, but it is imperative to recognize that Catholic clerics were genuinely anxious—more so than the authorities, who soberly tended to minimize the threat.
11. ASV, AESI pos. 794, fasc. 389, f. 52r.
12. ASV, ANI b. 23, fasc. 5, f. 17r (18 March 1933). Pius had difficulty even accepting the term "Protestantism." He does speak of groups that have rejected articles of faith and ceremonies the Roman church still embraces. These, he says, are groups that

affirm Protestantism, "as they call it." See the January 1928 encyclical *Mortalium Animos* 7 at http: //w2.vatican.va/content/pius-xi/en/encyclicals/documents/hf_p-xi_enc_19280106_mortalium-animos.html.

13. See Kertzer 2015, p. 220, on the meeting: "Pius brought up the subject he thought most pressing. Protestant proselytizing, he told a surprised Mussolini—who was not expecting this to be at the top of the agenda for the meeting—'is making progress in almost all of Italy's dioceses, as shown in a study that I had the bishops do. The Protestants are becoming ever bolder, and they speak of 'missions' they want to organize in Italy.' They were taking advantage of the concordat's unfortunate language, which referred to non-Catholic religions as 'admitted' cults. The pope had opposed that phrase, preferring that they be described as 'tolerated.' Mussolini pointed out that only 135,000 Protestants lived in Italy, 37,000 of them foreigners—a mere speck amid 42 million Catholics. The pope acknowledged that the Protestants were few but argued that the threat was nonetheless great. He handed the Duce a lengthy report on the question. Over the next years he would bombard the dictator with requests to keep the Protestants in check."
14. I have no evidence it did.
15. It is not impossible that Tacchi Venturi did take the information to Mussolini or that it reached the pope from Borgongini-Duca.
16. ASV, ANI b. 49, fasc. 2, f. 125r (containing materials dated 3, 9 April and May 1931, all handwritten pro memoriae by the nuncio). The folder also contains a report by the Commission of the Rhione Borgo on Protestant activity and presence on Via Aurelia (ASV, ANI b. 49, fasc. 2, ff. 131–32 [n.d.]) as well as a pamphlet entitled "Una Solenne Domanda: È l'anima tua Salvata?" (ASV, ANI b. 49, fasc. 2, ff. 128r–129v). The pamphlet has been stamped on the back with the following: Adunanza Evangelica, Via Aurelia 161 Rome. (While researching this book, I lived at Via Aurelia 145.) Borgongini-Duca annotated this in pencil, identifying the names of the Protestant ministers, the leaflets they distribute, and the names and the birth years of their two children, Emmanuela and Cristiano.
17. Borgongini, Pro-Memoria (ASV, ANI b. 49, fasc. 2, f. 126 [9 April 1931]).
18. "Una Solenne Domanda: È l'anima tua Salvata?" (ASV, ANI b. 49, fasc. 2, ff. 128r–129v).
19. ASV, ANI b. 49, fasc. 2, f. 129v.
20. ASV, ANI b. 49, fasc. 2, f. 129v.
21. ASV, ANI b. 49, fasc. 2, f. 132.
22. Borgongini, Pro-Memoria (ASV, ANI b. 49, fasc. 2, f. 127r–v [15 April 1931]).
23. Pizzardo to Borgongini-Duca (ASV, ANI b. 2, fasc. 49, f. 21 [15 February 1931]).
24. ASV, ANI b. 49, fasc. 2, f. 59.
25. Mario Crumelli to Pope Pius XI (ASV, ANI b. 49, fasc. 2, f. 120 [13 May 1931]). In their letter to Mussolini, the town council revealed that they were all also members of Catholic Action. They urged Mussolini to consider that Protestant propaganda of any kind was an offense to him as head of government and to a country whose national religion was the glory of the state. It would not be hard to guess whether their identity as members of Catholic Action and their assertion that Catholicism was the glory of the Italian state helped or hurt their cause with Il Duce.

26. Pope Pius XI to Mario Crumelli (ASV, ANI b. 49, fasc. 2, f. 119 [18 May 1931]).
27. See DeVecci to Grandi (ASMAE.SS. 1930, b. 11, f. 11 [25 June 1930]).
28. See Borgongini's notes on the pope's anguish (ASV, ANI b. 49, fasc. 2, ff. 15, 28–32 [15 February 1931]).
29. Where an ancient Roman villa, the so-called Villa Romana del Casale, dated to the third to fourth century BCE, exists. It is now a UNESCO heritage site. For a popular introduction, with photographs, see http://www.italia.it/en/travel-ideas/unesco-world-heritage-sites/piazza-armerina-the-villa-romana.html.
30. Archpriest D. Luigi Riggio Rutella, Assistentenza Ecclesiastica delle Associazioni Cattoliche della Matrice di Riesi to Agosto Ciriaci (ASV, ANI b. 49, fasc. 2, ff. 115–16 [4 April 1931]).
31. Rutella to Ciriaci (ASV, ANI fasc. 49/2, f. 115 [4 April 1931]).
32. Rutella to Ciriaci (ASV, ANI fasc. 49/2, ff. 115–16 [4 April 1931]).
33. Egidio Franchino to Pacelli (ASV, ANI b. 49, fasc. 2, ff. 108–9 [Feast of St. Joseph, 1931]). Emphasis added.
34. Mario Sturzo, Bishop of Piazza Armerina (ASV, ANI b. 49, fasc. 2, f. 9 [24 March 1931]).
35. Pizzardo to Borgongini-Duca (ASV, ANI b. 49, fasc. 2, f. 113 [23 April 1931]).
36. Report by Sargolini on Protestant propaganda in Italy, Allegato to Letter to Pacelli of 10 March 1931 (ASV, ANI b. 49, fasc. 2, ff. 28–34).
37. Sitting on the border of Umbria and within the Marches, the mountainous town of Camerino, home to one of the oldest universities in Europe, was one of which Sargolini would become suffragan bishop (1963–65), in which capacity he would later attend the Second, Third, and Fourth sessions of the Second Vatican Council. He was also for six years (1963–69) titular bishop of Lysias in Turkey. See discussion of Catholic Action in chapters 4 and 7.
38. The church he served still exists on a street that now bears his name: Vialetto Federico Maria Mistrorigo 6, Rome. See Dani 1958 for a collection of essays in honor of Padre Mistrorigo.
39. Father Federico Mistrorigo to Monsignor Sargolini (ASV, ANI b. 49, fasc. 2, ff. 48–49 [19 February 1931]).
40. Selvaggiani to Borgongini-Duca (ASV, ANI b. 49, fasc. 2, f. 51 [26 February 1931]). Following convention that attributes a report to the one who commissioned it, I will call this the Selvaggiani report.
41. See appendix 2 for one prepared for Tacchi Venturi, preserved in the Fondo TV in ARSI. I do not think the report was composed by Borgongini.
42. Report by Sargolini on Protestant propaganda in Italy, Allegato to Letter to Pacelli of 10 March 1931 (ASV, ANI b. 49, fasc. 2, ff. 28–34).
43. See Contarini 1538, *De emendanda ecclesiae.* Reformers used the self-critical remarks of this Catholic document to criticize the Roman church.
44. ASV, ANI b. 49, fasc. 2, f. 59. See Olin 1990, chapter 3.
45. ASV, ANI b. 49, fasc. 2, f. 59.
46. ASV, ANI b. 49, fasc. 2, ff. 29–30. Emphasis added.

47. See Giordani 1934, pp. 33–34, a theme expressed throughout many of his voluminous writings, above all in the journal *Fides*.
48. ASV, ANI b. 49, fasc. 2, ff. 28–30.
49. Pollard 2005, p. 111.
50. Sargolini sharpens this snapshot. In the Piedmont, above all in Turin, efforts at conversion were "intense in the city and some towns of the diocese." In Padua (the Veneto), the evangelical church, he was startled to report, had recruited four hundred members in recent years. "Many people" had been converted to the evangelical church in Bressanone. Had Christ not prophesied that many would come in his name and lead many astray? Even "a few Catholics" in the Veneto were, alarmingly, among those active in the church, which held its meetings in a room in a hotel (not uncommon, in the fascist period, for Protestant groups without church buildings). In Gorizia, "the Protestants propagandize a lot." To the dismay of authorities at the Vatican, they would do so there, successfully, for years to come. Indeed, it had an active "Center for Propaganda" in "a popular quarter" of the city (ASV, ANI b. 49, fasc. 2, ff. 28–34).
51. ASV, ANI b. 49, fasc. 2, ff. 28–32.
52. ASV, ANI b. 49, fasc. 2, f. 55.
53. The use of "heretic" and "heretical" is quite revealing. In a church led by a pope who looked back nostalgically to medieval Christendom, and even with some hope that it could be restored, the use of such terms suggested how threatening Protestants Pius thought evangelicals and Waldensians to be. In the Middle Ages the suppression of dissidents or apostates could be (and, in cultural memory, was always) swift. Moreover, in the most egregious cases, the suppression of heresy required collaboration between church and state. As in the Middle Ages, so in the fascist period, the conviction and determination of dissidents simply astonished Catholic bishops. Some Catholic prelates feared that their sheer energy, which stood in sharp contrast to the putative torpor of most diocesan clergy, would effect many conversions. Their origin in Britain and America suggested that they were wealthy; they would use that wealth to generate evangelical conversions, as in fact they did. To those given to conspiracy theories, those who were antisemitic, or those who feared communism, the arrival of the Anglo-American missionaries suggested a grand ambition: to convert Italy to Protestantism and to subvert fascism as well as to eradicate all traces of the Latin traditions.
54. Mitford 1987, p. 91, from her novel *The Pursuit of Love.* Mitford was "citing" the fictional seventeenth-century character, the Englishman Matthew Radlett.
55. The titles of others, one subtitled *Church and Mission in a Strange New World* (Murray, Williams, and Wright 2017) and the other *Christianity Outside the Box: Learning from Those Who Rocked the Boat* (Scotland and Kovoor, 2012) are worth pondering.
56. ASV, ANI b. 49, fasc. 2, f. 49.
57. In Puglia evangelical leaders had constructed a church and two halls "in the midst of the [Catholic] populace." They had also established a kindergarten. The splendor of Protestant churches was sometimes emphasized: Baptists had a "very beautiful" church in Reggio Calabria; from there "many evangelists [we]re diffused" (ASV, ANI b. 49, fasc. 2, f. 49). This is still the case. Many Assemblies of God churches in Italy are

hardly distinguishable, architecturally, from their surroundings, and most are marked with small, modest signs.

58. ASV, ANI b. 49, fasc. 2, f. 49.
59. ASV, ANI b. 49, fasc. 2, f. 53.
60. ASV, ANI b. 49, fasc. 2, f. 30.
61. ASV, ANI b. 49, fasc. 2, f. 54.
62. ASV, ANI b. 49, fasc. 2, f. 53.
63. ASV, ANI b. 49, fasc. 2, f. 56. On Monte Mario, see the extensive discussion below.
64. See discussion above.
65. Secrecy implicitly linked evangelicals with Freemasons, with whom Catholic polemicists often explicitly linked them. In fact, both the fascist regime and the Catholic church were deeply hostile to Freemasonry. It was long tied, politically, to the liberal regimes of prefascist Italy and, ideologically, to a program that was ferociously anti-Catholic, anticlerical, and secularizing. Pope Pius XI condemned the movement in 1864, as did Pope Leo in 1884. The Code of Canon Law (1917) also denounced it.
66. G. Miccoli, "Santa Sede, questione ebraica e anti-semitismo fra Otto e Novecento," in C. Vivianti, ed., *Storia D'italia: Annali 11 Gli Ebrei in Italia* (Turin: Einaudi, 1997), 1367–74.
67. Articles suggesting such would be published in *Difesa della Razza* 3/17, 5 July 1940. Thanks to David Kertzer for sending me images of this article.
68. Tinti, "Studio" (ARSI, Fondo TV, b. 22, fasc. 583, f. 9); Tacchi Venturi 1927, pp. 9–10 (ASV, ANI b. 49, fasc. 1, f. 8r–8v).
69. ASV, ANI b. 49, fasc. 2, f. 48.
70. ASV, ANI b. 49, fasc. 2, f. 34.
71. ASV, ANI b. 49, fasc. 2, f. 33. Conferences were held especially for women in Potenza (ASV, ANI b. 49, fasc. 2, f. 48).
72. ASV, ANI b. 49, fasc. 2, f. 56.
73. On women under fascism, see DeGrazia 1992; Meldini 1975; Perry Willson, "Women in Mussolini's Italy, 1922–1945," in Bosworth 2010, pp. 203–23.
74. ASV, ANI b. 49, fasc. 2, f. 31.
75. This is among the dubious charges made by the reports. There is good evidence that familial tension could be exaggerated as a way of justifying the criminalization of Pentecostalism (see chapter 8 below).
76. ASV, ANI b. 49, fasc. 2, f. 55.
77. As also is reported, e.g., in Campo Basso and Vallo Lucania, about which two towns it is said: "The activity of the Protestants had greatly intensified in the prior two years, especially through the work of women who have returned from America" (ASV, ANI b. 49 fasc. 2, f. 32). "Women, even the richest and most-talented ones," according to Bosworth, "could scarcely aspire to compete with men" in fascist Italy. See Bosworth 2014, p. 6.
78. ASV, ANI b. 49, fasc. 2, f. 53.
79. ASV, ANI b. 49, fasc. 2, f. 54.
80. ASV, ANI b. 49, fasc. 2, ff. 28, 29. The equivalent of 125,000 lire in today's terms, or perhaps 1,000 Euro.

81. Sargolini on Protestant propaganda in Italy, Allegato to Letter to Pacelli of 10 March 103. For central Italy in general (f. 29); a Waldensian Pastor gives subsidies to converts in Massa Carabbra (f. 30); in the towns of San Marco and Bisagnaro money is cited, simply, as the motive for conversions (f. 32); subsidies are distributed in Campania, Calabria, Palermo (ASV, ANI fasc. 2, ff. 31, 32, 33). "Works of benevolence," which may have encompassed direct gifts of cash, along with a broader spectrum of charitable actions are reported to have occurred in Rimini and Portogruaro (Tuscany). See f. 34 for mention of *mezzo della benificenza* and "intense activities" of *befana e soccorsi.*
82. ASV, ANI b. 49, fasc. 2, f. 33.
83. So frequently are the poor mentioned as recipients of gifts and the attention of Protestant recruiters, it would be otiose to cite multiple examples. The "lower class was recruited with special vigor in Pisa" (ASV, ANI b. 49, fasc. 2, f. 29). Overlapping with the poor were members of some occupations, particularly peasant farmers in Calabria, Sicily, Puglia, and Rimini in Emilia-Romagna (ff. 32, 33, 34). Also overlapping were those described as religiously ignorant, uneducated, or uncouth (*rozzo*), as in Civitavecchia (f. 29). Only in Turin, an industrial city, are workers mentioned as potential converts (f. 28).
84. As in Susa, in the Piedmont (ASV, ANI b. 49, fasc. 2, f. 28).
85. ASV, ANI b. 49, fasc. 2, f. 28.
86. ASV, ANI b. 49, fasc. 2, f. 57.
87. See Davis 2015, p. 5.
88. Mario Crumelli to Pope Pius XI (ASV, ANI b. 49, fasc. 2, f. 120 [13 May 1931]). This meeting is described further in ASV, ANI b. 49, fasc. 2, f. 119 [18 May 1931]).
89. ASV, ANI b. 49, fasc. 2, f. 33.
90. ASV, ANI b. 49, fasc. 2, f. 54.
91. As in a letter to Pope Pius XI from Giovanni Costantini, bishop of Luni, who refers to "il Capo della Missione Battista della Spezia per l'Italia, Sign. Amerigo Erberto Pullen" (Costantini to Pius XI, AESI 795/399, 19v [14 December 1935]). Getting his name right this time, Costantini had earlier written to the prefect of the Council for the Consistory that Protestant propaganda was continuing in an important city of his diocese, *"silenziosa, tenace, con piano preciso e ben organizzato e con grande abbondanza di mezzi.* Quasi tutta la attività è dovuta al Capo dei Battisti, Sign Arrigo Erberto PULLEN, inglese, e in parte, *ai fanatici Avventisti.* Un anno fa fu inaugurate una casa per asilo e per cure al mare nel piccolo paese di Tellaro, alla estremità orientale del golfo della *Spezia.* La casa, in estate, è occupata da bambini e giovenetti non del paese, ma della regione e, pare anche della Toscana" (Costantini to Serrafini, AESI 795/396, ff. 39–44 [28 October 1934]). The concern for Spezia, an important strategic and military site, and especially for youth targeted by proselytes, is typical.
92. See discussion of Tacchi Venturi and La Spezia, above, chapter 2.
93. ASV, ANI b. 49, fasc. 2, f. 53.
94. As in LeMarche (ASV, ANI b. 49, fasc. 2, f. 33) and Avellino (ASV, ANI b. 49, fasc. 2, f. 48). These reports together comprise an essential source for the discussion, below, of "apostate priests" then serving, in the eyes of Vatican cardinals, scandalously as well as illegally as Protestant pastors.

95. See discussion below, chapter 7.
96. ASV, ANI b. 49, fasc. 2, f. 57.
97. "In ogni caso I sacerdoti apostati o irretiti da censura non potranno essere assunti nè conservati in un insegnamento, in un officio od in un impiego, nei quali siano a contatto immediato col pubblico" (*Concordat* [1929], p. 62).
98. See Missirolli 1929, pp. 179–81, and discussion of "apostate priests" below.
99. As in Gorizia (ASV, ANI b. 49, fasc. 2, f. 29).
100. ASV, ANI b. 49 fasc. 2, f. 49. Another document in the archives of the Apostolic Nunciature indicates a trainsman was distributing, especially to students, a pamphlet entitled "Il Seminatore" on the Circumsvesuviana (ASV, ANI b. 49, fasc. 2, ff. 48–49 [19 February 1931]).
101. As in Turin (ASV, ANI b. 49, fasc. 2, f. 28) and Rome (ASV, ANI b. 49, fasc. 2, f. 33).
102. See J. Dagnino 2017, p. 175.
103. See Kertzer 2015, chapter 14.
104. See discussion below on Protestant propaganda.
105. ASV, ANI b. 49, fasc. 2, f. 57.
106. ASV, ANI b. 49, fasc. 2, f. 56. On modernism, see the discussion.
107. ASV, ANI b. 49, fasc. 2, f. 31. Mistrorigo reports tension between Wesleyan Methodists and Catholics in Dipignano in the province of Calabria (ASV, ANI b. 49, fasc. 2, f. 48).
108. See discussion below.
109. ASV, ANI b. 49, fasc. 2, f. 28.
110. Ebner 2011.
111. ASV, ANI b. 49, fasc. 2, f. 32.
112. "Catholic" Bibles recognize the authority and inspiration of the following seven "deuterocanonical" books: Tobit, Judith, 1 and 2 Maccabees, Wisdom, Sirach, and Baruch. Catholic Bibles also include sections in the books of Esther and Daniel. These are sometimes called the apocryphal books. Catholic Bibles include these; Protestant Bibles do not. Translations differ, with both Catholics and Protestants contending in the fascist era of tendentiousness in this respect. In addition, differences in modes of interpretation and whether an individual could freely and authentically interpret the Bible without authoritative guidance split the churches in our era and, to some degree, still do today. I discuss the polemical literature around this issue as well as Catholic attempts to suppress vendors of Protestant Bibles below.
113. Barone 2016, p. 33.
114. See below, chapter 8.
115. As, for example, in Calabria (f. 32), Sicily (f. 33), and Novara (f. 33) as well as the Piedmont (f. 28), Aquila (f. 30), Foggia/Puglia (ff. 31, 33), documents pertaining to which are all found in ASV, ANI b. 49, fasc. 2.
116. See Rochat 1990, pp. 30–31, for the public disorder charge and an illustrative letter from the parish priests of Filottranto (Ancona).
117. Rochat claims that "the reactions of the prefects were almost always favorable to the Catholic protests and almost always contrary to those of the Protestants" (Rochat 1990, p. 33). The claim is perhaps too vague to be discussed, but the reactions from the authorities were far too complex (and unpredictable) to be reduced in this way.

118. ASV, ANI b. 49, fasc. 2, f. 48.
119. See, e.g., the report by police in Calabria, who told him of two weddings celebrated locally "according to the Protestant rite" (ASV, ANI b. 49, fasc. 2, f. 48).
120. ASV, ANI b. 49, fasc. 2, f. 29.
121. ASV, ANI b. 49, fasc. 2, f. 29.
122. ASV, ANI b. 49, fasc. 2, f. 31.
123. That is, a priest who did not live in a *casa canonica,* or rectory, usually an insalubrious apartment he could not afford on the ultramodest stipend of roughly 1,500 lire per annum, or in the *casa paterna,* all too often with his mother. I discuss the poverty of many parish priests below.
124. By which the reports often meant lack of a canonical home, or rectory.
125. See Levi 1982.
126. ASV, ANI b. 49, fasc. 2, f. 49.
127. Or the Irpinia earthquake, which occurred in the early morning of 23 July 1930 and whose epicenter stood near the point at which the southern provinces of Apulia, Basilicata, and Campania intersected. More than fourteen hundred died; some five thousand to seven thousand were injured. Several large cities, including Salerno and Naples, were hit. The death toll would have been much higher had so many not been asleep in their fields, bringing in the wheat harvest. See "40 Years on, Why the Irpinia Earthquake Is Remembered as Italy's 'Worst Catastrophe,'" 23 November 2020, The Local, https://www.thelocal.it/20201123/40-years-on-why-the-irpinia-earthquake-is-remembered-as-italys-worst-catastrophe.
128. ASV, ANI b. 49, fasc. 2, f. 49.
129. Rochat 1990, p. 29.
130. Mistrorigo to Borgongini (ASV, ANI b. 49, fasc. 2 [19 February 1931]). Mistrorigo despaired that the church in Calabria had the resources, then, to resist the numerous, growing, and self-confident evangelical congregations. He observes that, around the time of his report, an opusculum had been published against the Protestants. But it "is not sufficient" as a means of combat (ASV, ANI b. 49, fasc. 2, f. 49).
131. ASV, ANI b. 49, fasc. 2, f. 38.
132. Rochat 1990, pp. 42–44.
133. Newspaper clips now found at ASV, ANI b. 49, fasc. 2, ff. 140–41. Pacelli confirms the verdict in his letter to Borgongini-Duca (ASV, ANI b. 49, fasc. 2, ff. 142–43 [15 March 1933]); as does Pizzardo in a later letter to the Apostolic Nuncio (ASV, ANI b. 49, fasc. 2, f. 144 [17 March 1933]).
134. Pacelli to Borgongini-Duca (ASV, ANI b. 49, fasc. 2, ff. 142v). Borgongini-Duca to Pacelli (AESI pos. 795, fasc. 395, f. 67 [8 March 1934]).

CHAPTER 5. A STUBBORN PROBLEM

1. Rochat 1990, pp. 217–24. I have published an article on the historiographical challenges presented by the diversity of archival sources in a recent monographic number of *Memoira e Ricerca.*
2. Leone 1972, pp. 95–114.

3. Leone 1972, p. 95.
4. See introduction to socioeconomic conditions of the Marsica in Leone 1972, pp. 95–98.
5. On the Torlonia family, see Felisini 2016.
6. *"Paghe di fame"* (Leone 1972, p. 97).
7. Leone 1972, p. 97.
8. Leone 1972, p. 96.
9. Leone 1972, p. 98.
10. This followed a two-year period (1927–29) during which the Villa was left, after the death on 14 April 1927 of the parish priest, without any religious assistance at all. Bagnoli occasionally sent substitute priests, whom the parish generally disliked; in turn, these priests complained to the Roman curia about the "indifferent [religious] comportment" of the parish (Leone 1972, p. 98). The complaints about religious indifference are difficult to credit, given the subsequent history of the parish. Bagnoli (1859–1945) had been ordained priest as a member of the Order of Discalced Carmelites in April 1885. He became bishop of Marsi in December 1910 and would remain so until his death in January 1945.
11. Spini 2007, pp. 166–71.
12. Both Leone 1972, p. 98, and Rochat 1990, p. 217, identify him as a Redemptorist priest. But by the time of his appointment to the parish of the Villa, he had left the order. Indeed, he announced that he was the founder of a new order, the Missionaries of the Mountains. For a brief description of Fr. Bernardino's career, put into the context of Marsican culture and religiosity, see Luongo 2003, pp. 570–94.
13. Founded by St. Alphonsus Maria Liguori in 1732 near Amalfi, the Redemptorists' (known formally as the Congregation of the Most Holy Redeemer) vocation was to be an order of itinerant preachers. Their homilies were to be simple and comprehensible to the poor. Finally, they were charged with taking special care of growing youth and established many parochial schools. Curiously, they were founded because, in the words of the founder of the Order, "the number of priests . . . is few," a neuralgic problem in the Marsica, and much of Meridional Italy, in the first quarter of the twentieth century. See Liguori 2004; Velocci 1994; and DeSpirito 2015.
14. See Davis 2015; and for a short, excellent treatment, see Davis, "A Tale of Two Italys?" in Jones and Pasquino 2015.
15. Amicucci had his reasons for remaining neutral. For his neutrality he became the target of (in Rochat's words) "una campagna violentissima" (Rochat 1990, p. 218; and see Allegato al Reporto del Prefetto dell'Aquila, ACS, G.1/Aquila [9 January 1932]). Tacchi Venturi, Jesuit missionaries, and Borgongini-Duca all requested that the mayor be removed, but the prefect of Aquila defended him and recommended that the Catholic authorities moderate their tone. Bagnoli and prelates from the Vatican would regard the lack of local cooperation from the political authorities with immense anger. At the end of the Second World War, Amicucci would later be charged with collaborating with the Germans. He attempted to defend himself, unsuccessfully, by arguing that he never intended to collaborate with the Germans but only with the Repubblica Sociale Italiana, which he regarded as the legitimate political authority in Italy after Mussolini's deposition. See Forno 2003a, p. 246.

16. Leone 1972, p. 98, suggests that the nuns were from the order Le Suore Figlie di S. Anna, founded in Piacenza, with the encouragement of Pius IX, in 1866 and given papal approval in 1892 (see Schwaiger 1997, pp. 215–16). Other evidence suggests they were not from that order and had not even completed a novitiate. Father Bernardino has since had a scuola materna in Rome dedicated to his memory. See Scuola dell'infanzia Padre Bernardino Mastroianni, ROMAPAESE, https://www.romapaese.it/risorsa/padre-bernardino-mastroianni/. In December 2016 a documentary film of his life and ministry, aptly entitled *Un Parroco Maestro,* was screened in Casalotti, where he had founded another *asilo.* See Roberta Sarzanini, "CASALOTTI: Proiezione del film documentario su Padre Bernardino Mastroianni," 6 December 2017, http://www.ilpungolo.org/2017/12/06/casalotti-proiezione-film-documentario-padre-bernardino-mastroianni/.
17. Rochat observes that the mayor, who remained neutral during the debate over the opening of the Methodist temple in the Villa, was depicted by Catholic polemicists as the instigator of the religious schism for reasons of rivalry with the bishops. See Rochat 1990, p. 218. In fact, although Rochat casts doubt on that claim, it was quite true (see below). The entire Amicucci family execrated the bishop.
18. Quoted in Leone 1972, p. 98.
19. Leone 1972, pp. 98–99. Some Catholic observers explicitly commented that the Villa made Fr. Bernardino an idol. See discussion below.
20. Rochat 1990, p. 217. See Schwaiger 1931, pp. 215–16.
21. It is hard not to agree with Leone that the villagers had staged an uprising against the conventional custodian and symbol of traditional Roman authority, though whether the mutiny counts as a revolution in Marxist terms, as Leone contends, may be questioned. See, e.g., Leone 1972, p. 100.
22. Leone 1972, pp. 100–101. While not untrue, it is not simply that the case of Fr. Bernardino provided the occasion for resistance. By the very nature of his formation with the Redemptorists and the character of his ministry, he enacted the sort of ministry for which Protestant pastors were known and Catholic priests, who saw their vocation largely in liturgical-mercenary terms—especially celebrating the Eucharist—as evangelical pastors did not. Appreciation for what is today called the social gospel was widespread and much deeper among Protestant than in European Catholic communities in the early twentieth century. Fr. Bernardino paved the way, then, for evangelical conversion by practicing an essentially Protestant pastorate while formally remaining a Catholic priest. Put another way, the Villa's appreciation for Fr. Bernardino was a way of recognizing and treasuring a new form of the meaning and implications of the Christian message.
23. See discussion of the vicissitudes of ex-priests in chapter 8.
24. See Lista dei Sacerdoti Apostati e Ministri Protestanti tratta dalle Informazioni Diocesane (ASV, SCC, SC b. 1, fasc. 1933, f. 1 [4 June 1933]). Ex-priests were feared and hated in the Vatican. They tended to be among the most critical Protestants, and they were despised for having broken vows and joined hands with heretical evangelical churches, many of which were filled with foreigners (*stranieri*), suspected of being unpatriotic and antifascist, teeming with spies, and intent on displacing Latin with Anglo-Saxon plutocratic culture.

25. Adjacent to the ground on which the Methodist church today stands.
26. Leone 1972, pp. 100–101. This means that roughly 50 percent of the community never attended an evangelical ceremony, and of those who did, the majority attended only the one described above.
27. Spini 2007, p. 167.
28. Rochat 1990, p. 217.
29. Spini 2007, p. 167.
30. Leone 1972, pp. 1–2.
31. Rochat 1990, p. 218, n. 42.
32. See Zanini 2015, p. 695. As I argue, Borgongini had so carefully cultivated the secretary of state and had achieved such an intimate relationship with him that Buffarini kept the nuncio informed. Indeed, the nuncio sometimes seems to have dictated to Buffarini the sorts of repressive measures he ought to enact.
33. Rochat 1990, p. 219.
34. Arpinati to Tacchi Venturi (ASV, ANI pos. 795, fasc. 39, f. 5 [16 January 1932]).
35. Tacchi Venturi to Pacelli (ASV, ANI pos. 795, fasc. 39, f. 4 [19 January 1932]).
36. Rochat 1990, p. 218. See Bagnoli's letter of 14 August 1931, reproduced in Leone 1972, pp. 118–20.
37. "In the sight of God," a common phrase in ecclesiastical Latin.
38. Borgongini-Duca to Pacelli (AESI pos. 795, fasc. 393, ff. 23v–24r [February 1934]).
39. Pacelli to Borgongini-Duca (AESI pos. 795, fasc. 393, f. 26r [10 February 1934]).
40. Borgongini-Duca to Pacelli (ASV, ANI b. 23, fasc. 5, f. 16r [18 March 1933]).
41. "Udienza Rocco" (ASV, ANI b. 49, fasc. 2, f. 104r [27 October 1931]).
42. Pro-Memoria by Pizzardo (AESI pos. 795, fasc. 393, f. 34r). The pro memoria was likely written in the spring or summer of 1934.
43. Borgongini-Duca to Pacelli (AESI pos. 795, fasc. 393, ff. 22r–v).
44. See Crivelli 1934, on which, deeply statistical in nature, Borgongini depended for his own pamphlet on Protestant proselytism. The typescripts for these publications were prepared for the Sacred Congregation of the Council and may now be found in their archives. See "Statistiche circa il proselitismo protestante: Stazioni e visite" (Vademecum per Sacerdoti) (ASV SCC, SC b. 1934, ff. 1, 2), which are acknowledged as received on 28 April 1934 (ASV SCC, SC b. 1934, f. 3).
45. "Udienza Rocco" (ASV, ANI b. 49, fasc. 2, f. 104v [27 October 1931]).
46. Reproduced in Spini 2007, p. 167.
47. I.e., the outcome of the dispute would determine whether the Roman church would stand or fall.
48. See Spini 2007, p. 167.
49. "Bravate metodiste in Abbruzzo" (*OR,* 11 February 1931).
50. See Rochat 1990, p. 221. Evangelicals were routinely charged by Catholic polemicists with encouraging, or at least allowing, the practice of abortion throughout the 1930s.
51. The word *rossi* may have been intended to suggest, in addition, that they were uneducated or uncouth.
52. Some charges that would, over the course of the 1930s, be leveled at virtually all evangelical communities included the reminder that the Methodists were foreigners, impe-

rialists, and thus enemies of Italy, that they sowed discord among families and villages (not untrue), and that they "bought souls with dollars" and the provision of other sorts of social services. In fact, there is good evidence that the relatively well-funded British and especially American Methodists *did* use subsidies and other sorts of economic or educational emoluments to encourage conversion. (Among other things, this whole episode in Italian history raises the question of what "conversion" meant in such a context.) Whether it was the venality of the villagers that led them to convert has been disputed, and, indeed, none of the local diocesan sources mentions it in connection with Villa San Sebastiano. To repeat, conversion, in this case, seems to have been almost wholly, in not entirely, earnest, motivated in large measure by religious yearnings if not unmixed with new, critical perspectives on Catholic practice, priesthood, and power.

53. Borgongini-Duca to Pacelli (AESI pos. 795, fasc. 393, ff. 22v [8 February 1934]).
54. An uninfluential text in its own day, the work, oddly, lives on in the world of social media. A Facebook page entitled "Apologetica Cattolica" has posted (in December 2012) the complete text of *Contro gli Errori dei Protestanti con la conferma scritturale alle singole risposte.* See https://www.facebook.com/apologeticacattolica.net/posts/p-vittorio-genovesi-s-j/466229340089251/. He also published, after the war, an anti-Catholic *Catechism* replete with responses to evangelical criticisms—in rhyme. Accessed 7 August 2018.
55. The only complete version of the poem is found among a collection online entitled "Poesia del Cattolicesimo integrale" at https://forum.termometropolitico.it/264015-poesie-del-cattolicesimo-integrale-2.html.
56. Genovesi to Bagnoli, original found in the appendix to Leone 1972, pp. 124–25.
57. See description of incidents in Leone 1972, p. 105.
58. See Leone 1972, p. 104.
59. Letter of Borgongini-Duca to Mussolini (AESI pos. 795, fasc. 393, ff. 27 r–v. [28 February 1934]). I have found no corroborating evidence of this claim.
60. Borgongini-Duca to Pacelli (AESI pos. 795, fasc. 393, ff. 37r–38r [1937]).
61. See Leone 1972, pp. 104–5.
62. Leone argues that ecclesiastical authorities in Avezzano had pressured Zardi to convert and that those who returned to Catholicism had shown "a complete inability to free themselves from traditional religious structures" (Leone 1972, pp. 109–110, 118–19). Intriguingly, two sources independently report that Zardi was, or at least claimed to be, a fascist, and it appears that he was recognized as such by the national government. In a letter to Pacelli, Borgongini reports that Zardi not only claimed to be a fascist. He also had an official fascist card (*tessera*). In addition, the bishop of Marsi, in a letter to Pizzardo, claims that Zardi "made a show of calling himself a Protestant fascist" and of insisting he was both fascist and Italian. This would have been quite unusual; Borgongini even implies that one could not be both non-Catholic and a fascist. Bagnoli to Pizzardo (AESI pos. 795, fasc. 393, f. 50 [17 January 1936]). Bagnoli adds here that governmental authorities wondered how "Protestant fascists" ought to be managed, presumably on the assumption that their fascist commitments should mitigate the severity of their treatment as Protestants.

63. Rochat 1990, pp. 222–24.
64. Rochat 1990, pp. 222–24.
65. The abbot, a military chaplain wounded in the Great War, was awarded several military medals before entering the Benedictine novitiate. A recent conference honoring him was held in Parma.
66. Abbot Coranati to Pope Pius XI (AESI pos. 795, fasc. 395, f. 66r [2 March 1936]).
67. Abbot Coranati to Pope Pius XI (AESI pos. 795, fasc. 395, f. 66r [2 March 1936]).
68. By the time of the investigation, Bagnoli had written to Pacelli several times about the immoralities of the Protestant community and his conviction that local authorities had been favoring the Protestants. This charge presents us with an interesting historiographical issue, as do so many issues connected with Villa San Sebastiano. Here Bagnoli suggests that local fascist authorities had been privileging evangelicals with building permits. At the same time, local Catholic families and especially the Conti charged Bagnoli with being insufficiently rigorous with evangelical missionaries and adepts, a charge brought by one of its members to the Vatican and to Borgongini. At first, it seems that both cannot be true and that each party is attempting to tar the other with the worst possible charge. Yet both parties at different times had "favored the Protestants." Chronology is critical here. Initially Bagnoli did everything he could to stop the construction of the Protestant temple. When his campaign failed, *then* he tried other tactics.
69. Abbot Coranati to Pope Pius XI (AESI pos. 795, fasc. 395, f. 66v).
70. Abbot Coranati to Pope Pius XI (AESI pos. 795, fasc. 395, f. 66v).
71. In a handwritten letter to Pacelli, Bagnoli says that he has learned that governmental authorities were pressing for the opening of a Protestant church in San Sebastiano. After writing in lurid (and perhaps not realistic) detail about the many immoralities of the local Protestant community, he writes: "In the face of such danger I feel obliged to add, to the many complaints already made, a complaint to the Head of Government" and leaves it to Pacelli to transmit his complaint to Mussolini. See AESI pos. 795, fasc. 393, f. 15r (24 August 1933). Needless to say, the letter hardly reflects the convictions of one habitually inclined to act on behalf of Protestants. The oddness of Bagnoli's letter was detected in a handwritten note to it by Pizzardo: "The letter of [His Excellency] Mons. Bagnoli to the Head of Government is conceived in terms so strange . . . that does not seem possible that it is presented through the Secretariat of State" (AESI pos. 795, fasc. 393, f. 16r [n.d.]).
72. "Egli si atteggia a difensore della fede cattolica ed A SUA CONFESSIONE è l'ispiratore dei ricorsi che di tanto in tanto giungono a Roma contro il Vescovo e contro il Parroco, che accusa di negligenza e di incapacità di fronte ai protestanti." Coronati capitalized the words having to do with Conti's admission (Abbot Coranati to Pope Pius XI [AESI pos. 795, fasc. 395, f. 65v]).
73. Abbot Coranati to Pope Pius XI (AESI pos. 795, fasc. 395, f. 65v).
74. See Codex Iuris Canonici, Can. 987.
75. Abbot Coranati to Pope Pius XI (AESI pos. 795, fasc. 395, f. 65v).
76. At the time, the Code of Canon Law in fact denied funeral rights and burial in a

church cemetery on the grounds that suicide was a mortal sin (a law that has since been modified). The most recent catechism of the Catholic church still forbids suicide. See *CCC* 2280–83.

77. Abbot Coranati to Pope Pius XI (AESI pos. 795, fasc. 395, f. 65v).
78. Abbot Coranati to Pope Pius XI (AESI pos. 795, fasc. 395, f. 65v).
79. Abbot Coranati to Pope Pius XI (AESI pos. 795, fasc. 395, f. 66r).
80. He also met with members of the Sacred Congregation of the Council.
81. Abbot Coranati to Pope Pius XI (AESI pos. 795, fasc. 395, f. 66r).
82. Abbot Coranati to Pope Pius XI (AESI pos. 795, fasc. 395, f. 66v).
83. Abbot Coranati to Pope Pius XI (AESI pos. 795, fasc. 395, f. 67rv).
84. Abbot Coranati to Pope Pius XI (AESI pos. 795, fasc. 395, f. 67r).
85. Abbot Coranati to Pope Pius XI (AESI pos. 795, fasc. 395, f. 67v). Again, the abbot puts Conti's lamentation in uppercase letters and underlines it.
86. Abbot Coranati to Pope Pius XI (AESI pos. 795, fasc. 395, f. 66v).
87. Abbot Coranati to Pope Pius XI (AESI pos. 795, fasc. 395, f. 67v).
88. Bagnoli to Pacelli (AESI pos. 795, fasc. 393, f. 52r [5 February 1936]).
89. Bellarini to Pacelli (AESI pos. 795, fasc. 393, f. 56r–v [24 February 1936]).
90. Bagnoli to Pacelli (AESI pos. 795, fasc. 393, 60r [27 February 1936]).
91. Leone says of this conversion that Zardi was "Ben pilotato della curia di Avezzano." Yet he cites a letter from Zardi to Igino Giordani in which Zardi declares: "*In piena libertà* e in piena purezza sono ritornato nella Chiesa dei vecchi." Leone asserts that, after the end of the Second World War, Zardi "returned to frequent evangelical environs and with the annoying insistence that distinguished him sought, without success, to be restored to the pastorate" (Leone 1972, pp. 110–11 and 110 n. 57; emphasis added).
92. Zardi to Pacelli (AESI pos. 795, fasc. 395, ff. 76r–v [26 June 1937]).
93. Pacelli to Zardi (AESI pos. 795, fasc. 393, f. 77r [n.d.]).
94. Fr. Ottaviano Ghigliotti to Pacelli (AESI pos. 795, fasc. 393, ff. 71r–73r [17 June 1937]).
95. Giordani's involvement in the anti-Protestant campaign is ironic, as he later became a key figure in the Focolare Movement, focused on ecumenical relations and church unity, which he had once deplored in his journal *Fides*. He became a precursor of the leading reformers at the Second Vatican Council, and later a peace activist.
96. Pizzardo to Giordani (AGMF–AIG1 [18 August 1936)]). Giordani had recently written Pacelli. Pizzardo reports that Ciriaci had already met with Zardi and adds, "he has succeeded at nothing." It is not clear what Pizzardo is referring to. In any case, the role of Giordani in the anti-Protestant campaign and especially an analysis of the character and impact of his writings is an important issue, one which I have started to investigate.
97. On Zardi, see "La pubblica abiura del protestantesimo del pastore Carlo Zardi," 7 January 2013, Misericordia io voglio e non sacrificio (blog), https://misericordiaiovoglionon sacrificio.blogspot.com/2013/01/la-pubblica-abiura-del-protestantesimo.html.
98. "Appunto" (AESI pos. 795, fasc. 400, f. 89 [19 January 1939]).
99. See Kertzer 2014, p. 351.

100. By "ended," I mean the Vatican and Jesuit sources go no further than the death of Pius XI in 1939. Other sources, from the Achivio Centrale dello Stato and ASMAE, bring the story forward into the 1940s.
101. Bellarini to Pope Pius XI (AESI pos. 795, fasc. 393, ff. 111v–12r).

CHAPTER 6. THE APOSTOLIC NUNCIO AND THE "FREE DISCUSSION" CLAUSE

1. Borgongini-Duca to Pacelli (AESI, pos. 795, fasc. 395, f. 67 [8 March 1934]).
2. See the statement of the Protestant jurist Mario Piacentini, "La legge 24 giugno 1929," in *Bilychnis* 35 (1929): "Questa legge è stata detta, giustamente, la Magna charta della libertà religiosa in Italia." See also Giuseppe LaScala, *Culti Ammessi, non più tollerati! Fascismo e Protestantismo* (Napoli: Tipografico Cav. Uff. F. Feola, 1933).
3. "Pro Memoria Intorno al Lavoro che i Protestanti vanno compiendo in Italia" (ASV, ANI b. 49, fasc. 2, ff. 344–46 [n.d.]). The document is unsigned, but at the top of the first page is the acronym AMDG: *Ad maiorem Dei gloriam* (To the Greater Glory of God), the motto of the Society of Jesus.
4. See ANI b. 49, fasc. 2, ff. 344.
5. Pro Memoria (ASV, ANI b. 2, fasc. 49, f. 344).
6. Reported in the first anonymous memorandum (ASV, ANI b. 49, fasc. 2, f. 343 [n.d.]); and in a letter from Borgongini-Duca to Pacelli on "Diffusione di bibbie protestanti" (ASV, ANI b. 49, fasc. 2, f. 354 [10 March 1937]).
7. She was the niece of the local mayor. See the Jesuit memorandum (ANI b. 49, fasc. 2, f. 344).
8. First Jesuit Memorandum (ASV, ANI b. 49, fasc. 2, f. 343 [n.d.]).
9. ASV, ANI, b. 49, fasc. 2, f. 346.
10. First Jesuit Memorandum (ASV, ANI b. 49, fasc. 2, f. 343 [n.d.]); Second Jesuit Memorandum (ASV, ANI b. 49, fasc. 2, f. 345 [n.d.]).
11. Second Jesuit Memorandum (ASV, ANI b. 49, fasc. 2, f. 346 [n.d.]).
12. From the December 1934 report of "Il Testimonio" (ASV, ANI b. 49, fasc. 2, f. 279).
13. ASV, ANI b. 49, fasc. 2, f. 343. At the same time, another, unnamed Jesuit from the Province of Napoli was, according to Borgongini, convicted on similar grounds by a Praetor (Pretore) in the Province of Naples. See Borgongini-Duca to Pacelli (ASV, ANI b. 49, fasc. 2, f. 282 [22 March 1935]).
14. Borgongini-Duca to Pacelli (ASV, ANI b. 49, fasc. 2, ff. 281–82 [22 March 1935]).
15. Borgongini-Duca to Pacelli (ASV, ANI b. 49, fasc. 2, f. 282).
16. ASV, ANI b. 49, fasc. 2, ff. 281–82.
17. Borgongini-Duca to Montecchi (ASV, ANI b. 49, fasc. 2, f. 347 [25 February 1936]). The same correspondence is found in the archives of the Sacred Congregation of the Council, in a folder entitled "Circa la diffusione di bibbie protestanti in Italia" (ASV, SCC, SC b. 1, fasc. 1936).
18. Borgongini-Duca to Pacelli, con allegato (AESI 795, fasc. 397, f. 4v, 8r [22 March 1935]).

19. Buffarini to Borgongini-Duca (ASV, ANI b. 49, fasc. 2, f. 349 [3 April 1936]).
20. Law N. 4917, dell 11. I. 1937.
21. Letter from Pizzardo to Borgongini-Duca (ASV, ANI b. 49, fasc. 2, f. 351 [28 February 1937]). The existence of the Beer decree was also reported to the director of *L'Osservatore Romano* from the paper's local correspondent in Acireale (AESI pos. 795 fasc. 399, f. 17v [n.d.]).
22. La Sacra Bibbia, translated by G. Diodati Lucchesi, professor of Hebrew at the Academy of Calvin, published a cura della Società Biblica Brittanica; or La Sacra Bibbia, Revised Version in Original Text by Dr. Giovanni Luzzi, now professor of the Waldensian Theological Faculty, Rome. Also published a cura della Soc. Bibl. Britt. See ASV, ANI b. 49, fasc. 2, f. 352 (1 November 1937).
23. Pizzardo to Borgongini-Duca (ASV, ANI b. 49, fasc. 2, f. 351 [28 February 1937]).
24. Borgongini-Duca to Pacelli (ASV, ANI b. 49, fasc. 2, ff. 353–55 [10 May 1937]).
25. Pizzardo to Borgongini-Duca (ASV, ANI b. 49, fasc. 2, f. 356 [20 March 1937]).
26. "Sincerità nella vendita delle Bibbie" (ASV, ANI b. 49, fasc. 2, f. 357).
27. Melomo to Bruno (AESI pos. 795, fasc. 393, ff. 81v–87v [31 December 1931]).
28. On Strappaveccia (sometimes misspelled Strappavecchia in archival sources), see Peyrot 1955; Rochat 1990, pp. 113–26.
29. Following his confinement, fourteen of Giancaspero's followers were surprised by a raid of carabinieri in May 1941 while they were meeting in a private house. They were given a warning. See Rochat 1990, pp. 269–70.
30. Rochat 1990, p. 241; and Langford 2015, pp. 76–77.
31. Strappaveccia à Sua Eccellenza il Prefetto di Bari (AESI pos. 795, fasc. 393, f. 88r [25 November 1931]). He adds that in Monopoli, "Catholic leaders incite people to throw stones, prosecute and insult these honest citizens about their faith."
32. AESI pos. 795, fasc. 395, f. 71v (8 March 1934).
33. Borgongini-Duca to Buffarini, Allegato al Rapporto 3269 della Nunziatura d'Italia (AESI pos. 795, fasc. 395, ff. 84–85 [12 March 1934]).
34. He also served as minister of education and was for long a parliamentary deputy. On Boselli, see Mack Smith 1997, pp. 204, 272–73, and passim. Mack is not easy on him: "an undistinguished trimmer from the right center," a "nonentity" than whom no one could be less unfit for war, and so forth.
35. See, e.g., Borgongini-Duca to Pizzardo (ASV, ANI b. 49, fasc. 2, f. 410 [9 July 1937]). There the nuncio deplores the activities of two Adventist pastors that contravene the "solemn words of Rocco and Boselli," not to mention "the honorable Benito Mussolini, who has condemned [propaganda] as an assault on the unity of the faith." He cites it also in his vade mecum on Protestant proselytism in Italy (see below) (ASV, ANI fasc. 2, ff. 495r, 497r).
36. See, e.g., two complaints from the clergy and archbishop of Piazza Armerina alleging expressions in the town of Riesi, a hotbed of Protestant activity, of hatred for the pope. Despite the laws and complaints by the bishop to the marshal of the Reale Carabinieri, "the Waldensians continue their propaganda" (AESI pos. 795, fasc. 397, ff. 40–41 [28 and 31 July 1935]).
37. Borgongini-Duca to Pacelli (AESI pos. 795, fasc. 395, ff. 71v–72v [8 March 1934]).

38. Garfinkel 2017, p. 389, where Rocco's comment is cited. See also International Business Publications 2018, p. 58.
39. See Garfinkel 2017, chap. 3; Belco, "Reading Crime," in Parati 2012, pp. 245–49.
40. Especially, he adds, when "the intolerant attitude of local Catholics endangered public order." Naturally, Catholic authorities and fascist prefects would have put it differently; they would have argued that evangelical meetings and propaganda jeopardized public order. See discussion of public meetings in Rochat 1990, pp. 141–45.
41. See, e.g., Peyrot 1950 and Peyrot 1955, written twenty years after the Circolare Buffarini had been issued.
42. Article 18 of the New Law on Public Security, at International Business Publications 2018, p. 58.
43. Memo, ASV, ANI b. 49, fasc. 2, 452r (10 March 1938).
44. Borgongini-Duca to Pacelli (AESI pos. 795, fasc. 395, f. 678 [March 1934]).
45. Borgongini to Montecchi (ASV, ANI b. 49, fasc. 2, ff. 501–4 [30 September 1938]).
46. *O.O.* 19, p. 33. The remark was made first to a group of journalists in Lausanne on 21 November 1922. Mussolini spoke, just after the March on Rome, of a spirit "profondamente religioso," which he described as "una forza fondamentale per la nazione e che quindi va difesa e rispettata." For commentary, see Scoppola 1976, p. 63; and Sale 2011, p. 23.
47. Borgongini to Pacelli (con allegato, Oggetto: Attività dei Protestanti e discorso del Capo del Governo) (AESI pos. 795, fasc. 395, f. 72v. [19 March 1934]).
48. Borgongini to Pacelli (AESI pos. 795, fasc. 395, f. 72v [19 March 1934]).
49. ASV, ANI b. 49, fasc. 2, ff. 479–503 (n.d.). The document and correspondence related to its publication can also be found in AESI pos. 795, fasc. 396, ff. 3r–8r (n.d.).
50. ASV, ANI b. 49, fasc. 2, folder 15, ff. 474–569. The reception includes reports and reviews by the press, who were in the dark about the identity of its author. Another copy of the pamphlet can be found in ASV, ANI b. 49, fasc. 2, ff. 283–308. In an appendix he reproduces twenty or so pages of the document (Rochat 1990, pp. 49–55).
51. Rochat discusses the document and transcribes some of it. Yet because he discovered it in secular archives, he was never able to divine its author. See Rochat 1990, pp. 36–37.
52. Crivelli 1934. He also composed a *Piccolo dizionario delle sette Protestanti* (Roma: La Civiltà Cattolica, 1945), which, if intended to be brief, still ran to 315 pages.
53. In mid-May Borgongini told Serafini that the manuscript had been "produced in a limited number of copies, as it was not destined for the public" (Borgongini to Serafini, ASV, ANI b. 49, fasc. 2, f. 478 [13 May 1934]).
54. Borgongini-Duca to Serafini (ASV, ANI b. 49, fasc. 2, f. 478 [14 May 1934]).
55. Borgongini-Duca to Cammarotta (ASV, ANI b. 49, fasc. 2, f. 312 [18 April 1935]). Borgongini habitually says he redacted the document. But the only part not written by him was the statistical part compiled by Father Crivelli. He was, in effect, its author.
56. ASV, ANI b. 49, fasc. 2, f. 265 (13 May 1934).
57. ASV, ANI b. 49, fasc. 2, f. 491r (p. 23).
58. AESI 795/395: f. 52.
59. Genesis 1:3; 2 Corinthians 4:6. *Proselitismo,* pp. 28–29 ASV, ANI b. 49, fasc. 2: 483v–484r.

60. ASV, ANI b. 49, fasc. 2, f. 482r–v (*Proselitismo,* pp. 28–29).
61. See especially ANI, ASV b. 48, fasc. 7, ff. 2, 14–27.
62. See *Annuario Pontificio per l'anno 1934* (Città del Vaticano: Tipografia Poliglotta Vaticana, 1934), pp. 747–84. See Moroni 1840, p. 22. I discuss Costantini's lengthy reports on the Pentecostal churches, whose meetings he would anonymously infiltrate on behalf of Borgongini, in chapter 7.
63. ANI, ASV b. 48, fasc. 7, f. 16r, Unnamed Parish Priest (n.d.). Probably written sometime in 1934–36.

CHAPTER 7. RESISTANCE, RESPITE—AND RETREAT

1. The report is found as a pamphlet in AESI pos. 795, fasc. 398, between folios 34 and 35.
2. De Felice IV, p. 248.
3. Scoppola 1973, p. 255.
4. On 23 July 1935 Cardinal Alessio Ascalesi, archbishop of Milan, wrote the secretary of state to notify him of the activities of Methodists in Portici and of the existence of a "Mother House" there. He also detailed the activities, which included warning the clergy and people of his archdiocese of the Methodist danger but acting in coordination with other bishops in the Campania. Pacelli soon wrote back. He told him that he had notified the Holy Father of all that Ascalesi had done to combat Protestant propaganda in this region and that "His Holiness had taken great satisfaction" in being apprised of Ascalesi's zeal and sent his compliments, along with his encouragement to continue his fruitful work. Pacelli to Ascalesi (AESI pos. 795, fasc. 397, ff. 38–39 [4 August 1935]).
5. Leonardo M. Bello, Ministro Generale dell'Ordine dei Frati Minori to the Holy Father. See "Intensa azione del T.O. francescano contro la propaganda protestante in Italia" (ASV, SCC, SC b. 1, fasc. 1935 [8 August 1934]).
6. Pizzardo to Borgongini-Duca (AESI pos. 795, fasc. 397, f. 27 [14 May 1935]).
7. Borgongini-Duca to Pacelli (AESI pos. 795, fasc. 397, f. 28 [24 May 1935]).
8. See correspondence at AESI pos. 795, fasc. 399, ff. 4r–7v (24 May 1935).
9. "Brevi cenni" (AESI pos. 765, fasc. 394, f. 41).
10. In that year the twenty-first canon issued by the Fourth Lateran Council, *Omnis Utriusque Sexus,* required. parishioners to communicate and confess at least annually. Although hailed as a "pastoral revolution," in fact the decree was widely ignored, in part because it remained for centuries, owing to poor clerical education (and, consequently, of deplorable or nonexistent lay catechesis) unknown. See Madigan 2015, pp. 310–12. It was not until the Council of Trent (1548–63) that bishops were required to establish seminaries in their dioceses. Even then, bishops often lacked the funds to obey the decree.
11. Bellarini to Pope Pius XI (AESI pos. 795. fasc. 393, ff. 11v–12r [1936]).
12. Monsignor Oddo Bernacchia, Bishop of Larino and Tremoli to Pizzardo (AESI pos. 795, fasc. 396, f. 20r [25 August 1934]).
13. Bernacchia to Pizzardo (AESI pos. 795, fasc. 396, f. 20r [25 August 1934]).
14. Paolone to Pacelli (AESI pos. 795, fasc. 396, ff. 18r–v [Spring/Summer 1934]).

15. *Nemo certe ignorat* and *Probe noscitis Venerabiles* were issued in 1852; *Cum nuper* and *Amantissimi Redemptoris* in 1858. For documents translated into English, see Vatican website at http://www.vatican.va/offices/papal_docs_list.html.
16. "Brevi cenni" (AESI pos. 765, fasc. 394, f. 39r).
17. Giovanni Costantini, Bishop of Luni, La Spezia to Giulio Serafini, Prefect of the Sacred Congregation of the Council (AESI pos. 795, fasc. 396, ff. 39r–44r [28 October 1934]).
18. See discussion below of Catholic polemical discussion of *indifferentismo,* caused in the polemicists' minds by Protestant Christianity and its acceptance of many sects as more or less equally valuable.
19. See appendix 6, "A 'Vast and Arduous Program': l'Unione Missionaria del Clero."
20. Bellarini's letter was connected to an investigation launched by Vatican authorities about the penetration of British Methodists in the diocese of Marsi.
21. The founder of the order, St. Giovanni Calabria, corresponded, in Latin, with no less a figure than C. S. Lewis. See their complete correspondence in Lewis et al. 2009. The order now ministers mainly to poor communities in the Philippines and India.
22. Bellarini to Pacelli (AESI pos. 795, fasc. 393, f. 13v).
23. In yet another handwritten note to Pacelli, Bellarini writes: "I would be willing to give even my blood and life to put an end to this Protestant question at the Villa" (AESI pos. 795, fasc. 393, f. 18v [3 August 1933]). In sharp contrast to his bishop and his Vatican superiors, Bellarini's concern is with his parish and the diocese of Marsi; he talks not about the end of the Protestant presence but of an issue that sadly divides his community.
24. Paolone to Pacelli (AESI pos. 795, fasc. 396, ff. 18r [Spring/Summer 1934]).
25. Bernacchia to Pizzardo (AESI pos. 795, fasc. 396, f. 20r [25 August 1934]). Bernacchia was bishop of Termoli from 1924 to 1962. Pizzardo did write back to the bishop indicating that he had passed on the issue of the priest's housing to the appropriate office. See Pizzardo to Bernacchia (AESI pos. 795, fasc. 396, f. 23r [9 September 1934]). The competent office was the Pontifical Office for Parochial Housing. Pizzardo received a letter from this office indicating the sort of housing the office was authorized to rent for the parish priest. See Ufficio Pontificio, Case Parrocchiali to Pizzardo (AESI pos. 795, fasc. 396, f. 24r [31 August 1934]).
26. See *Annuario pontificio per l'anno 1934* (Città del Vaticano: Tipografia Poliglotta Vaticana, 1934), p. 229.
27. Bishop of Rieti to Pizzardo (AESI pos. 795, fasc. 396, ff. 28–29r [28 September 1936]).
28. Costantini to Serafini, Prefect of the Sacred Congregation of the Council (AESI pos. 795, fasc. 396, ff. 39r–44r [28 October 1934]).
29. See Missirolli 1929, pp. 179–81. See also Cornaggia and Morello 1933, pp. 103–5, where the author argues (as, indeed, many ex-priests had) that the enforcement of Article 5 was cruel vengeance for Italy's recent anticlerical past as well as, or even more important than, the protection of the Catholic faith of their students. Again, like ex-priests themselves, Morello insists that apostate priests lived (or, in cases, ministered) as Christians, had their children baptized, and, if married, were wed in church.

30. This has roots deep in ancient history and is connected especially with Augustine's response to the Donatist Church in North Africa. For discussion, see Willis 2005, esp. chapter 6.
31. "Lista dei Sacerdoti Apostati e Ministri Protestanti tratta dalle Informazioni Diocesane (ASV, SCC, SC b. 1, fasc. 1933, f. 1 [4 June 1933]). See Appendix 7 for a transcription of Crivelli's complete list.
32. As was Giuseppe Verri. See letter from Giuseppe Castalli to Serafini (ASV, SCC, SV b. 1, fasc. 1936–37–38, f. 3 [25 May 1935]).
33. Pontificia Opera per La Preservazione della Fide e la Provvista di Nuove Chiese in Roma to Bruno, Seg. SCC (ASV, SCC, SC b. 1, fasc. 1936 [20 December 1934]).
34. Borgongini-Duca to Bruno (ASV, SCC, SC b. 1, 1936 [5 February 1935]).
35. Bruno to Borgongini-Duca (ASV, SCC, SC b. 1, 1936 [3 March 1935]).
36. See Pizzardo to Bruno (ASV, SCC, SC b. 1, 1936 [3 May 1935]).
37. "Circa l'ex prete *Lorenzo Palmieri,* ministro di setta battista a Gioia del Coole, dioces. di Bari" (ASV, SCC, SC b. 1, fasc. 1936).
38. Serafini to Pacelli (AESI pos. 795, fasc. 397, ff. 34r–v [28 June 1935]).
39. Pacelli to Serafini ("Circa l'ex prete *Lorenzo Palmieri,* ministro di setta battista a Gioia del Coole, dioces. di Bari") (ASV, SCC, SC b. 1, fasc. 1936, f. 3 [1 August 1935]).
40. Borgongini-Duca to Pacelli ("Circa l'ex prete *Lorenzo Palmieri,* ministro di setta battista a Gioia del Coole, dioces. di Bari") at ASV, SCC, SC b. 1, fasc. 1936, Allegato to Pacelli letter [23 July 1935]).
41. Bishop Domenico Petroni (1881–1978) of Rapolla (to Serafini) (ASV, SCC, SC b. 1, fasc. 1936–37–38, ff. 1–9 [21 November 1935]).
42. Borgongini-Duca to Buffarini (ASV, SCC, SC b. 1, fasc. 1936–37–38, Allegato to 30 June 1936 letter to Pacelli [28 June 1936]).
43. Borgongini-Duca to Pacelli (ASV, SCC, SC b. 1, fasc. 1936–37–38, ff. 10–11 [30 June 1936]).
44. Pacelli to Serafini (ASV, SCC, SC b. 1, fasc. 1936–37–38, f. 15 [23 March 1938]).
45. Borgongini-Duca to Pacelli (ASV, SCC, SC b. 1, fasc. 1936–37–38, Allegato al N. 15 [16 March 1938]).
46. Though Serafini had Crivelli examine the issue, and the Jesuit argued that, as Protestant ministers could perform weddings and as marriages so begun were approved by the state, an apostate ex-priest *was* an official of the state. See Crivelli to Bruno (ASV, SCC, SC b. 1, fasc. 1936–37–38, f. 13 [14 January 1938]).
47. Letter from Bp. Luigi Drago to Pacelli re pp in Civitavecchia (AESI pos. 795, fasc. 395, ff. 87–88 [3 May 1934]).
48. Drago to Serafini (ASV, SCC, SC b. 1, fasc. 1936–37–38, f. 8 [25 June 1937]).
49. AESI pos. 795, fasc. 398, ff. 3r–10v (Summer 1935).
50. G. Bruno Secretary of the Sacra Congregazione del Concilio to Pizzardo (AESI pos. 795, fasc. 398, f. 5r [6 August 1936]).
51. Borgongini-Duca to Mons. Giuseppe Malusardi, Undersec'y of the S. Cong. AA EE SS (AESI pos. 795, fasc. 398, f. r [20 August 1935]).
52. ASV, ANI b. 49, fasc. 2, f. 499 (p. 40).

CHAPTER 8. BORGONGINI AND THE PENTECOSTAL REPRESSION

1. Antonio Melomo to Borgongini-Duca (ASV, ANI b. 48, fasc. 7, ff. 2r–3r [23 February 1932]).
2. Antonio Melomo to Borgongini-Duca (ASV, ANI b. 48, fasc. 7, ff. 2r–3r [23 February 1932]).
3. ASV, ANI b. 48, fasc. 7, f. 2r.
4. Those who had a special veneration for Mary, according to the bishop, possessed an ancient painting that had miraculously washed up on the shores of Monopoli (ASV, ANI b. 48, fasc. 7, f. 2r).
5. Melomo to Borgongini (ASV, ANI b. 48, fasc. 7, ff. 2r–3r).
6. ASV, ANI b. 48, fasc. 7, f. 2r.
7. ASV, ANI b. 48, fasc. 7, ff. 6r–27r (3 December 1934).
8. The decree was to remain in place for twenty years, until 1955—a full eight years after the Republican Constitution had granted religious freedom in Italy. See Zanini 2015, p. 686.
9. Costantini, Report (ASV, ANI b. 48, fasc. 7, f. 5 [3 December 1934]).
10. Costantini, Report (ASV, ANI b. 48, fasc. 7, ff. 5–7 [3 December 1934]).
11. Parham's authoritative biographer reports that rumors began to circulate around Parham in January 1907, when he suddenly left Texas for a northeastern tour. By 1908 his "awful sin," sodomy, was being discussed, and Parham himself was "disfellowshipped" by a "large segment of the Texas organization" of Pentecostals, now being directed by others. The private rumors became public when Parham's arrest was reported in the *San Antonio Light* on 19 July. He was charged, though never convicted, of what was a crime in Texas in 1907. Though Parham lost national standing in national Pentecostal circles, he remained active in midwestern Pentecostal circles. See Goff 1988, esp. chap. 6.
12. Ebner also observes: "With its adulation of masculinity and its obsession with maintaining strict gender differentiation, Fascism harbored an elevated level of hostility toward homosexuality. . . . [A]t the core of the Fascist totalitarian state's project to remake the Italian male there operated an antimodel: the effeminate 'pederast'" (Ebner 2011, pp. 211–12).
13. ASV, ANI b. 48, fasc. 7, f. 6r.
14. In Acts 2:13 those speaking "in tongues" at Pentecost are ridiculed for having consumed too much wine.
15. ASV, ANI b. 48, fasc. 7, ff. 8r, 14r, 15r.
16. As was the case, according to the testimony of the parish priest of the parish of Addolorata in S. Bonosa (ASV, ANI b. 48, fasc. 7, f. 16r).
17. See, e.g., the report by the parish priest of Addolorata in S. Bonosa, relying on the putative testimony of those who witnessed it, suggests *nocivo alla salute.* Of course, *this* could suggest a circularity, as the priest "reports" on the reports of others, who may have alleged damage to health (ASV, ANI b. 48, fasc. 7, f. 16).
18. ASV, ANI b. 48, fasc. 7, f. 12r.
19. ASV, ANI b. 48, fasc. 7, f. 15r. Battisti refers to Strappaveccia as "Spaccavaccia" in his report.

20. By his own admission: see Gal. 1:13–14; Phil. 3:6; Acts 8:1–3; by the author of Luke–Acts, see Acts 7:58–60 and 22:20.
21. ASV, ANI b. 48, fasc. 7, f. 6r.
22. ASV, ANI b. 48, fasc. 7, f. 6r.
23. ASV, ANI b. 48, fasc. 7, f. 6r.
24. ASV, ANI b. 48, fasc. 7, ff. 14r.
25. ASV, ANI b. 48, fasc. 7, ff. 15r.
26. ASV, ANI b. 48, fasc. 7, ff. 17r.
27. As, according to the testimony of the parish priest of the parish of Addolorata in S. Bonosa, sometimes occurred (ASV, ANI b. 48, fasc. 7, ff. 16r).
28. As recounted in Rochat 1980, pp. 113–14.
29. ASV, ANI b. 48, fasc. 7, f. 20r (28 February 1934).
30. ASV, ANI b. 48, fasc. 7, f. 21r.
31. ASV, ANI b. 48, fasc. 7, f. 7r.
32. ASV, ANI b. 48, fasc. 7, f. 18r.
33. ASV, ANI b. 48, fasc. 7, f. 9r.
34. ASV, ANI b. 48, fasc. 7, f. 11r.
35. In the tiny *quartiere coppedè* district of Rome between the Villa Borghese and the Villa Savoia.
36. ASV, ANI b. 48, fasc. 7, f. 11r.
37. See Browning 2014, especially pp. 424–28.
38. Zanini 2015, p. 691.
39. See Borgongini 1919; Tamborini 1919.
40. See the interesting comment in the secretary of state archives, however. Giordani is identified as one who "dirige il movimento antiprotestantico" (AESI, Italia IV, pos. 795 P.O., fasc. 398, ff. 39r–v). It is true that Giordani was perhaps, as editor and prolific contributor to *Fides,* the leading anti-Protestant writer in the campaign. Indeed, Pacelli once praised him for the quality of his writings and as a leader of Italian writers. Pizzardo to Giordani (AGMF–AIG1 [18 August 1936]).
41. Borgongini to Pacelli (AESI pos. 795, fasc. 395, f. 71 [19 March 1934]); and Borgongini to Buffarini (AESI pos. 795, fasc. 395, f. 75, Allegato to the Report of the Apostolic Nuncio [12 March 1934]).
42. Borgongini to Pacelli (AESI pos. 795, fasc. 395, f. 71 [19 March 1934]).
43. "Le legge garentisce ai protestanti il libero esercizio del loro culto per i loro adepti, ma non *li autorizza ad inquietari I* buoni campagnoli, perchè lascino la religione cattolica ed entrino nelle loro chiesuole. La legge italiana non autorizza questo proselitismo. . . . La discussion è un dibatto scientifico. . . . La relazione della Commisione del Senato sulla Legge dei culti ammessi dice testualmente che la discussion non deve essere 'publica perturbazione ed insidia contro la fede altrui, tanto piu' se la propaganda popolarmente si diffonde fra cete ignoranti ed inconsci e fra le disparazioni della povertà e id patimenti delle miserie occulte e vergognose" (Relazione Boselli, 18 June 1929). . . . "Tutto . . . è vera aggressione alla religione cattolica, proprio come lo deprecava la relazione senatoriale dell'On. Boselli" (AESI 795 pos. 395, ff. 71v–76v [13 February 1934]).

44. Borgongini-Duca to Buffarini (AESI 795 pos. 395, f. 75r–76r [13 March 1934]), Allegato to Letter from Borgongini to Pacelli (AESI 795 pos. 395, f. 72v [19 March 1934]).
45. Letter from Borgongini to Pacelli (AESI 795, pos. 395, f. 72r [19 March 1934]).
46. Letter from Borgongini to Pacelli (AESI 795, pos. 395, f. 72v [19 March 1934]). Emphasis added.
47. Costantini to Borgongini (ASV, ANI b. 48, fasc. 7, f. 36r).
48. Costantini to Borgongini (ASV, ANI b. 48, fasc. 7, f. 36r).
49. Costantini to Borgongini (ASV, ANI b. 48, fasc. 7, f. 36r).
50. See Ebner 2010, pp. 217–18.
51. Costantini to Borgongini (ASV, ANI b. 48, fasc. 7, f. 38r).
52. Costantini to Borgongini (ASV, ANI b. 48, fasc. 7, f. 36r).
53. Costantini to Borgongini (ASV, ANI b. 48, fasc. 7, f. 41r).
54. Costantini to Borgongini (ASV, ANI b. 48, fasc. 7, f. 39r).
55. Costantini to Borgongini (ASV, ANI b. 48, fasc. 7, f. 37r).
56. Costantini to Borgongini (ASV, ANI b. 48, fasc. 7, f. 37r).
57. Borgongini to Pacelli (ASV, ANI b. 48, fasc. 7, f. 41r). I take the term from Jeremy Cohen, who popularized the use of "hermeneutical Jew" in Cohen 1999. See his statement: "In order to meet their particular needs, Christian theology and exegesis created a Jew of their own. . . . [T]he origins, the character, and the role of the hermeneutical Jew derive from a theological agenda encompassing much more than the Jews themselves. . . . [M]y interest lies with the hermeneutically crafted Jew . . . and his distinguishing characteristics" (pp. 2–5).
58. Buffarini to Borgongini (ASV, ANI b. 48, fasc. 2, f. 42 [9 April 1935]).
59. Borgongini to Pacelli (ASV, ANI b. 48, fasc. 7, ff. 44–45 [3 April 1945]).
60. Borgongini-Duca to Luigi Cardinal Lavitrano, Archbishop of Palermo (ASV ANI b. 49, fasc. 2, f. 330v [30 April 1935]). Emphasis added.

CHAPTER 9. STALEMATE

1. Relazione della SCC al Santo Padre, "Località dove maggiore è il proselitismo protestante in Italia" (ASV, ANI b. 49, fasc. 2, ff. 374–76 [16 November 1936]).
2. Bartolini 2008, pp. 33–34.
3. Apostolic Nunciature to Pizzardo (AESI pos. 795, fasc. 395, f. 45r–v [12 December 1935]).
4. Paolo Galeazzi to Bruno (AESI pos. 795, fasc. 395, f. 49 [24 February 1936]).
5. Bruno to Pacelli (AESI pos. 795, fasc. 395, f. 48 [16 March 1936]).
6. Borgongini-Duca to Pizzardo (AESI pos. 795, fasc. 397, f. 52 [28 March 1936]). Bruno thanks Pizzardo for involving the effective nuncio at AESI pos. 795, fasc. 397, f. 57 (10 June 1936).
7. Pizzardo to Borgongini-Duca (ASV, ANI b. 2, fasc. 49, f. 372 con allegato from Sacra Congregatio Concilii [12 March 1937]). Pizzardo concludes his letter by repeating a suggestion that would have a future, if not a terribly effective one: that more Catholic churches be built in order to neutralize the Protestant danger. In a later letter to Borgongini, he would suggest again "costruzione di chiese al fine di fronteggiare la

propaganda protestante" (ASV, ANI b. 49, fasc. 2, f. 410 [9 July 1937]). According to his own testimony, expressed in a rescript to Pacelli in early July 1937, Borgongini examined "with that attentive care, that a topic so serious demands" the condensed reports of the thirteen bishops. Given Borgongini's near obsession with the issue of Protestant activity—especially in relation to the law on permitted cults—and that he took nearly three months to respond to Pacelli, this is certainly true. (In the meantime, he had also independently taken the time to write the bishops of Foggia and Taranto, like a teacher writing a dunning letter to rebellious schoolboys, to submit their overdue reports.) He also responded to Pacelli, on the basis of the condensed reports, in a nine-page letter. Yet the nuncio wanted more; he wanted to understand local conditions better. In order to achieve clarity, the nuncio asked Pacelli if he could receive the unedited letters sent to the Sacred Congregation of the Council. Three days later Pizzardo asked the council to send Borgongini all the reports received by Serafini. It was late in the summer when the nuncio made the request, so it was not until 21 September 1937 that the undersecretary of the council sent him all the reports transmitted to his dicastery. Now Borgongini had the full *incarto.*

8. "Propaganda Protestante in Italia," Allegato 3 (ASV, ANI b. 49, fasc. 2, ff. 416–25 [12 March 1937]). His was the only report not sent by a bishop.
9. Of an Adventist pastor vending propagandistic materials in Bologna, Ghetti remarks: "This pastor may neither propagandize nor proselytize, as these activities are prohibited by art. 28 of the Statuto del Regno, which defends in Catholic Italy the conscience of its citizens; from art. 5 of the Law of 24 June 1929, no. 1159 . . . which does not recognize peddlers as ministers."
10. ASV, ANI b. 1, fasc. 2, f. 416 (19 August 1937).
11. ASV, ANI b. 1, fasc. 2, f. 416 (19 August 1937).
12. Ghetti reports that at least two families purchased an Adventist periodical under the assumption that it was a publication of Catholic missionary organizations (see ASV, ANI b. 1, fasc. 2, ff. 417–18 [19 August 1937]).
13. ASV, ANI b. 1, fasc. 2, f. 416 (19 August 1937).
14. ASV, ANI b. 1, fasc. 2, f. 417 (19 August 1937).
15. Neufeld 1996, 62.1.
16. Crivelli 1938, pp. 222–23.
17. "Sarebbe una grande provvidenza se l'Autorita' civilie desse ordini maggioramente precisi circa l'interpretazione e l'osservanze delle leggi del Concordato, tutelando cosi nel modo piu' scrupoloso gli interessi della unita' religiosa del nostro popolo, pegno piu' sicura dell'unita' nazionale, e provvendo affinche' venga impedito questo dilagarsi di eresie straniere tanto doloroso ed umiliante per noi cattolici e Italiani" (Ghetti report, ASV, ANI b. 1, fasc. 2, f. 417 [19 August 1937]). Notice the grammatical parallelism of Catholicism and Italian national identity.
18. As Rochat has pointed out, the use of the Catholic word "oratory" could be used as justification for denying approval. See Rochat 1990, p. 141.
19. Borgongini-Duca to Pacelli (AESI pos. 795, fasc. 398, f. 16r–16v [26 June 1936]).
20. ASV, ANI b. 49, fasc. 2, f. 418. Lippolis's address is given as Via Farini 10. Lippolis is said "gia' fatto alcune vittime dell'errore" and to have held at least weekly visits and

conversations at the homes of several families (ASV, ANI b. 1, fasc. 2, f. 418). Ghetti transcribes the letter he had sent to the questore di Bologna (ASV, ANI b. 1, fasc. 2, ff. 419–20 [11 December 1936]) complaining of Lippolis.

21. ASV, ANI b. 1, fasc. 2, ff. 419–20 (11 December 1936).
22. ASV, ANI b. 49, fasc. 2, f. 424.
23. Margotti to Serafini (ASV, ANI b. 49, fasc. 2, f. 415 [11 September 1937]).
24. Tacchi Venturi to Pizzardo (AESI pos. 795, fasc. 399, f. 61 [16 March 1937]).
25. Pizzardo to Borgongini, con allegato from Sacra Congregatio Concilii (ASV, ANI b. 49/2, f. 372 [12 March 1937]).
26. "Osservazioni" in "Circa la relazioni degli Ordini sul proselitismo protestante" (ASV, SCC, SC b. 1, fasc. 1936 [1 August 1936]).

EPILOGUE

1. See Kertzer 2015, pp. 86–88, for analysis.
2. See Kertzer 2015, especially part 3 for a comprehensive discussion of the sources of the pope's dissatisfaction.
3. Zanini 2017.

APPENDIXES

1. AESI pos. 795, fasc. 400, ff. 51–52.
2. AESI pos. 795, fasc. 400, ff. 47r–v.
3. The blessing of a church bell by pouring water over it. Because a priest administered water in the blessing, it came to be called a baptism.
4. A form of the Rosary consisting of seven (rather than five) decades in honor of the seven joys of Mary.
5. "And blessed is the fruit of thy womb, Jesus" (from Elizabeth's greeting to Mary in Luke 1:42).
6. *Professio fidei Tridentina,* issued in 1564. Authorized by Pius IV with the bull *Benedictus Deus* (1565). Considered today by the church as one of four authoritative creeds.
7. These last lines in bold were bracketed in red with an indication that Testa came from Agrigento.
8. ARSI, TB b. 22, fasc. 583, ff. 22–30 (n.d.).
9. Pugliatti to Pius XI. The Codice ended up in the archives of the Apostolic Nuncio. See ASV ANI b. 49, fasc. 2, ff. 152–57.
10. Note the link made between antifascism and anti-Catholicism ("hypocritical religious infiltration").
11. AESI pos. 795, P.O. fasc. 394, ff. 38r–39r (1927–38; likely ca. 1934–35).
12. Probably meant to be *confutazione.*
13. "School."
14. "Conferenze di S. Vincenzo": Società di S. Vincenzo de' Paoli is a charitable Catholic organization founded in 1833 in Paris by Federico Ozanam.

15. "Far un po' di cagnare": "make noise," "to alarm" police or other public authority.
16. AESI pos. 795, fasc. 395, ff. 3r–5r.
17. Bovelli to Serafini (ASV, SCC, SC b. 1, fasc. 1936, f. 12 [2 April 1934]). It was in this letter that the archbishop described the program of the Missionary Union as "vast and arduous."
18. Bovelli to Bruno (ASV, SCC, SC b. 1, fasc. 1936, f. 10 [16 July 1934]).
19. Words used by Serafini in a pro memoria of his audience with Pius XI, 12 September 1932 ("Schiera volante dei Missionari per la difesa della Fede contro la propaganda dei Protestanti in Italia," ASV, SCC, SC b. 1, fasc. 1936, f. 3 [13 September 1932]). Over the course of the fall and early winter of 1932 Giuseppe Bruno, the secretary of the Sacred Congregation of the Council, sent letters to the superiors of each of these orders, indicating how the religious would interact with the bishops in the dioceses in which they worked, how many religious priests could be active in each Italian province and so forth, to which the ministers general of these orders responded with enthusiasm (ASV, SCC, SC b. 1, fasc. 1936, ff. 2–15 [November–December 1932]). A "Constitution" for the mission was drawn up and approved by Pius XI in an audience with Serafini on 2 August 1932 (ASV, SCC, SC b. 1, fasc. 1936, f. 1 [2 August 1932]).
20. See Letters from the Superiors and Ministers General in 1933–34, ASV, SCC, SC b. 1, fasc. 1936, folder entitled "Circa il proselitismo protestante in Italia e le schiere missionarie." The subsequent folder, with the same title, contains many letters of approval from diocesan bishops as well, most from early summer 1935.
21. Bovelli would later describe the Missionary Union as following "the August suggestion of the Holy Father." See Bovelli to Schiarappa (ASV, SCC, SC b. 1, fasc. 1936, f. 14 [21 February 1935]).
22. See "Pro-Memoria" on "Schiere Volanto di Missionari" for Bruno's program (ASV, SCC, SC b. 1, fasc. 1936, ff. 2 [9 September 1932]). "Dopo aver avuto conoscenza del Pro-Memoria del P. Crivelli del 7 corrente mese, si è benignamente degnato di approvare in massima le proposte in esso formulate contro il proselitismo protestante, con particolare attenzione per l'idea di costituzione di 'Schiere volanti di Missionari,' *ideata da Crivelli*" ("Circa il proselitismo protestante in Italia e le schiere missionarie" (ASV, SCC, SC b. 1, fasc. 1936 [13 September 1932]). Emphasis added.
23. *Programmata pro-Scholis de protestantismo in Pontificia Universitatis Gregoriana* (Rome: Ex Typis Pont. Univers. Gregorianae, 1934). Document may be found in ASV, SCC, SC b. 1, fasc. 1936.
24. ASV, SCC, SC b. 1, fasc. 1936, pp. 5–6.
25. In Mark 6:7 and Luke 10:1 Jesus sends out disciples to preach in pairs.
26. "Considerazioni riservate del pericolo protesante in Italia" (ASV, SCC, SC b. 1, fasc. 1936 [13 February 1935]). The Canadian document was published in Ottawa in 1933 by the Canadian Bureau of Statistics by the authority of H. H. Stevens, M.P. Minister of Trade and Commerce.
27. For what it is worth, this folder is separated from others by a black ribbon tied around it.
28. See Bruno to Ciarappa (ASV, SCC, SC b. 1, fasc. 1936, f. 9 [4 July 1934]).

29. Bovelli to Serafini (ASV, SCC, SC b. 1, fasc. 1936 [2 April 1934]).
30. Entitled *Rivista dell'Unione Missionaria del Clero in Italia,* the March–April 1935 number may be found as the last item in "L'Unione Missionaria del Clero" (ASV, SCC, SC b. 1, fasc. 1936).
31. See Mons. Adelfo Ciarappa, Direttore Nazionale, Unione Missionaria del Clero in Italia to G. Bruno ("L'Unione Missionaria del Clero," ASV, SCC, SC b. 1, fasc. 1936, f. 10 [19 July 1934], con allegato with information and advice for the missionaries); and Bovelli to Serafini ("L'Unione Missionaria del Clero," ASV, SCC, SC b. 1, fasc. 1936, f. 12 [5 December 1934]).
32. Manueletto per I Sacerdoti dell'Unione Missionaria del Clero (Rome: Via di Propaganda 1c, 1945).
33. Ciarappa to Bruno ("L'Unione Missionaria del Clero," ASV, SCC, SC b. 1, fasc. 1936, f. 14 [21 February 1935]).
34. In one letter Ciarappa writes as "National Director" and refers to Bovelli as "President" of the Missionary Union ("L'Unione Missionaria del Clero," ASV, SCC, SC b. 1, fasc. 1936, f. 12 [5 December 1934]). In another letter Bovelli writes as president and refers to a letter he wrote to the Director (ASV, SCC, SC b. 1, fasc. 1936, f. 18 [5 December 1934]).
35. Pacelli to Serafini (ASV, SCC, SC b. 1, fasc. 1936, f. 6 [26 March 1934]).
36. Bovelli to Pius XI (ASV, SCC, SC b. 1, fasc. 1936, f. 5 [18 March 1934]). The audience with the pope was held on 14 March 1934.
37. It is found, without explanation, in the middle of the folder ("L'Unione Missionaria del Clero," ASV, SCC, SC b. 1, fasc. 1936, immediately after f. 8). Bovelli later would report that "more than 40,000 had signed on" (ASV, SCC, SC b. 1, fasc. 1936), Allegato 1 to Ciarappa to Bruno ("L'Unione Missionaria del Clero," ASV, SCC, SC b. 1, fasc. 1936, f. 17 [13 March 1935]). Bovelli's Allegato is dated 14 March 1934.
38. In a folder whose name replicated the title of his pamphlet: "Il Proselitismo protestante in Italia e l'Unione Missionaria del Clero," Allegato to Bovelli to Serafini (28 May 1934, just a month or so after its publication).
39. Bovelli to Serafini ("Circa la XIII Settimana di Studi Missionari a Bari," ASV, SCC, SC b. 1, fasc. 1936, f. 1 [10 September 1935]). Serafini wrote to Bovelli the letter he requested, saying he was with them "spiritually" ("Circa la XIII Settimana di Studi Missionari a Bari," ASV, SCC, SC b. 1, fasc. 1936, f. 2 [15 September 1935]).
40. Crivelli to Bruno_List of Apostate Priests_31 dic 1932 (ASV, Sacra Congregazione del Concilio, Sezione Catechista, b. 1—*Protestanti.*)

Bibliography

Ackroyd, P. 1998. *The Life of Thomas More.* Julio Mario Santo Domingo Collection. New York: Nan A. Talese/Doubleday.

Adamson, W. L. 2014. "Fascism and Political Religion in Italy: A Reassessment." *Contemporary European History* 23 (1): 43–73.

Agostino Gemelli, Francescano. 1959. Milan: Società Editrice Vita e Pensiero.

Alvarez, D. J. 2002. *Spies in the Vatican: Espionage and Intrigue from Napoleon to the Holocaust.* Lawrence: University Press of Kansas.

"Ancora sull'opera Protestante in Italia." 1920. *CC* 71: 427.

Anderson, M. C. 1998. "'What's to Be Done with 'Em?' Images of Mexican Cultural Backwardness, Racial Limitations, and Moral Decrepitude in the United States Press, 1913–1915." *Mexican Studies/Estudios Mexicanos* 14 (1): 23–70.

Anderson, R. M. 1992. *Vision of the Disinherited: The Making of American Pentecostalism.* Eugene, OR: Wipf and Stock.

Anderson, Robin, and Alfredo C. Ottaviani. 1978. *St. Pius V: A Brief Account of His Life, Times, Virtues and Miracles.* Rockford, IL: TAN Books.

Angold, M., ed. 2006. *Eastern Christianity.* The Cambridge History of Christianity. Cambridge: Cambridge University Press.

"Appello di un Protestante al Papa per la ristaurazione del Diritto Internazionale, L'." 1919. *CC* 70: 89.

Apostleship of Prayer (Organization). 1982. *Messenger of the Sacred Heart.* Toronto: Apostleship of Prayer.

Aquilante, S. 1998. *Chiese e stato nell'Italia che cambia: il ruolo del protestantesimo.* Turin: Claudiana.

Aramini, D. 2015. "The Myth of 'Christian Rome' and the Institute of Roman Studies: An Attempted Synthesis of Fascism and Catholicism." *Journal of Contemporary History* 50 (2): 188–214.

Aresi, L. 2003. *La pentecoste rinnovata: i primi anni di vita del movimento pentecostale italiano.* Milan: Società Editrice Vita e Pensiero.

Armistead, D. 1987. *Cristiani in divisa: un secolo di storia dell'esercito della salvezza fra gli italiani (1887–1987).* Turin: Claudiana.

Armstrong, G., and I. N. Wood. 2000. International Medieval Congress. International Medieval Research 7. *Christianizing Peoples and Converting Individuals.* Turnhout: Brepols.

Aronica, F. 2003. *D. Brizio Casciola tra nazionalismo e fascismo.* Roma: Ed. SPES.

Arthur, W. 1860. *Italy in Transition: Public Scenes and Private Opinions in the Spring of 1860; Illustrated by Official Documents from the Papal Archives of the Revolted Legations.* New York: Harper and Brothers.

Astorri, R. 2000. "Il trattato di amicizia, commercio, navigazione tra Italia e Stati Uniti: la questione della libertà religiosa e i rapporti tra Italia e Santa Sede. *Studi in Onore di Francesco Finocchiaro.* Padua: CEDAM.

Atkins, Gaius Glenn, and Frederick Louis Fagley. 1942. *History of American Congregationalism.* Boston: Pilgrim Press.

Audenino, P. 2009. *Il prezzo della libertà: Gaetano Salvemini in esilio (1925–1949).* Soveria Mannelli: Rubbettino.

Avalle, V., and U. Avalle. 2004. *Non tenterai il signore: diario di un prete di montagna.* Ivrea (TO): Priuli and Verlucca.

Baird, R. 1845. *Sketches of Protestantism in Italy, Past and Present: Including a Notice of the Origin, History, and Present State of the Waldenses.* Glasgow: William Collins Sons.

Baldwin, P. 1990. "Social Interpretations of Nazism: Renewing a Tradition." *Journal of Contemporary History* 25 (1): 5–37. Retrieved October 25, 2020, from http://www.jstor.org/stable/260719.

Balestra, P. 2006. *Pietro Balestra: lettere circolari, 1902–1911.* Cagliari: Zonza.

Barclay, W. C. 1949. *History of Methodist Missions.* Edited by J. T. Copplestone and John Tremayne. New York: Board of Missions and Church Extension of the Methodist Church.

Barclay, W. C., and J. T. Copplestone. 1957. *History of Methodist Missions: The Methodist Episcopal Church, 1845–1939.* 4 vols. Volume 3: *Widening Horizons, 1845–95.* Volume 4: J. T. Copplestone. 1949. *Twentieth-Century Perspectives, 1896–1939.* New York: Board of Missions and Church Extension of the Methodist Church.

Barnett, S. J. 1999. "Where Was Your Church before Luther? Claims for the Antiquity of Protestantism Examined." *Church History* 68 (1): 14–41.

Barone, D. 2016. *Beyond Memory: Italian Protestants in Italy and America.* Albany: State University of New York Press.

Barra, F. 1978. *Chiesa e società in Irpinia dall'unità al fascismo.* Roma: La Goliardica.

Bartolini, Stefano, and Roberto Barontini. 2008. *Fascismo antislavo: Il tentativo di "Bonifica Etnica" al confine nord orientale.* Pistoia: Istituto Storico della Resistenza e dell'età contemporanea di Pistoia.

Bates, David, Edoardo D'Angelo, and Elisabeth M. C. Van Houts. 2018. *People, Texts and Artefacts: Cultural Transmission in the Medieval Norman Worlds.* London: Institute of Historical Research, University of London.

Bergen, D. L. 1996. *Twisted Cross: The German Christian Movement in the Third Reich.* Chapel Hill: University of North Carolina Press.

Bernauer, J. W., and R. A. Maryks. 2014. *"The Tragic Couple": Encounters between Jews and Jesuits.* Leiden: Brill, 2014.

Besant, A. 1920. *Annie Besant: An Autobiography,* 2d ed. London: Fisher.

Besier, G. 2007. *The Holy See and Hitler's Germany.* Edited by F. Piombo. Houndmills, Basingstoke, Hampshire: Palgrave Macmillan, 2007.

Besier, Gerhard, and Katerzyna Stokłosa. 2016. *Jehovah's Witnesses in Europe: Past and Present.* Volume I/1 and I/2. Newcastle upon Tyne: Cambridge Scholars Publishing.

Binchy, D. A. 1941. *Church and State in Fascist Italy.* Edited by Royal Institute of International Affairs. London: Oxford University Press.

Binfield, Clyde, and World Alliance of YMCAs. 1991. *This Has Been Tomorrow: The World Alliance of YMCAs since 1955.* Geneva: World Alliance of Young Men's Christian Associations.

Birnstein, U. 2013. *Toleranz und scheiterhaufen: das Leben des Michael Servet.* Göttingen: Vandenhoeck and Ruprecht.

Black, C. F. 2004. *Church, Religion and Society in Early Modern Italy.* London: Palgrave Macmillan.

Blet, P. 1999. *Pie XII e la Seconde Guerre Mondiale.* English: *Pius XII and the Second World War: According to the Archives of the Vatican.* New York: Paulist Press.

Blet, Pierre, Angelo Martini, and Burkhart Schneider. 1968. *The Holy See and the War in Europe: March 1939–August 1940.* Washington, D.C.: Corpus Books.

Blinkhorn, M. 2000. *Fascism and the Right in Europe, 1919–1945.* Harlow: Longman.

Bocci, M. 2003. *Agostino Gemelli rettore e francescano: Chiesa, regime, democrazia.* Brescia: Morcelliana.

Bogdan, H., and J. Snoek. 2014. *Handbook of Freemasonry.* Leiden: Brill.

Borgongini-Duca, F. 1919. *Il profilo di S. Agostino e la genesi della dottrina agostiniana intorno al peccato originale: saggio critico su due scritti del Prof. Ernesto Buonaiuti della R. Università di Roma.* Rome: Libreria Editrice Spithoever.

Bosworth, R. J. B. 2005. *Mussolini's Italy: Life under the Fascist Dictatorship, 1915–1945.* London: Allen Lane.

———, ed. 2010. *The Oxford Handbook of Fascism.* Oxford: Oxford University Press.

———. 2014. *Mussolini.* New ed. London: Bloomsbury.

Box, Z., and I. Saz. 2011. "Spanish Fascism as a Political Religion (1931–1941)." *Politics, Religion and Ideology* 12 (4): 371–89.

Bracco, R. 1990? *Persecuzione in Italia: ricordi e bozzetti.* Rome: Rinascita Spirituale.

Bresso, P. 1979. "Mondo cattolico, fascismo e minoranze religiose: il caso Pinerolese." *Chiesa, azione cattolica e fascismo nell' Italia settentrionale durante il pontificato i Pio II (1922–1939): Atti del quinto Convegno di storia della chiesa, Torreglia 25–27 marzo 1977.* Milan.

Brezzi, Camillo, and Pietro Scoppola. 2002. *Democrazia e cultura religiosa: studi in onore di Pietro Scoppola.* Bologna: Il Mulino.

Brown, J. W. 1890. *An Italian Campaign; or, The Evangelical Movement in Italy, 1845–1887.* Edited by R. W. Stewart. London: Hodder and Stoughton.

Brown, S. J., and T. Tackett, eds. 2006. *Enlightenment, Reawakening and Revolution 1660–1815.* The Cambridge History of Christianity. Cambridge: Cambridge University Press.

Browning, C. R. 2014. *The Origins of the Final Solution: The Evolution of Nazi Jewish Policy, September 1939–March 1942.* Lincoln: University of Nebraska Press.

Burgess, S. M., and G. B. McGee, eds. 1988. *Dictionary of Pentecostal and Charismatic Movements.* Grand Rapids: Zondervan.

Burt, W. 1909. *Europe and Methodism.* New York: Eaton and Mains.

Butler, Jonathan M., and Ronald L. Numbers. 1993. *The Disappointed: Millerism and Millenarianism in the Nineteenth Century.* Knoxville: University of Tennessee Press.

Butticci, Annalisa. 2016. *African Pentecostals in Catholic Europe: The Politics of Presence in the Twenty-First Century.* Cambridge: Harvard University Press.

Caglioti, D. L. 2006. *Vite parallele: una minoranza protestante nell'Italia dell'ottocento.* Bologna: Il Mulino.

Cajetan, T. D. V. 1978. *Cajetan Responds: A Reader in Reformation Controversy.* Edited by J. Wicks. Washington, DC: Catholic University of America Press.

Calvez, J. 1965. *The Social Thought of John XXIII: Mater et Magistra.* Chicago: H. Regnery.

Calvino, I. 2003. *The Hermit in Paris: Autobiographical Writings.* Edited by M. L. McLaughlin. New York: Pantheon Books.

Cameron, E. 1986. *The Reformation of the Heretics: The Waldenses of the Alps, 1480–1580.* Oxford: Clarendon Press.

———. 2000. *Waldenses: Rejections of Holy Church in Medieval Europe.* Oxford: Blackwell Publishers.

———. 2016. *Bibles in Italian and Spanish.* Cambridge: Cambridge University Press.

Campbell, A. 1843. *The Christian System, in Reference to the Union of Christians and a Restoration of Primitive Christianity, as Pleaded in the Current Reformation.* Birmingham: Publishing Committee of Churches of Christ.

Campbell, Alexander, W. K. Pendleton, and Charles Louis Loos. 1976. *The Millennial Harbinger.* Joplin, MO: College Press.

Campi, E. 2001. Review of *The Protestant Reformation in Sixteenth-Century Italy*, by Salvatore Caponetto. *Journal of Ecclesiastical History* 52 (4): 740–741.

Canali, M. 2004. *Le spie del regime.* Bologna: Il Mulino.

———. 2009. "The Matteotti Murder and the Origins of Mussolini's Totalitarian Fascist Regime in Italy." *Journal of Modern Italian Studies* 14 (2): 143–67.

Cannistraro, Philip V., and Brian R. Sullivan. 1993. *Il Duce's Other Woman.* New York: William Morrow.

Cantimori, D. 2006. *Eretici italiani del cinquecento.* Milan: Il Giornale.

Caponetto, S. 1997. *La riforma protestante nell'Italia del Cinquecento.* Turin: Claudiana.

Capozzi, F. C. 1918. *Protestantism and the Latin Soul.* Philadelphia: Winston.

Carlen, C. 1951. *Guide to the Documents of Pius XII, 1939–1949.* Westminster, MD: Newman Press.

———. 1958. *Dictionary of Papal Pronouncements, Leo XIII to Pius XII, 1878–1957.* New York: P. J. Kenedy.

Carli-Ballola, R. 1953. *L'azione cattolica alla conquista dell'Italia.* Milan: Edizioni Avanti!

Casanova, J. 1994. *Public Religions in the Modern World.* Chicago: University of Chicago Press.

Casiday, A., and F. W. Norris, eds. 2007. *Constantine to C.600.* The Cambridge History of Christianity. Cambridge: Cambridge University Press.

Castiglione, M. 1972. *Aspetti della diffusione del movimento pentecostale in Puglia.* Palermo: Flaccovio.

———. 1978. "Marginalitá religiosa e dinamica culturale: spunti per una analisi di movimenti acattolici contemporanei nel mezzogiorno." *Storia e cultura del mezzogiorno. Studi in memoria di Umberto Caldora.*

Castro, S. 2011. *Egidio reale tra Italia, Svizzera e Europa.* Milan: Francoangeli.

Catholic Church, official documents of:

———, *Acta Apostolicae Sedis.* 1909– . *Acta Apostolicae Sedis; Commentarium Officiale.*

———, *Annuario pontificio.* 1860–. Rome: Tipografia Poliglotta Vaticana.

———, *Codex iuris.* 1917. *Codex iuris canonici Pii X Pontificis Maximi: Iussu digestus benedicti Papae XV auctoritate promulgatus.* Edited by P. Gasparri. Rome: Typis Polyglottis.

———, *Mediator Dei.* 1948. *Mediator Dei.* English: *Mediator Dei: Encyclical Letter of Pope Pius XII on the Sacred Liturgy. With Discussion Club Outline.* Edited by G. C. Treacy. New York: Paulist Press. Vatican edition of treaty here: http://www.vatican.va/content/pius-xii/en/encyclicals/documents/hf_p-xii_enc_20111947_mediator-dei.html.

———, *Summi Pontificatus.* 1939. *Summi Pontificatus: Encyclical Letter of Pope Pius XII on the Function of the State in the Modern World* (Official Vatican English Translation with Discussion Study Club Outline); *Encyclical Letter of Pope Pius XII on the Function of the State.* Washington, DC: National Catholic Welfare Conference. Vatican edition online at http://www.vatican.va/content/pius-xii/en/encyclicals/documents/hf_p-xii_enc_20101939_summi-pontificatus.html.

———, *Treaty and Concordat.* 1929. *Treaty and Concordat between the Holy See and Italy; Official Documents.* By Vittorio Emanuele III. Edited by the National Catholic Welfare Conference. Washington, DC: National Catholic Welfare Conference.

Ceci, L. 2017. *The Vatican and Mussolini's Italy.* Leiden: Brill.

Centro, D. M. 1980. *Storia della massoneria: Testi estudi.* Turin: EDI.

Cesana, T. 1978. *Fra Agostino Gemelli: dalla nascita alla professione religiosa, 1878–1904.* Milan: Biblioteca Francescana.

Chiarini, F. 1999. *Storia delle chiese metodiste in Italia (1859–1915).* Turin: Claudiana.

———, S. Carile, and G. Spini. 1997. *Il metodismo italiano.* Turin: Claudiana.

———, L. Giorgi, and G. Spini. 1990. *Movimenti evangelici in Italia dall'unità ad oggi: studi e ricerche.* Turin: Claudiana.

"Chiesa protestante nel Terzo Reich, La." 1935. *CC* 86: 138. From F. C. Church. 1974. *The Italian Reformers, 1534–1564.* First published in 1932. New York: Columbia University Press.

Cianfarra, C. M. 1945. *The War and the Vatican.* London: Oates and Washbourne.

Cleaves, R. W. 1977. *The Story of the Federation: Congregationalism 1960–1976.* Swansea: J. Penry.

Cohen, J. 1999. *Living Letters of the Law: Ideas of the Jew in Medieval Christianity.* Berkeley: University of California Press.

Collins, J. J., B. McGinn, and S. J. Stein. 1998. *The Encyclopedia of Apocalypticism.* New York: Continuum.

Comba, A. 2000. *Valdesi e massoneria due minoranze a confronto.* Turin: Claudiana.

Comba, E. 1930. *Storia dei Valdesi.* Torre Pellice: Claudiana.

"Condition of the Pope." 1930. *Time* 16 (2): 60.

Condizione giuridica di Roma e sinti in Italia, La. Vol. 1. 2011. Milan: Giuffrè.

Contarini, Gasparo. 1538. *Consilium Delectorum Cardinalium et Aliorum Praelatorum de Emendanda Ecclesia: S.D.N.D Paul III. Ipso Jubente Conscriptum, e Exhibitum Anno MDXXXVIII.* [Argentorati (Strasbourg)].

Conti, F. 2003. *Storia della massoneria italiana: dal Risorgimento al fascismo.* Bologna: Il Mulino.

"Contraddizioni della propaganda protestante in Italia, Le." 1932. *CC* 83: 521.

Coppa, F. J. 2005. "Italy: The Church and the Risorgimento." In *The Cambridge History of Christianity: World Christianities, c. 1815–c. 1914.* Edited by S. Gilley and B. Stanley. Cambridge: Cambridge University Press.

———. 2006. *The Papacy, the Jews, and the Holocaust.* Washington, DC: Catholic University of America Press.

———. 2012. *Controversial Concordats: The Vatican's Relations with Napoleon, Mussolini, and Hitler.* Washington, DC: Catholic University of America Press.

Copplestone, J. T. 1949. *Twentieth-Century Perspectives, 1896–1939.* Volume 4: *History of Methodist Missions: The Methodist Episcopal Church, 1845–1939.* New York: Board of Missions and Church Extension of the Methodist Church.

———. 1973. *The Methodist Episcopal Church, 1896–39.* 4 vols. New York: Board of Global Ministries and United Methodist Church.

Corallo, M. 1945. *La poesia Latina di Vittorio Genovesi.* Milan: Società Editrice Vita e Pensiero.

Cornaggia Medici, L., and V. Morello 1933. *Lettera aperta al Senatore Vincenzo Morello (Rastignac): il conflitto dopo la conciliazione.* 3d ed. Con risposta di Rastignac all'autore. Florence: G. Giannini.

Corrigan, J. 1991. *The Prism of Piety: Catholick Congregational Clergy at the Beginning of the Enlightenment.* New York: Oxford University Press.

Courtois, Gaston, ed. 1961. *The States of Perfection According to the Teaching of the Church: Papal Documents from Leo XIII to Pius XII.* Westminster, MD: Newman Press.

Creech, J. 1996. "Visions of Glory: The Place of the Azusa Street Revival in Pentecostal History." *Church History* 65 (3): 405–24.

Crippa, L. 1994. "Alfredo Ildefonso Card. Schuster O.S.B. Saggio Bibliografico." *Benedictina* 41: 13–39.

Cristiani d'Italia. 1. 1. 2011a. Rome: Istituto della Enciclopedia Italiana.

———. 2011b. Rome: Istituto della Enciclopedia Italiana.

———. 2011c. Rome: Istituto della Enciclopedia Italiana.

Crivelli, C. 1934. *Sètte e società Protestanti in Italia.* 2d ed. Aggiornata Edition. Rome: n.p.

———. 1938. *I Protestanti in Italia:* Isola del Liri: Macioce and Pisani.

———. 1944. *Protestanti e Cristiani orientali.* Rome: La Civiltà Catolica.

———, and Pontificio Collegio Pio latino americano. 1931. *Los protestantes y la América latina, conferencias, acusaciones, respuestas.* Isola del Liri: Soc. tip. A. Macioce and Pisani.

Croce, B. 1929. *Italian Liberals and the Lateran Treaties. I. Speech by Benedetto Croce to the Senate, May 24th, 1929. II. Anonymous Pamphlet Clandestinely Circulating Throughout Italy. August 1929.* London: Victor Printing.

Cumbo, E. C. 2000. "'Your Old Men Will Dream Dreams': The Italian Pentecostal Experience in Canada, 1912–1945." *Journal of American Ethnic History* 19 (3): 35–81.

Dagnino, J., and Z. G. Barański. 2012. "The Intellectuals of Italian Catholic Action and the Sacralisation of Politics in 1930s Europe." *Contemporary European History* 21 (2): 215–33.

———. 2017. *Faith and Fascism: Catholic Intellectuals in Italy, 1925–43.* London: Palgrave Macmillan.

D'Agostino, P. R. 2004. *Rome in America: Transnational Catholic Ideology from the Risorgimento to Fascism.* Chapel Hill: University of North Carolina Press.

Dalmas, D., and A. Strumia. 2000. *Una resistenza spirituale: conscientia 1922–1927.* Turin: Claudiana.

Damsteegt, P. G. 1995. *Foundations of the Seventh-Day Adventist Message and Mission.* Grand Rapids: Andrews University Press.

D'Angelo, A., F. Tosi, S. Dominici, and Istituto Nazionale di Studi Romani. 2005. *Lettere pastorali dei Cardinali Suburbicari: 1870–1958.* Rome: Istituto Nazionale di Studi Romani.

Dani, Aristide, Federico M. Mistrorigo, and Luciano Rossi. 1958. *Studi in onore di Federico M. Mistrorigo.* Vicenza: Comune.

Davis, John A. 2010. *The Jews of San Nicandro.* New Haven: Yale University Press.

———. 2015. *A Tale of Two Italys? The "Southern Question" Past and Present.* In *The Oxford Handbook of Italian Politics,* edited by Erik Jones and Gianfranco Pasquino, 53–68. Oxford: Oxford University Press.

De Cesaris, V. 2010. *Vaticano, fascismo e questione razziale.* Milan: Guerini Studio.

De Felice, R. 1965. *Mussolini.* Turin: Einaudi.

De Grazia, V. 1992. *How Fascism Ruled Women: Italy, 1922–1945.* Berkeley: University of California Press.

Delzell, C. F. 1961. *Mussolini's Enemies: The Italian Anti-Fascist Resistance.* Princeton: Princeton University Press.

De Meo, G. 1980. "*Granel di sale": un secolo di storia della Chiesa Cristiana Avventista del 7° giorno in Italia (1864–1964).* Turin: Claudiana.

Demofonti, L. 2004. "The Study of Giorgio Spini on Protestantism in Italy." *Studi Storici* 45 (2): 581–99.

De Vita, L. 2008. *La missione evangelica zigana: una minoranza italiana.* Edited by L. Frezza and A. Iovino. Napoli: Guida.

Denzinger, H. 1854. *Enchiridion symbolorum et definitionum: quae de rebus fidei et morum a conciliis oecumenicis et summis pontificibus emanarunt.* Edited by Catholic Church, 2d ed., Aucta et Emendata. Wirceburgi: Sumptibus Stahelianis.

Desprat, J. 2011. *Henri IV: L'homme de la tolérance.* Paris: Garnier.

Digiovanni, S. 2013. *The Second Founder: Bishop Martin J. O'Connor and the Pontifical North American College.* Bloomington, IN: Trafford.

Di Girolamo, B. 1879. *Trionfo della chiesa cattolica sul liberalismo moderno ossia apologia della vera chiesa di Gesù Cristo contro gli errori che il nuovo liberalismo ha riprodotto dal protestantesimo e da fonti cotali.* Naples: Tipografia Dell'accademia Reale delle Scienze.

"Di Lucca il Protestante Don Giovanni." 1934. *CC* 85: 40.

Dinapoli, T. P., ed. 2000. *The Italian Jewish Experience.* Stony Brook, NY: Forum Italicum.

Di Porto, B. 1998. "Valdesi ed Ebrei: le due storiche minoranze religiose dal Risorgimento alla repubblica." *La rassegna mensile di Israel* 64 (1): 7–12.

"Di scuole della chiesa d'Inghilterra." 1884. *CC* 6: 113.

"Dizionario Storico del movimento cattolico in Italia 1860–1980." 1982. *CC* 133 (4): 402.

Domenico, R. P. 2002. *The Regions of Italy: A Reference Guide to History and Culture.* Westport, CT: Greenwood.

———. 2005a. "Cattolicesimo e totalitarismo: chiese e culture religiose tra le Due Guerre Mondiali (Italia, Spagna, Francia)." *Catholic Historical Review* 91 (4): 839–41.

———. 2005b. "'For the Cause of Christ Here in Italy': America's Protestant Challenge in Italy and the Cultural Ambiguity of the Cold War." *Diplomatic History* 29 (4): 625–54.

"Dovere dei Cattolici di fronte alla propaganda Protestante in Italia, Il." 1932. *CC* 83: 328.

Dowling, M. 1999. *Fisher of Men: A Life of John Fisher, 1469–1535.* Basingstoke, Hampshire: Macmillan.

Doyle, B. 1991. "Do Catholics Have a Built-In Fear of the Masons?" *U.S. Catholic* 56 (3): 28.

Duce, A. 2006. *La Santa Sede e la questione ebraica, 1933–1945.* Rome: Studium.

Duggan, C. 2013. *Fascist Voices: An Intimate History of Mussolini's Italy.* New York: Oxford University Press.

Dunnage, J. 2012. *Mussolini's Policemen: Behaviour, Ideology and Institutional Culture in Representation and Practice.* Manchester: Manchester University Press.

"Ed e Protestante!" 1874. *CC* 3: 671.

Ebner, M. R. 2006. "The Political Police and Denunciation during Fascism: A Review of Recent Historical Literature." *Journal of Modern Italian Studies* 11 (2): 209–26.

———. 2014. *Ordinary Violence in Mussolini's Italy.* Cambridge: Cambridge University Press.

Eck, J. 1976. *Enchiridion of Commonplaces of John Eck against Martin Luther and His Followers.* Edited by F. L. Battles. Pittsburgh: Duquesne University Press.

Edwards, B. 2013. *With God on Our Side: British Christian Responses to the Spanish Civil War.* Newcastle upon Tyne: Cambridge Scholars Publishing.

Edwards, M. U. 1994. *Printing, Propaganda, and Martin Luther.* Berkeley: University of California Press.

Evensen, B. J. 2003. *God's Man or the Gilded Age: D. L. Moody and the Rise of Modern Mass Evangelism.* New York: Oxford University Press.

Fabiani, R. 1978. *I Massoni in Italia.* Rome: L'Espresso.

Fabre, G. 2005. *Mussolini razzista: dal socialismo al fascismo: La formazione di un antisemita.* Milan: Garzanti.

Farber, D. R. 2013. *Everybody Ought to Be Rich: The Life and Times of John J. Raskob, Capitalist.* Oxford: Oxford University Press.

Fattorini, E. 2011. *Hitler, Mussolini and the Vatican: Pope Pius XI and the Speech That Was Never Made.* Translated by C. Ipsen. Cambridge: Polity Press.

Federzone, L. 1926. *Venti mesi di azione coloniale.* Milan: A. Mondadori.

Feinstein, W. 2003. *The Civilization of the Holocaust in Italy: Poets, Artists, Saints, Anti-Semites.* Madison, NJ: Fairleigh Dickinson University Press.

Feldman, L. H. 1996. *Jew and Gentile in the Ancient World: Attitudes and Interactions from Alexander to Justinian.* Princeton: Princeton University Press.

Felisini, D. 2016. *Alessandro Torlonia: The Pope's Banker.* Palgrave Studies in the History of Finance. Cham, Switzerland: Palgrave Macmillan.

Ferrara, R. 2007. *Movimenti evangelici in Sicilia dal Risorgimento al fascismo.* Soveria Mannelli: Rubbettino.

Ferrari, M. 1994. *Catalogo storico della Editrice Vita e Pensiero, 1914–1994.* Milan: Società Editrice Vita e Pensiero.

Fiorentino, C. M. 1999. *All'ombra di Pietro: la chiesa cattolica e lo spionaggio fascista in Vaticano: 1929–1939.* Florence: Le Lettere.

Forno, M. 2003a. *Fascismo e informazione: Ermanno amicucci e la rivoluzione giornalistica incompiuta (1922–1945).* Alessandria: Edizione dell'Orso.

———. 2003b. "La stampa cattolica alla prova del fascismo." *Contemporanea* 6 (4): 621–46.

Fortson, J. L. 1943. *How to Make Friends for Your Church: A Manual on Public Relations.* New York: Association Press.

"Francia: Succursale di propaganda protestante nella Corsica." 1853. *CC* 1: 215.

Franzinelli, M. 1999. *I tentacoli dell'ovra: agenti, collaboratori e vittime della polizia politica fascista.* Turin: Bollati Boringhieri.

Frattini, E. 2008. *The Entity: Five Centuries of Secret Vatican Espionage.* Translated by D. Cluster. New York: St. Martin's Press.

Freitag, S. 2003. *Exiles from European Revolutions: Refugees in Mid-Victorian England.* Oxford: Berghahn Books.

Friedländer, S. 1997. *Nazi Germany and the Jews.* Vol. 1, *The Years of Persecution, 1933–1939.* New York: HarperCollins.

Friedman, J. 1978. *Michael Servetus: A Case Study in Total Heresy.* Geneva: Droz.

Frugoni, A. 1954. *Arnaldo da Brescia nelle fonti del secolo XII.* Rome: Nella Sede Dell'istituto.

———, M. Pegrari, O. Capitani, C. Frugoni, and M. Bianchini. 1991. *Arnaldo da Brescia e il suo tempo.* 6th ed. Brescia: Fondazione Banca credito agrario bresciano, Istituto di cultura Giovanni Folonari.

Fucci, F. 1985. *Le polizie di Mussolini: la repressione dell'antifascismo nel "ventennio."* Milan: Mursia.

Fullam, R. B., ed. 1956. *The Popes on Youth: Principles for Forming and Guiding Youth from Popes Leo XIII to Pius XII.* Buffalo, NY: Canisius High School.

Furiozzi, G. B. 2003. "Free-Masonry and Protestantism in Italy, 1700–1900." *Risorgimento* 55 (1): 69–76.

Gabriel, K., C. Spiess, and K. Winkler. 2010. *Religionsfreiheit und pluralismus: entwicklungslinien eines Katholischen lernprozesses.* Paderborn: Schöningh.

Gagliano, S. 2013. "Socialismo. Evangelismo. Meridionalismo (1893–1915)." In *Il protestantesimo italiano nel mezzogiorno tra otto e novecento,* edited by Stefano Gagliano, 39–59. Milan: Biblion Edizione.

———. 2015. *150 Anni di presenza battista in Italia (1863–2013): atti del convegno organizzato dall'associazione Piero Guicciardini e dall'Unione Cristiana Evangelica Battista d'Italia: Roma, 22–23 Ottobre 2013.* Milan: Biblion Edizioni.

Gallagher, C. R. 2008. *Vatican Secret Diplomacy: Joseph P. Hurley and Pope Pius XII.* New Haven: Yale University Press.

Gangale, Giuseppe, and Alberto Cavaglion. 1991. *Revival.* Palermo: Sellerio.

Garfinkel, P. 2017. *Criminal Law in Liberal and Fascist Italy.* Cambridge: Cambridge University Press.

Gariglio, B. 1976. *Cattolici democratici e clerico-fascisti: il mondo cattolico Torinese alla prova del fascismo (1922–1927).* Bologna: Il Mulino.

Gaudio, A. 1995. *Scuola, chiesa e fascismo: la scuola cattolica in Italia durante il fascismo: 1922–1943.* Brescia: La Scuola.

Gaustad, E. S. 1974. *The Rise of Adventism: Religion and Society in Mid-Nineteenth-Century America.* New York: Harper and Row.

Gavazzi, A. 1877. *The Priest in Absolution: An Exposure.* London: Simpkin, Marshall.

Gazzetta Ufficiale della Repubblica Italiana. 1975. Rome: Istituto Poligrafico e Zecca dello Stato.

Gemelli, A., O.F.M. 1934. *Il protestantesimo e l'Italia.* Pp. 469–71. Milan: Società Editrice Vita e Pensiero.

Genovesi, V. 1933. *Alla chiesa credo, ai protestanti no! Catechismo cattolico antiprotestantico.* Roma: Messaggero del S. Cuore.

Gentile, E. 1993. *Il culto del littorio: la sacralizzazione della politica nell'Italia fascista.* Rome: Laterza.

———. 1996a. *Le origini dell'ideologia fascista (1918–1925).* Bologna: Il Mulino.

———. 1996b. *The Sacralization of Politics in Fascist Italy.* Cambridge: Harvard University Press.

———. 2001. *Le religioni della politica: fra democrazie e totalitarismi.* Rome: GLF Editori Laterza.

———. 2004. "Fascism, Totalitarianism and Political Religion: Definitions and Critical Reflections on Criticism of an Interpretation." *Totalitarian Movements and Political Religions* 5 (3): 326–75.

———. 2005. *Fascismo: storia e interpretazione.* Roma: Laterza.

———. 2010. *Contro Cesare: cristianesimo e totalitarismo nell'epoca dei fascismi.* Milan: Feltrinelli.

———, and Italy Parlamento Senato, Archivio Storico. 2002. *Il totalitarismo alla conquista della camera alta: inventari e documenti dell'unione nazionale fascista del senato e delle carte suardo.* Soveria Mannelli (Catanzaro): Rubbettino.

———, C. Tumminelli, G. D. Sanctis, and Istituto Superiori G. T. Giordani. 1929. *Enciclopedia italiana di scienze, lettere ed arti.* Rome: Istituto Giovanni Treccani.

George, T., ed. 2004. *Mr Moody and the Evangelical Tradition.* London: T and T Clark.

Germinario, F. 2009. *Fascismo e antisemitismo: progetto razziale e ideologia totalitaria.* Rome: Laterza.

Ghiron, M. 1935. *Mario Piacentini, i culti ammessi nello stato italiano . . .* Milan: Hoepli Editore.

Giacchi, O. 1934. *La legislazione italiana sui culti ammessi.* Milan: Società Editrice Vita e Pensiero.

Giacomo, L. 2012. "Pius XI: Keywords." International Conference Milan 2009. Edited by Alberto Guasco and Raffaella Perin. *Revue de l'histoire des religions* (4): 571.

Gibson, J. 1909. *The Waldenses.* 3d ed. Edinburgh: The Religious Tract and Book Society of Scotland.

Gilley, S., and B. Stanley, eds. 2005. *World Christianities, c. 1815–c. 1914.* The Cambridge History of Christianity. Cambridge: Cambridge University Press.

Gillette, A. 2002. *Racial Theories in Fascist Italy.* London: Routledge.

Giordani, I. 1930. *Crisi protestante e unità della chiesa.* Brescia: Morcelliana.

———. 1943. *I protestanti alla conquista d'Italia.* Milan: Società Editrice Vita e Pensiero.

———. 1945. *La rivolta cattolica.* 3d ed. Rome: Coletti.

Giuntella, M. C. 2000. *La fuci tra modernismo, partito popolare e fascismo.* Rome: Edizioni Studium.

Gladden, W. 1881. *Protestantism in Italy.* New York: n.p.

Godman, P. 2004. *Hitler and the Vatican: Inside the Secret Archives That Reveal the Complete Story of the Nazis and the Church.* New York: Free Press.

Goff, J. R. 1988. *Fields White unto Harvest: Charles F. Parham and the Missionary Origins of Pentecostalism.* Fayetteville: University of Arkansas Press.

Goldman, S. 2009. *Zeal for Zion: Christians, Jews, and the Idea of the Promised Land.* Chapel Hill: University of North Carolina Press.

Gooch, J. 2014. *The Italian Army and the First World War.* Cambridge: Cambridge University Press.

Good, James I. 1910. *Famous Places of the Reformed Churches: A Religious Guidebook to Europe.* Edited by Marcus A. Brownson. Philadelphia: Heidelberg Press.

Grant, F. 1961. "Religio licita." *Texte und untersuchungen zur geschichte der altchristlichen literatur* 79: 84.

Grasso, D. 1952. "Ciò che un Protestante ha trovato a Roma." *CC* 103: 666.

Graves, C., ed. 1940. *The Pope Speaks: Being a Compilation of His Allocutions, Messages, Broadcasts, Addresses, and Encyclicals since His Accession to the Holy See, Together with a Biography and Current Precis.* London: Faber and Faber.

Grazia, V. D. 1993. *How Fascism Ruled Women: Italy, 1922–1945.* Berkeley: University of California Press.

Greenaway, G. W. 1978. *Arnold of Brescia.* New York: AMS Press.

Greene, A. C. 2016. *No Depression in Heaven: The Great Depression, the New Deal, and the Transformation of Religion in the Delta.* Oxford: Oxford University Press.

Gregor, A. J. 2005. *Mussolini's Intellectuals: Fascist Social and Political Thought.* Princeton: Princeton University Press.

Gregory, Brad S. 1999. *Salvation at Stake: Christian Martyrdom in Early Modern Europe.* Cambridge: Harvard University Press.

Griffin, R. 2013. *Fascism, Totalitarianism and Political Religion.* Abingdon-on-Thames, UK: Taylor and Francis.

Guasco, A. 2013a. *Cattolici e fascisti: la Santa Sede e la politica italiana all'alba del regime (1919–1925).* Bologna: Il Mulino.

———. 2013b. "Tra segretaria di stato e regime fascista: Mons. F. Borgongini Duca e la nunziatura in Italia in le gouvernement pontifical sous Pie XI." Edited by Laura Pettinaroli. Rome: Ecole française de Rome, 2013.

Guerra, A. J. 1992. "The Conversion of Marcus Aurelius and Justin Martyr: The Purpose, Genre, and Content of the First Apology." *The Second Century* 9 (3): 171.

Gunnemann, Louis H., and Charles Shelby Rooks. 1999. *The Shaping of the United Church of Christ: An Essay in the History of American Christianity.* Cleveland: United Church Press.

Hanson, R. P. C. 1988. *The Search for the Christian Doctrine of God: The Arian Controversy 318–381.* Edinburgh: T. and T. Clark.

Harrell, D. E. 1966. *Quest for a Christian America: The Disciples of Christ and American Society to 1866.* Nashville: Disciples of Christ Historical Society.

Hattersley, Roy, and Jeff Bellamy. 2005. *Blood and Fire: The Story of William and Catherine Booth and Their Salvation Army.* London: Royal National Institute of the Blind.

Hearley, J. 1929. *Pope or Mussolini.* Edited by Catholic Church in Italy. New York: Macaulay.

Hedlund, R. E. 1970. *The Protestant Movement in Italy: Its Progress, Problems, and Prospects.* South Pasadena: William Carey Library.

Heitzenrater, R. P. 1989. *Mirror and Memory: Reflections on Early Methodism.* Nashville: Kingswood Books.

Hempton, D. 2005. *Methodism: Empire of the Spirit.* New Haven: Yale University Press.

Hillerbrand, H. J. 2004. *Encyclopedia of Protestantism.* 4 vols. London: Routledge.

Hofstadter, R. 1967. *The Paranoid Style in American Politics and Other Essays.* New York: Vintage Books.

Holden, A. 2012. *Jehovah's Witnesses: Portrait of a Contemporary Religious Movement.* London: Routledge.

Holland, J. 2003. *Modern Catholic Social Teaching: The Popes Confront the Industrial Age, 1740–1958.* New York: Paulist Press.

Hollenweger, W. J. 1997. *Pentecostalism: Origins and Developments Worldwide.* Peabody, MA: Hendrickson.

Homer, M. W. 2006. "Seeking Primitive Christianity in the Waldensian Valleys: Protestants, Mormons, Adventists and Jehovah's Witnesses in Italy." *Nova Religio: The Journal of Alternative and Emergent Religions* 9 (4): 5–53.

Hopkins, C. H. 1980. *John R. Mott 1865–1955: A Biography.* Grand Rapids: Eerdmans.

Horn, D. G. 1994. *Social Bodies: Science, Reproduction, and Italian Modernity.* Princeton: Princeton University Press.

Horridge, G. K. 1993. *The Salvation Army: Origins and Early Days: 1865–1900.* Godalming, Surrey: Ammonite Books.

Hsia, R. P., ed. 2007. *Reform and Expansion 1500–1660.* The Cambridge History of Christianity. Cambridge: Cambridge University Press.

Hughes, Richard T., and R. L. Roberts. 2000. *The Churches of Christ.* Westport, CT: Greenwood Press.

"I. Dall'osso, su Roma primitiva e gli scavi di Monte Mario." 1924. *Rivista di filologia e di istruzione classica* 52: 130.

International Business Publications. 2018. *Italy: Justice System and National Police Handbook,* vol. 1. Washington, DC: International Business Publications.

Introvigne, M. 2013. *L'isola che c'è: le comunità Protestanti in Sicilia.* Edited by L. Zoccatelli, P. Zoccatelli, A. Maira, G. Scaringella, and M. Ibanisteanu. Caltanissetta: Lussografica.

Iovino, A. 2014. *Alfonso Melluso: il giovane saggio del Pentecostalismo italiano.* Chieti Scalo: GBU.

Ireland, J. 1911. "Methodist Episcopal Church in Italy." *North American Review* 193 (1): 121.

Jedin, H., P. Dolan, and D. L. Holland, eds. 1993. *The Early Church: An Abridgment of History of the Church.* Vols. 1–3. New York: Crossroad.

Jodock, D. 2000. *Catholicism Contending with Modernity: Roman Catholic Modernism and Anti-Modernism in Historical Context.* Cambridge: Cambridge University Press.

Joerges, C., and N. S. Ghaleigh. 2003. *Darker Legacies of Law in Europe: The Shadow of National Socialism and Fascism over Europe and Its Legal Traditions.* Oxford: Hart Publishing.

Jones, E., and G. Pasquino, eds. 2015. *The Oxford Handbook of Italian Politics.* Oxford: Oxford University Press.

Kaiser, W., and H. Wohnout. 2004. *Political Catholicism in Europe, 1918–45.* London: Routledge.

Kaminsky, H. 2004. *A History of the Hussite Revolution.* Eugene, OR: Wipf and Stock.

Kay, W. K., and A. E. Dyer. 2011. *European Pentecostalism.* Leiden: Brill.

Keltie, John Scott, and Isaac Parker Anderson Renwick. 1903. *The Statesman's Year-Book: Statistical and Historical Annual of the States of the World for the Year 1903.* Palgrave Connect (Online Service).

Kent, P. C. 1981. *The Pope and the Duce: The International Impact of the Lateran Agreements.* New York: St. Martin's Press.

———. 1988. "A Tale of Two Popes: Pius XI, Pius XII and the Rome–Berlin Axis." *Journal of Contemporary History* 23 (4): 589–608.

———. 2002. *The Lonely Cold War of Pope Pius XII: The Roman Catholic Church and the Division of Europe, 1943–1950.* Montreal: McGill-Queen's University Press.

Kertzer, D. I. 1997. *The Kidnapping of Edgardo Mortara.* New York: Alfred Knopf.

———. 2002. *Unholy War: The Vatican's Role in the Rise of Modern Anti-Semitism.* London: Macmillan.

———. 2006. *Prisoner of the Vatican: The Popes, the Kings, and Garibaldi's Rebels in the Struggle to Rule Modern Italy.* Boston: Mariner Books.

———. 2007. *The Popes against the Jews: The Vatican's Role in the Rise of Modern Anti-Semitism.* New York: Alfred A. Knopf.

———. 2014. *The Pope and Mussolini: The Secret History of Pius XI and the Rise of Fascism in Europe.* New York: Random House.

———. 2018. *The Pope Who Would Be King: The Exile of Pius IX and the Emergence of Modern Europe.* New York: Random House.

Killinger, C. 2010. "Gaetano Salvemini: Antifascism in Thought and Action." *Journal of Modern Italian Studies* 15 (5): 657–77.

Kissack, R. 1960. *Methodists in Italy.* London: Cargate Press.

Knight, G. R. 2005. *Historical Sketches of Foreign Missions.* Berrien Springs, MI: Andrews University Press.

Koenig, H. C., and National Catholic Welfare Conference, eds. 1943. *Principles for Peace: Selections from Papal Documents, Leo XIII to Pius XII, Edited for the Bishops' Committee on the Pope's Peace Points.* Washington, DC: National Catholic Welfare Conference.

Köhler, W. 2017. *Zwingli und Luther: ihr streit über das Abendmahl nach seinen politischen und religiösen beziehungennband 2* [Munich]: Gütersloher Verlagshaus. Die Vision einer Neuen Welt.

Kohn, D. 1988. *The Darwinian Heritage.* Princeton: Princeton University Press.

Land, G. 1998. *Adventism in America.* Berrien Springs, MI: Andrews University Press.

Langford, P. 2015. *Roberto Esposito: Law, Community and the Political.* Abingdon-on-Thames, UK: Taylor and Francis.

Lanna, D. 1934. *Offensiva Protestante e difesa Cattolica.* Milan: Società Editrice Vita e Pensiero.

La Rovere, L. 2014. "Interpretations of Fascism as a Political Religion in Post-Fascist Italy (1943–1948)." *Politics, Religion and Ideology* 15 (1): 23–44.

Latourette, K. S. 1941. *A History of the Expansion of Christianity.* Volume 4 of *The Great Century, A.D. 1800–1914.* London: Eyre and Spottiswoode.

———. 1957. *World Service.* New York: Association Press.

———. 1959. *The Nineteenth Century in Europe: The Protestant and Eastern Churches.* New York: Harper.

"Lavoro Protestante in Italia, Il." 1919. *CC* 70: 230.

Lefebvre, G. 2005. *The Coming of the French Revolution.* Translated and with a preface by R. R. Palmer. With a new introduction by Timothy Tackett. Princeton: Princeton University Press.

Lentini, G. 2008. *Pio XI, l'italia e Mussolini.* Rome: Città Nuova.

Leonardi, R. 1989. *Italian Christian Democracy: The Politics of Dominance.* Edited by D. A. Wertman. Basingstoke, Hampshire: Palgrave Macmillan.

Leone, A. R. 1972. "Villa San Sebastiano: una comunità Evangelica nel periodo fascista." *Bollettino della Società di Studi Valdesi* 132: 95–114.

Levi, C. 1982. *Christ Stopped at Eboli.* New York: Penguin.

Levy, R. S. 2005. *Antisemitism: A Historical Encyclopedia of Prejudice and Persecution.* Santa Barbara: ABC-CLIO.

Lewis, C. S., G. Calabria, and M. Moynihan, eds. 2009. *The Latin Letters of C. S. Lewis.* South Bend, IN: St. Augustine's Press.

Leziroli, G., ed. 2004. *Dalla legge sui culti ammessi al progetto di legge sulla libertà religiosa (1 Marzo 2002): atti del Convegno di Ferrara del 25–26 Ottobre 2002.* Naples: Jovene.

Lias, J. J. 1888. "The Catholic Reform Movement in Italy." *The Spectator* 61: 264.

Liedtke, Rainer, and Stephan Wendehorst. 1999. *The Emancipation of Catholics, Jews and Protestants: Minorities and the Nation State in Nineteenth-Century Europe.* Manchester: Manchester University Press.

Liguori, A. M. de. 2004. *Carteggio.* Edited by G. Orlandi and Istituto Storico Redentorista. Rome: Edizione di Storia e Litteratura.

Linder, Robert Dean, Daniel G. Reid, Bruce Leon Shelley, and Harry S. Stout. 1991. *Dictionary of Christianity in America.* Downers Grove, IL: InterVarsity Press.

Littlefield, W. 1931. "The Dispute with Fascism." *Current History* 35 (1): 29.

Livingston, M. A. 2014. *The Fascists and the Jews of Italy: Mussolini's Race Laws, 1938–1943.* Cambridge: Cambridge University Press.

Locher, G. W. 1969. *Huldrych Zwingli in neuer Sicht Zehn Beitr. Zur Theol. D. Zuericher Reformation.* Stuttgart: Zwingli-Verl.

Lorè, M. 2008. *Antisemitismo e razzismo ne la difesa della razza, 1938–1943.* Soveria Mannelli: Rubbettino.

Luconi, S. 2001. "The Response of Italian Americans to Fascist Antisemitism." *Patterns of Prejudice* 35 (3): 3–24.

———. 2004. *The Italian-American Vote in Providence, Rhode Island, 1916–1948.* Madison, NJ: Fairleigh Dickinson University Press.

Luongo, G. 2002. *La Terra dei Marsi: Cristianesimo, cultura, istituzioni: atti del Convegno di Avezzano, 24–26 Settembre 1998.* Rome: Viella.

Luzzi, G. 1913. *The Struggle for Christian Truth in Italy.* New York: Fleming H. Revell.

———. 1914. *The Waldensian Church: Her Work, Her Difficulties, Her Hopes.* New York: Dodd, Mead.

Lyttelton, A. 2002. *Liberal and Fascist Italy: 1900–1945.* Oxford: Oxford University Press.

Mack Smith, D. 1997. *Modern Italy: A Political History.* Ann Arbor: University of Michigan Press.

Macleod, D. I. 1983. *Building Character in the American Boy: The Boy Scouts, YMCA, and Their Forerunners, 1870–1920.* Madison: University of Wisconsin Press.

Madigan, K. 2015. *Medieval Christianity: A New History.* New Haven: Yale University Press.

Madonna, M. 2012. *Profili Storici del Diritto di Libertà Religiosa Nell'italia Post-Unitaria.* Tricase (Lecce): Libellula Edizioni.

Maghenzani, S., and Convegno di Studi sulla Riforma e Sui Movimenti Religiosi in Italia (51st: 2011, Torre Pellice). 2012. *Il Protestantesimo Italiano nel Risorgimento: Influenze, miti, identità: atti del LI Convegno di studi sulla riforma e sui movimenti religiosi in Italia: Torre Pellice, 2–4 Settembre 2011.* Turin: Claudiana.

Mangano, A. 1917. *Religious Work among Italians in America: A Survey for the Home Missions Council.* Missionary Education Movement of the United States and Canada, Home Missions Council (U.S.). Edited by Immigrant Work Committee and Home Missions Council. New York: Published for the Immigrant Work Committee of the Home Missions Council; Missionary Education Movement of the United States and Canada.

Marino, G. C. 1995. *La repubblica della forza: Mario Scelba e le passioni del suo tempo.* Milan: F. Angeli.

Martina, G. 1978. *La chiesa nell'età dell'assolutismo, del liberalismo, del totalitarismo.* 3d ed. Brescia: Morcelliana, 1978.

Maryks, R. A. 2012. *"Pouring Jewish Water into Fascist Wine": Untold Stories of (Catholic) Jews from the Archive of Mussolini's Jesuit Pietro Tacchi Venturi.* Edited by P. Tacchi Venturi. Leiden: Brill.

Maselli, D. 1974. *Tra risveglio e millennio: storia delle Chiese Cristiane Dei Fratelli: 1836–1886.* Turin: Claudiana.

———. 1978. *Libertà della parola: storia delle chiese Cristiane dei Fratelli, 1886–1946.* Turin: Claudiana.

———. 2003. *Storia dei Battisti Italiani: 1873–1923.* Turin: Claudiana.

———, and Carlo Ghidelli. 2004. *La Società Biblica Britannica e Forestiera: 200 anni di storia in Italia.* Roma: Società Biblica Britannica e Forestiera.

———, and Anna Maffei. 2003. *Storia dei Battisti Italiani: 1873–1923.* Turin: Claudiana.

Mastantuoni, A. 2012. *Bilychnis: una rivista tra fede e ragione, 1912–1931.* Turin: Claudiana.

Mazzella, O. 1930. *La vera chiesa e le false chiese: il Protestantesimo è vera chiesa? è vera religione?* Taranto: STAT.

Mazzini, E. 2013. *Ostilità convergenti: stampa diocesana, razzismo e antisemitismo nell'Italia fascista (1937–1939).* Naples: Edizioni Scientifiche Italiane.

Mazzonis, F., and Istituto Luigi Sturzo. 1997. *Cattolici, chiesa e resistenza in Abruzzo.* Bologna: Il Mulino.

McAllister, Lester G., and William Edward Tucker. 1995. *Journey in Faith: A History of the Christian Church (Disciples of Christ).* St. Louis: Chalice Press.

McDermott, T. 1946. *Keeper of the Keys: A Life of Pope Pius XII.* Milwaukee: Bruce Publishing.

McGinn, B. 1994. *Antichrist: Two Thousand Years of the Human Fascination with Evil.* San Francisco: HarperSanFrancisco.

McGrath, Alister E., and Darren C. Marks. 2007. "Italian Protestantism to the Present Day." Chapter 14 in *The Blackwell Companion to Protestantism.* Malden, MA: Blackwell.

McInerny, R. M. 2001. *The Defamation of Pius XII.* South Bend: St. Augustine's Press.

McLaughlin, P. J. 1952. *Prove della esistenza di Dio (22 Novembre 1951).* English: *Modern Science and God.* Dublin: Clonmore and Reynolds.

McLeod, H., ed. 2006. *World Christianities, c. 1914–c. 2000.* The Cambridge History of Christianity. Cambridge: Cambridge University Press.

Meldini, P. 1975. *Sposa e madre esemplare: ideologia e politica della donna e della famiglia durante il fascismo.* Florence: Guaraldi.

Melloni, A. 2013. *Tutto e niente: i Cristiani d'Italia alla prova della storia.* Rome: Laterza.

"Methodists and the Pope." 1910. *Current Literature* 48: 256–60.

"Methodists on the Hills of Rome." 1921. *Literary Digest* 70: 28–29.

Michel, P. 2017. *Religions, Nations, and Transnationalism in Multiple Modernities.* Edited by A. Possamai and B. S. Turner. New York: Palgrave Macmillan.

Michelson, E. 2013. *The Pulpit and the Press in Reformation Italy.* Cambridge: Harvard University Press.

Milton, John. 2007. *The Complete Poetry and Essential Prose of John Milton.* Edited by William Kerrigan, John Peter Rumrich, and Stephen M. Fallon. New York: Modern Library.

Minoni, Anthony J. 1999. *The Popes against Modern Errors: 16 Papal Documents.* Rockford, IL: Tan Books.

Missiroli, M. 1929. *Date a Cesare: La Politica Religiosa di Mussolini, con Documenti Inediti.* Roma: Libreria del Littorio.

Mitchell, M. M., and F. M. Young, eds. 2006. *Origins to Constantine.* The Cambridge History of Christianity. Cambridge: Cambridge University Press.

Mitford, N. 1987. *The Nancy Mitford Omnibus.* Harmondsworth: Penguin Books U.A.

Mola, A. A. 1993. *Storia della Massoneria Italiana dalle origini ai nostri giorni.* 3d ed. Milan: Bompiani.

Molnár, Amedeo, Valdo Vinay, and Augusto Armand Hugon. 1989. *Storia dei Valdesi / (1532–1848) / Augusto Armand Hugon.* 2d ed. Turin: Claudiana.

Moore, R. Laurence, and Maurizio Vaudagna, eds. 2003. *The American Century in Europe.* Ithaca: Cornell University Press.

Moretti, M. 1928. *La propaganda del Protestantesimo in Italia contro l'unità religiosa.* Milan: Società Editrice Vita e Pensiero.

Moro, Renato. 1997. "L'opposizione Cattolica al Metodismo tra anni venti e anni trenta." In *Il metodismo Italiano,* edited by Franco Chiarini, 131–80. Turin: Claudiana.

———. 1998. "Pregiudizio religioso e ideologia: antiebraismo e antiprotestantesimo nel cattolicesimo italiano fra le due guerre." *Le Carte* 3: 17–65.

———. 2002. "Antiprotestantesimo cattolico alla settimana sociale del 1928." In *Democrazia e cultura religiosa: studi in onore di Pietro Scoppola.* Edited by Camillo Brezzi, Carlo Felice Casula, Agostino Giovagnoli, and Andrea Riccardi, 231–70. Bologna: Il Mulino.

Moroni, G. 1840. *Dizionario di erudizione storico-ecclesiastica da S. Pietro Sino ai nostri giorni.* Venice: Tipografia Emiliana.

Morton, J. 2010. *Spies of the First World War: Under Cover for King and Kaiser.* Richmond, UK: National Archives.

Moser, F. G., and G. Teglio. 1853. *Antidoto contro l'empio tentativo dominante d'introdurre il protestantesimo in Italia, ossia, scelte di prediche sulla vera chiesa e sulla falsità delle sette divise da essa.* Mantova: Presso L'editore Bortolo Balbiani.

Mottu, H. 1977. *Religione popolare in un'ottica protestante: Gramsci, cultura subalterna e lotte contadine.* Edited by M. Castiglione. Turin: Claudiana.

Müller, M. 2007. *The Catholic Dogma: "Extra ecclesiam nullus omnino salvatur." . . . "Error, cui non resititur, approbatur; et veritas, cum minime defensatur, opprimitur."* Hartford, CT: Catholic Authors Press.

Muollo, Giuseppe, and Paola Mele. 1998. *Ariano Irpino: città dei Normanni.* Viterbo: Betagamma.

Murdoch, N. 2014. *Origins of the Salvation Army.* Eugene, OR: Wipf and Stock.

Murray, Stewart. *Post-Christendom: Church and Mission in a Strange New World.* Eugene, OR: Cascade Books.

Murri, R. 1915. "Italy, the Vatican, and the European War." *Contemporary Review* 107: 167–177.

Mussolini, B. 1933. "The Doctrine of Fascism." *Living Age (1897–1941)* 345 (4406): 235–244.

———. 1934. *Scritti e discorsi di Benito Mussolini.* Edited by V. Piccoli, C. Ravasio, and B. Damiani. Milan: Hoepli Editore.

———. 1951. *Opera omnia / A cura di Edoardo e Duilio Susmel.* Florence: La Fenice.

Muston, A. 1853. *The Israel of the Alps: A History of the Persecutions of the Waldenses.* London: Ingram, Cooke.

Naughton, J. W. 1943. *Pius XII on World Problems.* New York: American Press.

Nelis, J., A. Morelli, and D. Praet, eds. 2015. *Catholicism and Fascism in Europe 1918–1945.* Hildesheim: Georg Olms.

Neufeld, D. 1996. *Seventh-Day Adventist Encyclopedia.* 2nd rev. ed., Commentary reference series; vols. 10–11. Hagerstown, MD: Review and Herald Publishing Association.

Newman, John Henry. 2016. *Apologia Pro Vita Sua: Being a History of His Religious Opinions.* Edited by Martin J. Svaglic. Oxford: Clarendon Press.

Noble, T. F. X. 1984. *The Republic of St. Peter: The Birth of the Papal State, 680–825.* Philadelphia: University of Pennsylvania Press.

———, and J. M. H. Smith, eds. 2008. *Early Medieval Christianities, c. 600–c. 1100.* The Cambridge History of Christianity. Cambridge: Cambridge University Press.

Nogueira, E. 1958. *Igreja e o estado em Portugal.* Lisbon: SNI.

"Non-Aryan Nordics." 1938. *The Spectator* 161: 289.

North, F. M., and E. Hawks. 1923. "Methodists on Monte Mario." *Outlook* (1893) 134: 637–38.

"Nuovo movimento Protestante, Un." 1938. *CC* 89: 13. From *La propaganda protestantica e l'opera primaria della preservazione della fede in Roma nel XXV anniversario della sua fondazione (1899–1924).* Book Review, 1924. Rome: Typographia Vaticana.

Oakley, F. 1991. *The Western Church in the Later Middle Ages.* Ithaca: Cornell University Press.

Obermann, H. A., and P. L. Nyhus. 2002. *Forerunners of the Revolution: The Shape of Late Medieval Thought.* Cambridge: Clarke.

O'Brien, A. 1982. "Italian Youth in Conflict: Catholic Action and Fascist Italy, 1929–1931." *Catholic Historical Review* 68 (4): 625.

Olin, J. C. 1990. *Catholic Reform: From Cardinal Ximenes to the Council of Trent, 1495–1563: An Essay with Illustrative Documents and a Brief Study of St. Ignatius Loyola.* New York: Fordham University Press.

Orano, P. 1935. *Cesare Maria De Vecchi di Val Cismon.* Rome: Casa Editrice Pinciana, XIII.

O'Reilly, C. T. 2007. *The Jews of Italy, 1938–1945: An Analysis of Revisionist Histories.* Jefferson, NC: McFarland.

Ortenberg, V. 1992. *The English Church and the Continent in the Tenth and Eleventh Centuries: Cultural, Spiritual, and Artistic Exchanges.* Oxford: Clarendon Press.

O'Shea, P. D. 2008. *A Cross Too Heavy: Eugenio Pacelli, Politics and the Jews of Europe, 1917–1943.* Dural Delivery Centre, NSW: Rosenberg Publishing.

Pace, E. 2010. *Le religioni pentecostali.* Rome: Carocci.

Paiano, Maria. 2011. "Contro 'l'invadente eresia Protestante': l'opera della preservazione della fede in Roma (1899–1930)." In *Chiesa cattolica e minoranze in Italia nella prima meta' del novecento,* edited by Raffaella Perin, 27–103. Rome: Viella.

Painter, B. W. 1990. "Renzo de Felice and the Historiography of Italian Fascism." *American Historical Review* 95 (2): 391–405.

Parati, G. 2012. *New Perspectives in Italian Cultural Studies: Definition, Theory, and Accented Practices.* Madison, NJ: Fairleigh Dickinson University Press.

Parish, H. L. 2005. *Monks, Miracles and Magic: Reformation Representations of the Medieval Church.* London: Routledge.

Parlato, V. 1991. *Le intese con le confessioni acattoliche: i contenuti.* Turin: Giappichelli.

Parsons, T. 1942. "Some Sociological Aspects of the Fascist Movements." *Social Forces* 21 (1): 138.

Partner, P. 1972. *The Lands of St. Peter: The Papal State in the Middle Ages and the Early Renaissance.* Berkeley: University of California Press.

Paschetto, E., P. Sbaffi, and E. Rivoir. 1990. *Evangelici in Italia: documenti delle chiese Battiste, Metodiste e Valdesi, 1961–1990.* Turin: Claudiana.

Paul, R. S. 1987. *Freedom with Order: The Doctrine of the Church in the United Church of Christ.* New York: United Church Press.

Pavan, I. 2009. "An Unexpected Betrayal? The Italian Jewish Community Facing Fascist Persecution." *Holocaust Studies* 15 (1–2): 127–44.

Paxton, Robert O. 2004. *The Anatomy of Fascism.* London: Allen Lane.

Pecorari, Paolo. 1979a. "Chiesa, azione cattolica e fascismo nell'Italia settentrionale durante il pontificato di Pio XI (1922–1939)." Atti del Quinto Convegno di Storia della Chiesa, Torreglia, 25–27 March 1977. Paper presented at the Convegno di Storia della Chiesa in Italia.

———, ed. 1979b. *Chiesa, azione cattolica e fascismo nell'Italia settentrionale durante il pontificato di Pio XI (1922–1939): Atti del Quinto Convegno di Storia della Chiesa, Torreglia, 25–27 Marzo 1977.* Convegno di Storia della Chiesa in Italia. Milan: Società Editrice Vita e Pensiero.

Penco, G. 1986. *Storia della chiesa in Italia nell'età contemporanea.* Milan: Jaca Book.

Penna, A. 1981. *Il Protestantesimo: la sfida degli evangelici in Italia e nel mondo.* Edited by S. Ronchi. Milan: Feltrinelli.

Pennacchini, P. 2012. *La Santa Sede e il fascismo in conflitto per l'azione cattolica.* Città del Vaticano: Libreria Editrice Vaticana.

Perin, R. 2010. "Pregiudizio antiebraico e antiprotestante: Alcuni riflessi sull'atteggiamento della chiesa verso il fascismo." In *Pius XI: Keywords,* edited by Alberto Guasco and Raffaella Perin, pp. 147–62. Berlin: LIT Verlag.

———. 2011. *Chiesa cattolica e minoranze in Italia nella prima metà del novecento: il caso Veneto a confronto.* Rome: Viella.

———. 2013. "Santa Sede e minoranze evangeliche in Italia durante il fascismo." *Storia e problemi contemporanei* 26 (62): 79–98.

Peters, E., 1936. *The 1917 Pio-Benedictine Code of Canon Law: In English Translation with Extensive Scholarly Apparatus.* Reprint 2001. San Francisco: Ignatius Press.

Peyrot, G. 1950. *Le riunioni religiose e l'esercizio del culto nelle norme attualment vigenti in Italia.* Torre Pellice: Claudiana.

———. 1955. *La circolare Buffarini–Guidi e i pentecostali.* Rome: Associazione Italiana per la Libertá ella Cultura.

———. 1956. *La condizione dei protestanti in Italia: prolusione tenuta alla Facoltà Valdese di Teologia di Roma il 3. XI. 1956 in occasione dell'inaugurazione del CII anno accademico.* Rome: Tipografia U. Quintily.

———. 1957. *Religious Liberty and Conditions of Evangelical People in Italy.* Federal Council of Evangelical Churches in Italy. Rome: Tipografia Ferraiolo.

———. 1977. *Gli evangelici nei loro rapporti con lo stato dal fascismo ad oggi.* Torre Pellice: Società di Studi Valdesi.

Phayer, M. 2000. *The Catholic Church and the Holocaust, 1930–1965.* Bloomington: Indiana University Press.

———. 2008. *Pius XII, the Holocaust, and the Cold War.* Bloomington: Indiana University Press.

Piacentini, M. 1929. *La legge 24 giugno 1929 N. 1159, contenente disposizioni sull'esercizio dei culti ammessi nello stato, e sul matrimonio celebrato davanti ai Ministri dei Culti Medesimi.* Rome: Bilychnis.

———. 1934. *I culti ammessi nello stato italiano.* Milan: Hoepli.

———. 1940. *Nel decennale della legge sui culti ammessi.* Florence: C. Cya.

Piccioli, P. 2000. "I testimoni di Geova durante il regime fascista." *Studi Storici* 41 (1): 191–229.

Pieri, P. 1974. In *Pietro Badoglio: [di] P. Pieri, [ed.] G. Rochat.* Torino: Unione tipografico–editrice torinese.

Piggott, Henry J., Febe Cavazzutti Rossi, Theodore Caro Piggott, Thomas Durley, and Orietta Zamparini. 2002. *Henry James Piggott: vita e lettere.* Turin: Claudiana.

Pinotti, F. 2007. *Fratelli d'Italia.* Edited by BUR Futuropassato. Milan: Biblioteca Universale Rizzoli.

Pinto, A. C. 1995. *Salazar's Dictatorship and European Fascism: Problems of Interpretation.* Boulder: Social Science Monographs.

———. 2011. *Rethinking the Nature of Fascism: Comparative Perspectives.* New York: Palgrave Macmillan.

———. 2012. *The Nature of Fascism Revisited.* Boulder: Social Science Monographs.

Piola, A. 1968. *Stato e chiesa dopo il concilio: saggi.* Milan: A. Giuffrè.

Pius XI. 1960. Ed. D. Berdetto. *Discorsi di Pio XI.* Città del Vaticano: Libreria Vaticana Editrice.

Poggi, G. 1967. *Catholic Action in Italy: The Sociology of a Sponsored Organization.* Stanford: Stanford University Press.

Polasky, J. L. 1995. *The Democratic Socialism of Emile Vandervelde: Between Reform and Revolution.* Washington, DC: Berg.

Pollard, John F. 1989. "Post-War Italy: The Papal State of the Twentieth Century." In *The Legacy of Fascism: Lectures Delivered at the University of Glasgow,* edited by Eileen A. Millar. Glasgow: University of Glasgow, Department of Italian.

———. 2005. *Money and the Rise of the Modern Papacy: Financing the Vatican, 1850–1950.* Cambridge: Cambridge University Press.

———. 2006. "The Papacy." In *The Cambridge History of Christianity: World Christianities, c. 1914—c. 2000,* edited by H. McLeod, 27–49. Cambridge: Cambridge University Press.

———. 2014. *The Papacy in the Age of Totalitarianism, 1914–1958.* Oxford: Oxford University Press.

Posner, G. L. 2015. *God's Bankers: A History of Money and Power at the Vatican.* New York: Simon and Schuster.

Protestant Evangelism among Italians in America. 1975. The Italian American Experience. New York: Arno Press.

"Protestants in Italy." 1931. *Time* 18 (10): 43.

"Protestants in Italy." 1957. *Time* 69 (16): 70.

Pugliese, S. G. 2004. *Fascism, Anti-Fascism, and the Resistance in Italy: 1919 to the Present.* Lanham, MD: Rowan and Littlefield.

Purdy, W. A. 1966. *The Church on the Move: The Characters and Policies of Pius XII and John XXIII.* London: Hollis and Carter.

Puzzo, D. A. 1959. "Gaetano Salvemini: An Historiographical Essay." *Journal of the History of Ideas* 20 (2): 217–35.

Rauschenbusch, W. 1960. *A Theology for the Social Gospel.* London: Forgotten Books.

"Reformation in Italy." 1837. *North American Review* 44 (1): 153–78.

Regan, G. 2004. *More Military Blunders.* London: Carlton.

Reuter, H. 1875. *Geschichte der religiösen aufklärung im mittelalter, vom ende des achten jahrhunderts bis zum anfange des vierzehnten, Von Hermann Reuter.* Berlin: W. Hertz.

Rhodes, A. R. E. 1973. *The Vatican in the Age of the Dictators, 1922–1945.* London: Hodder and Stoughton.

Riall, L. 2009. *Risorgimento: The History of Italy from Napoleon to Nation-State.* Basingstoke, Hampshire: Palgrave Macmillan.

Ricca, P. 2011. "Minoranze Cristiane nell'Italia unita." In *Cristiani d'Italia: chiese, società, Stato, 1861–2011,* 2 vols. Vol. 1. Rome: Istituto della Enciclopedia italiana.

Riccardi, A. 1979. *Roma città sacra?: dalla conciliazione all'operazione sturzo.* Milan: Società Editrice Vita e Pensiero.

Rittner, C., and J. K. Roth, eds. 2002. *Pope Pius XII and the Holocaust.* London: Leicester University Press.

Robert, D. 1986. "The Origin of the Student Volunteer Watchword: "The Evangelization of the World in This Generation." *International Bulletin of Missionary Research* 10 (4): 146.

Roberts, D. D. 2006. *The Totalitarian Experiment in Twentieth-Century Europe: Understanding the Poverty of Great Politics.* London: Routledge.

Rocco, A. 1926. *The Political Doctrine of Fascism.* Edited by D. Bigongiari. New York: Carnegie Endowment for International Peace, Division of Intercourse and Education.

Rochat, G. 1990. *Regime fascista e chiese evangeliche: direttive e articolazioni del controllo e della repressione.* Turin: Claudiana.

———. 1996. *I cappellani Valdesi.* Torre Pellice: Società di Studi Valdesi.

Roldán, V. 2009. *Il rinnovamento carismatico cattolico: uno studio comparativo Argentina–Italia.* Milan: Francoangeli.

Rosapepe, G. 1960. *Inquisizione addomesticata.* Bari: Laterza.

Rowe, D. L. 2008. *God's Strange Work: William Miller and the End of the World.* Grand Rapids: Eerdmans.

Rubin, M., and W. Simons, eds. 2009. *Christianity in Western Europe, C.1100–C.1500.* The Cambridge History of Christianity. Cambridge: Cambridge University Press.

Sabry, M. I. 2017. *The Development of Socialism, Social Democracy and Communism: Historical, Political and Socioeconomic Perspectives.* Bingley, UK: Emerald Publishing.

Sale, G. 2001. *"La Civiltà Cattolica" nella crisi modernista (1900–1907): fra transigentismo politico e integralismo dottrinale.* Milan: Jaca Book.

———. 2004. *Hitler, la Santa Sede e gli Ebrei: con documenti dell'archivo segreto Vaticano.* Milan: Jaca Book.

———. 2009. *Le leggi razziali in Italia e il Vaticano.* Milan: Jaca Book.

———. 2011. *La chiesa di Mussolini: i rapporti tra fascismo e religione.* Milan: Rizzoli.

Salvation Army. 1986. *The Doctrines of the Salvation Army.* Toronto: n.p.

Sánchez, J. M. 2002. *Pius XII and the Holocaust: Understanding the Controversy.* Washington, DC: Catholic University of America Press.

Sandidge, J. L. 1987. *Roman Catholic–Pentecostal Dialogue (1977–1982): A Study in Developing Ecumenism.* New York: Lang.

Santini, L. 1955. *Alessandro Gavazzi: aspetti del problema religioso del Risorgimento.* Modena: Tipografia Modenese.

———. 1961. *Dalla Riforma al Risorgimento: protestantesimo e unità d'Italia.* Torre Pellice: Società di Studi Valdesi.

———. 1981. *Gli evangelici italiani negli anni della crisi, 1918–1948.* Torre Pellice: Società di Studi Valdesi.

———, A. Artissi, and G. Capezzani. 1969. *Minoranze religiose in Italia.* Rome: Edizioni Religioni oggi.

Saresella, D. 2011. *Cattolici a sinistra: dal modernismo ai giorni nostri.* Rome: Laterza.

Sarfatti, M. 2000. *Gli Ebrei nell'Italia fascista: vicende, identità, persecuzione.* Turin: G. Einaudi.

Scaduto, M. 1956. "P. Pietro Tacchi Venturi." *Archivum Historicum Societatis Iesu* 25: 755.

Scaramuccia, F. 1999. *Un'avventura di fede: l'opera missionaria di Edward Clarke (1820–1912).* Turin: Claudiana.

Schembs, K. 2013. "Fascist Youth Organizations and Propaganda in a Transnational Perspective: Balilla and Gioventù Italiana del Littorio All'estero in Argentina (1922–1955). *Amnis* 12.

Schwaiger, G. 1997. *La vita religiosa dalle origini ai nostri giorni: dizionario.* Milan: Edizioni San Paolo.

Scoppola, P. 1973. *Il fascismo e le minoranze religiose.* In *Il fascismo e le autonomie locali,* ed. S. Fontana, 331–68. Bologna: Il Mulino.

———. 1976. *La chiesa e il fascismo: documenti e interpretazioni.* Bari: Laterza.

Scotland, N., and G. Kovoor. 2012. *Christianity Outside the Box: Learning from Those Who Rocked the Boat.* Eugene, OR: Cascade Books.

Sell, A. P. F. 1986. *Saints: Visible, Orderly and Catholic: The Congregational Idea of the Church.* Geneva: World Alliance of Reformed Churches.

Seventh-Day Adventist Encyclopedia. 1996. Hagerstown, MD: Review and Herald Publishing Association.

Sharkey, H. J. 2013. *Cultural Conversions: Unexpected Consequences of Christian Missionary Encounters in the Middle East, Africa, and South Asia.* Syracuse: Syracuse University Press.

Sienkiewicz, H. 1993. *Quo Vadis?* Edited by W. S. Kuniczak. New York: Hippocrene.

Simonsohn, S., and Pontifical Institute of Mediaeval Studies, eds. 1990. *The Apostolic See and the Jews.* Toronto: Pontifical Institute of Mediaeval Studies.

Simpson, C., and Mazal Holocaust Collection. 1993. *The Splendid Blond Beast: Money, Law, and Genocide in the Twentieth Century.* New York: Grove Press.

Smit, J. O. 1950. *Angelic Shepherd: The Life of Pope Pius XII.* New York: Dodd, Mead.

Smith, M. A. 1976. *The Church under Siege.* Downers Grove, IL: InterVarsity Press.

Smith, N. D. 1987. *Roots, Renewal and the Brethren.* Exeter: Paternoster Press.

Snape, M. 2006. "The Great War." In *The Cambridge History of Christianity: World Christianities, c. 1914–c. 2000,* edited by H. McLeod, 129–50. Cambridge: Cambridge University Press.

Spadolini, G. 1988. *Italia di minoranza: lotta politica e cultura dal 1915 a oggi.* Florence: F. Le Monnier.

Spalding, A. W. 1977. *Origin and History of Seventh Day Adventists.* Washington, DC: Review and Herald Publishing Association.

Spini, G. 1965. *I protestanti in Italia.* Marchirolo (Varese): Edizioni Uomini Nuovi.

———. 1971. *L'evangelo e il berretto frigio: storia della chiesa cristiana libera in Italia 1870–1904.* Turin: Claudiana.

———. 1989. *Risorgimento e protestanti.* New revised edition. Milan: Il saggiatore.

———. 1994. *Studi sull'evangelismo italiano tra otto e novecento.* Turin: Claudiana.

———. 2002. *Italia liberale e protestanti.* Turin: Claudiana.

———. 2005. *Il protestantesimo italiano del novecento.* Edited by Istituto Italiano per gli Studi Filosofici. Naples: La Città del Sole.

———. 2007. *Italia di Mussolini e protestanti.* In S. Gagliano and C. A. Ciampi, eds. Turin: Claudiana.

———, Luigi Firpo, Delio Cantimori. 1959. *Ginevra e l'Italia: raccolta di studi promossa dalla Facoltà Valdese di Teologia di Roma.* Florence: Sansoni.

Spinka, M. 1968. *John Hus: A Biography.* Princeton: Princeton University Press.

Stackpole, E. S. 1894. *4 1/2 Years in the Italy Mission: A Criticism of Missionary Methods.* Lewiston, ME: Printed at the Journal Office.

Stark, R., and L. Iannaccone. 1997. "Why the Jehovah's Witnesses Grow So Rapidly." *Journal of Contemporary Religion* 12 (2): 133–57.

Steigmann-Gall, R. 2003. *The Holy Reich: Nazi Conceptions of Christianity, 1919–1945.* Cambridge: Cambridge University Press.

Stoops, R. F., and J. V. Hills. 2012. *The Acts of Peter.* Salem, OR: Polebridge Press.

Street, B. V. 2001. *Literacy and Development: Ethnographic Perspectives.* New York: Routledge.

Stretti, M. 1998. *Il movimento Pentecostale: le Assemblee di Dio in Italia.* Turin: Claudiana.

———. 2016. *L'impronta nella storia.* Italy: Youcanprint.

Suardo, G. 1926. *Mussolini e le corporazioni con uno scritto di S. E. il Conte Suardo e il testo completo della legge e del regolamento sindacale.* Mantova: Edizioni Palasino.

Sweet, J. J. T. 1980. *Iron Arm: The Mechanization of Mussolini's Army, 1920–1940.* Westport, CT: Greenwood Press.

Sylvain, R. 1962. *Alessandro Gavassi, 1809–1889: clerc, garibaldien, prédicant des eux mondes.* Québec: Le Centre Pédagogique.

Synan, V. 1987. *The Holiness-Pentecostal Movement in the United States.* Grand Rapids: Eerdmans.

Tacchi Venturi [pseud. Veritas]. 1927. *Il pericolo protestante: in appendice La bibbia.* Bari: Scuola tipografia Salesiana.

———. 1950. *Storia della compagnia di Gesù in Italia.* In P. Tacchi Venturi and M. Scaduto, eds. Rome: Società Editrice Dante Alighieri; Civiltà Cattolica, 1910.

Talbot, G. 2007. *Censorship in Fascist Italy, 1922–43.* New York: Palgrave Macmillan.

Tamborini, A. 1919. "Genesi della dottrina di S. Agostino intorno al peccato originale." *Rivista di filosofia neo-scolastica* 11 (4): 496–503.

Taplin, Mark, et al. 2003. *The Italian Reformers and the Zurich Church, C.1540–1620.* London: Routledge.

Taradel, R. 2000. *La segregazione amichevole: la "Civiltà Cattolica" e la questione ebraica, 1850–1945.* Edited by B. Raggi and R. Di Segni. Rome: Editori Riuniti.

Thayer, Donlu, and W. Cole Durham. 2016. *Religion and Equality: Law in Conflict.* Abingdon-on-Thames, UK: Taylor and Francis.

Thayer, Donlu, Javier Martínez Torrón, and W. Cole Durham, Congress of the International Academy of Comparative Law. 2015. *Religion and the Secular State: National Reports/La religion et l'état laïque: Rapports Nationaux.* Madrid: Servicio de Publicaciones de la Facultad de Derecho de la Universidad Complutense de Madrid.

Thompson, D. 2006. "Ecumenism." In *The Cambridge History of Christianity: World Christianities, c. 1914–c. 2000,* edited by H. McLeod, 50–70. Cambridge: Cambridge University Press.

Tinti, F. M. 1897. *La vigilanza speciale dell'autorità di P.S.: studio teorico-pratico.* Ivrea: L. Garda.

Tittmann, H. H. 2004. *Inside the Vatican of Pius XII: The Memoir of an American Diplomat during World War II.* New York: Image Books/Doubleday.

Toppi, F. S. 1999. *E mi sarete testimoni: il movimento Pentecostale e le Assemblee di Dio in Italia.* Rome: ADI-Media.

Tourn, G. 2011. *Risorgimento e chiese cristiane.* Turin: Claudiana.

Trafeli, D. 2015. *Il Ticino, l'antifascismo e la filosofia: Tommaso Gallarati Scotti, Stefano Jacini, Alessandro Casati.* Pisa: Edizioni ETS.

Traniello, F. 2007. *Religione cattolica e stato nazionale: dal Risorgimento al secondo dopoguerra.* Bologna: Il Mulino.

Tripodi, N. 1959. *I patti lateranensi e il fascismo.* Bologna: Capelli.

Truman, H. S., and Pope Pius XII. 1953. *Correspondence between President Truman and Pope Pius XII.* New York: n.p.

Turco, D. 2005. *Memoria religiosa e identità sociale: la religiosità in una comunità del mezzogiorno.* Soveria Mannelli: Rubbettino.

Vecoli, R. J. 1969. "Prelates and Peasants: Italian Immigrants and the Catholic Church." *Journal of Social History* 2 (3): 217–268.

Velocci, G. 1994. *Sant'alfonso de Liguori: un maestro di vita cristiana.* Cinisello Balsamo: Edizione Paoline.

Ventura, A. 2013. *Il fascismo e gli Ebrei: il razzismo antisemita nell'ideologia e nella politica del regime.* Rome: Donzelli.

Venzi, F. 2008. *Massoneria e fascismo: dall'intesa cordiale alla distruzione delle logge: come nasce una "Guerra Di Religione," 1921–1925.* Roma: Castelvecchi.

Veritas. 1927. *Il pericolo protestante; in appendice la Bibbia.* Bari: Sucola Tipografia Salesiana.

Vernon, S. M. 1910. "Reply to Archbishop Ireland on the Methodist Episcopal Church of America in Italy." *North American Review* 192: 188–201.

Verrill, A. H. 1931. *The Inquisition.* New York: D. Appleton.

Veuillot, P. 1957. *The Catholic Priesthood According to the Teaching of the Church: Papal Documents from Pius X to Pius XII.* Dublin: Gill and Son.

Viallet, J. 1985. *La chiesa valdese di fronte allo stato fascista.* Turin: Claudiana.

Vianello, M. 1950. *Cattolicismo e settarismo: lettera pastorale per la S. Quaresima dell'Anno Santo 1950.* Perugia: Tipografia Panti.

Villa, A. 2004. *Ebrei in fuga: chiesa e leggi razziali nel Basso Piemonte, 1938–1945.* Brescia: Morcelliana.

Villani, G., and E. Dalla Costa. 1992. *Giorni di guerra, 1943–1945: lettere al vescovo.* Florence: Libreria Editrice Fiorentina.

Villis, T. 2013. *British Catholics and Fascism: Religious Identity and Political Extremism between the Wars.* Basingstoke, Hampshire: Palgrave Macmillan.

Vinay, V. 1955. *Facoltà valdese di teologia, 1855–1955.* Torre Pellice: Claudiana.

———. 1961a. *Evangelici italiani esuli a Londra durante il Risorgimento.* Turin: Claudiana.

———. 1961b. *Il Nuovo Testamento della Repubblica Romana 1849: la copia della Biblioteca del Museo Britannico. Estratto dalla rivista "Protestantesimo."* Rome: Ferraiolo.

———. 1965. *La comunità cristiana e la trasmissione della sua fede.* Roma: s.n.

Vincent, M. 2015. "Ungodly Subjects: Protestants in National-Catholic Spain, 1939–53." *European History Quarterly* 45 (1): 108–31.

Wacker, G. 2001. *Heaven Below: Early Pentecostals and American Culture.* Cambridge: Harvard University Press.

Walker, P. J. 2001. *Pulling the Devil's Kingdom Down: The Salvation Army in Victorian Britain.* Berkeley: University of California Press.

Ward, J. M. 2013. *Priest, Politician, Collaborator: Jozef Tiso and the Making of Fascist Slovakia.* Ithaca: Cornell University Press.

Webster, R. A. 1960. *The Cross and the Fasces: Christian Democracy and Fascism in Italy.* Stanford: Stanford University Press.

Weinstein, D. 2011. *Savonarola: The Rise and Fall of a Renaissance Prophet.* New Haven: Yale University Press.

Weisbord, R. G., and W. P. Sillanpoa. 1992. *The Chief Rabbi, the Pope, and the Holocaust: An Era in Vatican–Jewish Relations.* New Brunswick, NJ: Transaction Publishers.

Weiss, B. 1993. *Understanding Italo Calvino.* Columbia: University of South Carolina Press.

White, P. 1992. *Predestination, Policy and Polemic: Conflict and Consensus in the English Church from the Reformation to the Civil War.* Cambridge: Cambridge University Press.

Willis, G. G. 2005. *Saint Augustine and the Donatist Controversy.* Eugene, OR: Wipf and Stock.

Winehouse, I. 1959. *The Assemblies of God: A Popular Survey.* New York: Vantage Press.

Wiseman, N. P. 1880. *Fabiola, or, the Church of the Catacombs.* New York: P. O'Shea.

Wistrich, R. S., and S. Della Pergola. 1995. *Fascist Antisemitism and the Italian Jews.* Jerusalem: Vidal Sassoon International Center for the Study of Antisemitism, Avraham Harman Institute of Contemporary Jewry, Hebrew University of Jerusalem.

Witte, John, and Richard C. Martin. 2008. *Sharing the Book: Religious Perspectives on the Rights and Wrongs of Proselytism.* Eugene, OR: Wipf and Stock.

Wolf, H. 2010. *Pope and Devil: The Vatican's Archives and the Third Reich.* Edited by K. Kronenberg. Cambridge: Harvard University Press, 2010.

Wolff, R. J. 1990. *Between Pope and Duce: Catholic Students in Fascist Italy.* New York: P. Lang.

Womack, David A., and Francesco Toppi. 1989. *Le radici del movimento pentecostale.* Rome: ADI-Media.

Wood, L. J. S. 1923. "Methodists in Rome." *Catholic World (1865)* 117: 647–59.

Woodward, K. L. 1990. *Making Saints: How the Catholic Church Determines Who Becomes a Saint, Who Doesn't, and Why.* New York: Simon and Schuster.

World Council of Churches, Commission on Inter-Church Aid, Refugee and World Service. 1984. *The Churches in Italy.* Geneva: Commission on Inter-Church Aid, Refugee and World Service.

Worthen, M. 2014. *Apostles of Reason: The Crisis of Authority in American Evangelicalism.* New York: Oxford University Press.

Young, D. "Pentecostals in Italy, Sicily, and Calabria." *Journal of the European Pentecostal Theological Association* 34 (1): 55–60.

Zagheni, G. 2006. *La croce e il fascio: i cattolici italiani e la dittatura.* Cinisello Balsamo, Milan: San Paolo.

Zanini, P. 2015. "Twenty Years of Persecution of Pentecostalism in Italy: 1935–1955." *Journal of Modern Italian Studies* 20 (5): 686–707.

Zimmerman, J. D. 2005. *Jews in Italy under Fascist and Nazi Rule, 1922–1945.* New York: Cambridge University Press.

Zuccotti, S. 2000. *Under His Very Windows: The Vatican and the Holocaust in Italy.* New Haven: Yale University Press.

Index